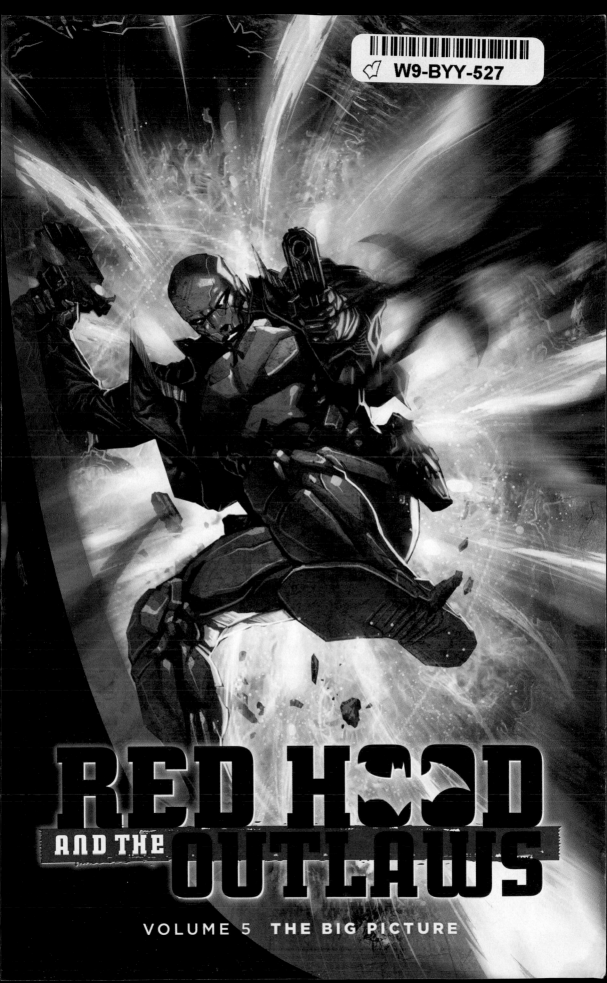

RED HOOD
AND THE OUTLAWS

VOLUME 5   THE BIG PICTURE

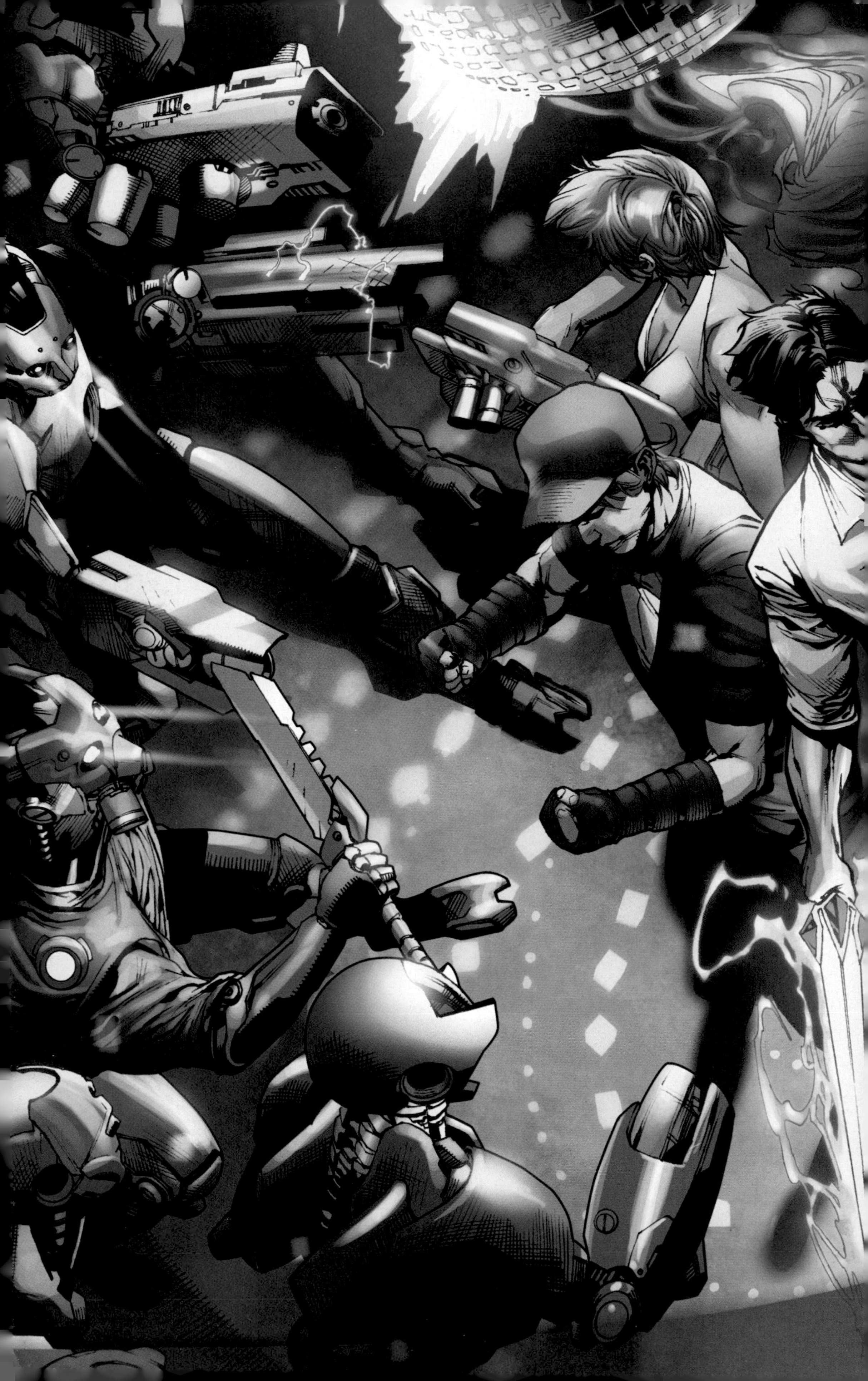

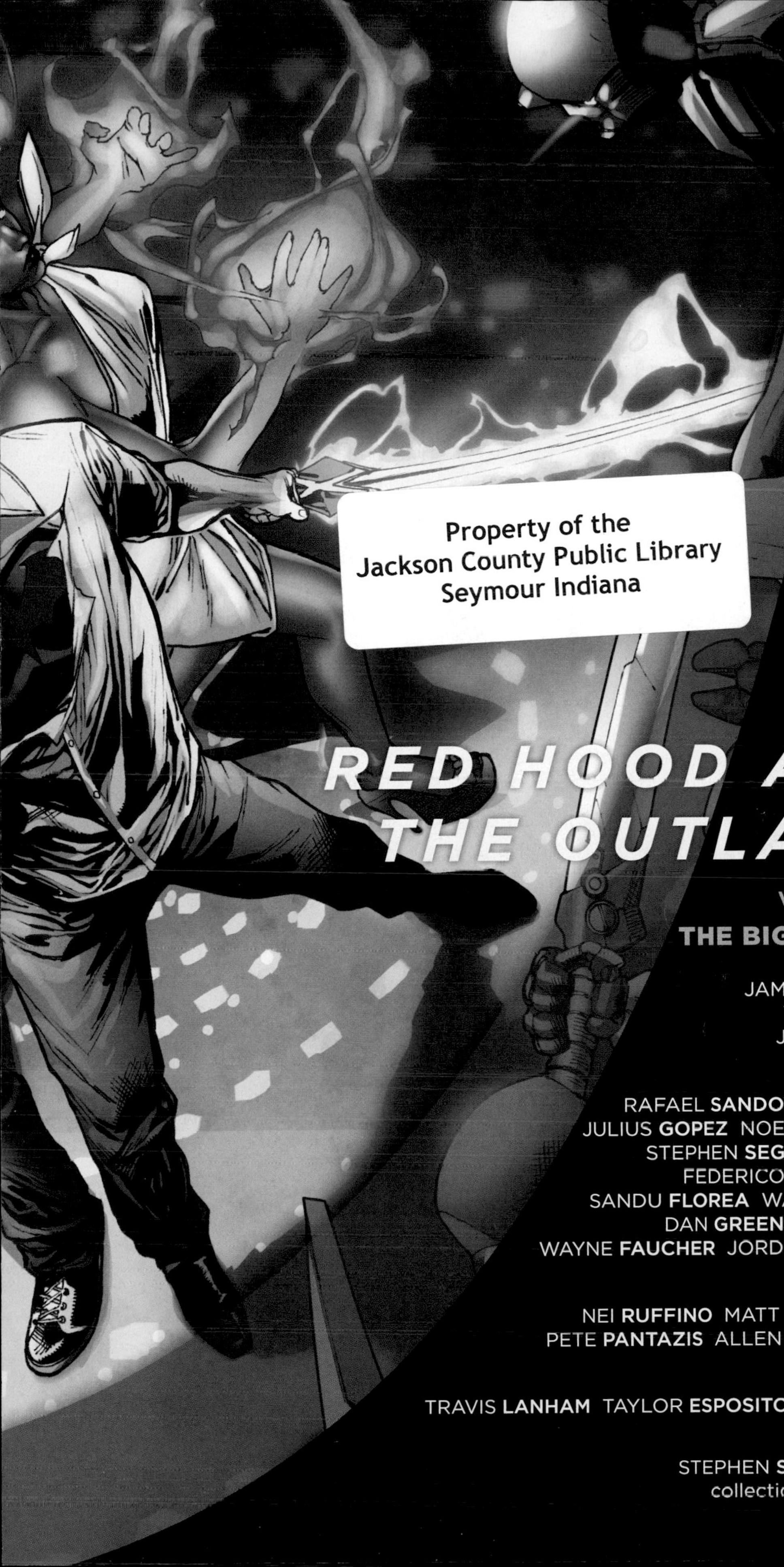

RED HOOD AND THE OUTLAWS

VOLUME 5
THE BIG PICTURE

JAMES **TYNION IV**
WILL **PFEIFER**
JOE **KEATINGE**
writers

RAFAEL **SANDOVAL** RB **SILVA**
JULIUS **GOPEZ** NOEL **RODRIGUEZ**
STEPHEN **SEGOVIA** **RICKEN**
FEDERICO **DALLOCCHIO**
SANDU **FLOREA** WALDEN **WONG**
DAN **GREEN** PAUL **NEARY**
WAYNE **FAUCHER** JORDI **TARRAGONA**
artists

NEI **RUFFINO** MATT **YACKEY** **HI-FI**
PETE **PANTAZIS** ALLEN **PASSALAQUA**
colorists

TRAVIS **LANHAM** TAYLOR **ESPOSITO** DEZI **SIENTY**
letterers

STEPHEN **SEGOVIA** **HI-FI**
collection cover artists

EDDIE BERGANZA MIKE COTTON DARREN SHAN Editors – Original Series RICKEY PURDIN Associate Editor – Original Series
ANTHONY MARQUES Assistant Editor – Original Series JEREMY BENT Editor
ROBBIN BROSTERMAN Design Director – Books ROBBIE BIEDERMAN Publication Design

BOB HARRAS Senior VP – Editor-in-Chief, DC Comics

DIANE NELSON President DAN DIDIO and JIM LEE Co-Publishers GEOFF JOHNS Chief Creative Officer
AMIT DESAI Senior VP – Marketing and Franchise Management
AMY GENKINS Senior VP – Business and Legal Affairs NAIRI GARDINER Senior VP – Finance
JEFF BOISON VP – Publishing Planning MARK CHIARELLO VP – Art Direction and Design
JOHN CUNNINGHAM VP – Marketing TERRI CUNNINGHAM VP – Editorial Administration
LARRY GANEM VP – Talent Relations and Services ALISON GILL Senior VP – Manufacturing and Operations
HANK KANALZ Senior VP – Vertigo and Integrated Publishing JAY KOGAN VP – Business and Legal Affairs, Publishing
JACK MAHAN VP – Business Affairs, Talent NICK NAPOLITANO VP – Manufacturing Administration SUE POHJA VP – Book Sales
FRED RUIZ VP – Manufacturing Operations COURTNEY SIMMONS Senior VP – Publicity BOB WAYNE Senior VP – Sales

RED HOOD AND THE OUTLAWS VOLUME 5: THE BIG PICTURE

DC Comics, 1700 Broadway, New York, NY 10019
A Warner Bros. Entertainment Company.
Printed by RR Donnelley, Owensville, MO, USA.   11/7/14 First Printing.

ISBN: 978-1-4012-5048-5

SUSTAINABLE
FORESTRY
INITIATIVE

Certified Chain of Custody
20% Certified Forest Content,
80% Certified Sourcing
www.sfiprogram.org
SFI-01042
APPLIES TO TEXT STOCK ONLY

Library of Congress Cataloging-in-Publication Data

Tynion, James, IV, author.
Red Hood and the Outlaws. Volume 5 / James Tynion IV, writer ; Julius Gopez, artist.
pages cm. — (The New 52!)

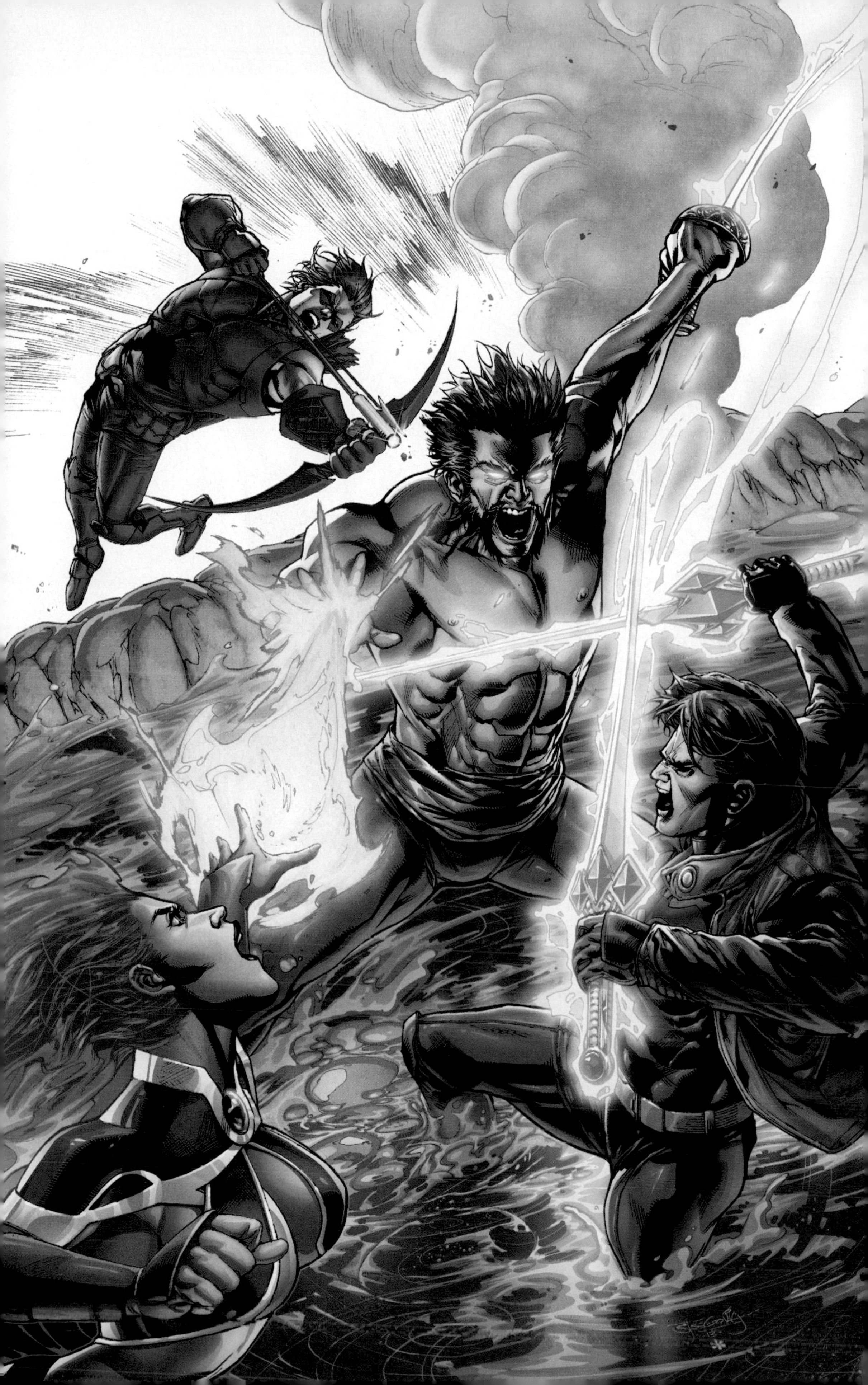

DEMONS

JAMES TYNION IV writer **JULIUS GOPEZ** and **NOEL RODRIGUEZ** pencillers **SANDU FLOREA, WALDEN WONG** and **DAN GREEN** inkers
NEI RUFFINO colorist **TRAVIS LANHAM** letterer cover art by **STEPHEN SEGOVIA** and **HI-FI**

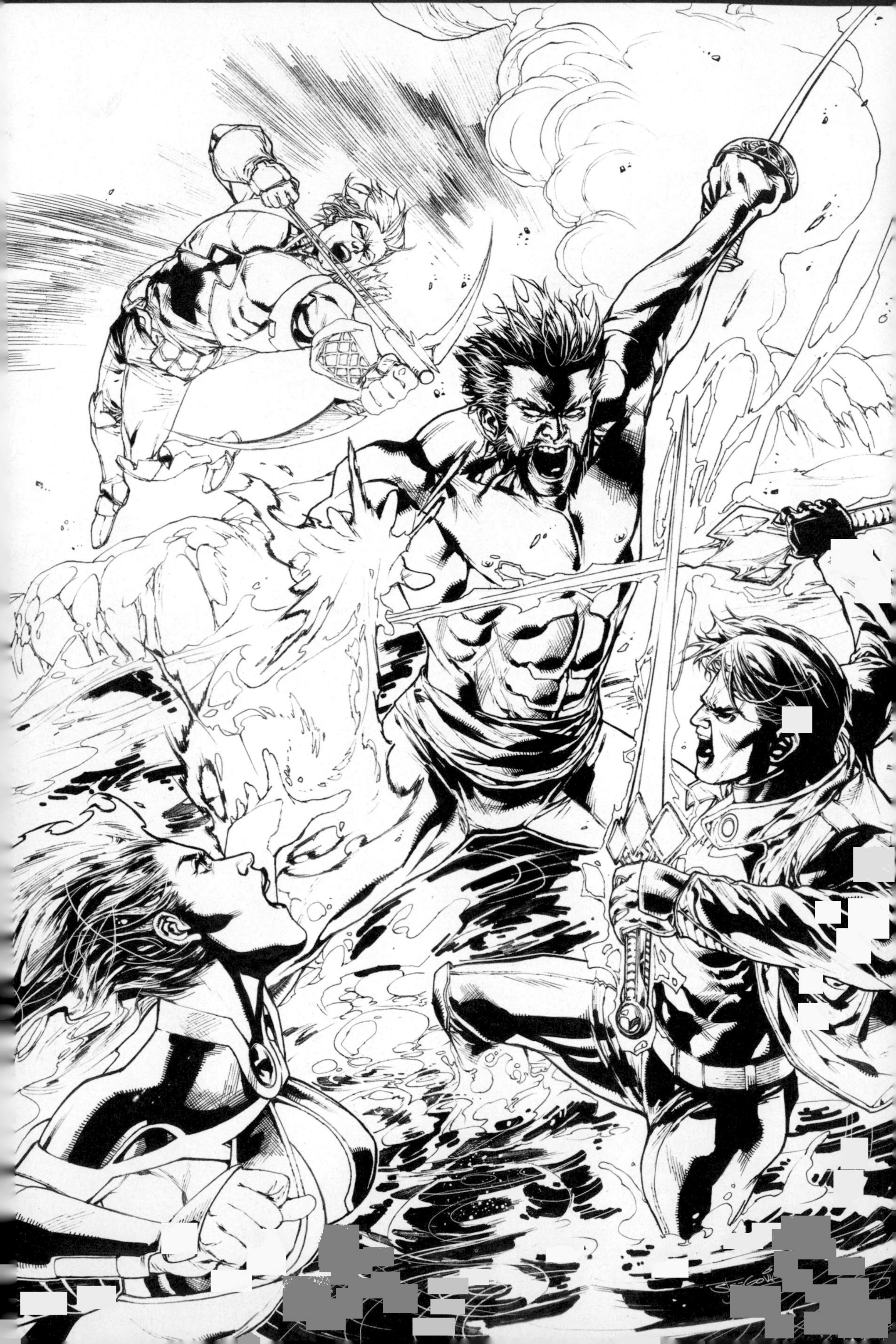

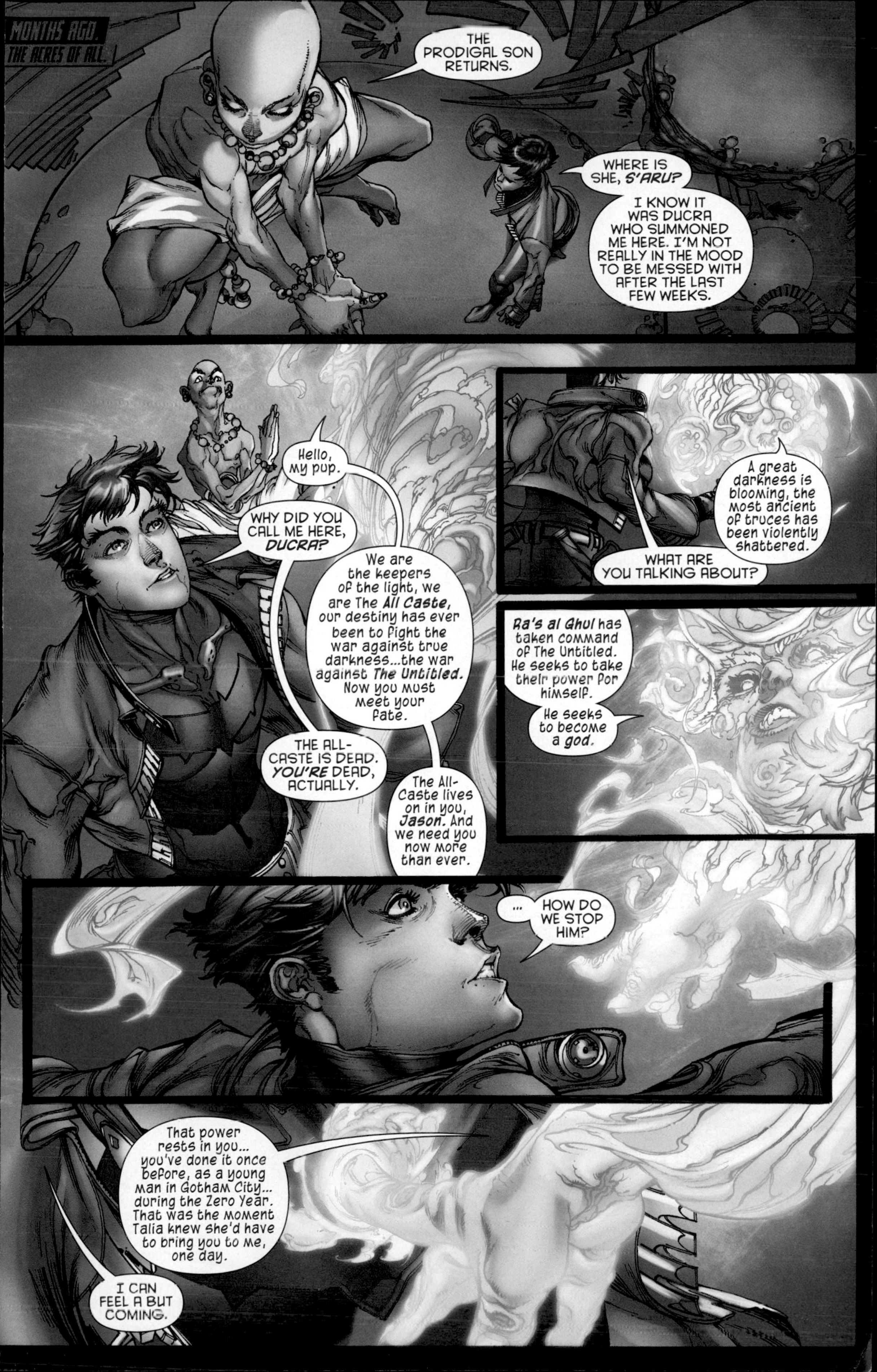
MONTHS AGO. THE ACRES OF ALL.
THE PRODIGAL SON RETURNS.
WHERE IS SHE, S'ARU?
I KNOW IT WAS DUCRA WHO SUMMONED ME HERE. I'M NOT REALLY IN THE MOOD TO BE MESSED WITH AFTER THE LAST FEW WEEKS.
Hello, my pup.
WHY DID YOU CALL ME HERE, DUCRA?
We are the keepers of the light, we are The All Caste, our destiny has ever been to fight the war against true darkness...the war against The Untitled. Now you must meet your fate.
THE ALL-CASTE IS DEAD. YOU'RE DEAD, ACTUALLY.
The All-Caste lives on in you, Jason. And we need you now more than ever.
A great darkness is blooming, the most ancient of truces has been violently shattered.
WHAT ARE YOU TALKING ABOUT?
Ra's al Ghul has taken command of The Untitled. He seeks to take their power for himself.
He seeks to become a god.
... HOW DO WE STOP HIM?
That power rests in you... you've done it once before, as a young man in Gotham City... during the Zero Year. That was the moment Talia knew she'd have to bring you to me, one day.
I CAN FEEL A BUT COMING.

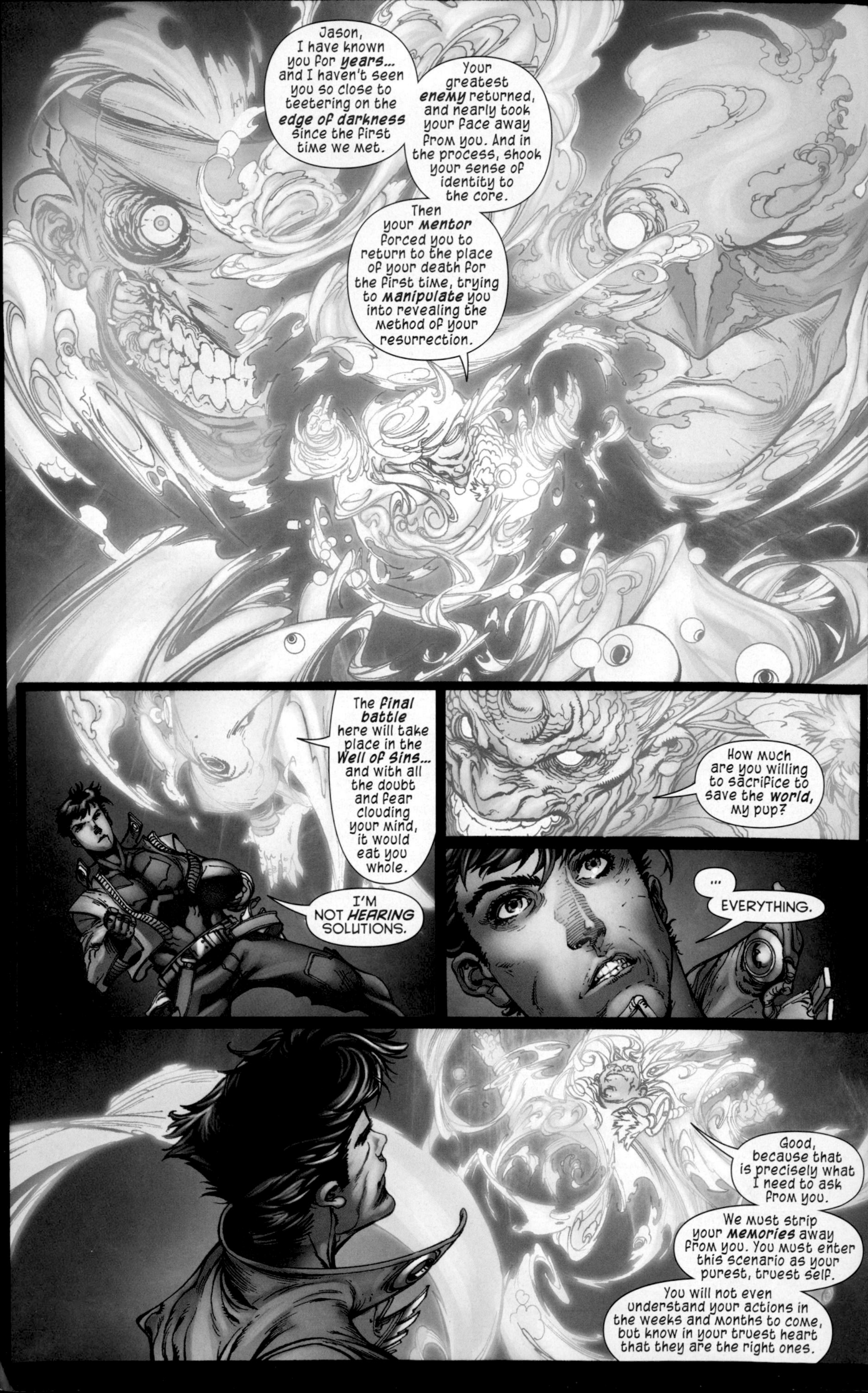
Jason, I have known you for *years...* and I haven't seen you so close to teetering on the *edge of darkness* since the first time we met.
Your greatest *enemy* returned, and nearly took your face away from you. And in the process, shook your sense of identity to the core.
Then your *mentor* forced you to return to the place of your death for the first time, trying to *manipulate* you into revealing the method of your resurrection.
The *final battle* here will take place in the *Well of Sins...* and with all the doubt and fear clouding your mind, it would eat you whole.
I'M NOT *HEARING* SOLUTIONS.
How much are you willing to sacrifice to save the *world,* my pup?
... EVERYTHING.
Good, because that is precisely what I need to ask from you.
We must strip your *memories* away from you. You must enter this scenario as your purest, truest self.
You will not even understand your actions in the weeks and months to come, but know in your truest heart that they are the right ones.

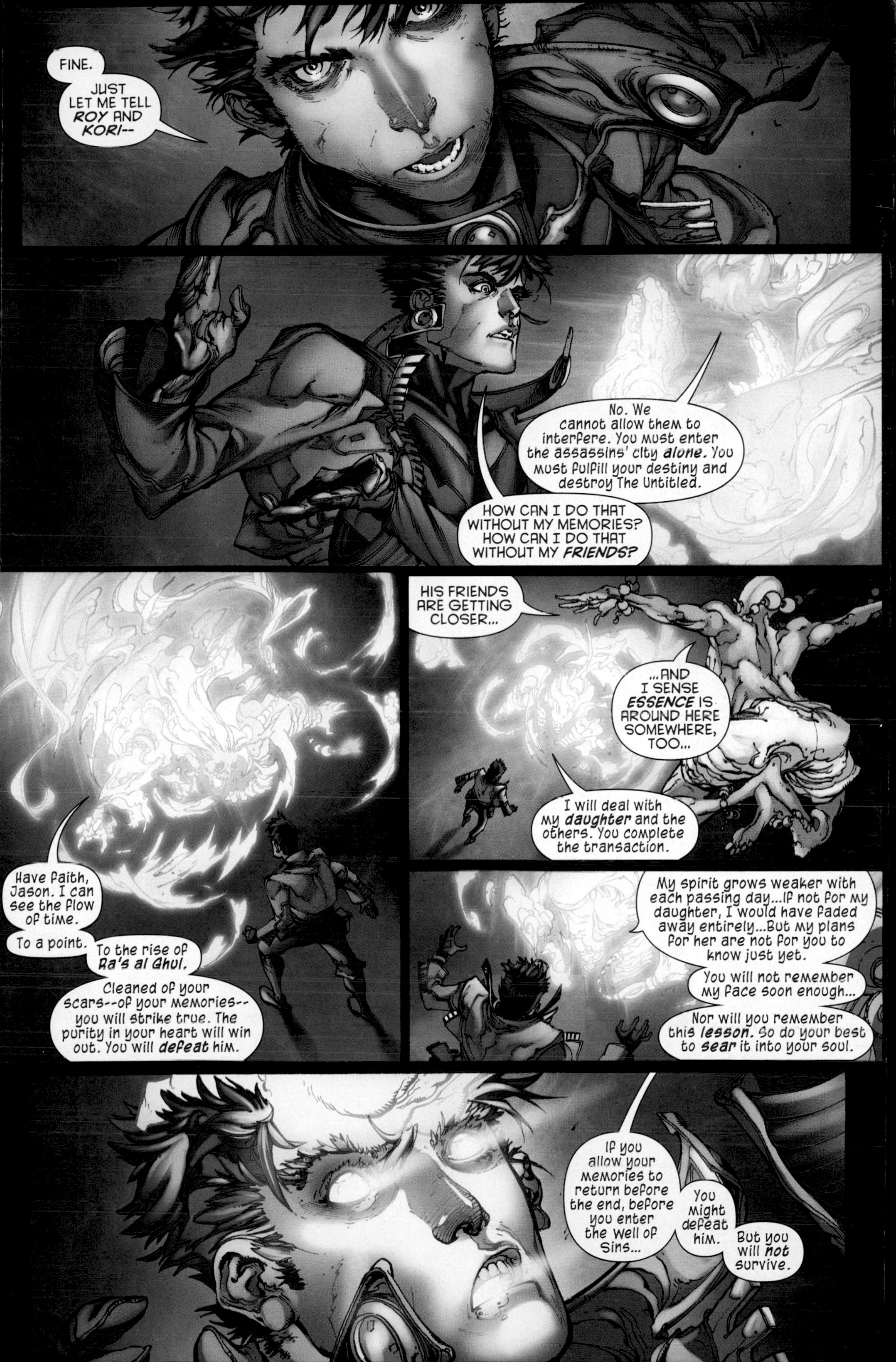
FINE.
JUST LET ME TELL ROY AND KORI--
No. We cannot allow them to interfere. You must enter the assassins' city alone. You must fulfill your destiny and destroy The Untitled.
HOW CAN I DO THAT WITHOUT MY MEMORIES? HOW CAN I DO THAT WITHOUT MY FRIENDS?
HIS FRIENDS ARE GETTING CLOSER...
...AND I SENSE ESSENCE IS AROUND HERE SOMEWHERE, TOO...
I will deal with my daughter and the others. You complete the transaction.
Have faith, Jason. I can see the flow of time.
To a point.
To the rise of Ra's al Ghul.
Cleaned of your scars--of your memories--you will strike true. The purity in your heart will win out. You will defeat him.
My spirit grows weaker with each passing day...If not for my daughter, I would have faded away entirely...But my plans for her are not for you to know just yet.
You will not remember my face soon enough...
Nor will you remember this lesson. So do your best to sear it into your soul.
If you allow your memories to return before the end, before you enter the Well of Sins...
You might defeat him.
But you will not survive.

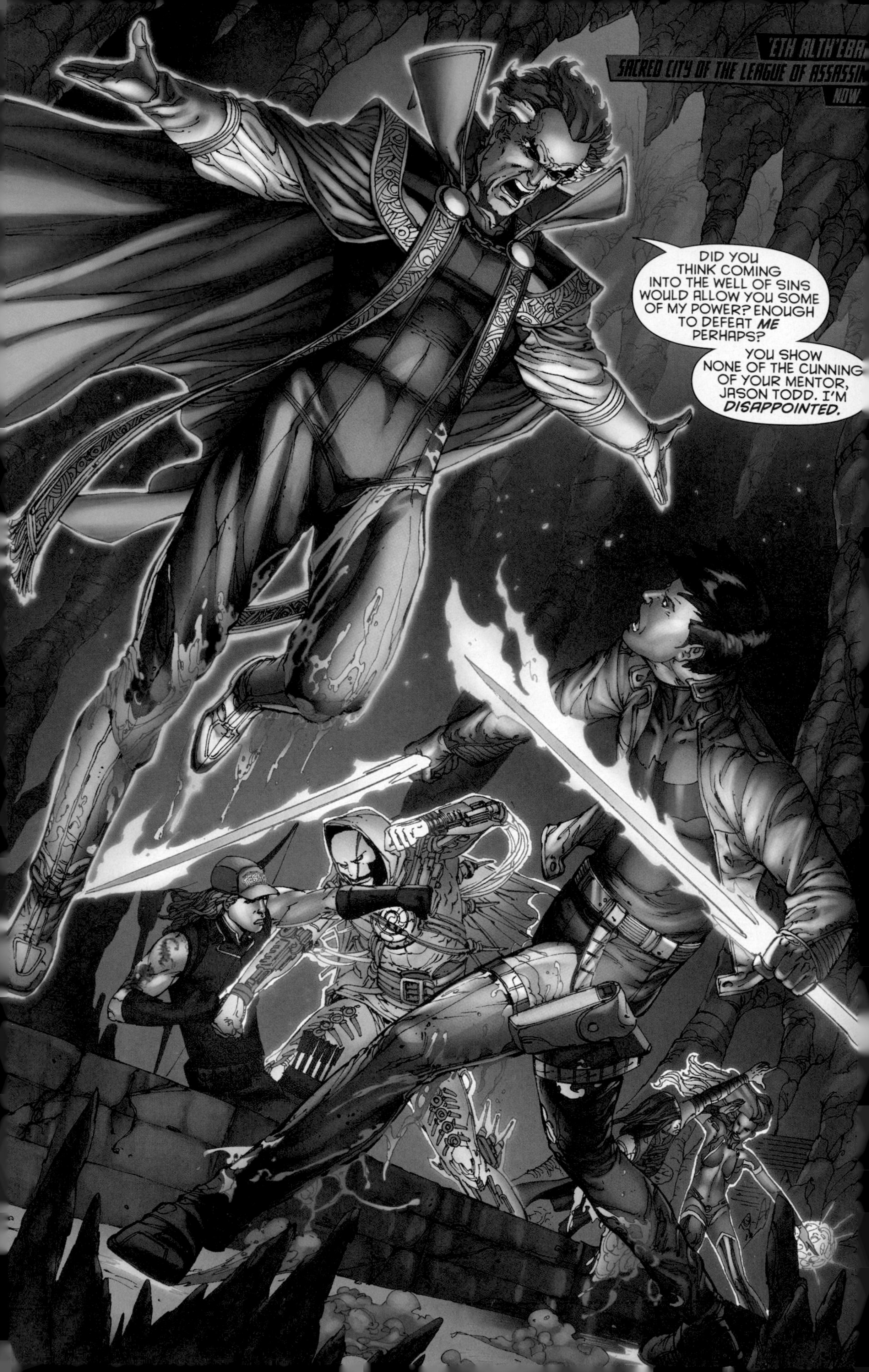
'ETH ALTH'EBA
SACRED CITY OF THE LEAGUE OF ASSASSI
NOW.
DID YOU THINK COMING INTO THE WELL OF SINS WOULD ALLOW YOU SOME OF MY POWER? ENOUGH TO DEFEAT *ME* PERHAPS?
YOU SHOW NONE OF THE CUNNING OF YOUR MENTOR, JASON TODD. I'M *DISAPPOINTED.*

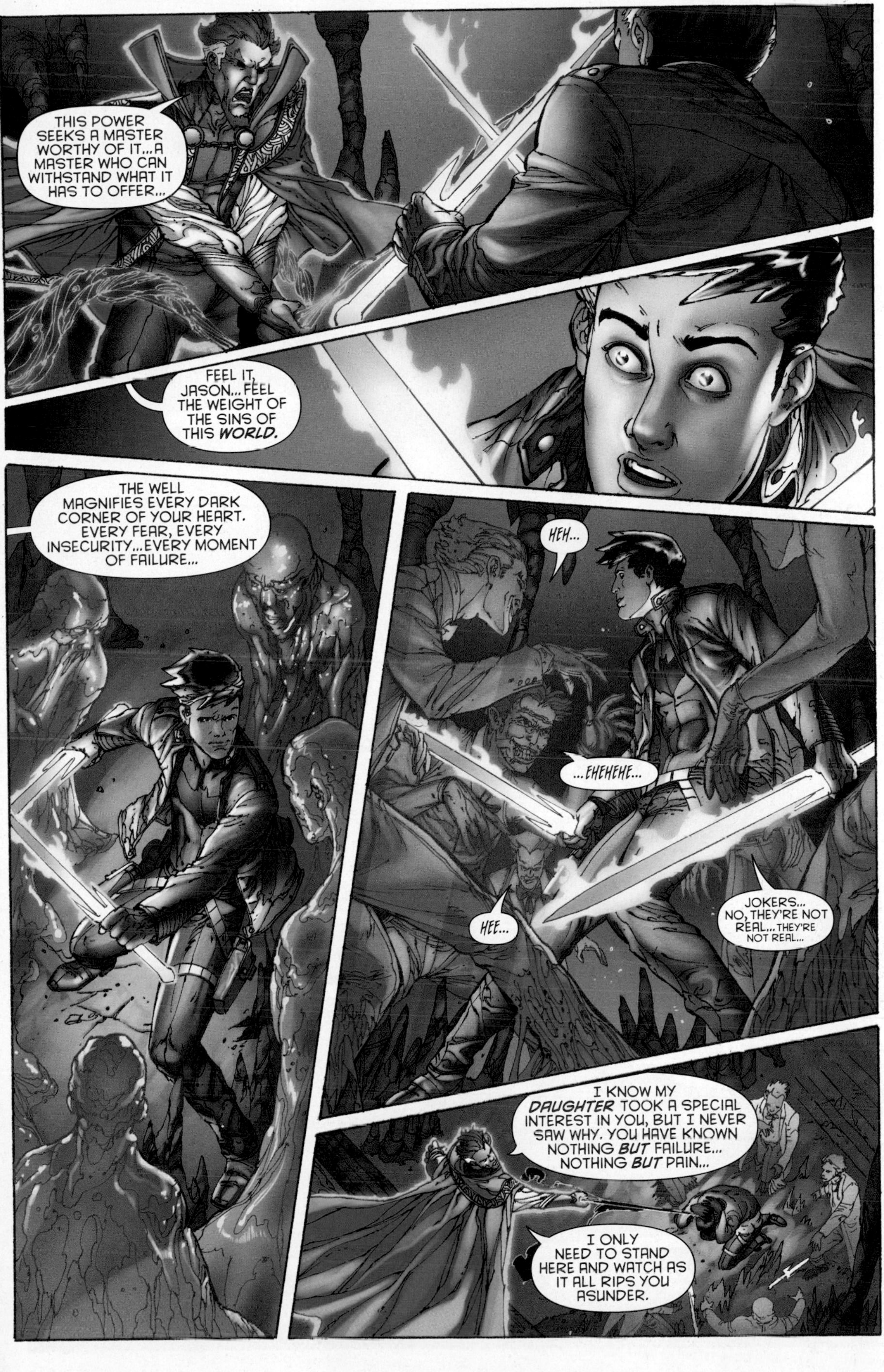
THIS POWER SEEKS A MASTER WORTHY OF IT...A MASTER WHO CAN WITHSTAND WHAT IT HAS TO OFFER...
FEEL IT, JASON...FEEL THE WEIGHT OF THE SINS OF THIS WORLD.
THE WELL MAGNIFIES EVERY DARK CORNER OF YOUR HEART. EVERY FEAR, EVERY INSECURITY...EVERY MOMENT OF FAILURE...
HEH...
...EHEHEHE...
HEE...
JOKERS... NO, THEY'RE NOT REAL... THEY'RE NOT REAL...
I KNOW MY DAUGHTER TOOK A SPECIAL INTEREST IN YOU, BUT I NEVER SAW WHY. YOU HAVE KNOWN NOTHING BUT FAILURE... NOTHING BUT PAIN...
I ONLY NEED TO STAND HERE AND WATCH AS IT ALL RIPS YOU ASUNDER.

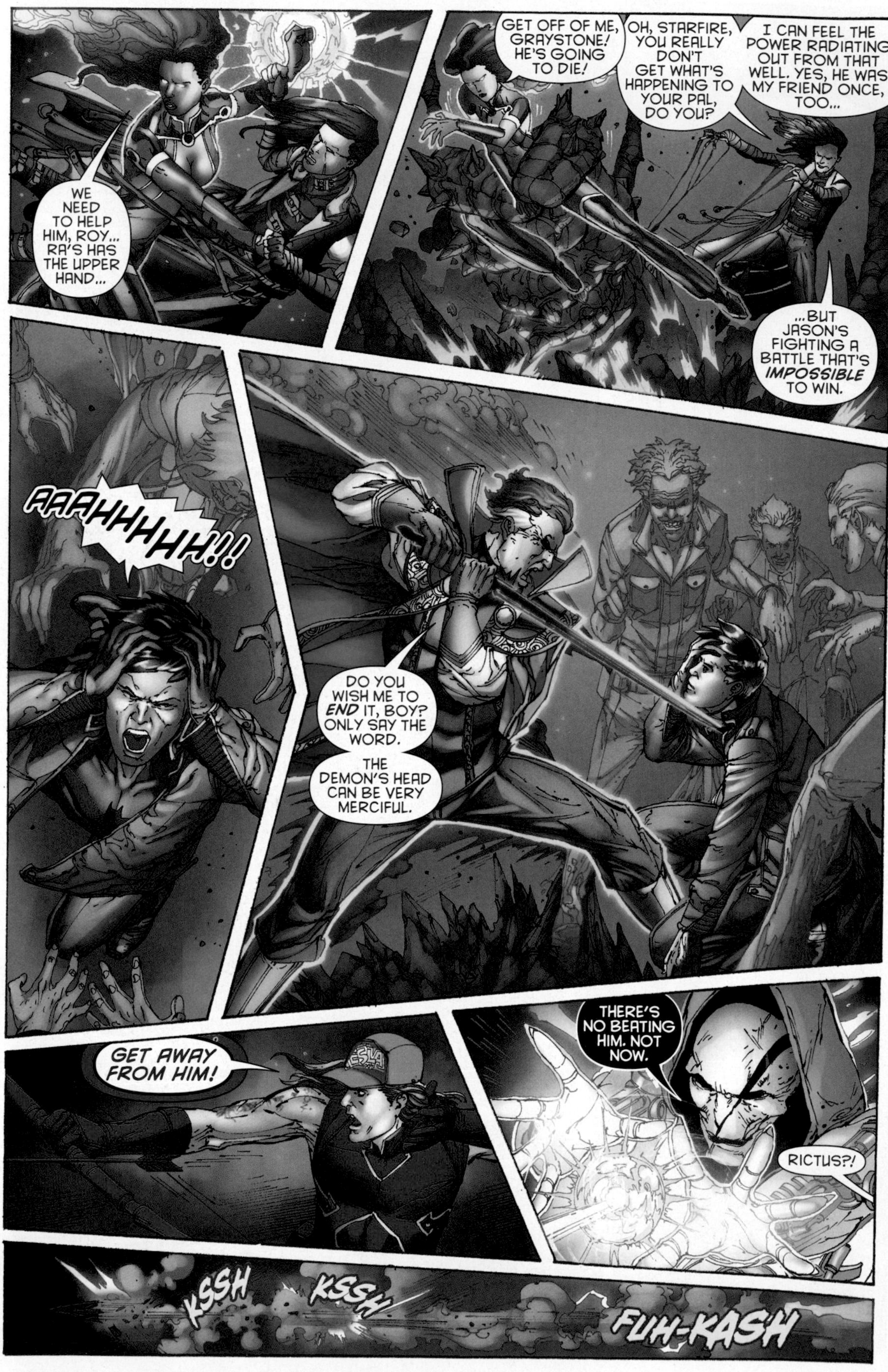
WE NEED TO HELP HIM, ROY... RA'S HAS THE UPPER HAND...
GET OFF OF ME, GRAYSTONE! HE'S GOING TO DIE!
OH, STARFIRE, YOU REALLY DON'T GET WHAT'S HAPPENING TO YOUR PAL, DO YOU?
I CAN FEEL THE POWER RADIATING OUT FROM THAT WELL. YES, HE WAS MY FRIEND ONCE, TOO...
...BUT JASON'S FIGHTING A BATTLE THAT'S IMPOSSIBLE TO WIN.
AAAHHHHHH!!!
DO YOU WISH ME TO END IT, BOY? ONLY SAY THE WORD.
THE DEMON'S HEAD CAN BE VERY MERCIFUL.
GET AWAY FROM HIM!
THERE'S NO BEATING HIM. NOT NOW.
RICTUS?!
KSSH
KSSH
FUH-KASH

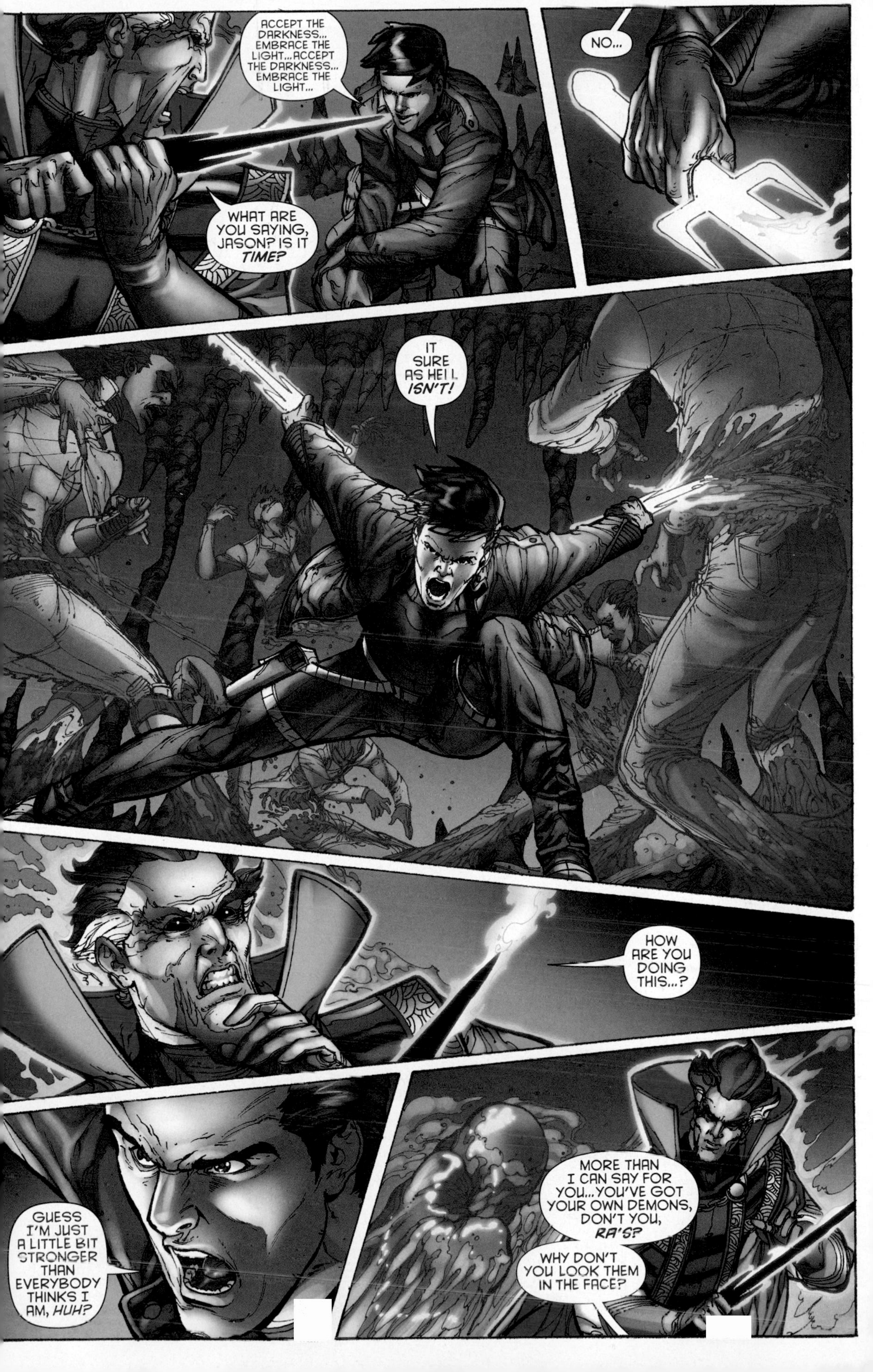
ACCEPT THE DARKNESS... EMBRACE THE LIGHT...ACCEPT THE DARKNESS... EMBRACE THE LIGHT...
WHAT ARE YOU SAYING, JASON? IS IT TIME?
NO...
IT SURE AS HELL ISN'T!
HOW ARE YOU DOING THIS...?
GUESS I'M JUST A LITTLE BIT STRONGER THAN EVERYBODY THINKS I AM, HUH?
MORE THAN I CAN SAY FOR YOU...YOU'VE GOT YOUR OWN DEMONS, DON'T YOU, RA'S?
WHY DON'T YOU LOOK THEM IN THE FACE?

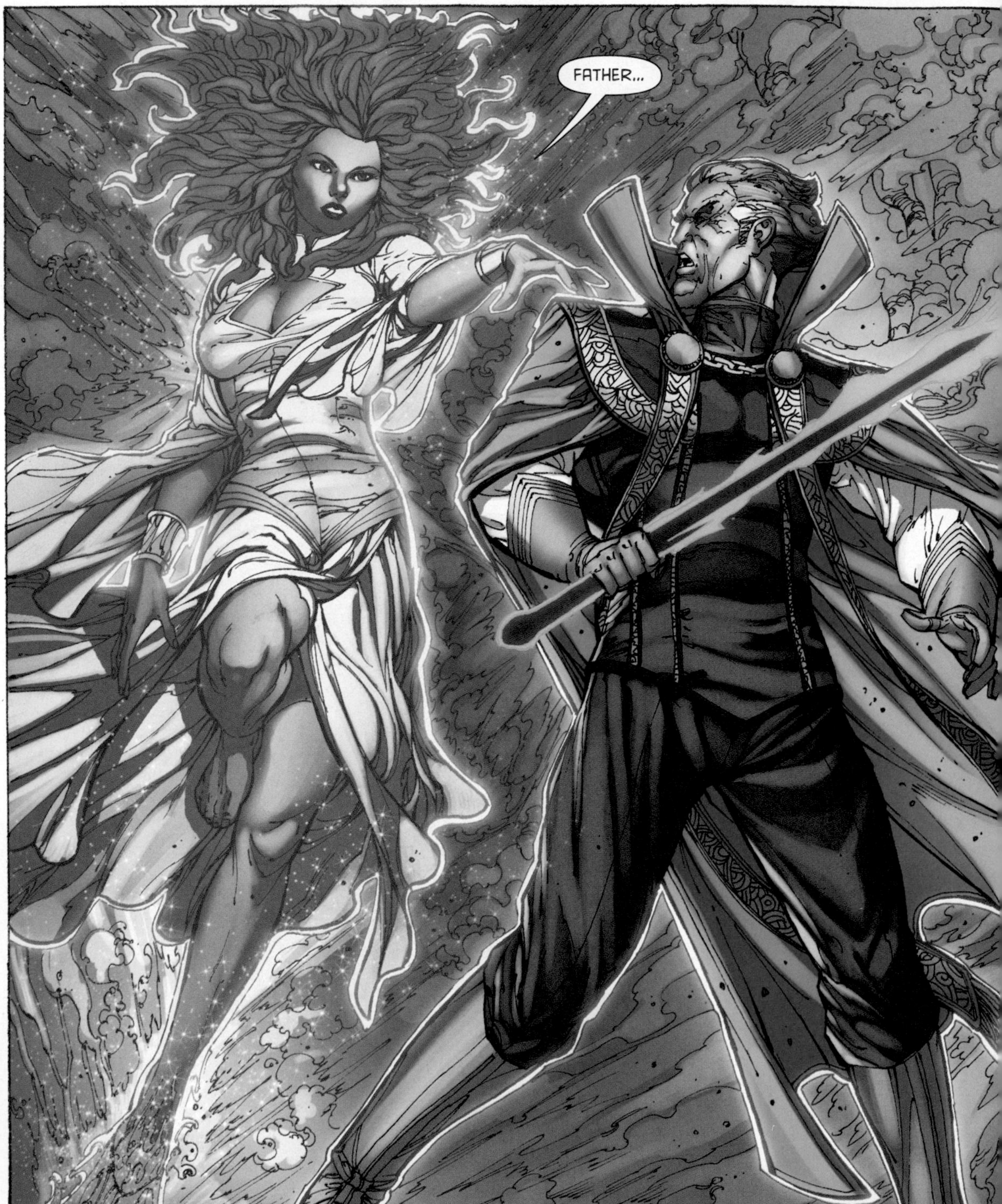
FATHER...

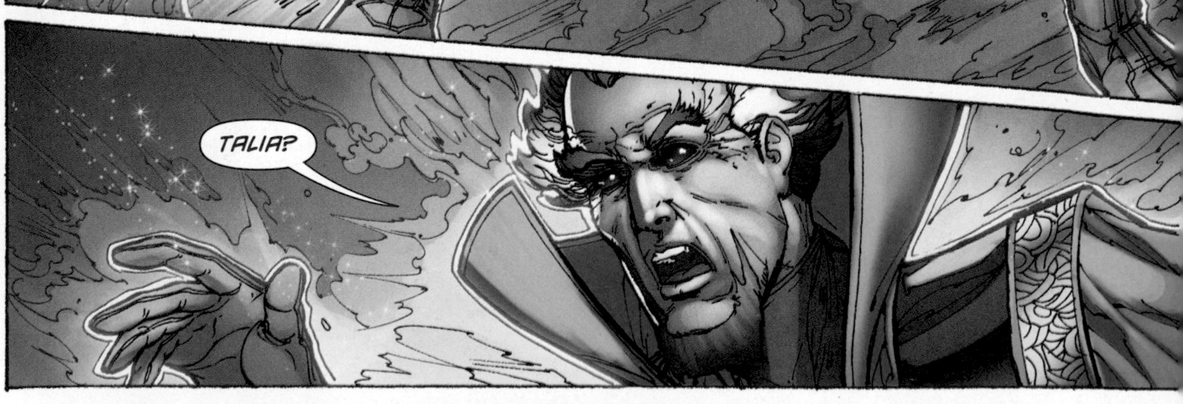
TALIA?

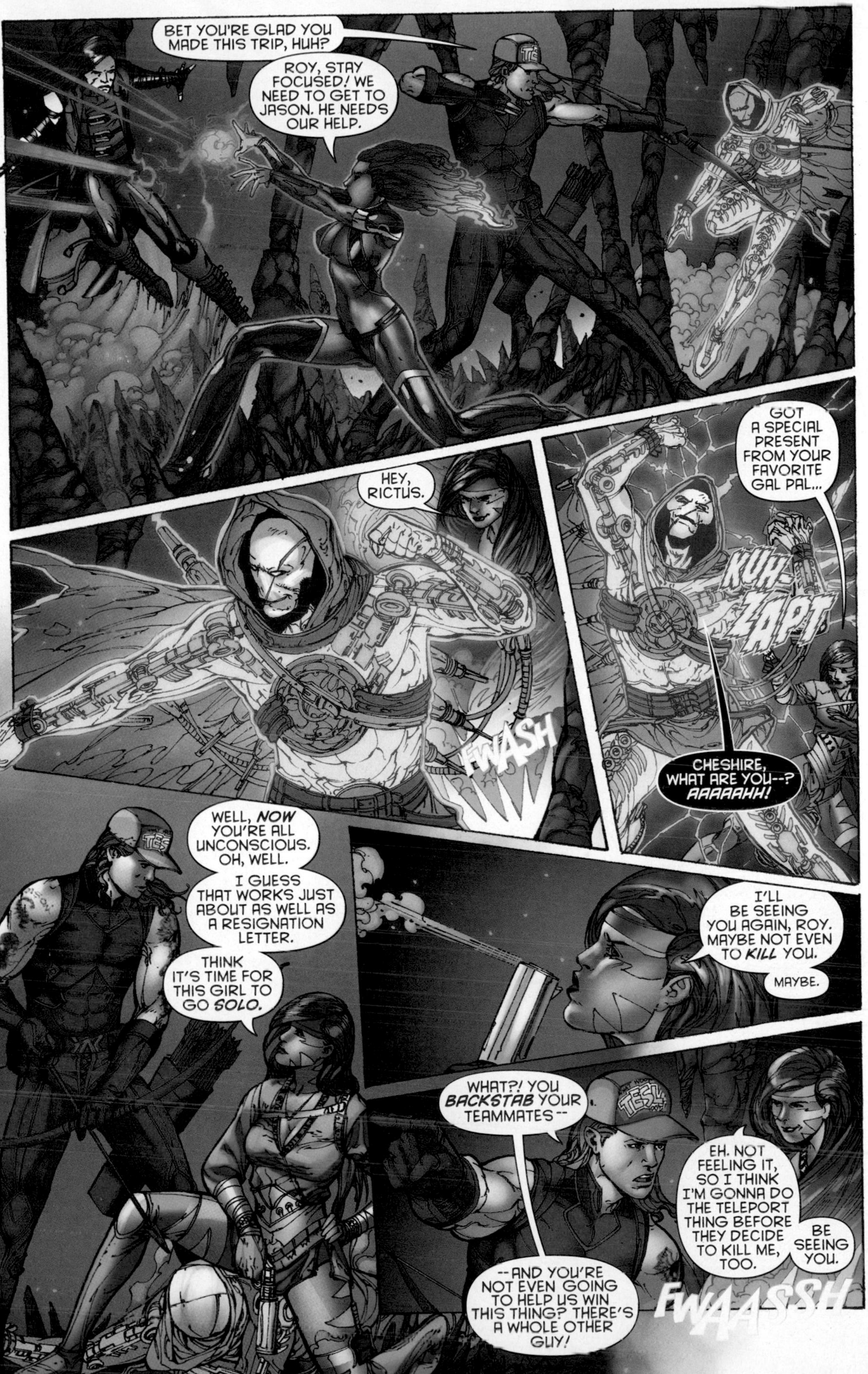
BET YOU'RE GLAD YOU MADE THIS TRIP, HUH?
ROY, STAY FOCUSED! WE NEED TO GET TO JASON. HE NEEDS OUR HELP.
HEY, RICTUS.
FWASH
GOT A SPECIAL PRESENT FROM YOUR FAVORITE GAL PAL...
KUH-ZAPT
CHESHIRE, WHAT ARE YOU--? AAAAAHH!
WELL, NOW YOU'RE ALL UNCONSCIOUS. OH, WELL.
I GUESS THAT WORKS JUST ABOUT AS WELL AS A RESIGNATION LETTER.
THINK IT'S TIME FOR THIS GIRL TO GO SOLO.
I'LL BE SEEING YOU AGAIN, ROY. MAYBE NOT EVEN TO KILL YOU.
MAYBE.
WHAT?! YOU BACKSTAB YOUR TEAMMATES--
--AND YOU'RE NOT EVEN GOING TO HELP US WIN THIS THING? THERE'S A WHOLE OTHER GUY!
EH. NOT FEELING IT, SO I THINK I'M GONNA DO THE TELEPORT THING BEFORE THEY DECIDE TO KILL ME, TOO.
BE SEEING YOU.
FWAASSH

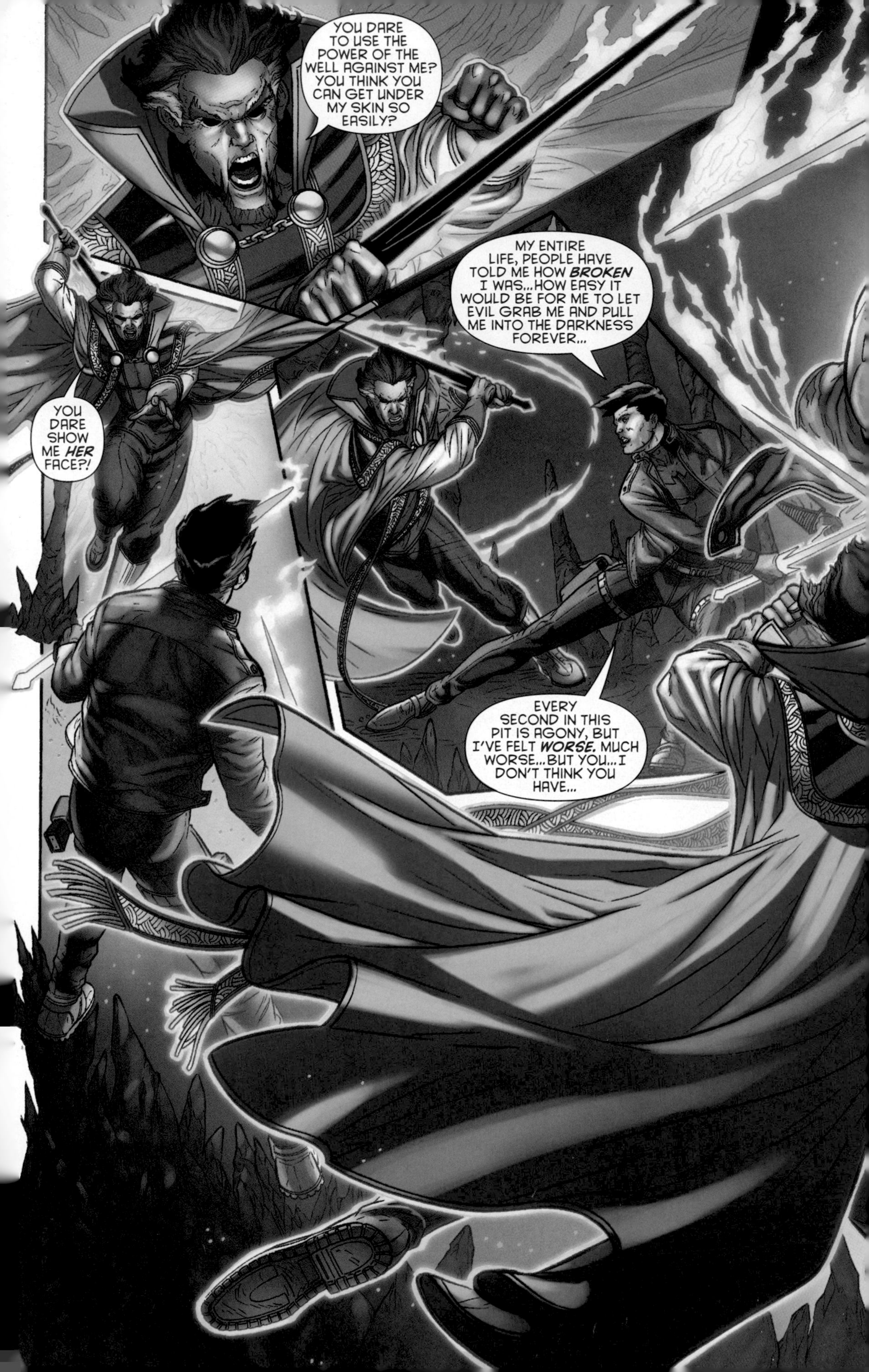
YOU DARE TO USE THE POWER OF THE WELL AGAINST ME? YOU THINK YOU CAN GET UNDER MY SKIN SO EASILY?
YOU DARE SHOW ME HER FACE?!
MY ENTIRE LIFE, PEOPLE HAVE TOLD ME HOW BROKEN I WAS...HOW EASY IT WOULD BE FOR ME TO LET EVIL GRAB ME AND PULL ME INTO THE DARKNESS FOREVER...
EVERY SECOND IN THIS PIT IS AGONY, BUT I'VE FELT WORSE. MUCH WORSE...BUT YOU...I DON'T THINK YOU HAVE...

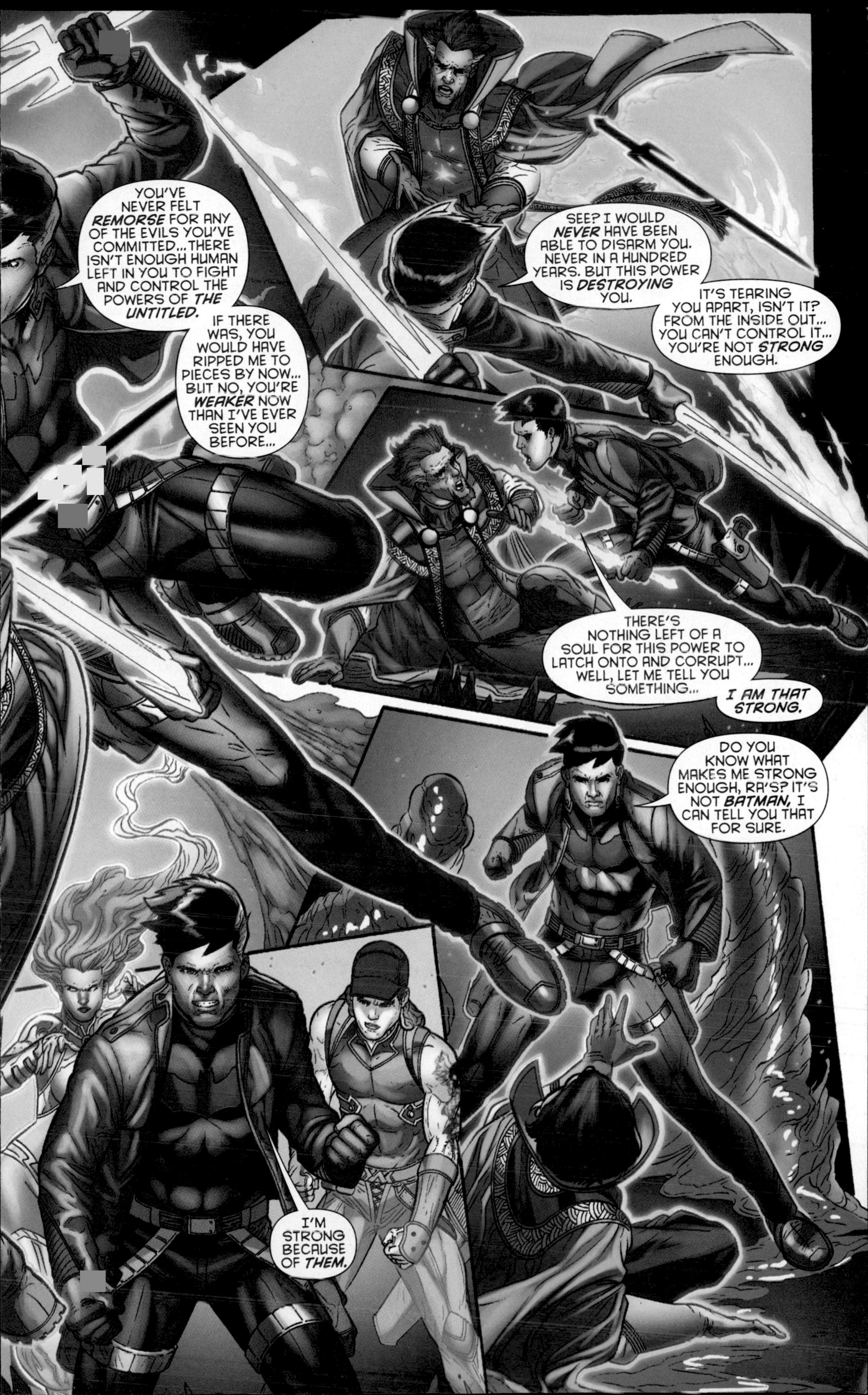

YOU'VE NEVER FELT REMORSE FOR ANY OF THE EVILS YOU'VE COMMITTED... THERE ISN'T ENOUGH HUMAN LEFT IN YOU TO FIGHT AND CONTROL THE POWERS OF THE UNTITLED.
IF THERE WAS, YOU WOULD HAVE RIPPED ME TO PIECES BY NOW... BUT NO, YOU'RE WEAKER NOW THAN I'VE EVER SEEN YOU BEFORE...
SEE? I WOULD NEVER HAVE BEEN ABLE TO DISARM YOU. NEVER IN A HUNDRED YEARS. BUT THIS POWER IS DESTROYING YOU.
IT'S TEARING YOU APART, ISN'T IT? FROM THE INSIDE OUT... YOU CAN'T CONTROL IT... YOU'RE NOT STRONG ENOUGH.
THERE'S NOTHING LEFT OF A SOUL FOR THIS POWER TO LATCH ONTO AND CORRUPT... WELL, LET ME TELL YOU SOMETHING...
I AM THAT STRONG.
DO YOU KNOW WHAT MAKES ME STRONG ENOUGH, RA'S? IT'S NOT BATMAN, I CAN TELL YOU THAT FOR SURE.
I'M STRONG BECAUSE OF THEM.

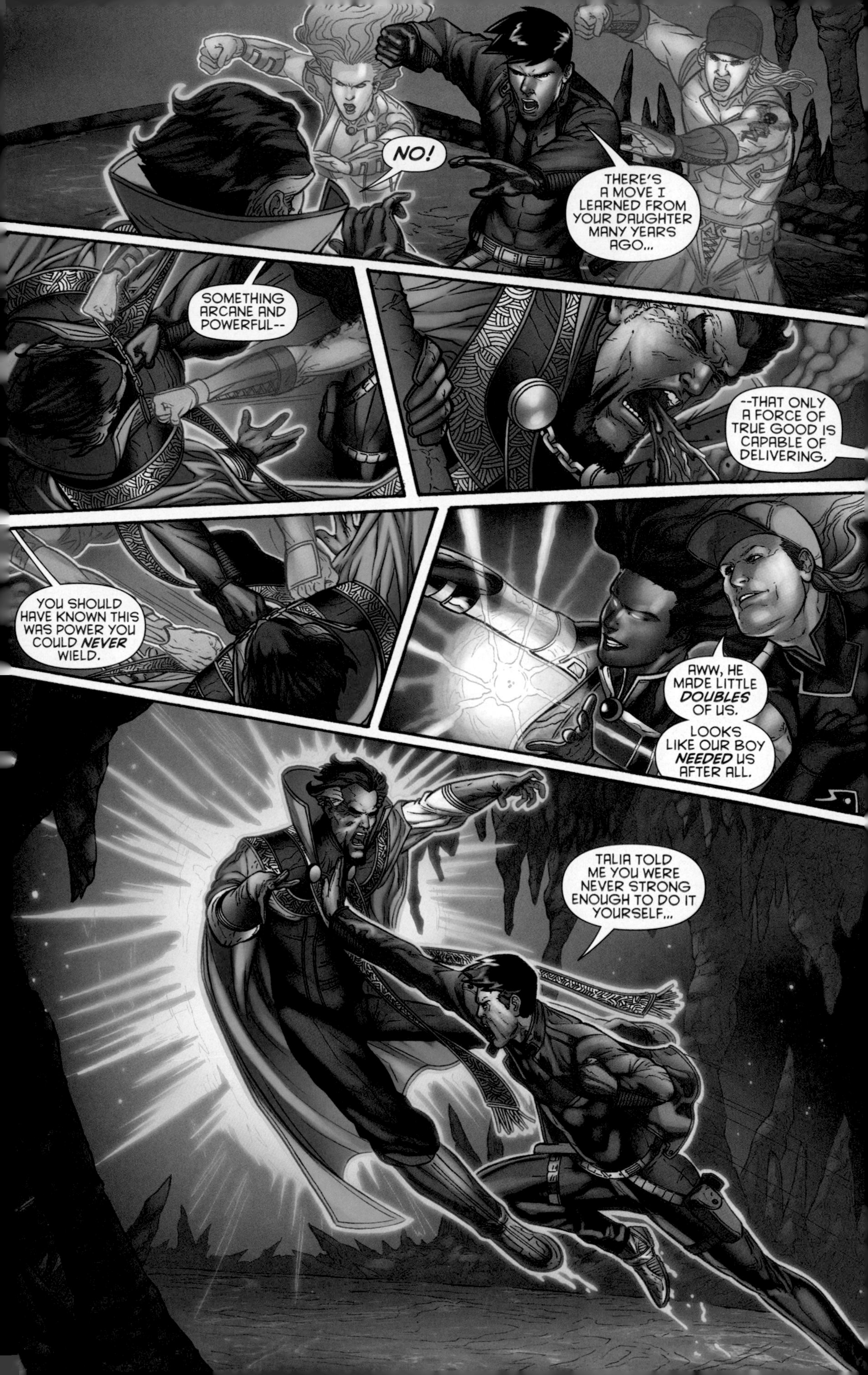
NO!
THERE'S A MOVE I LEARNED FROM YOUR DAUGHTER MANY YEARS AGO...
SOMETHING ARCANE AND POWERFUL--
--THAT ONLY A FORCE OF TRUE GOOD IS CAPABLE OF DELIVERING.
YOU SHOULD HAVE KNOWN THIS WAS POWER YOU COULD NEVER WIELD.
AWW, HE MADE LITTLE DOUBLES OF US.
LOOKS LIKE OUR BOY NEEDED US AFTER ALL.
TALIA TOLD ME YOU WERE NEVER STRONG ENOUGH TO DO IT YOURSELF...

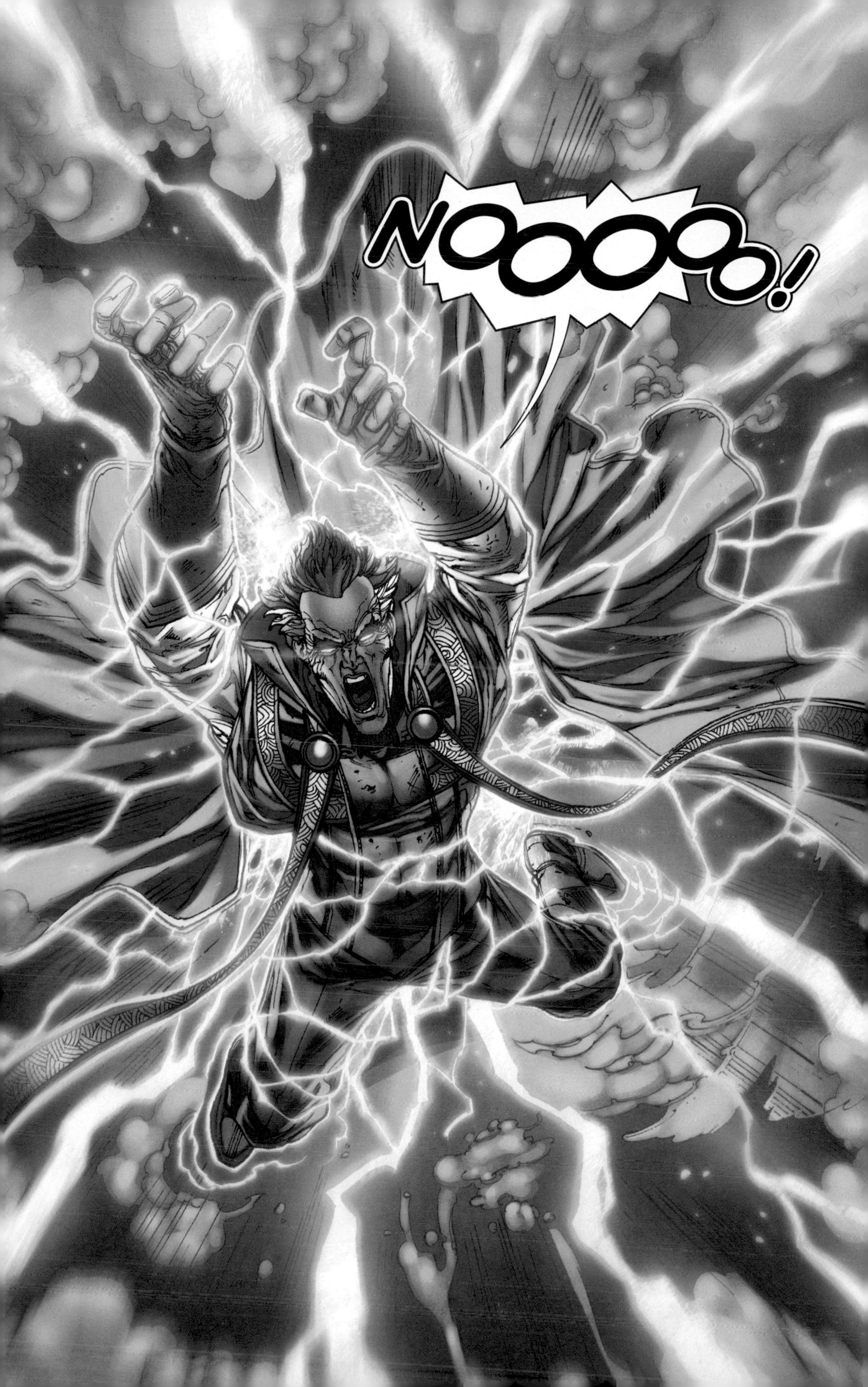
NOOOOO!

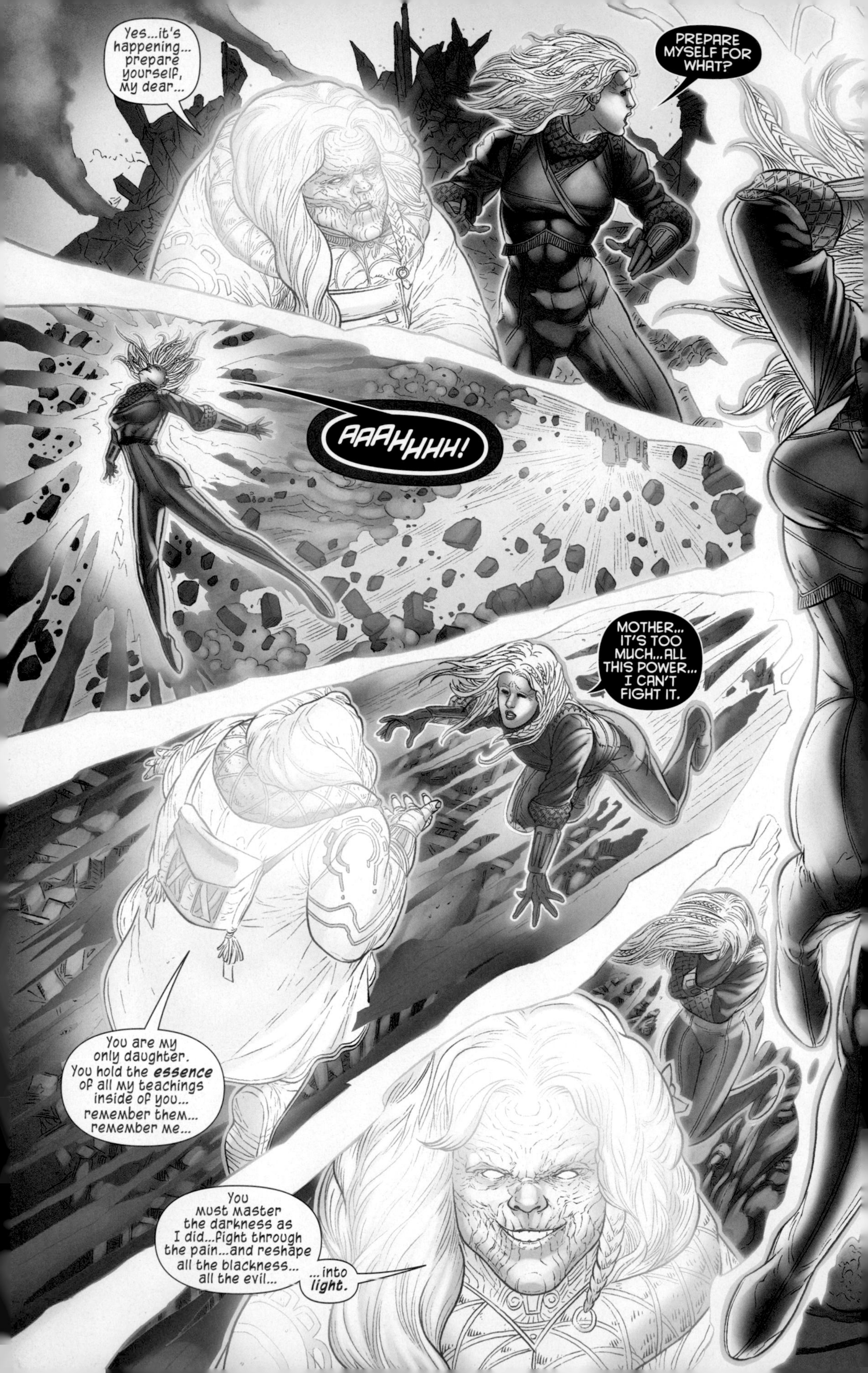
Yes...it's happening... prepare yourself, my dear...
PREPARE MYSELF FOR WHAT?
AAAHHHH!
MOTHER... IT'S TOO MUCH...ALL THIS POWER... I CAN'T FIGHT IT.
You are my only daughter. You hold the essence of all my teachings inside of you... remember them... remember me...
You must master the darkness as I did...fight through the pain...and reshape all the blackness... all the evil...
...into light.

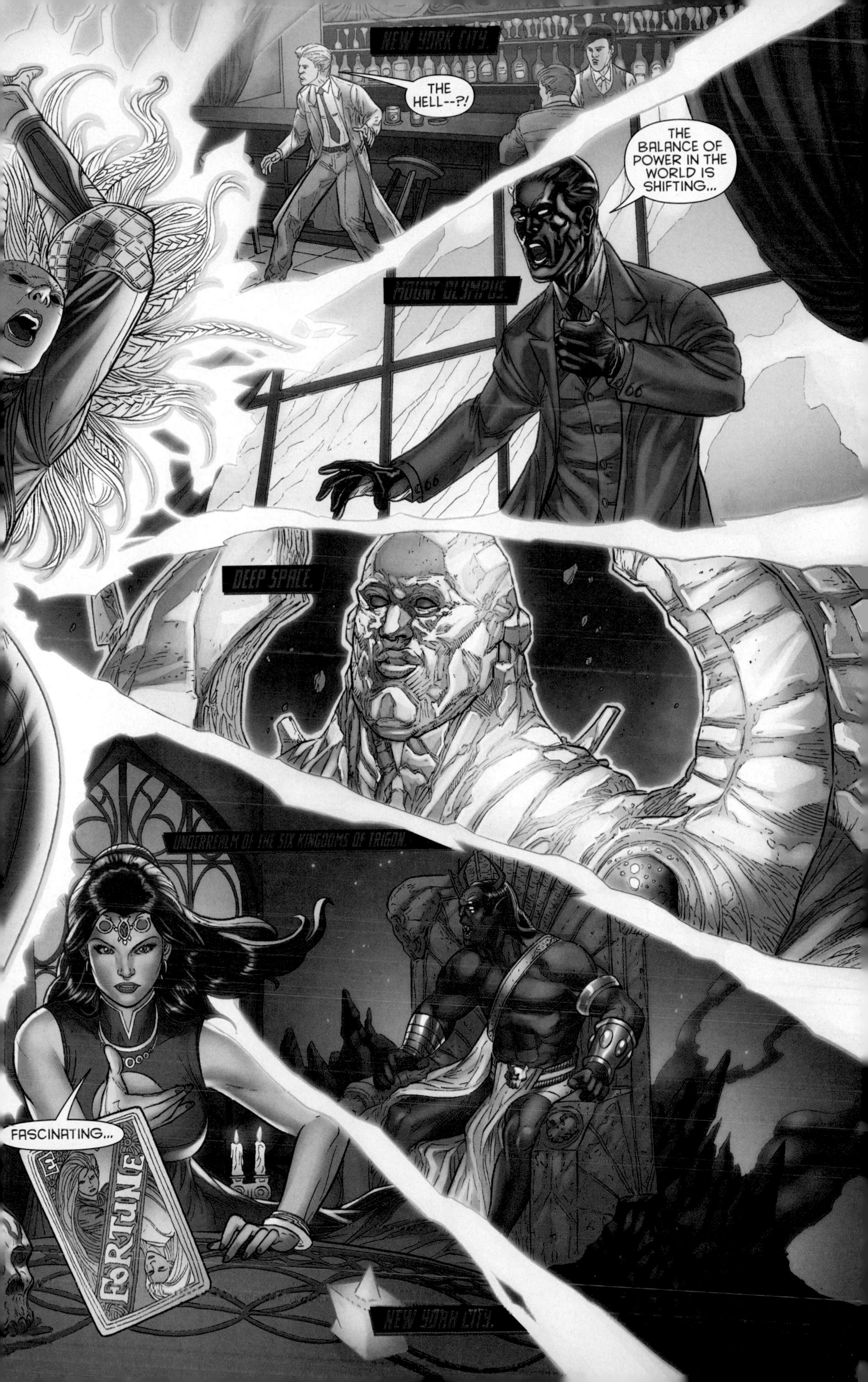

NEW YORK CITY.
THE HELL--?!
THE BALANCE OF POWER IN THE WORLD IS SHIFTING...
MOUNT OLYMPUS.
DEEP SPACE.
UNDERREALM OF THE SIX KINGDOMS OF TRIGON.
FASCINATING...
FORTUNE
NEW YORK CITY.

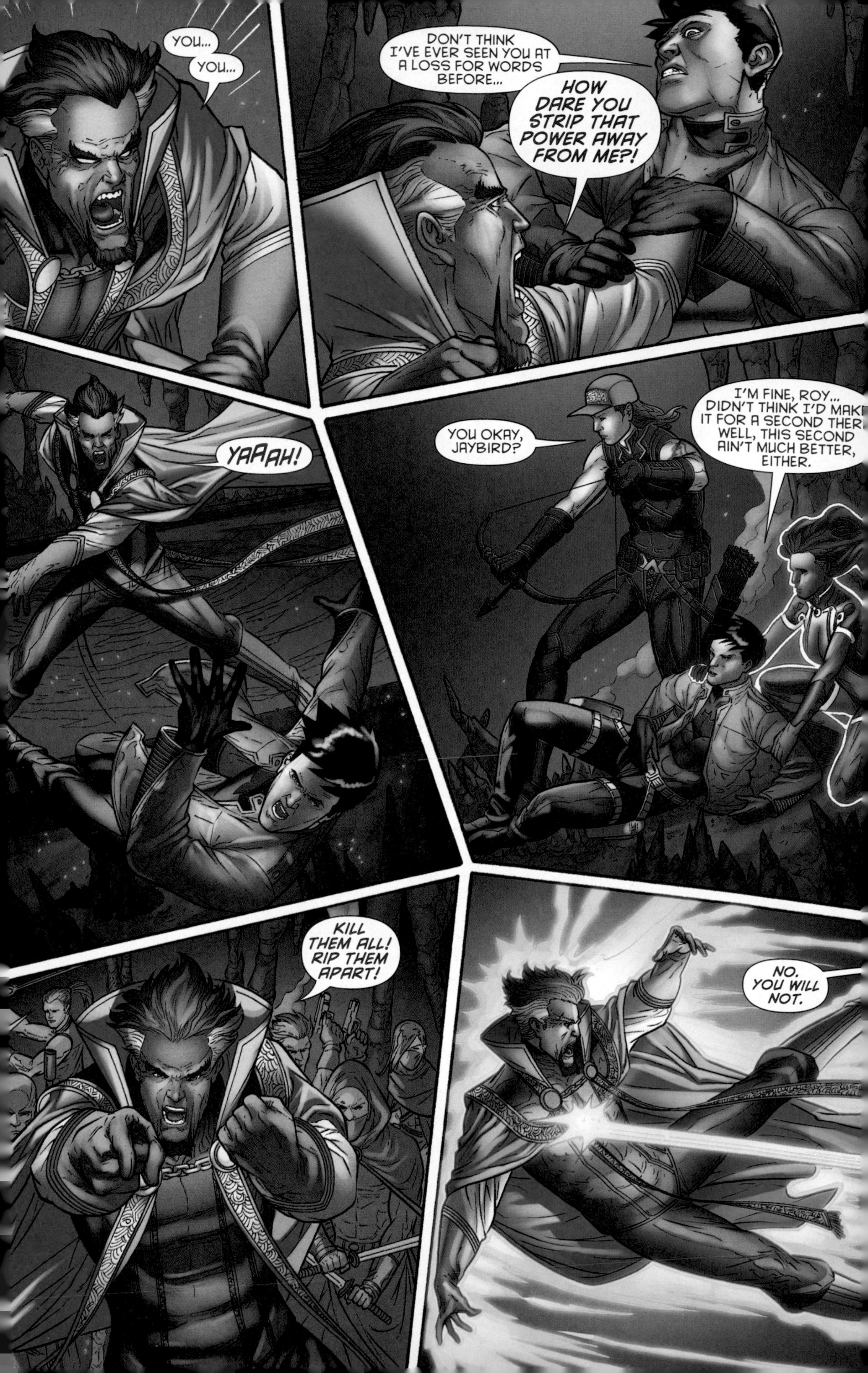
YOU...
YOU...
DON'T THINK I'VE EVER SEEN YOU AT A LOSS FOR WORDS BEFORE...
HOW DARE YOU STRIP THAT POWER AWAY FROM ME?!
YAAAAH!
YOU OKAY, JAYBIRD?
I'M FINE, ROY... DIDN'T THINK I'D MAKE IT FOR A SECOND THERE. WELL, THIS SECOND AIN'T MUCH BETTER, EITHER.
KILL THEM ALL! RIP THEM APART!
NO. YOU WILL NOT.

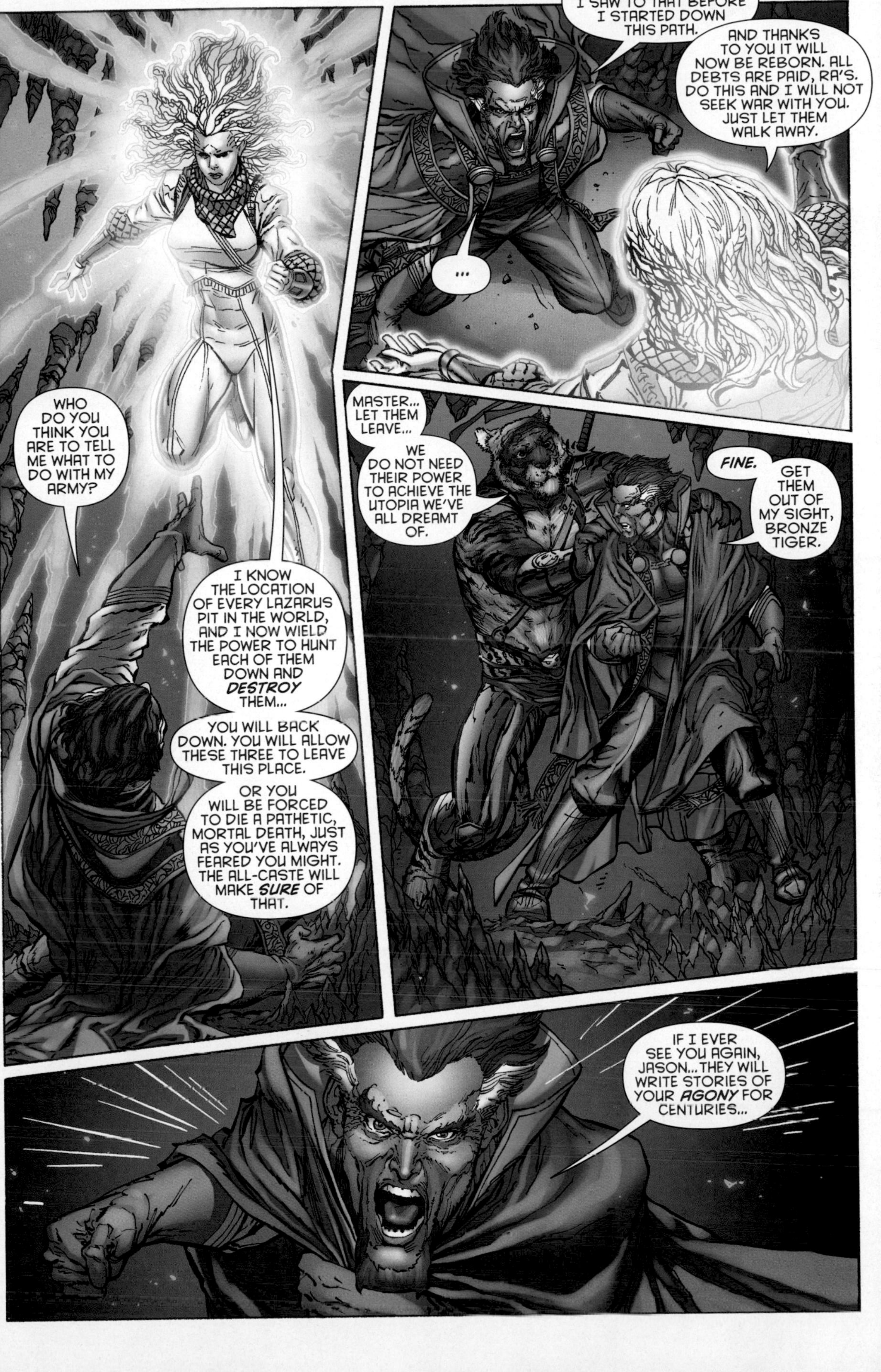

THE ALL CASTE HAS BEEN DESTROYED... I SAW TO THAT BEFORE I STARTED DOWN THIS PATH.
AND THANKS TO YOU IT WILL NOW BE REBORN. ALL DEBTS ARE PAID, RA'S. DO THIS AND I WILL NOT SEEK WAR WITH YOU. JUST LET THEM WALK AWAY.
...
WHO DO YOU THINK YOU ARE TO TELL ME WHAT TO DO WITH MY ARMY?
I KNOW THE LOCATION OF EVERY LAZARUS PIT IN THE WORLD, AND I NOW WIELD THE POWER TO HUNT EACH OF THEM DOWN AND ***DESTROY*** THEM...
YOU WILL BACK DOWN. YOU WILL ALLOW THESE THREE TO LEAVE THIS PLACE.
OR YOU WILL BE FORCED TO DIE A PATHETIC, MORTAL DEATH, JUST AS YOU'VE ALWAYS FEARED YOU MIGHT. THE ALL-CASTE WILL MAKE ***SURE*** OF THAT.
MASTER... LET THEM LEAVE...
WE DO NOT NEED THEIR POWER TO ACHIEVE THE UTOPIA WE'VE ALL DREAMT OF.
FINE.
GET THEM OUT OF MY SIGHT, BRONZE TIGER.
IF I EVER SEE YOU AGAIN, JASON... THEY WILL WRITE STORIES OF YOUR ***AGONY*** FOR CENTURIES...

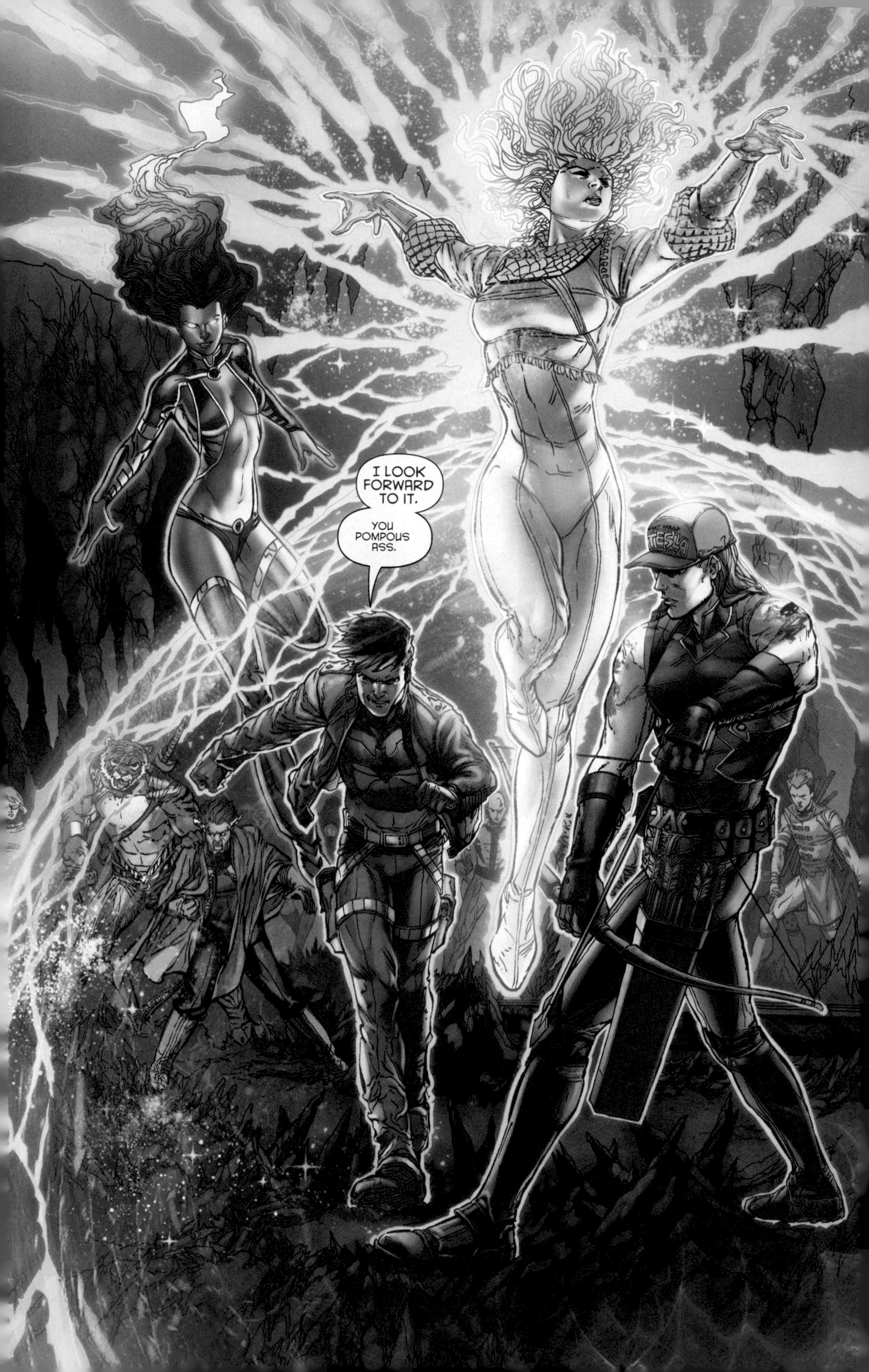
I LOOK FORWARD TO IT.
YOU POMPOUS ASS.
TESLA

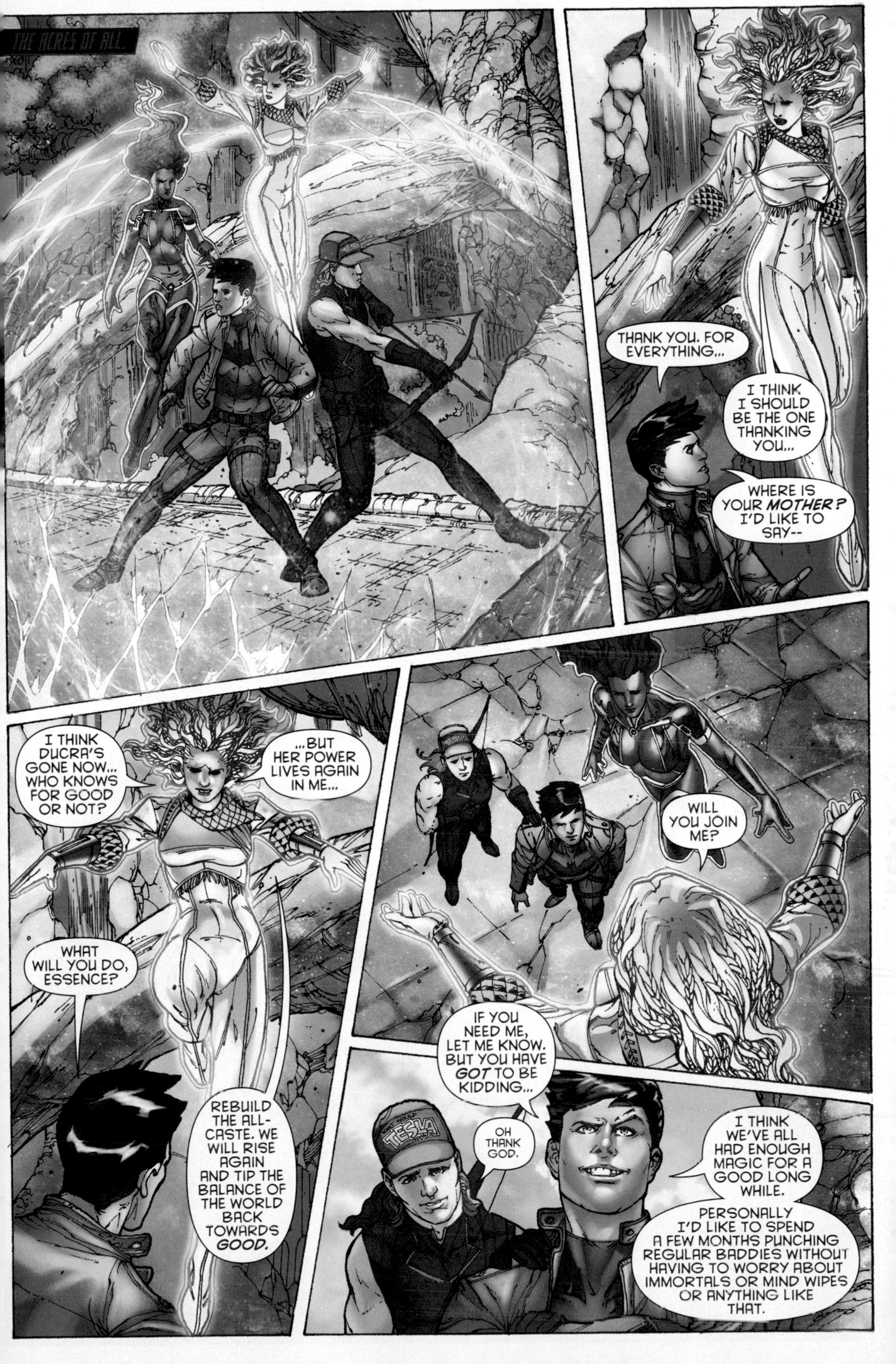
THE ACRES OF ALL.
THANK YOU. FOR EVERYTHING...
I THINK I SHOULD BE THE ONE THANKING YOU...
WHERE IS YOUR MOTHER? I'D LIKE TO SAY--
I THINK DUCRA'S GONE NOW... WHO KNOWS FOR GOOD OR NOT?
...BUT HER POWER LIVES AGAIN IN ME...
WHAT WILL YOU DO, ESSENCE?
REBUILD THE ALL-CASTE. WE WILL RISE AGAIN AND TIP THE BALANCE OF THE WORLD BACK TOWARDS GOOD.
WILL YOU JOIN ME?
IF YOU NEED ME, LET ME KNOW. BUT YOU HAVE GOT TO BE KIDDING...
OH THANK GOD.
I THINK WE'VE ALL HAD ENOUGH MAGIC FOR A GOOD LONG WHILE.
PERSONALLY I'D LIKE TO SPEND A FEW MONTHS PUNCHING REGULAR BADDIES WITHOUT HAVING TO WORRY ABOUT IMMORTALS OR MIND WIPES OR ANYTHING LIKE THAT.

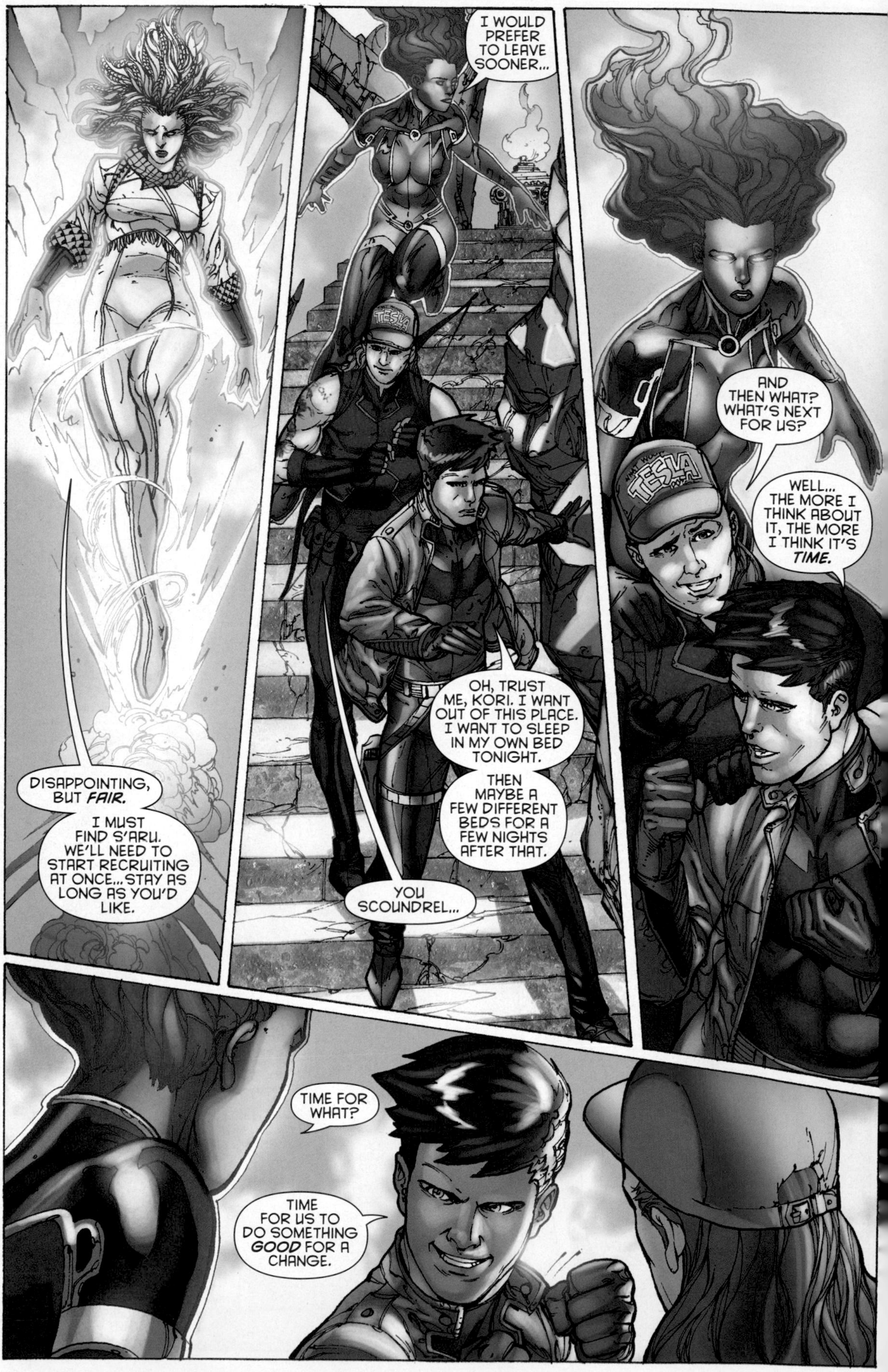

DISAPPOINTING, BUT FAIR.
I MUST FIND S'ARU. WE'LL NEED TO START RECRUITING AT ONCE... STAY AS LONG AS YOU'D LIKE.
I WOULD PREFER TO LEAVE SOONER...
OH, TRUST ME, KORI. I WANT OUT OF THIS PLACE. I WANT TO SLEEP IN MY OWN BED TONIGHT.
THEN MAYBE A FEW DIFFERENT BEDS FOR A FEW NIGHTS AFTER THAT.
YOU SCOUNDREL...
TESLA
AND THEN WHAT? WHAT'S NEXT FOR US?
WELL... THE MORE I THINK ABOUT IT, THE MORE I THINK IT'S TIME.
TESLA
TIME FOR WHAT?
TIME FOR US TO DO SOMETHING GOOD FOR A CHANGE.

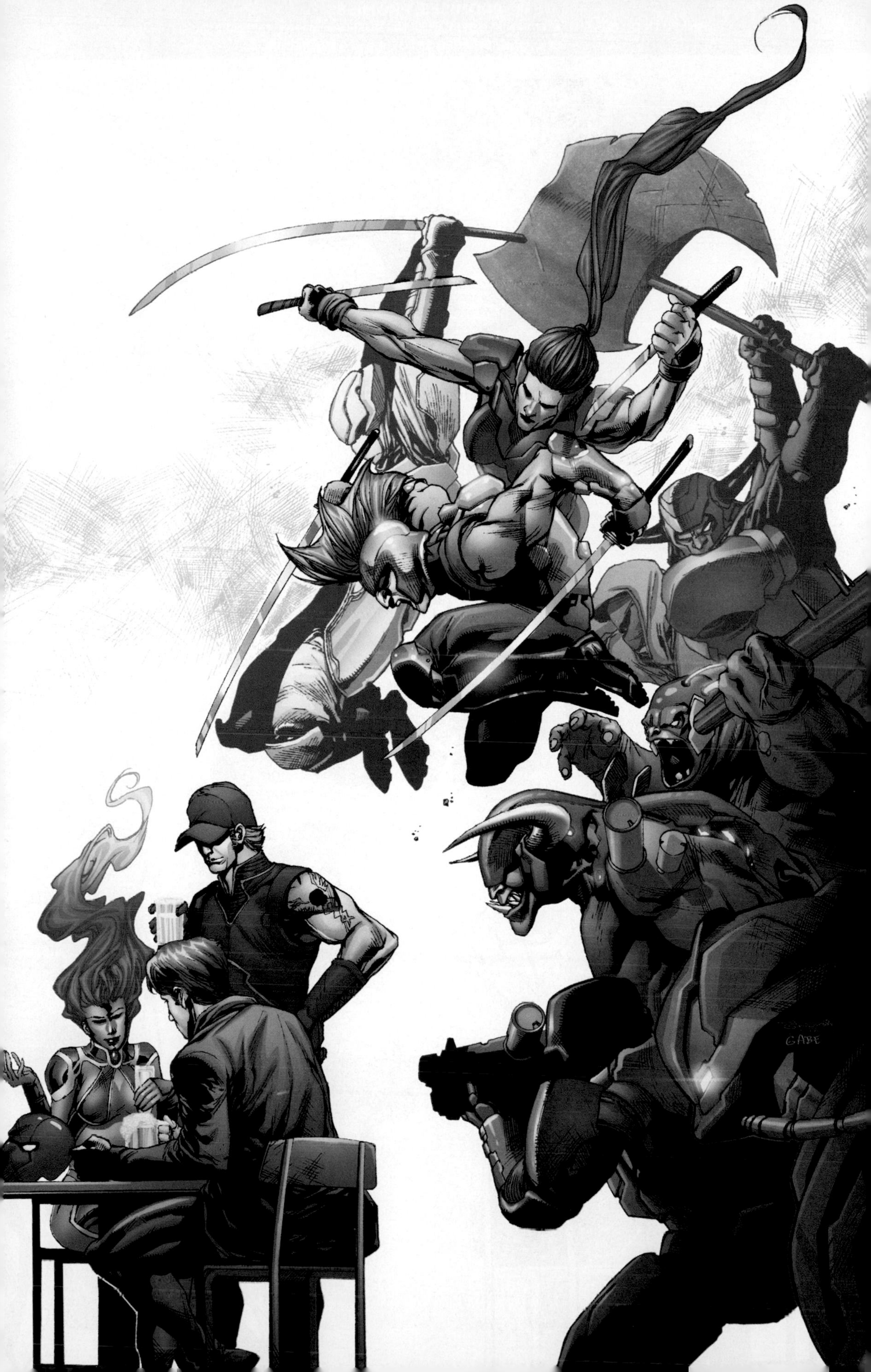
GABE

PROMISES, PROMISES

JAMES TYNION IV writer **STEPHEN SEGOVIA** artist **NEI RUFFINO** colorist **TAYLOR ESPOSITO** letterer
cover art by **STEPHEN SEGOVIA** and **GABE ELTAEB**

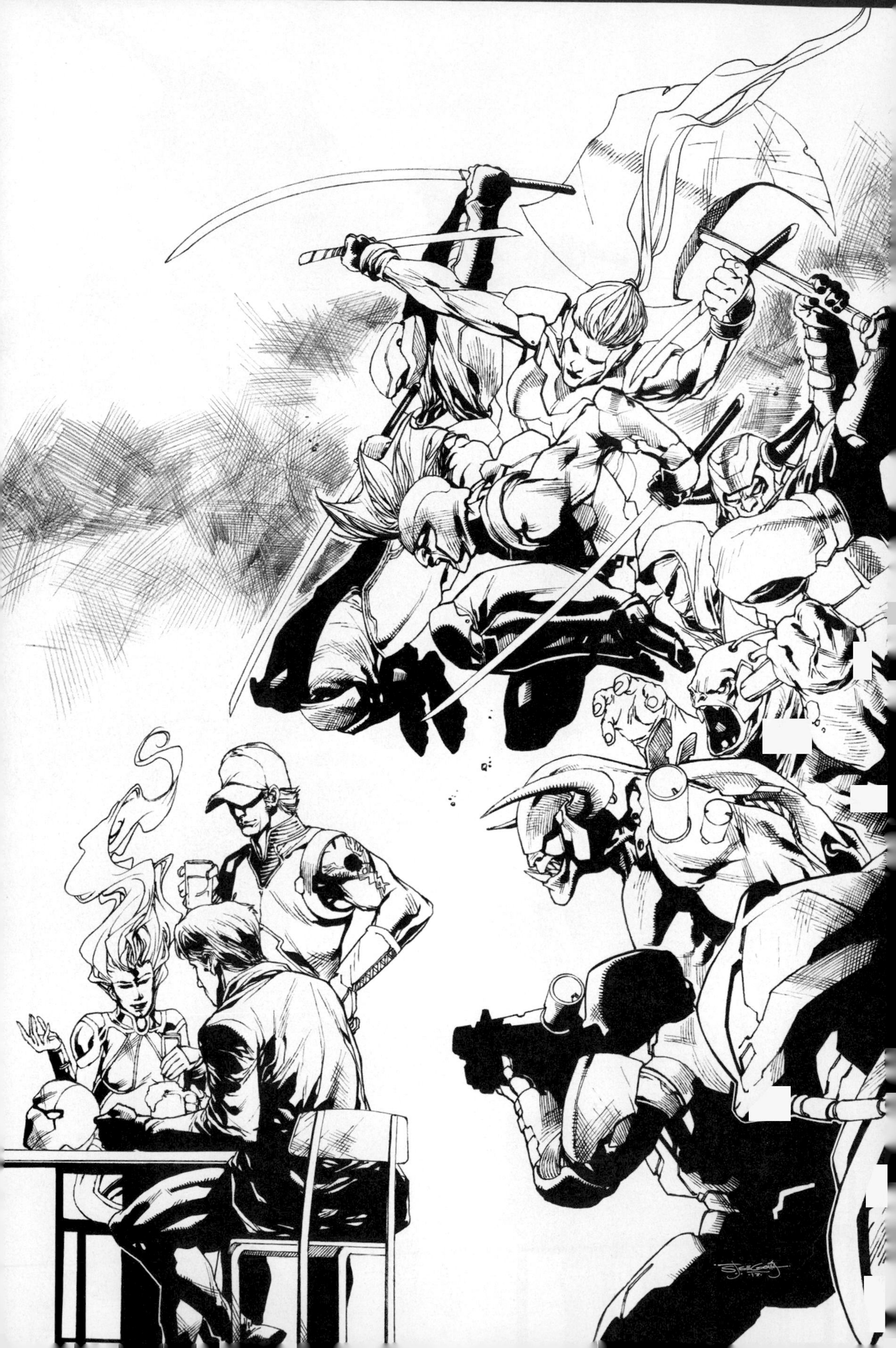

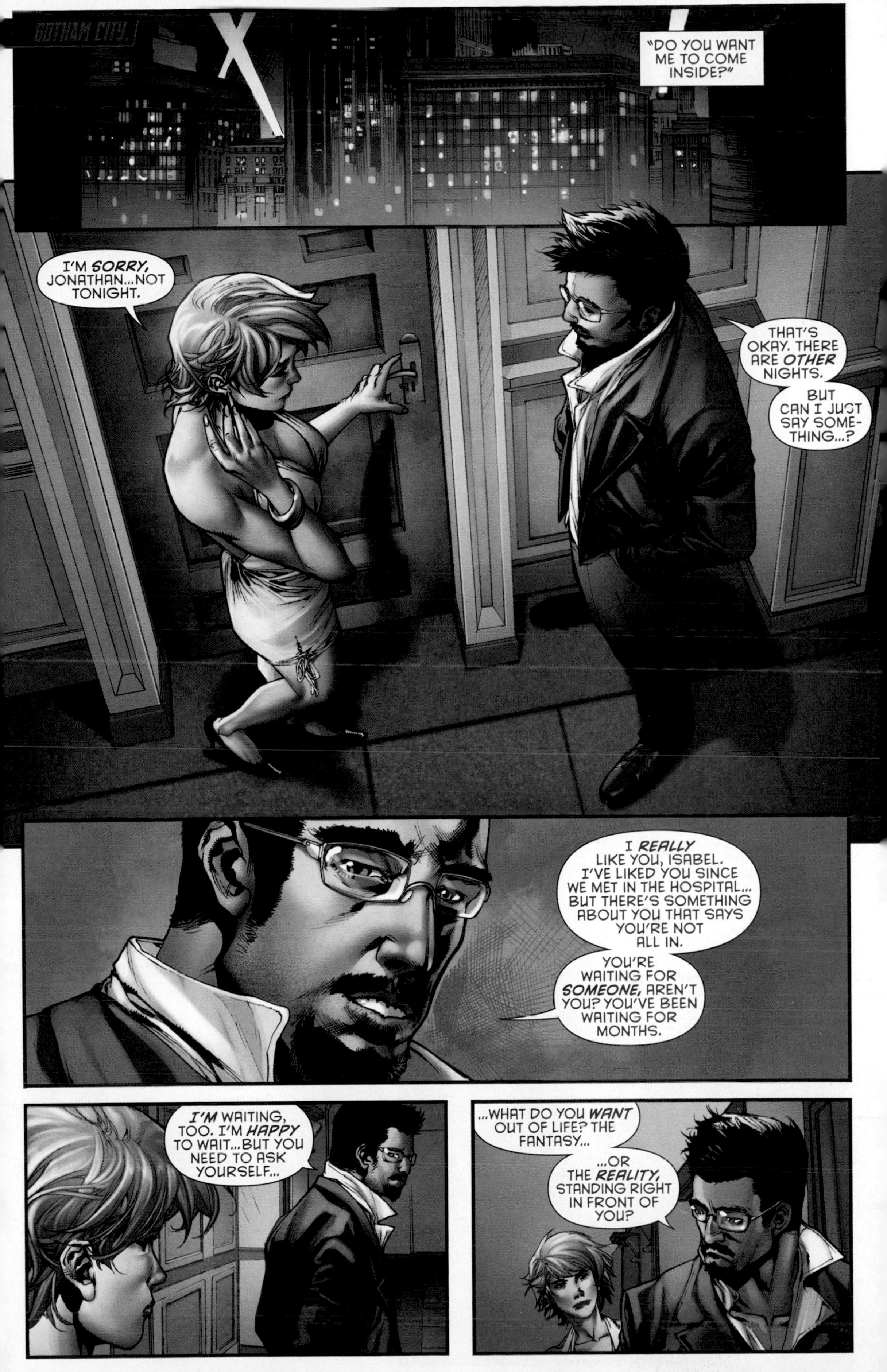
GOTHAM CITY.
"DO YOU WANT ME TO COME INSIDE?"
I'M SORRY, JONATHAN...NOT TONIGHT.
THAT'S OKAY. THERE ARE OTHER NIGHTS.
BUT CAN I JUST SAY SOMETHING...?
I REALLY LIKE YOU, ISABEL. I'VE LIKED YOU SINCE WE MET IN THE HOSPITAL... BUT THERE'S SOMETHING ABOUT YOU THAT SAYS YOU'RE NOT ALL IN.
YOU'RE WAITING FOR SOMEONE, AREN'T YOU? YOU'VE BEEN WAITING FOR MONTHS.
I'M WAITING, TOO. I'M HAPPY TO WAIT...BUT YOU NEED TO ASK YOURSELF...
...WHAT DO YOU WANT OUT OF LIFE? THE FANTASY...
...OR THE REALITY, STANDING RIGHT IN FRONT OF YOU?

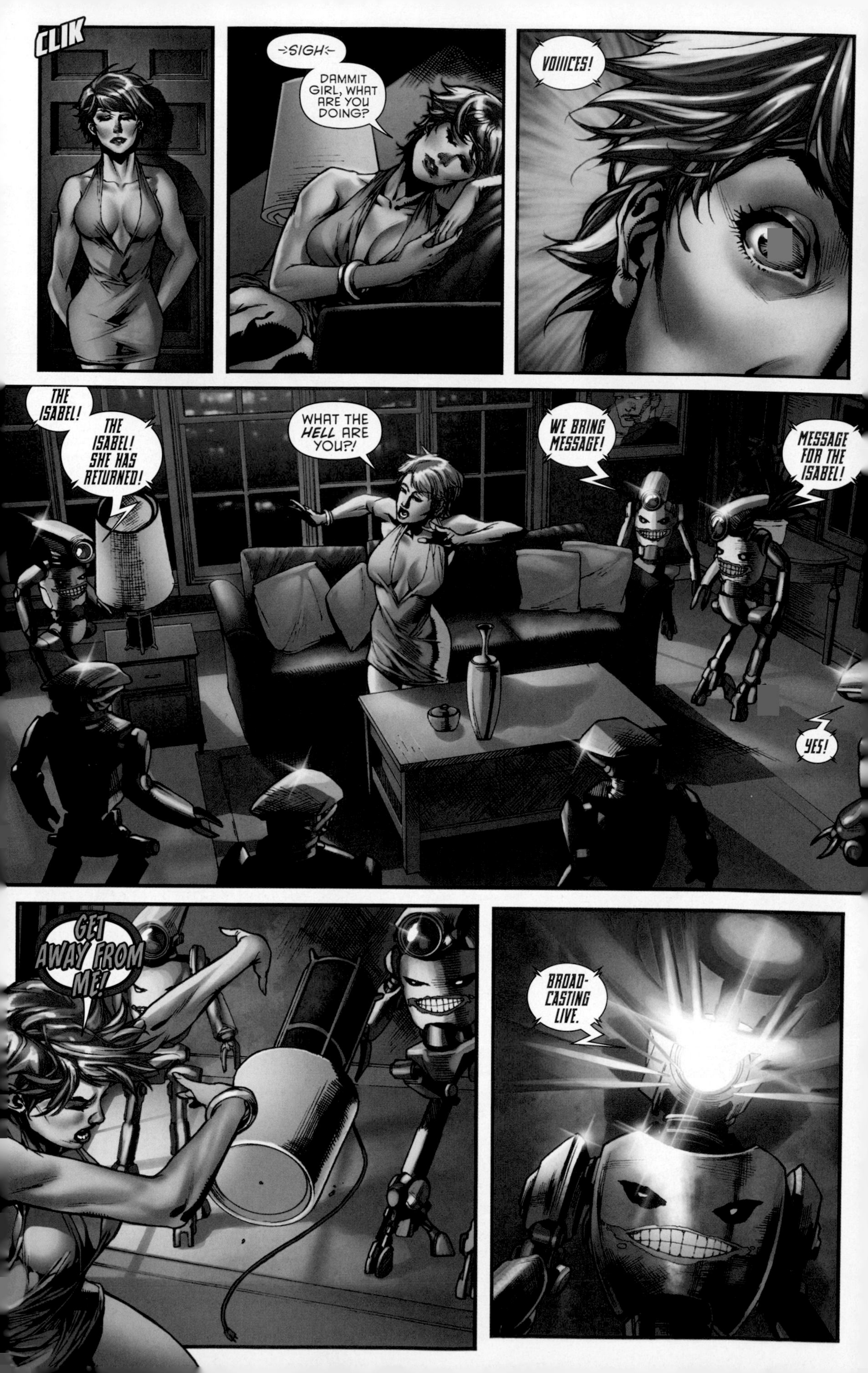
CLIK
-SIGH-
DAMMIT GIRL, WHAT ARE YOU DOING?
VOIIICES!
THE ISABEL!
THE ISABEL! SHE HAS RETURNED!
WHAT THE HELL ARE YOU?!
WE BRING MESSAGE!
MESSAGE FOR THE ISABEL!
YES!
GET AWAY FROM ME!
BROAD-CASTING LIVE.

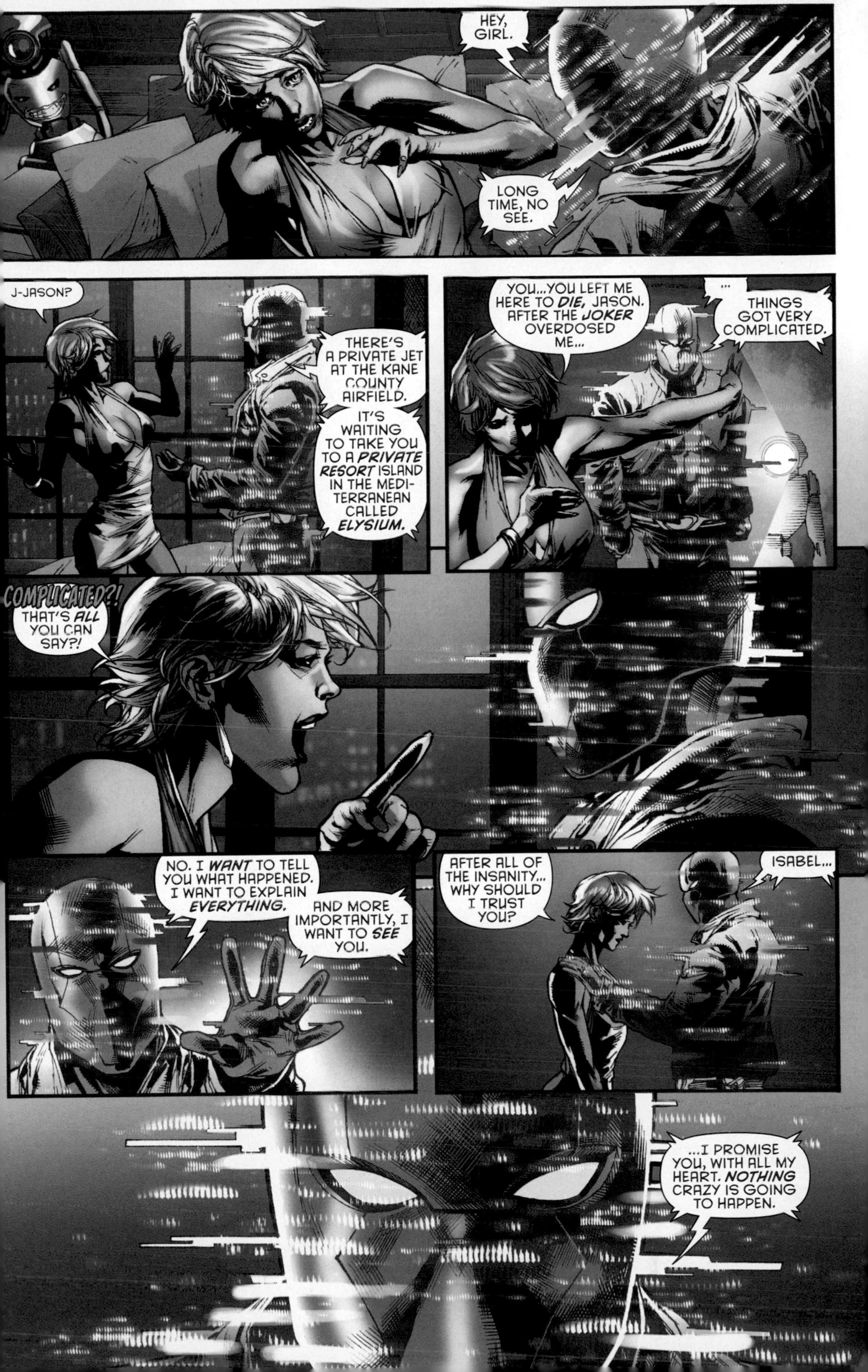
HEY, GIRL.
LONG TIME, NO SEE.
J-JASON?
THERE'S A PRIVATE JET AT THE KANE COUNTY AIRFIELD.
IT'S WAITING TO TAKE YOU TO A *PRIVATE RESORT* ISLAND IN THE MEDI-TERRANEAN CALLED *ELYSIUM.*
YOU...YOU LEFT ME HERE TO *DIE,* JASON. AFTER THE *JOKER* OVERDOSED ME...
...
THINGS GOT VERY COMPLICATED.
COMPLICATED?!
THAT'S *ALL* YOU CAN SAY?!
NO. I *WANT* TO TELL YOU WHAT HAPPENED. I WANT TO EXPLAIN *EVERYTHING.*
AND MORE IMPORTANTLY, I WANT TO *SEE* YOU.
AFTER ALL OF THE INSANITY... WHY SHOULD I TRUST YOU?
ISABEL...
...I PROMISE YOU, WITH ALL MY HEART. *NOTHING* CRAZY IS GOING TO HAPPEN.

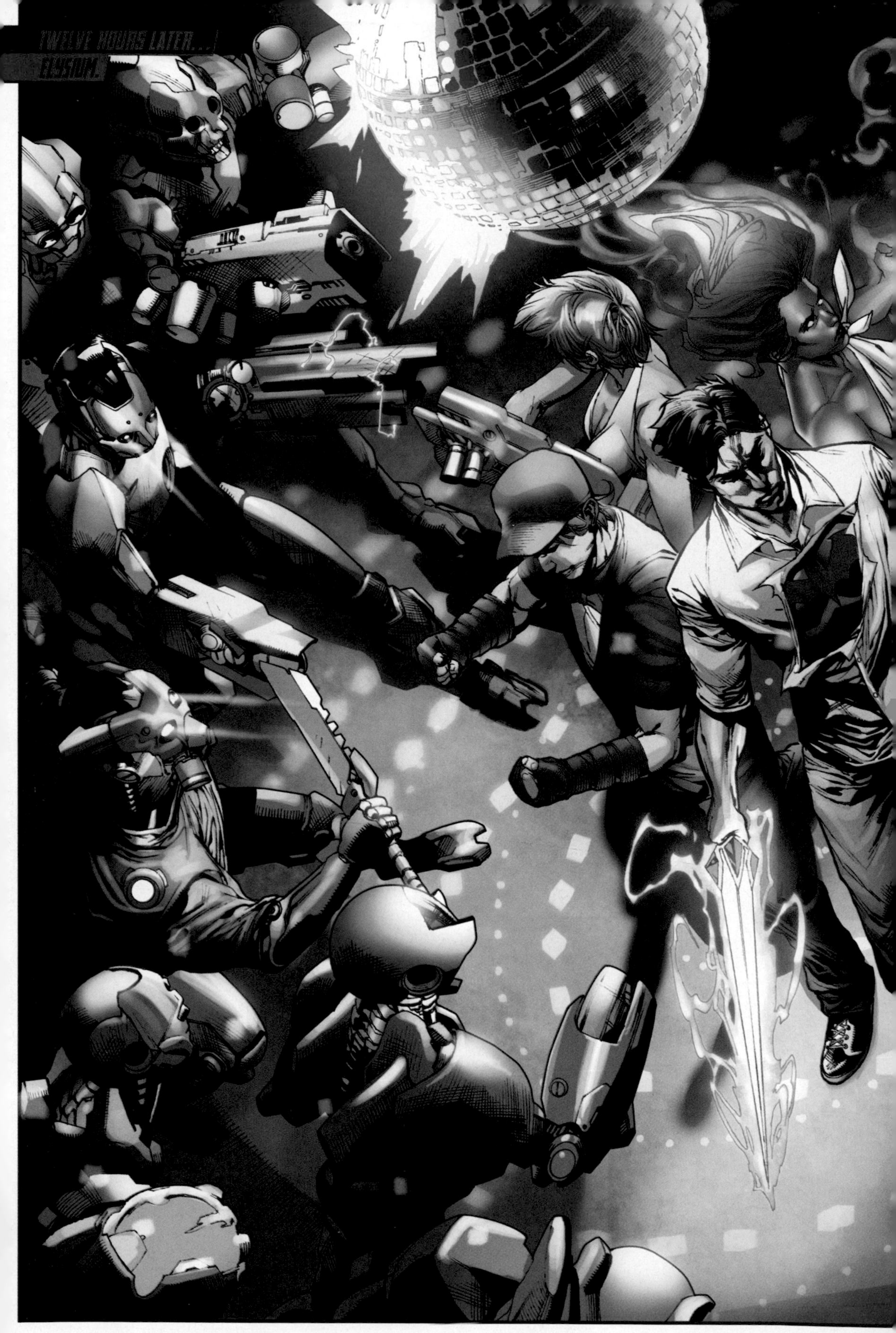
TWELVE HOURS LATER...
ELYSIUM.

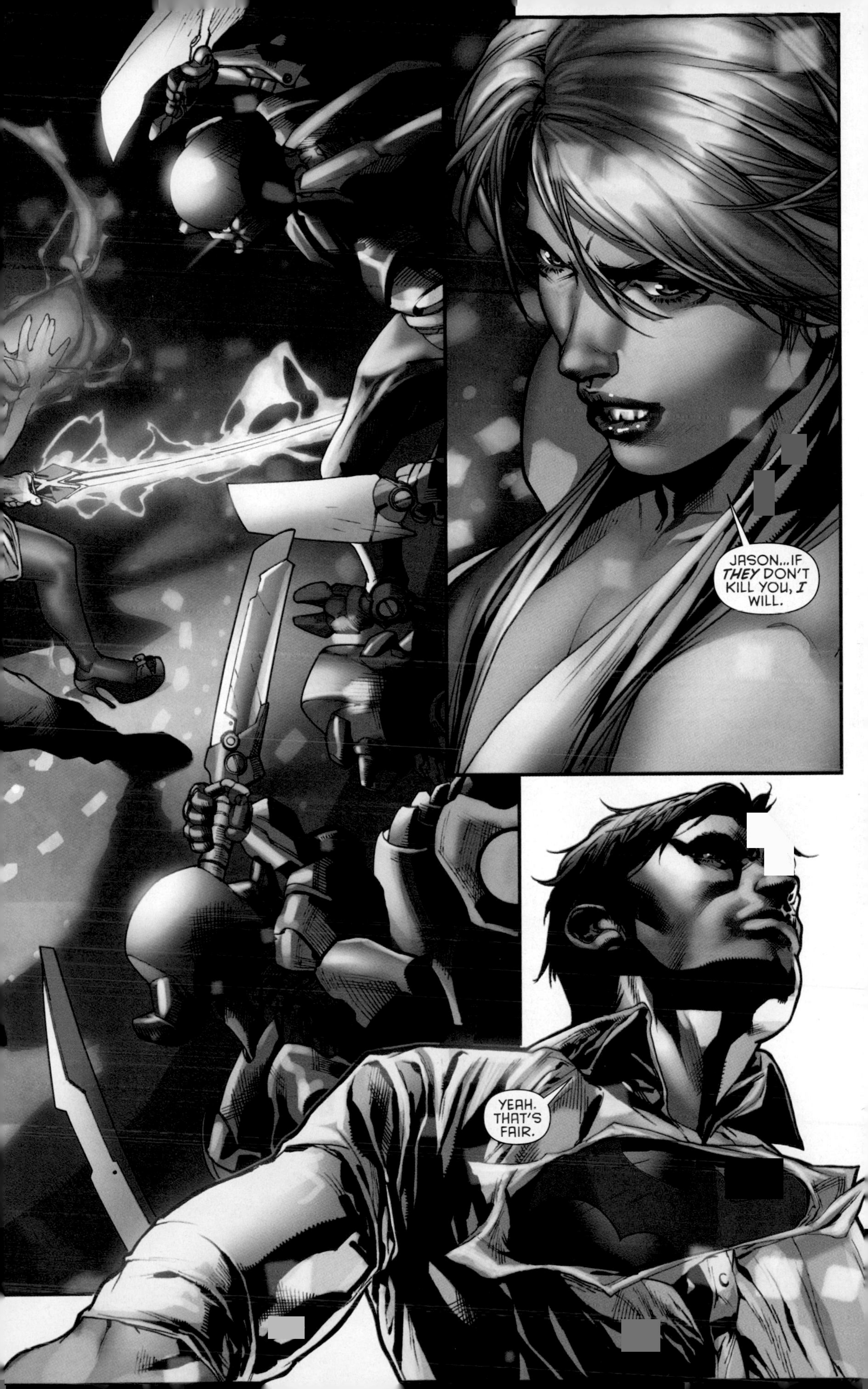
JASON...IF THEY DON'T KILL YOU, I WILL.
YEAH. THAT'S FAIR.

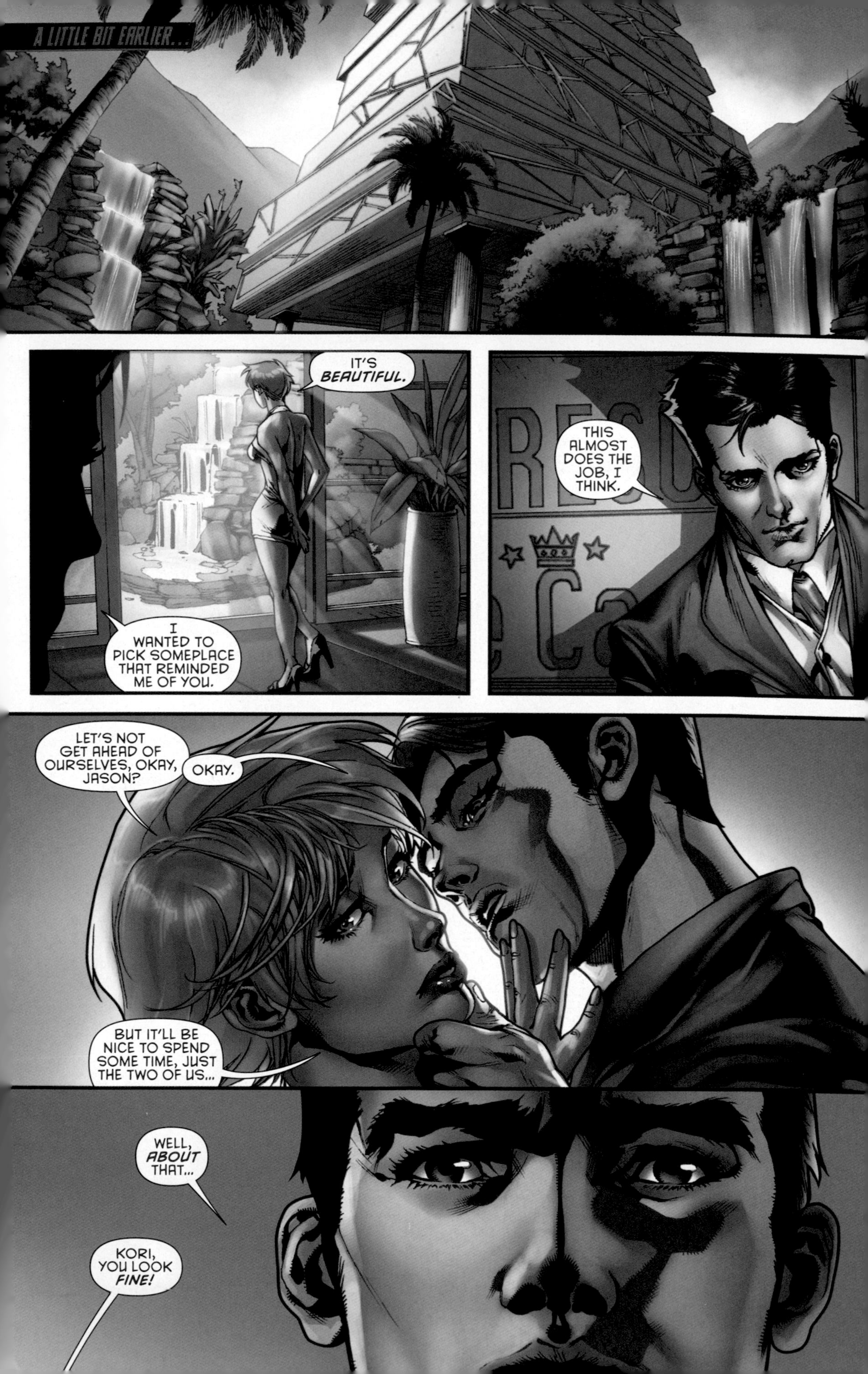

A LITTLE BIT EARLIER...
IT'S BEAUTIFUL.
I WANTED TO PICK SOMEPLACE THAT REMINDED ME OF YOU.
THIS ALMOST DOES THE JOB, I THINK.
LET'S NOT GET AHEAD OF OURSELVES, OKAY, JASON?
OKAY.
BUT IT'LL BE NICE TO SPEND SOME TIME, JUST THE TWO OF US...
WELL, ABOUT THAT...
KORI, YOU LOOK FINE!

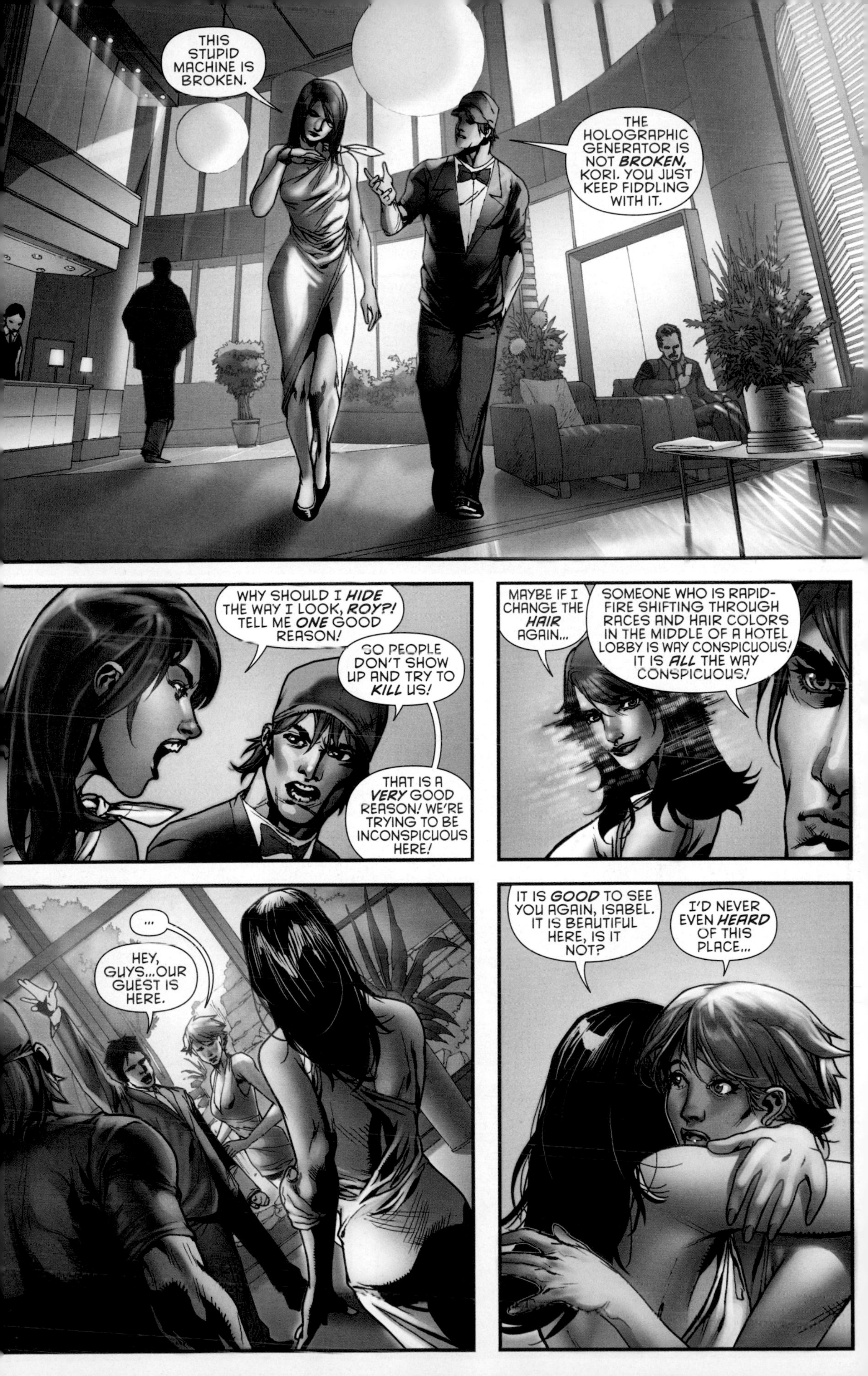

THIS STUPID MACHINE IS BROKEN.
THE HOLOGRAPHIC GENERATOR IS NOT BROKEN, KORI. YOU JUST KEEP FIDDLING WITH IT.
WHY SHOULD I HIDE THE WAY I LOOK, ROY?! TELL ME ONE GOOD REASON!
SO PEOPLE DON'T SHOW UP AND TRY TO KILL US!
THAT IS A VERY GOOD REASON! WE'RE TRYING TO BE INCONSPICUOUS HERE!
MAYBE IF I CHANGE THE HAIR AGAIN...
SOMEONE WHO IS RAPID-FIRE SHIFTING THROUGH RACES AND HAIR COLORS IN THE MIDDLE OF A HOTEL LOBBY IS WAY CONSPICUOUS! IT IS ALL THE WAY CONSPICUOUS!
...
HEY, GUYS...OUR GUEST IS HERE.
IT IS GOOD TO SEE YOU AGAIN, ISABEL. IT IS BEAUTIFUL HERE, IS IT NOT?
I'D NEVER EVEN HEARD OF THIS PLACE...

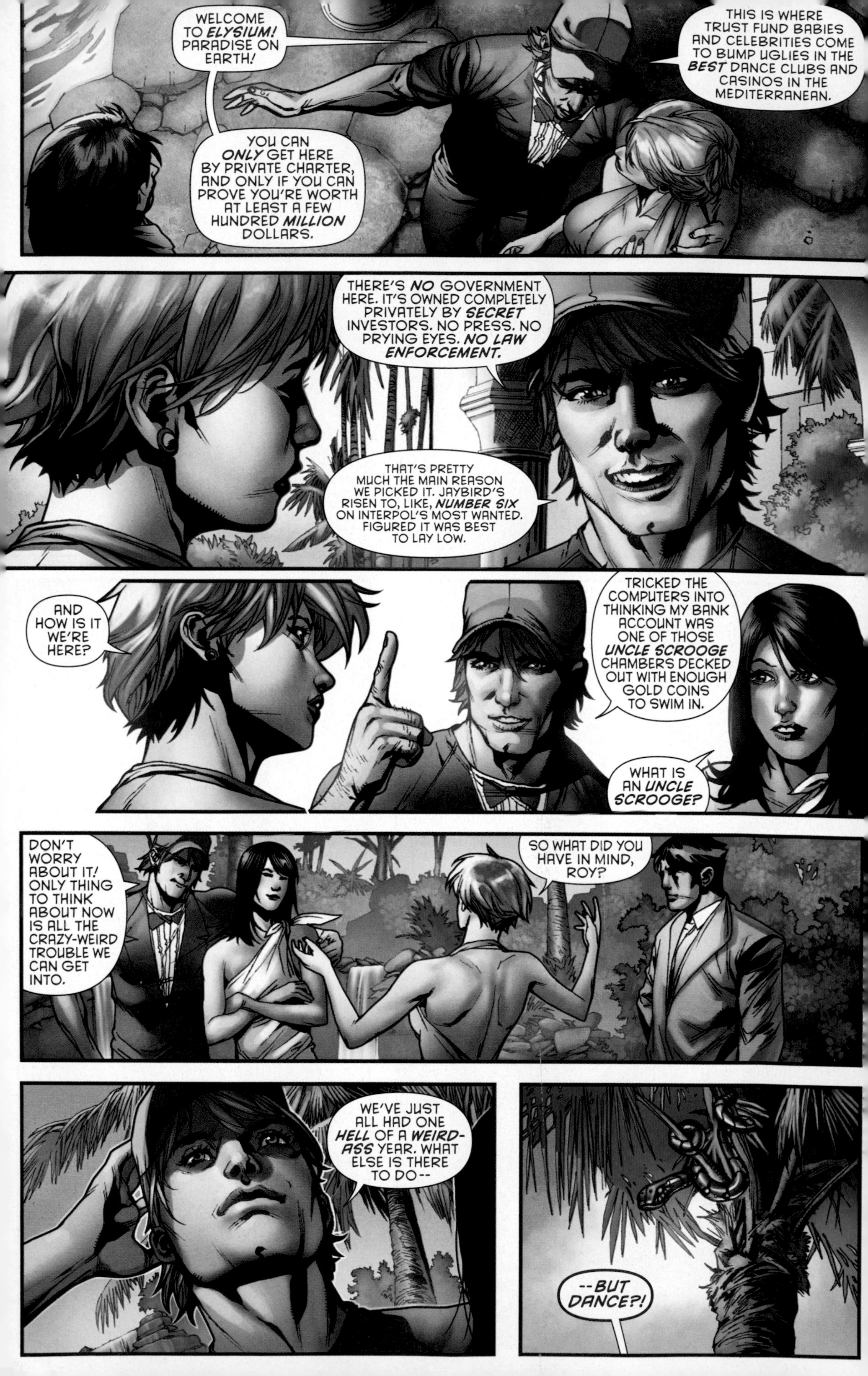
WELCOME TO ELYSIUM! PARADISE ON EARTH!
YOU CAN ONLY GET HERE BY PRIVATE CHARTER, AND ONLY IF YOU CAN PROVE YOU'RE WORTH AT LEAST A FEW HUNDRED MILLION DOLLARS.
THIS IS WHERE TRUST FUND BABIES AND CELEBRITIES COME TO BUMP UGLIES IN THE BEST DANCE CLUBS AND CASINOS IN THE MEDITERRANEAN.
THERE'S NO GOVERNMENT HERE. IT'S OWNED COMPLETELY PRIVATELY BY SECRET INVESTORS. NO PRESS. NO PRYING EYES. NO LAW ENFORCEMENT.
THAT'S PRETTY MUCH THE MAIN REASON WE PICKED IT. JAYBIRD'S RISEN TO, LIKE, NUMBER SIX ON INTERPOL'S MOST WANTED. FIGURED IT WAS BEST TO LAY LOW.
AND HOW IS IT WE'RE HERE?
TRICKED THE COMPUTERS INTO THINKING MY BANK ACCOUNT WAS ONE OF THOSE UNCLE SCROOGE CHAMBERS DECKED OUT WITH ENOUGH GOLD COINS TO SWIM IN.
WHAT IS AN UNCLE SCROOGE?
DON'T WORRY ABOUT IT! ONLY THING TO THINK ABOUT NOW IS ALL THE CRAZY-WEIRD TROUBLE WE CAN GET INTO.
SO WHAT DID YOU HAVE IN MIND, ROY?
WE'VE JUST ALL HAD ONE HELL OF A WEIRD-ASS YEAR. WHAT ELSE IS THERE TO DO--
--BUT DANCE?!

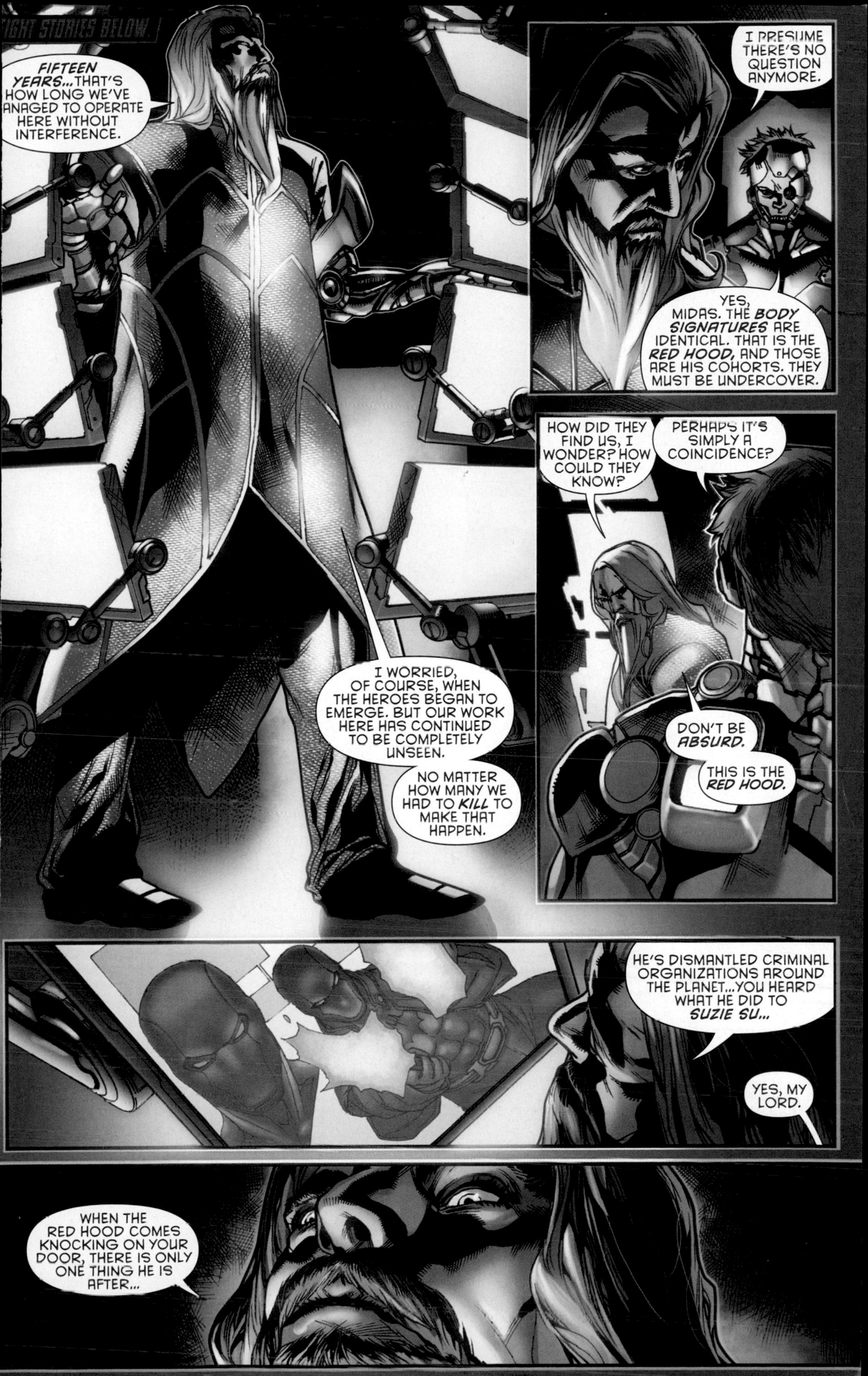

...EIGHT STORIES BELOW.
FIFTEEN YEARS... THAT'S HOW LONG WE'VE MANAGED TO OPERATE HERE WITHOUT INTERFERENCE.
I PRESUME THERE'S NO QUESTION ANYMORE.
YES, MIDAS. THE BODY SIGNATURES ARE IDENTICAL. THAT IS THE RED HOOD, AND THOSE ARE HIS COHORTS. THEY MUST BE UNDERCOVER.
I WORRIED, OF COURSE, WHEN THE HEROES BEGAN TO EMERGE. BUT OUR WORK HERE HAS CONTINUED TO BE COMPLETELY UNSEEN.
NO MATTER HOW MANY WE HAD TO KILL TO MAKE THAT HAPPEN.
HOW DID THEY FIND US, I WONDER? HOW COULD THEY KNOW?
PERHAPS IT'S SIMPLY A COINCIDENCE?
DON'T BE ABSURD.
THIS IS THE RED HOOD.
HE'S DISMANTLED CRIMINAL ORGANIZATIONS AROUND THE PLANET... YOU HEARD WHAT HE DID TO SUZIE SU...
YES, MY LORD.
WHEN THE RED HOOD COMES KNOCKING ON YOUR DOOR, THERE IS ONLY ONE THING HE IS AFTER...

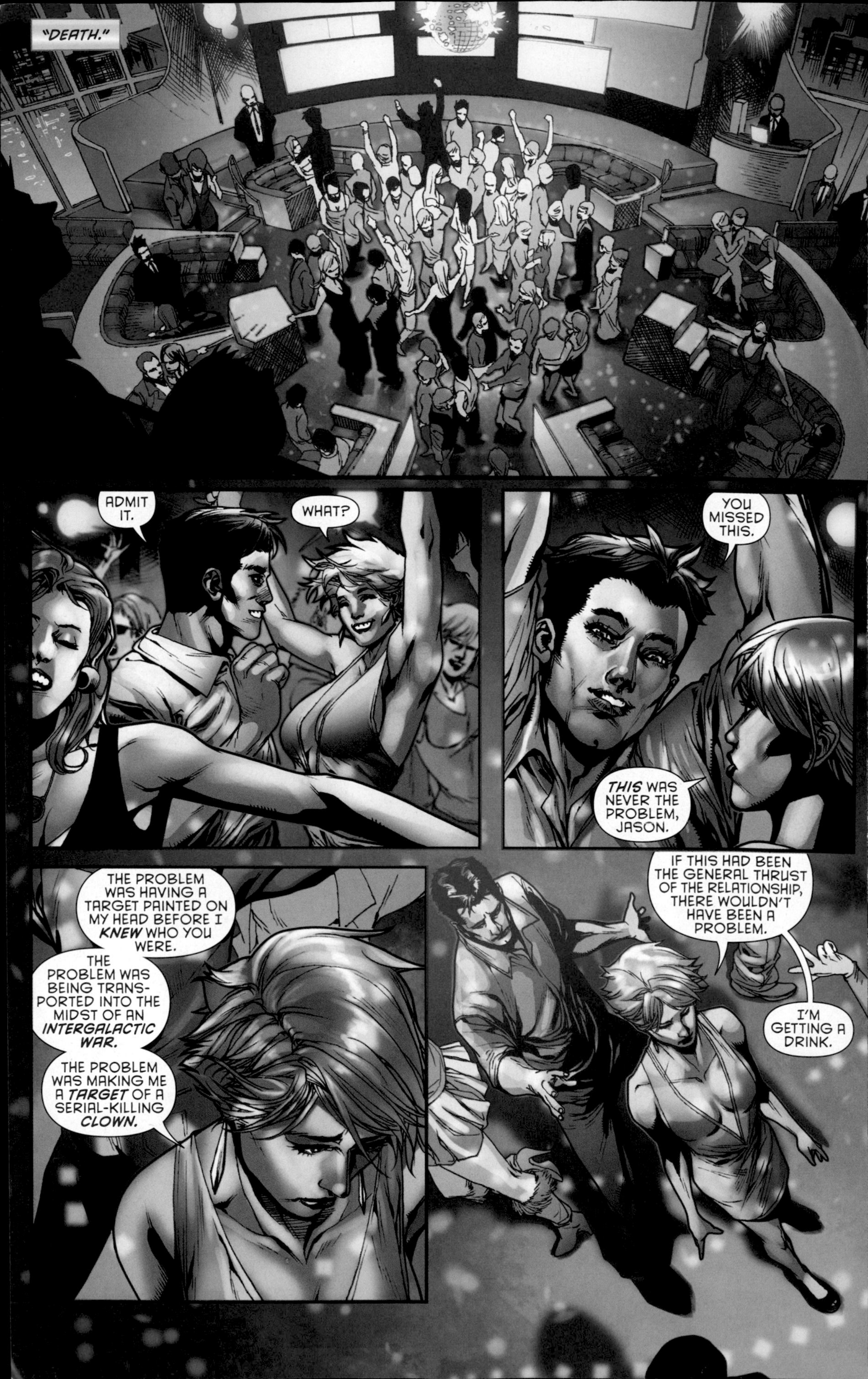
"DEATH."
ADMIT IT.
WHAT?
YOU MISSED THIS.
THIS WAS NEVER THE PROBLEM, JASON.
THE PROBLEM WAS HAVING A TARGET PAINTED ON MY HEAD BEFORE I KNEW WHO YOU WERE.
THE PROBLEM WAS BEING TRANS-PORTED INTO THE MIDST OF AN INTERGALACTIC WAR.
THE PROBLEM WAS MAKING ME A TARGET OF A SERIAL-KILLING CLOWN.
IF THIS HAD BEEN THE GENERAL THRUST OF THE RELATIONSHIP, THERE WOULDN'T HAVE BEEN A PROBLEM.
I'M GETTING A DRINK.

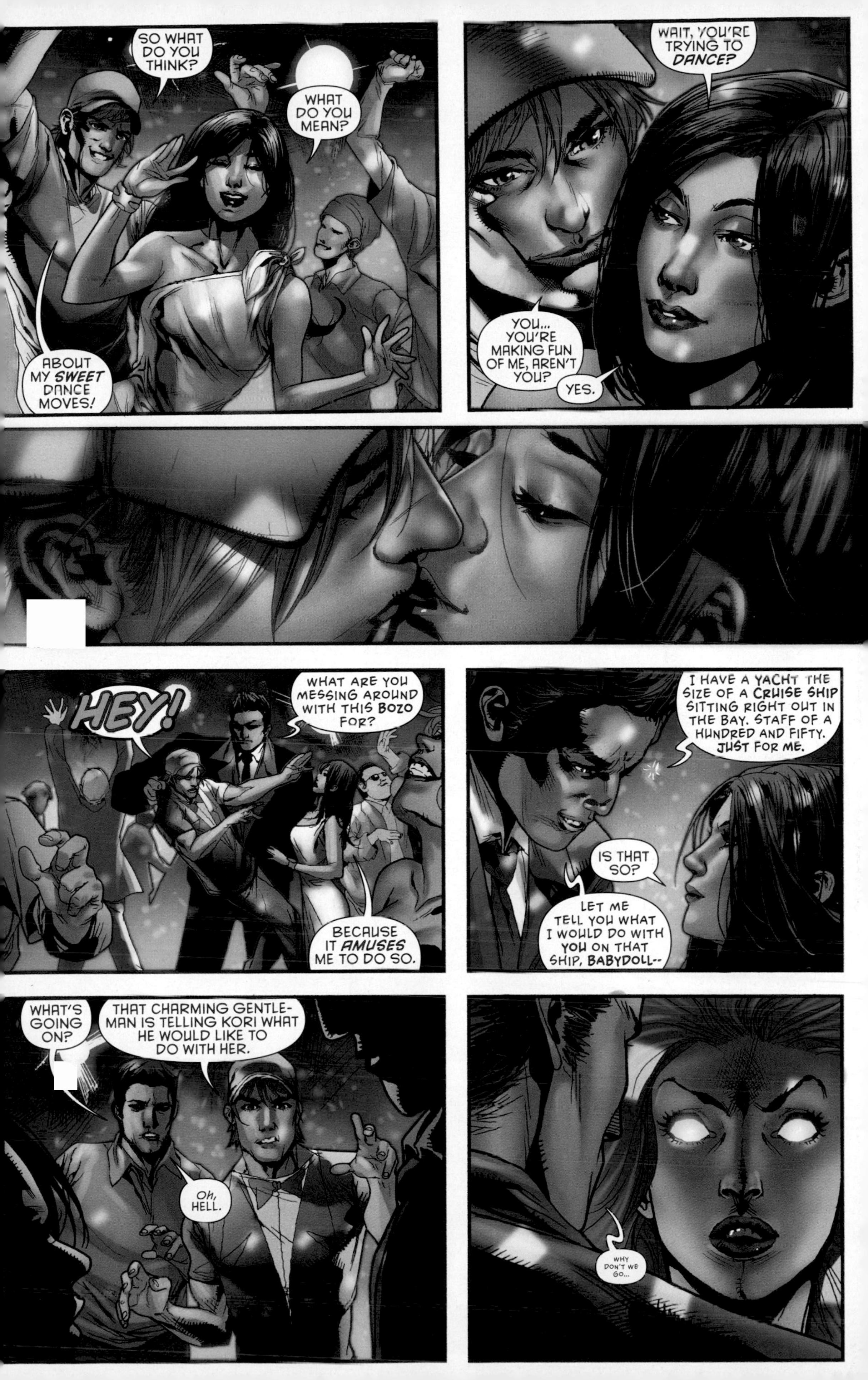

SO WHAT DO YOU THINK?
WHAT DO YOU MEAN?
ABOUT MY SWEET DANCE MOVES!
WAIT, YOU'RE TRYING TO DANCE?
YOU... YOU'RE MAKING FUN OF ME, AREN'T YOU?
YES.
HEY!
WHAT ARE YOU MESSING AROUND WITH THIS BOZO FOR?
BECAUSE IT AMUSES ME TO DO SO.
I HAVE A YACHT THE SIZE OF A CRUISE SHIP SITTING RIGHT OUT IN THE BAY. STAFF OF A HUNDRED AND FIFTY. JUST FOR ME.
IS THAT SO?
LET ME TELL YOU WHAT I WOULD DO WITH YOU ON THAT SHIP, BABYDOLL--
WHAT'S GOING ON?
THAT CHARMING GENTLEMAN IS TELLING KORI WHAT HE WOULD LIKE TO DO WITH HER.
OH, HELL.
WHY DON'T WE GO...

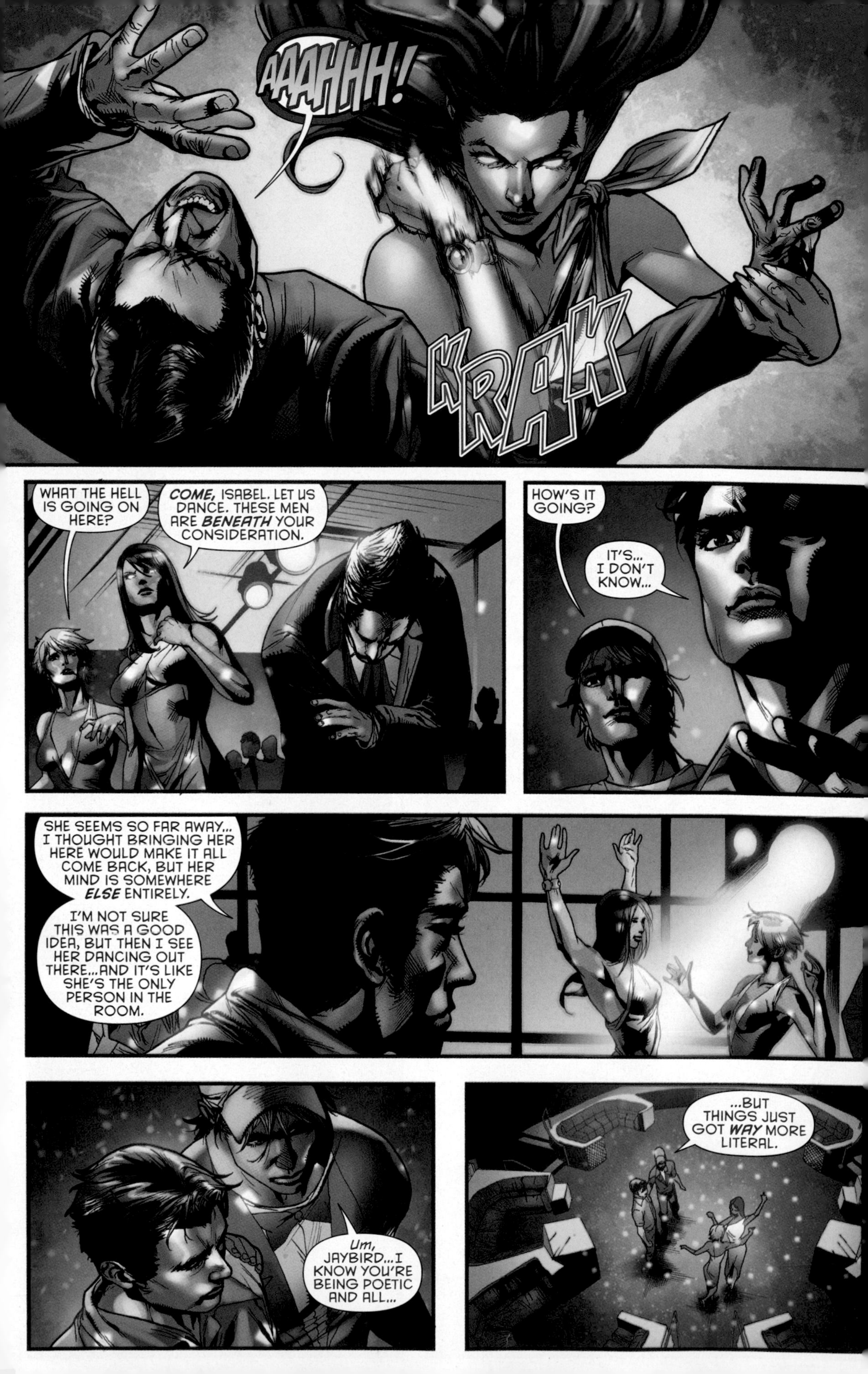
AAAHHH!
KRAK
WHAT THE HELL IS GOING ON HERE?
COME, ISABEL. LET US DANCE. THESE MEN ARE BENEATH YOUR CONSIDERATION.
HOW'S IT GOING?
IT'S... I DON'T KNOW...
SHE SEEMS SO FAR AWAY... I THOUGHT BRINGING HER HERE WOULD MAKE IT ALL COME BACK, BUT HER MIND IS SOMEWHERE ELSE ENTIRELY.
I'M NOT SURE THIS WAS A GOOD IDEA, BUT THEN I SEE HER DANCING OUT THERE...AND IT'S LIKE SHE'S THE ONLY PERSON IN THE ROOM.
Um, JAYBIRD...I KNOW YOU'RE BEING POETIC AND ALL...
...BUT THINGS JUST GOT WAY MORE LITERAL.

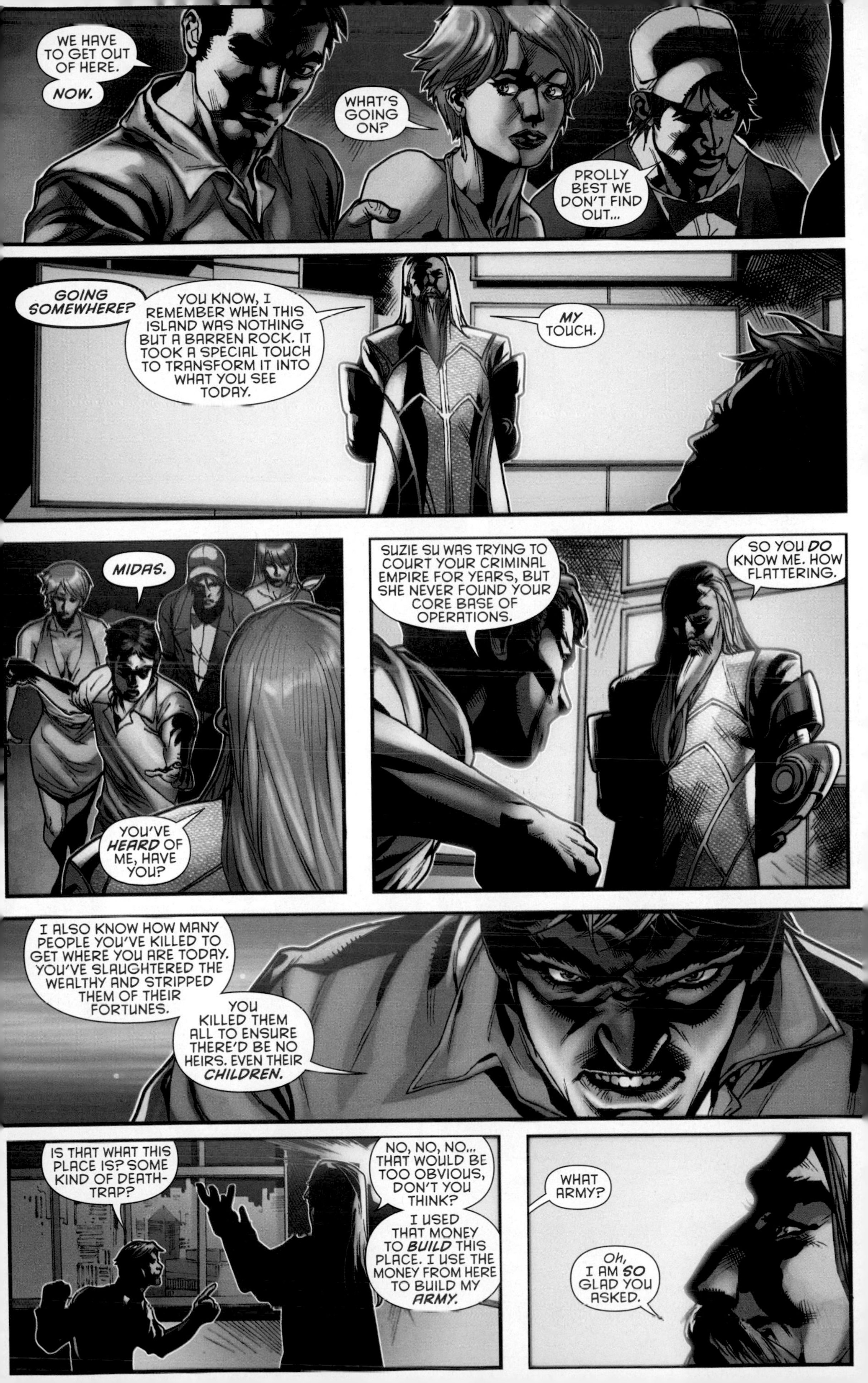
WE HAVE TO GET OUT OF HERE.
NOW.
WHAT'S GOING ON?
PROLLY BEST WE DON'T FIND OUT...
GOING SOMEWHERE?
YOU KNOW, I REMEMBER WHEN THIS ISLAND WAS NOTHING BUT A BARREN ROCK. IT TOOK A SPECIAL TOUCH TO TRANSFORM IT INTO WHAT YOU SEE TODAY.
MY TOUCH.
MIDAS.
YOU'VE HEARD OF ME, HAVE YOU?
SUZIE SU WAS TRYING TO COURT YOUR CRIMINAL EMPIRE FOR YEARS, BUT SHE NEVER FOUND YOUR CORE BASE OF OPERATIONS.
SO YOU DO KNOW ME. HOW FLATTERING.
I ALSO KNOW HOW MANY PEOPLE YOU'VE KILLED TO GET WHERE YOU ARE TODAY. YOU'VE SLAUGHTERED THE WEALTHY AND STRIPPED THEM OF THEIR FORTUNES.
YOU KILLED THEM ALL TO ENSURE THERE'D BE NO HEIRS. EVEN THEIR CHILDREN.
IS THAT WHAT THIS PLACE IS? SOME KIND OF DEATH-TRAP?
NO, NO, NO... THAT WOULD BE TOO OBVIOUS, DON'T YOU THINK?
I USED THAT MONEY TO BUILD THIS PLACE. I USE THE MONEY FROM HERE TO BUILD MY ARMY.
WHAT ARMY?
Oh, I AM SO GLAD YOU ASKED.

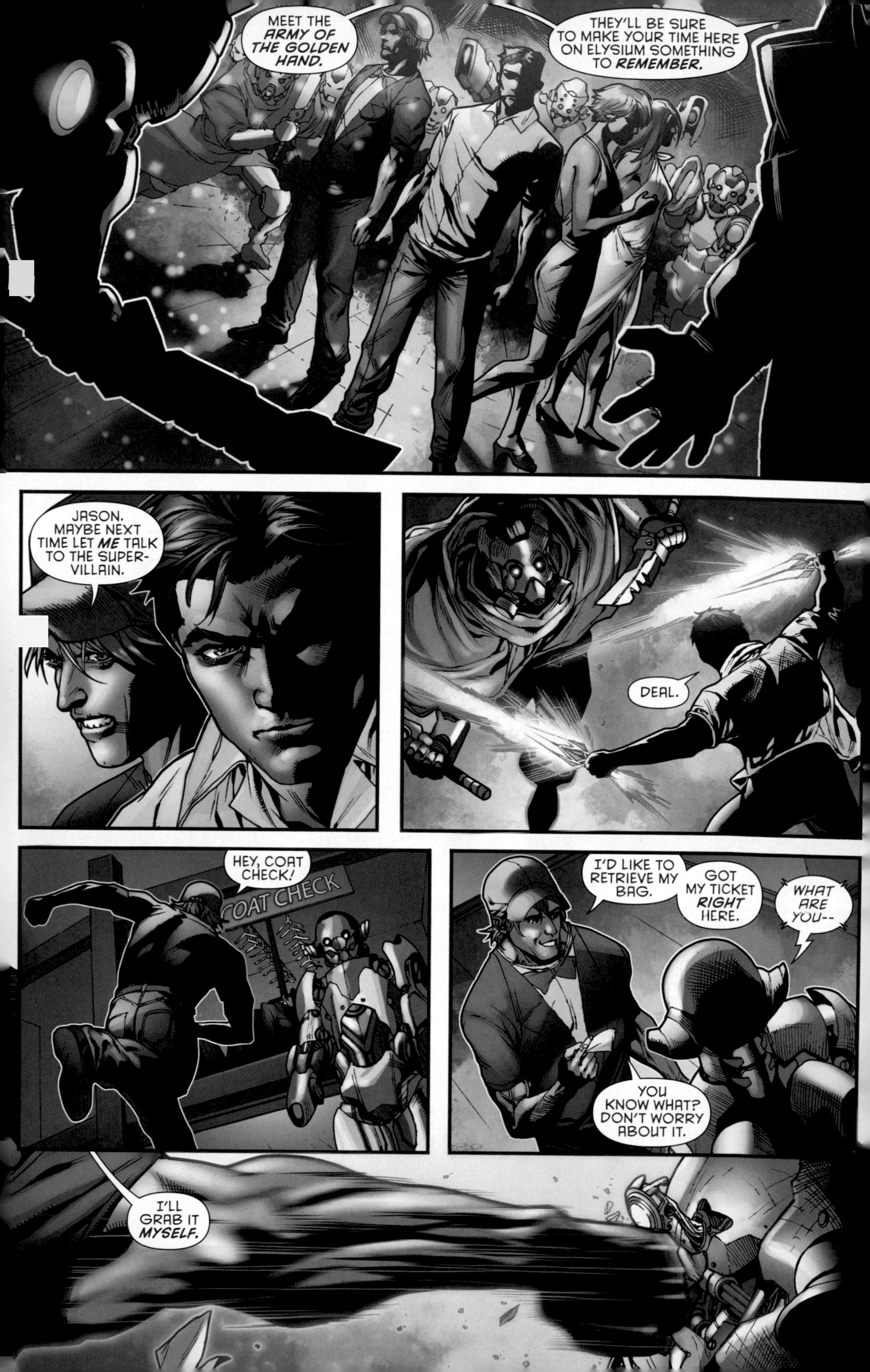
MEET THE ARMY OF THE GOLDEN HAND.
THEY'LL BE SURE TO MAKE YOUR TIME HERE ON ELYSIUM SOMETHING TO REMEMBER.
JASON. MAYBE NEXT TIME LET ME TALK TO THE SUPER-VILLAIN.
DEAL.
HEY, COAT CHECK!
COAT CHECK
I'D LIKE TO RETRIEVE MY BAG.
GOT MY TICKET RIGHT HERE.
WHAT ARE YOU--
YOU KNOW WHAT? DON'T WORRY ABOUT IT.
I'LL GRAB IT MYSELF.

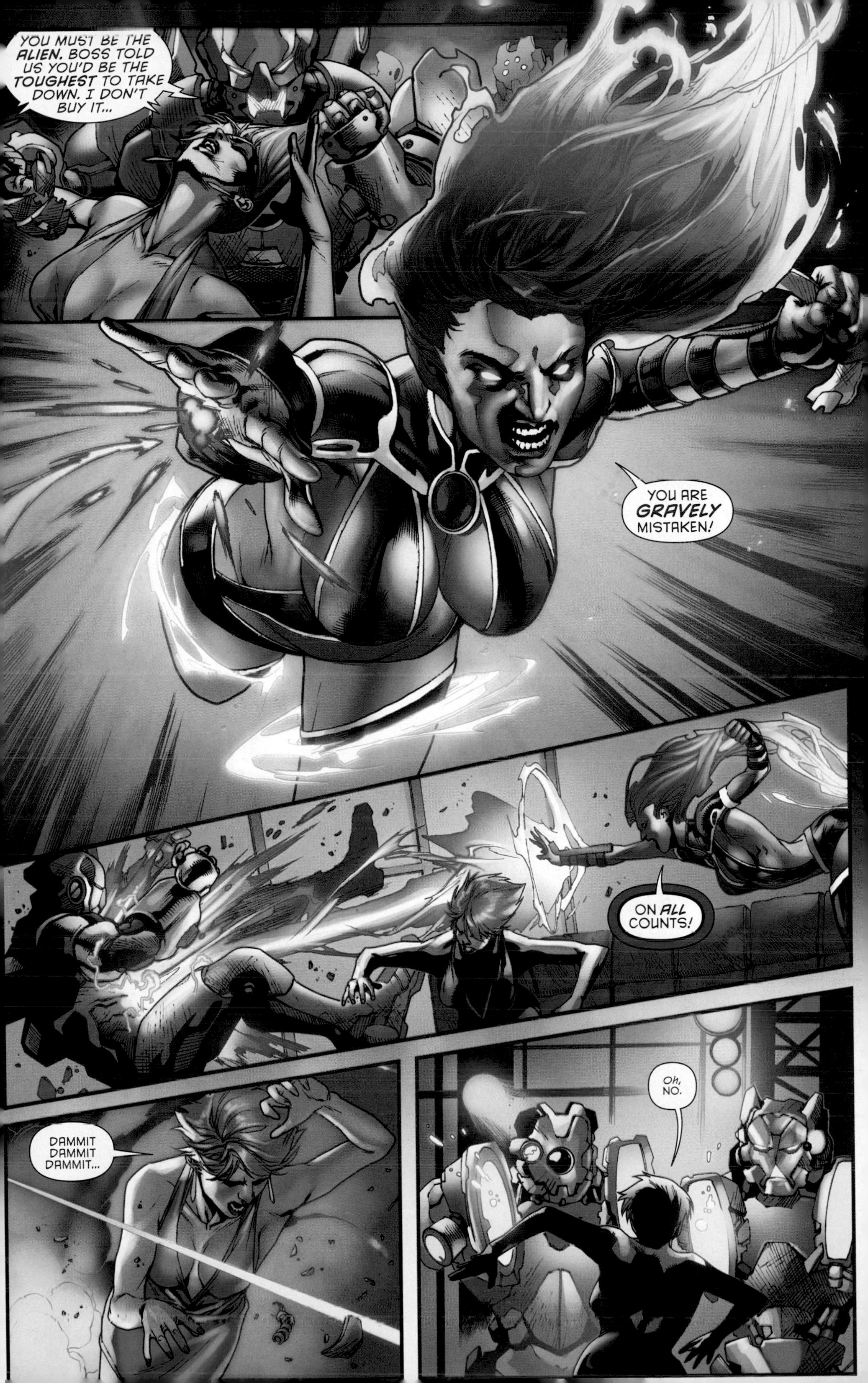
YOU MUST BE THE ALIEN. BOSS TOLD US YOU'D BE THE TOUGHEST TO TAKE DOWN. I DON'T BUY IT...
YOU ARE GRAVELY MISTAKEN!
ON ALL COUNTS!
DAMMIT DAMMIT DAMMIT...
OH, NO.

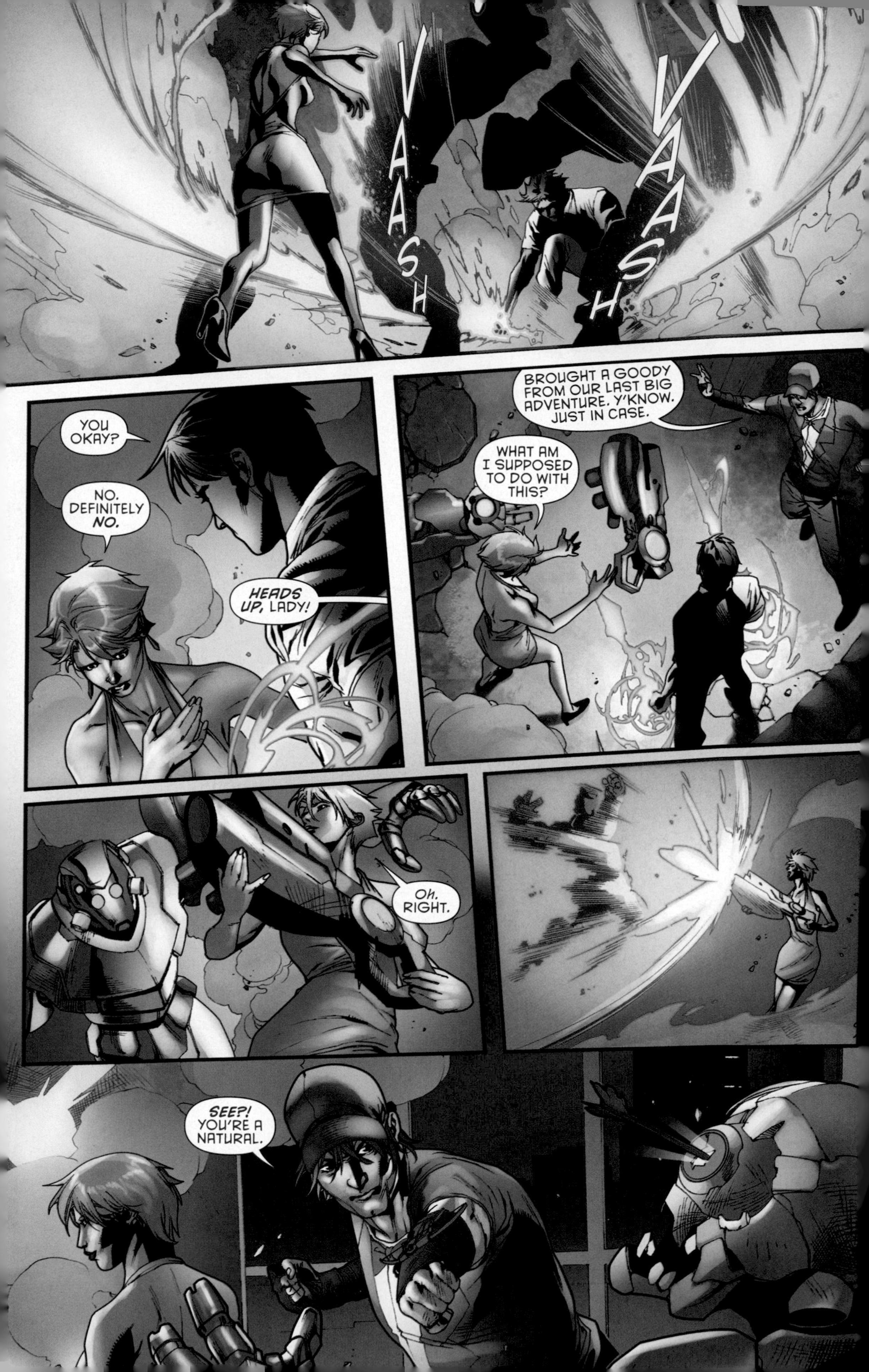
VAASH
VAASH
YOU OKAY?
NO. DEFINITELY NO.
HEADS UP, LADY!
BROUGHT A GOODY FROM OUR LAST BIG ADVENTURE. Y'KNOW. JUST IN CASE.
WHAT AM I SUPPOSED TO DO WITH THIS?
Oh. RIGHT.
SEE?! YOU'RE A NATURAL.

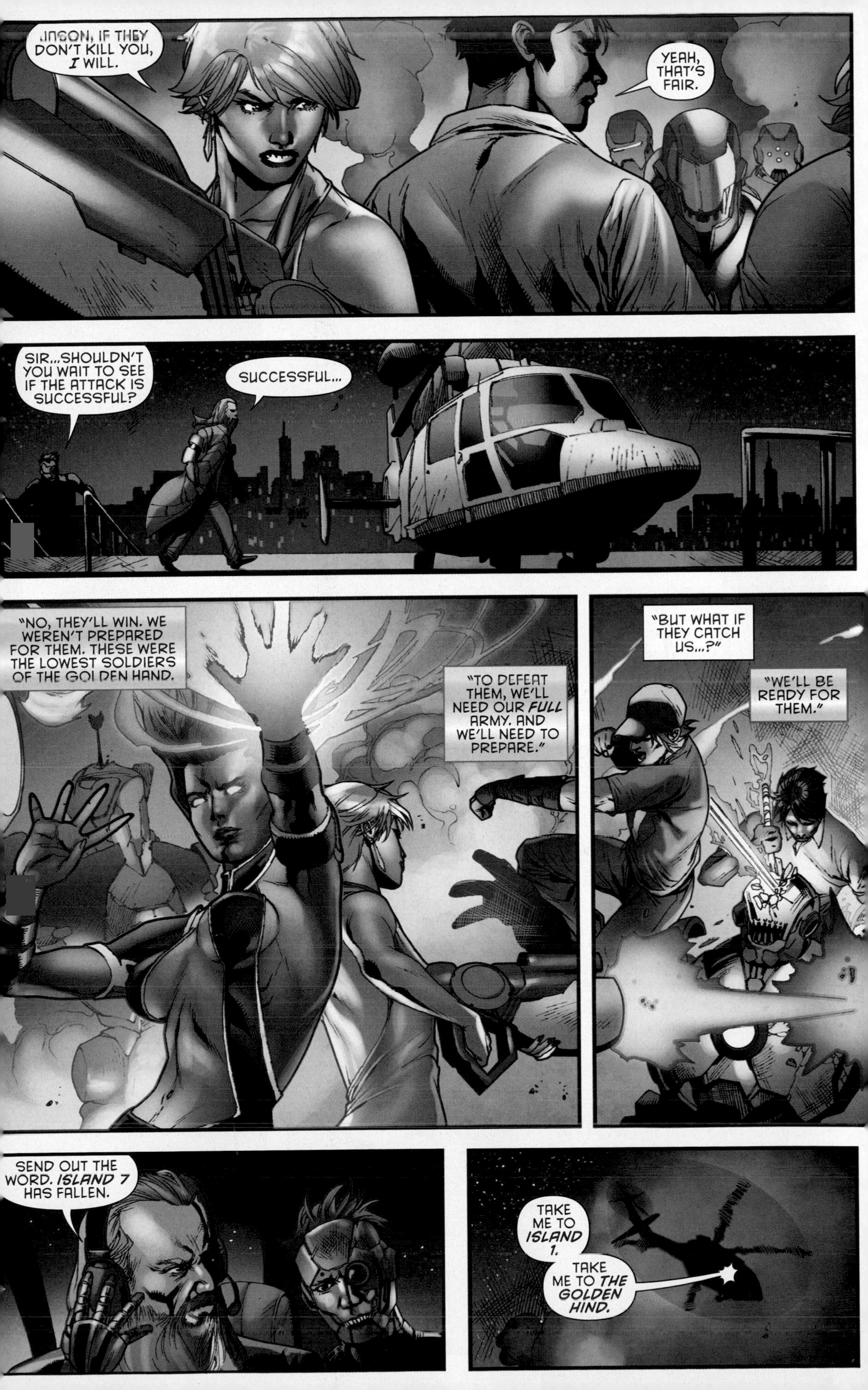
JASON, IF THEY DON'T KILL YOU, *I* WILL.
YEAH, THAT'S FAIR.
SIR...SHOULDN'T YOU WAIT TO SEE IF THE ATTACK IS SUCCESSFUL?
SUCCESSFUL...
"NO, THEY'LL WIN. WE WEREN'T PREPARED FOR THEM. THESE WERE THE LOWEST SOLDIERS OF THE GOLDEN HAND.
"TO DEFEAT THEM, WE'LL NEED OUR *FULL* ARMY. AND WE'LL NEED TO PREPARE."
"BUT WHAT IF THEY CATCH US...?"
"WE'LL BE READY FOR THEM."
SEND OUT THE WORD. *ISLAND 7* HAS FALLEN.
TAKE ME TO *ISLAND 1.*
TAKE ME TO *THE GOLDEN HIND.*

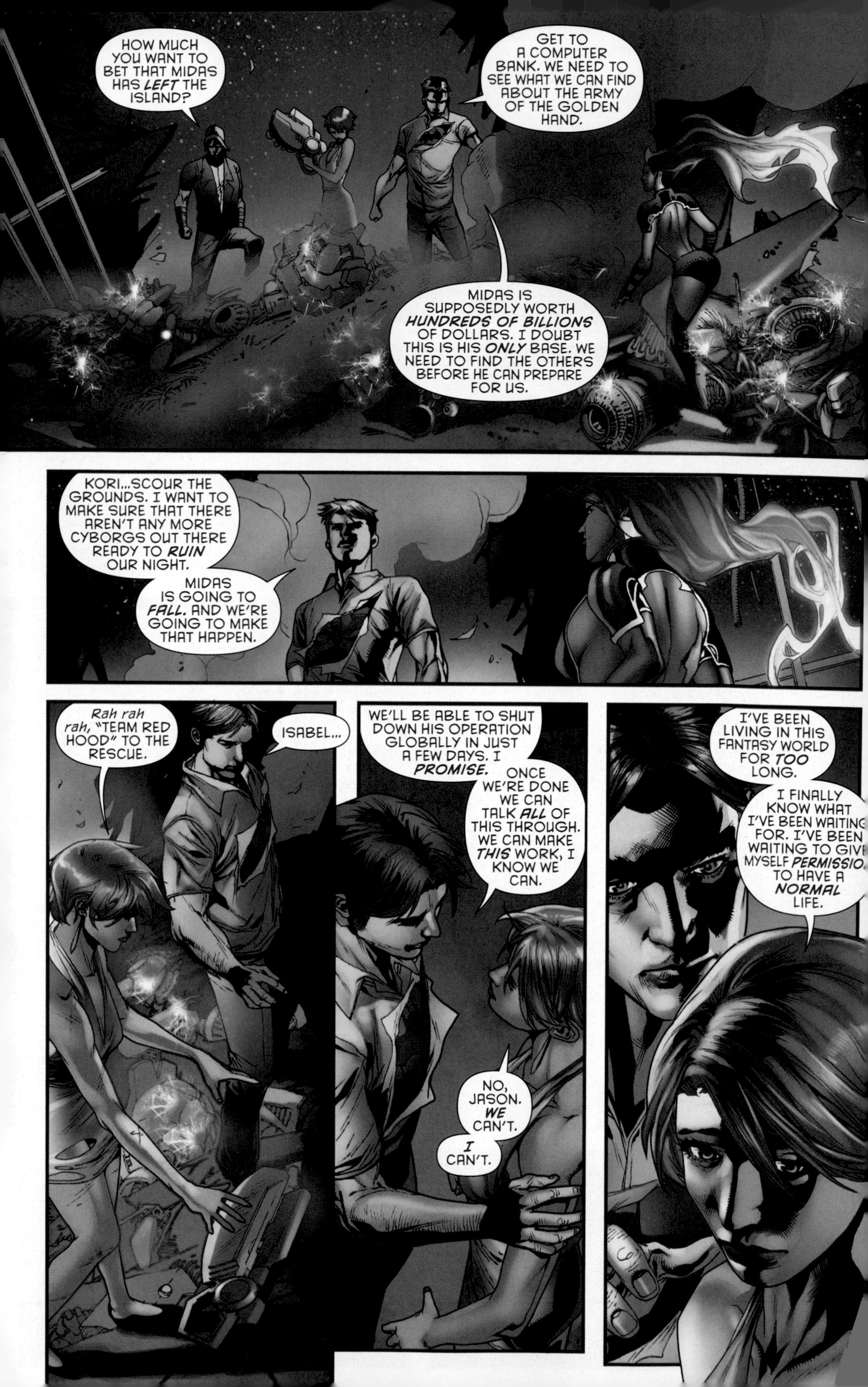
HOW MUCH YOU WANT TO BET THAT MIDAS HAS *LEFT* THE ISLAND?
GET TO A COMPUTER BANK. WE NEED TO SEE WHAT WE CAN FIND ABOUT THE ARMY OF THE GOLDEN HAND.
MIDAS IS SUPPOSEDLY WORTH ***HUNDREDS OF BILLIONS*** OF DOLLARS. I DOUBT THIS IS HIS *ONLY* BASE. WE NEED TO FIND THE OTHERS BEFORE HE CAN PREPARE FOR US.
KORI...SCOUR THE GROUNDS. I WANT TO MAKE SURE THAT THERE AREN'T ANY MORE CYBORGS OUT THERE READY TO *RUIN* OUR NIGHT.
MIDAS IS GOING TO *FALL*. AND WE'RE GOING TO MAKE THAT HAPPEN.
Rah rah rah, "TEAM RED HOOD" TO THE RESCUE.
ISABEL...
WE'LL BE ABLE TO SHUT DOWN HIS OPERATION GLOBALLY IN JUST A FEW DAYS. I ***PROMISE.***
ONCE WE'RE DONE WE CAN TALK *ALL* OF THIS THROUGH. WE CAN MAKE *THIS* WORK, I KNOW WE CAN.
NO, JASON. ***WE*** CAN'T.
I CAN'T.
I'VE BEEN LIVING IN THIS FANTASY WORLD FOR *TOO* LONG.
I FINALLY KNOW WHAT I'VE BEEN WAITING FOR. I'VE BEEN WAITING TO GIVE MYSELF *PERMISSION* TO HAVE A ***NORMAL*** LIFE.

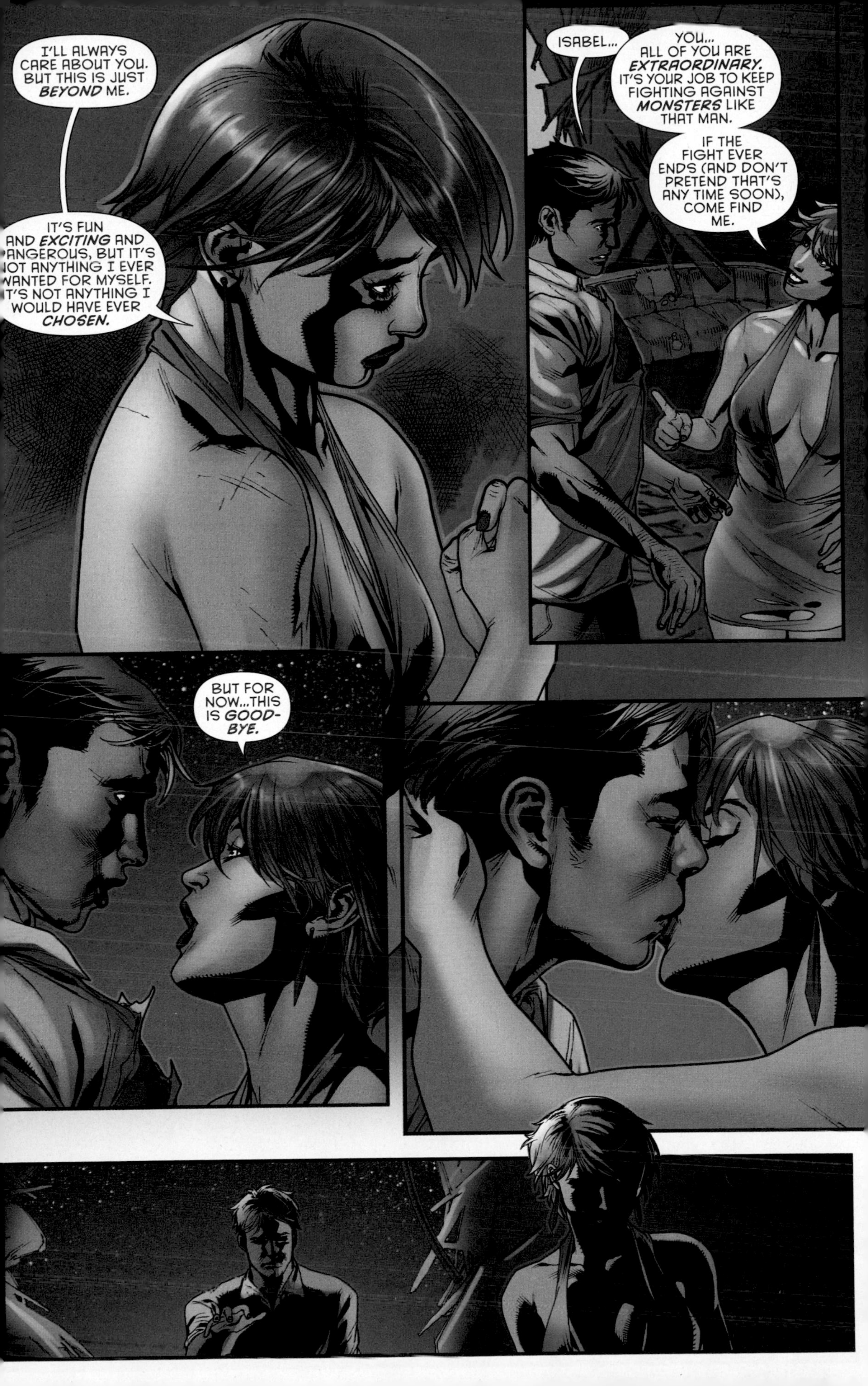
I'LL ALWAYS CARE ABOUT YOU. BUT THIS IS JUST BEYOND ME.
IT'S FUN AND EXCITING AND DANGEROUS, BUT IT'S NOT ANYTHING I EVER WANTED FOR MYSELF. IT'S NOT ANYTHING I WOULD HAVE EVER CHOSEN.
ISABEL...
YOU... ALL OF YOU ARE EXTRAORDINARY. IT'S YOUR JOB TO KEEP FIGHTING AGAINST MONSTERS LIKE THAT MAN.
IF THE FIGHT EVER ENDS (AND DON'T PRETEND THAT'S ANY TIME SOON), COME FIND ME.
BUT FOR NOW...THIS IS GOOD-BYE.

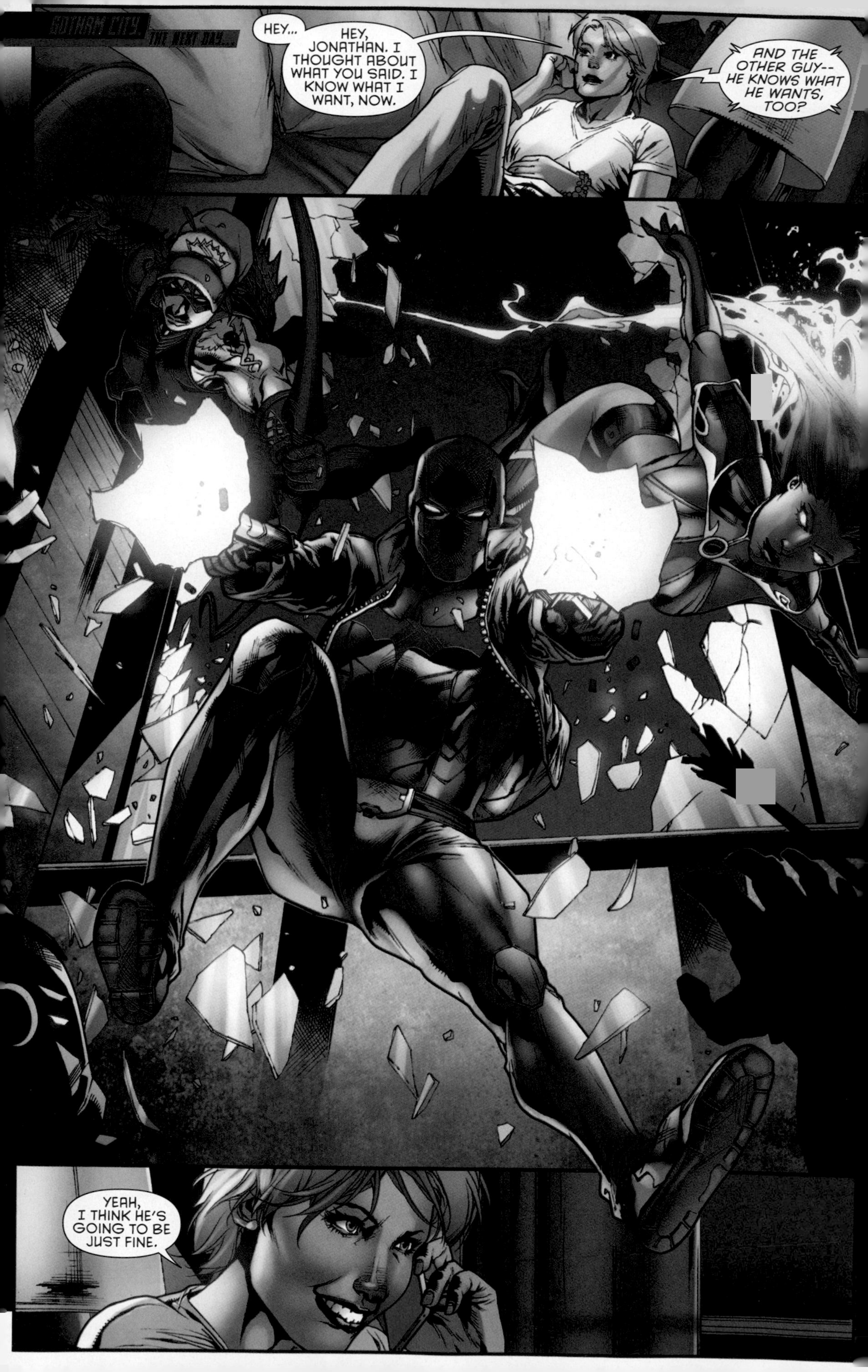
GOTHAM CITY.
THE NEXT DAY...
HEY...
HEY, JONATHAN. I THOUGHT ABOUT WHAT YOU SAID. I KNOW WHAT I WANT, NOW.
AND THE OTHER GUY-- HE KNOWS WHAT HE WANTS, TOO?
YEAH, I THINK HE'S GOING TO BE JUST FINE.

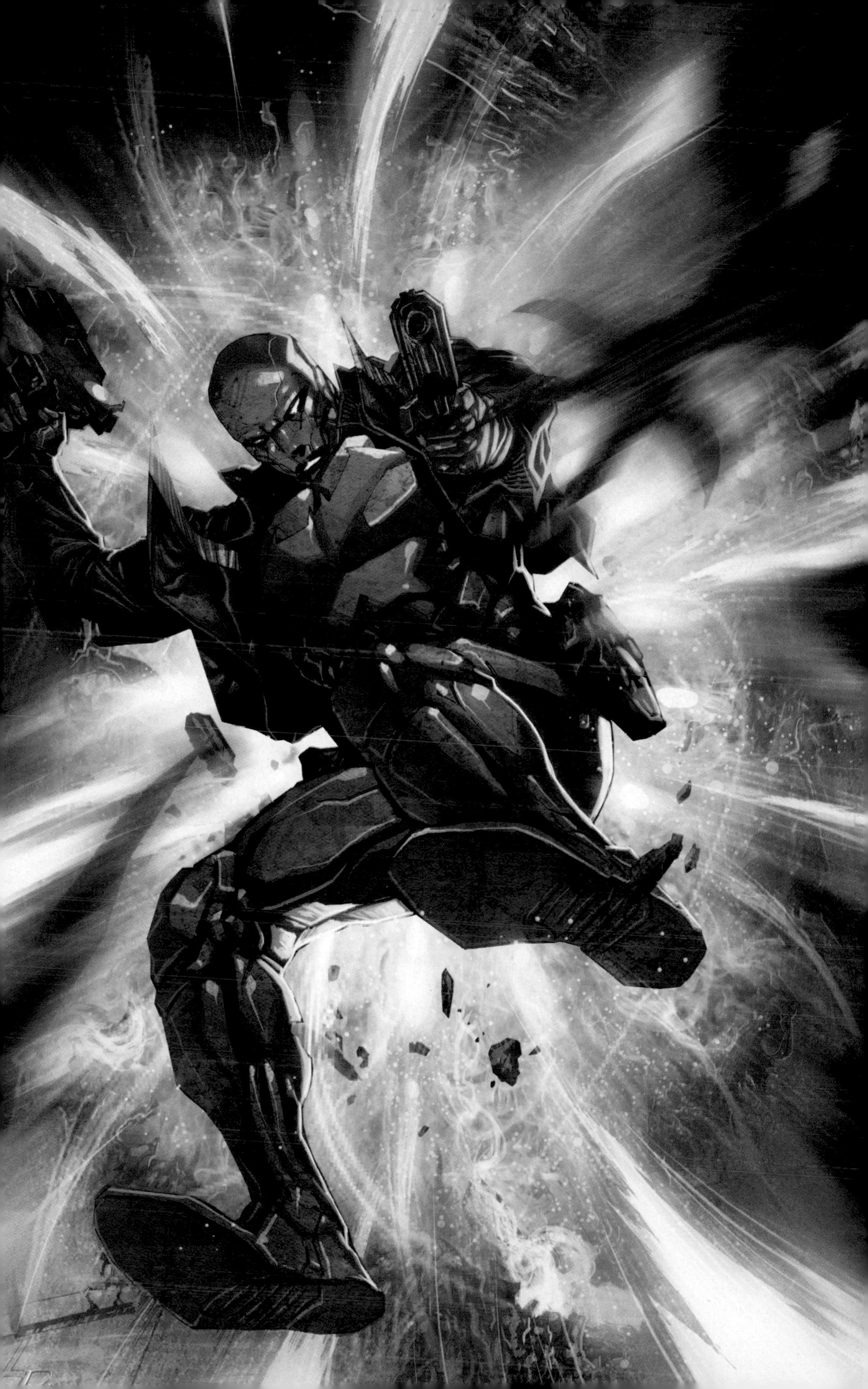

THE BIG PICTURE: PART ONE

WILL PFEIFER writer **RAFAEL SANDOVAL** penciller **PAUL NEARY** and **JORDI TARRAGONA** inkers **MATT YACKEY** colorist **TAYLOR ESPOSITO** letterer cover art by **PHILIP TAN** and **ROMULO FAJARDO, JR**

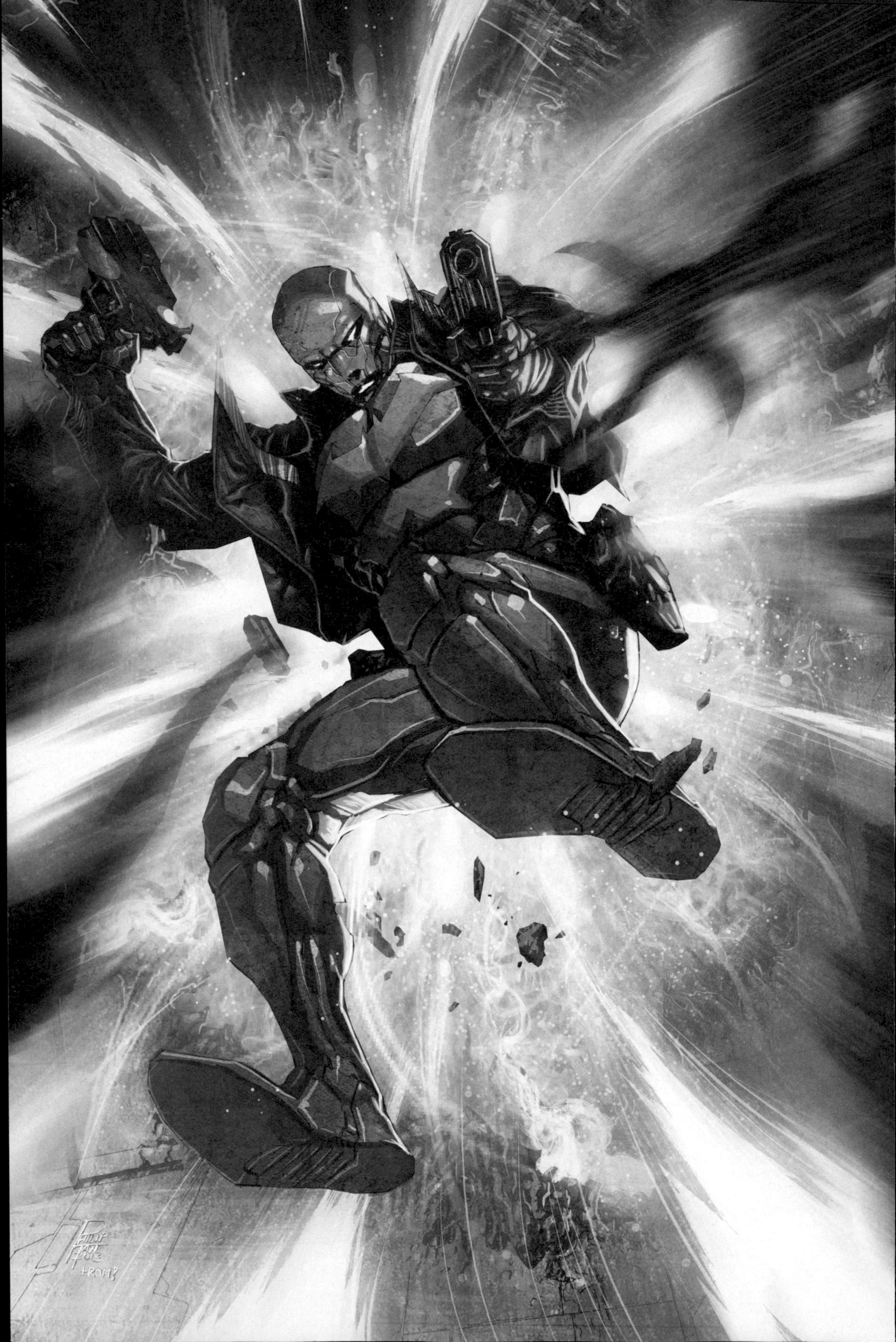

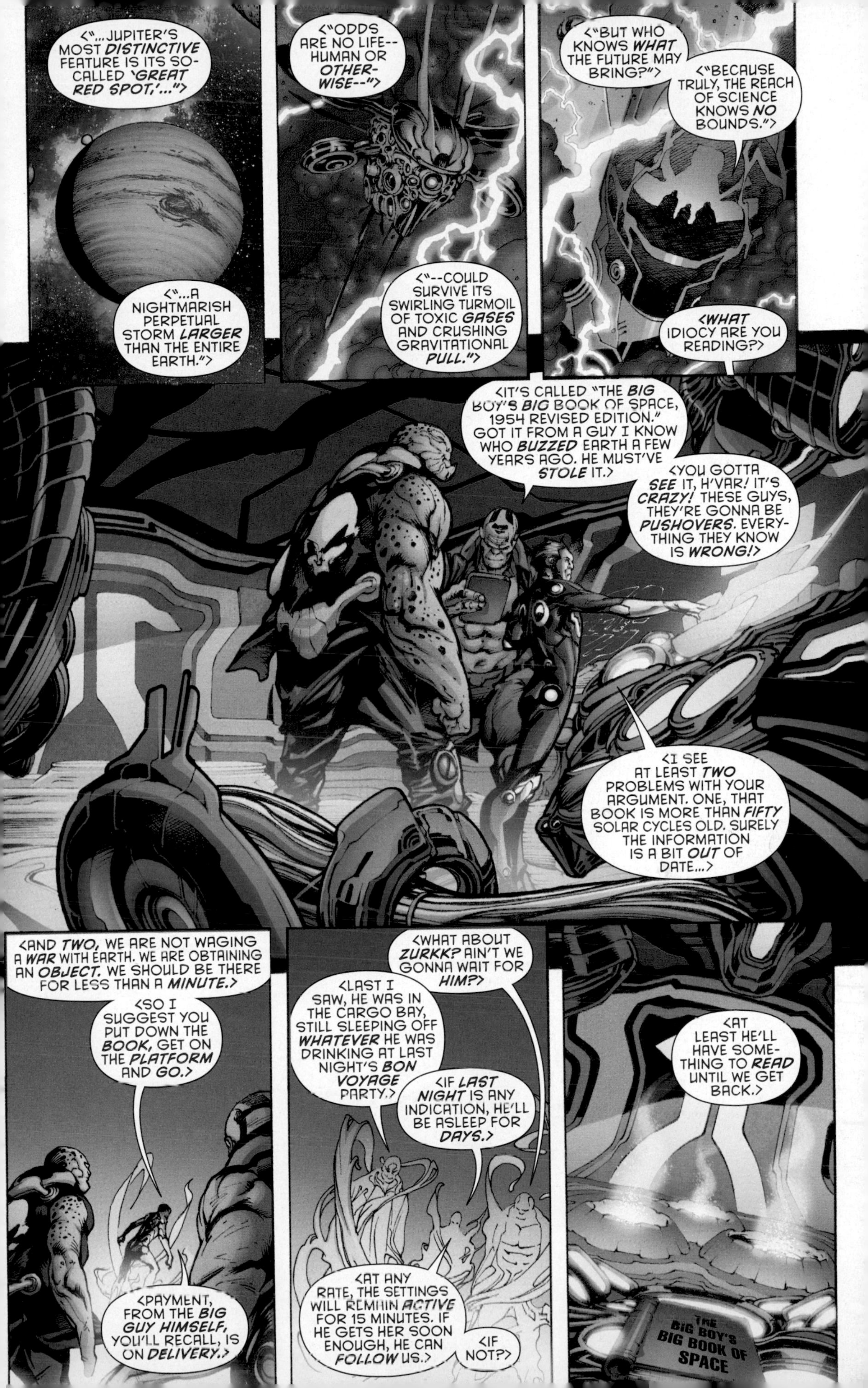
<"...JUPITER'S MOST DISTINCTIVE FEATURE IS ITS SO-CALLED 'GREAT RED SPOT,'...">
<"...A NIGHTMARISH PERPETUAL STORM LARGER THAN THE ENTIRE EARTH.">
<"ODDS ARE NO LIFE-- HUMAN OR OTHER-WISE--">
<"--COULD SURVIVE ITS SWIRLING TURMOIL OF TOXIC GASES AND CRUSHING GRAVITATIONAL PULL.">
<"BUT WHO KNOWS WHAT THE FUTURE MAY BRING?">
<"BECAUSE TRULY, THE REACH OF SCIENCE KNOWS NO BOUNDS.">
<WHAT IDIOCY ARE YOU READING?>
<IT'S CALLED "THE BIG BOY'S BIG BOOK OF SPACE, 1954 REVISED EDITION." GOT IT FROM A GUY I KNOW WHO BUZZED EARTH A FEW YEARS AGO. HE MUST'VE STOLE IT.>
<YOU GOTTA SEE IT, H'VAR! IT'S CRAZY! THESE GUYS, THEY'RE GONNA BE PUSHOVERS. EVERY-THING THEY KNOW IS WRONG!>
<I SEE AT LEAST TWO PROBLEMS WITH YOUR ARGUMENT. ONE, THAT BOOK IS MORE THAN FIFTY SOLAR CYCLES OLD. SURELY THE INFORMATION IS A BIT OUT OF DATE...>
<AND TWO, WE ARE NOT WAGING A WAR WITH EARTH. WE ARE OBTAINING AN OBJECT. WE SHOULD BE THERE FOR LESS THAN A MINUTE.>
<SO I SUGGEST YOU PUT DOWN THE BOOK, GET ON THE PLATFORM AND GO.>
<PAYMENT, FROM THE BIG GUY HIMSELF, YOU'LL RECALL, IS ON DELIVERY.>
<WHAT ABOUT ZURKK? AIN'T WE GONNA WAIT FOR HIM?>
<LAST I SAW, HE WAS IN THE CARGO BAY, STILL SLEEPING OFF WHATEVER HE WAS DRINKING AT LAST NIGHT'S BON VOYAGE PARTY.>
<IF LAST NIGHT IS ANY INDICATION, HE'LL BE ASLEEP FOR DAYS.>
<AT ANY RATE, THE SETTINGS WILL REMAIN ACTIVE FOR 15 MINUTES. IF HE GETS HER SOON ENOUGH, HE CAN FOLLOW US.>
<IF NOT?>
<AT LEAST HE'LL HAVE SOME-THING TO READ UNTIL WE GET BACK.>
THE BIG BOY'S BIG BOOK OF SPACE

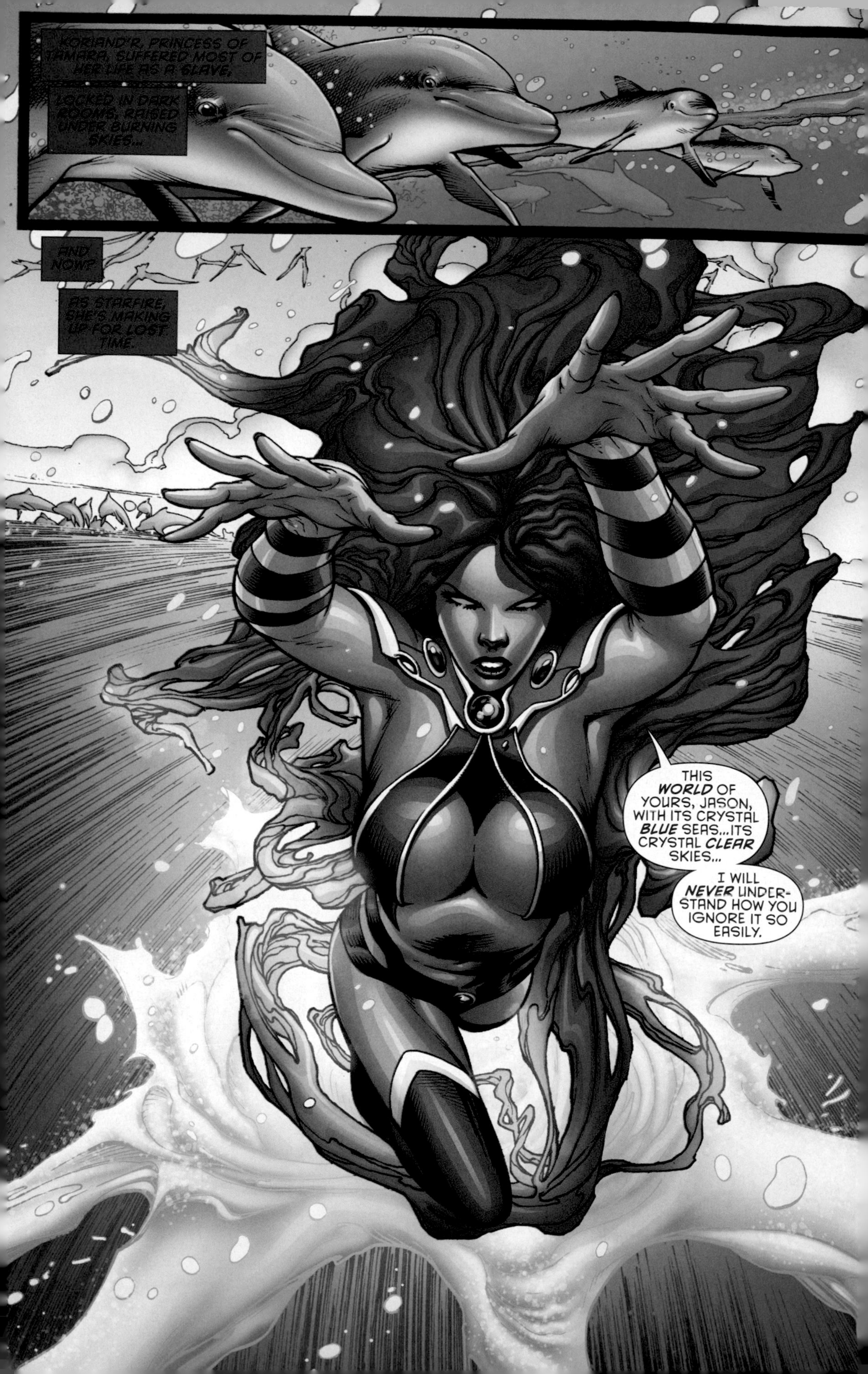
KORIAND'R, PRINCESS OF TAMARA, SUFFERED MOST OF HER LIFE AS A SLAVE,
LOCKED IN DARK ROOMS, RAISED UNDER BURNING SKIES...
AND NOW?
AS STARFIRE, SHE'S MAKING UP FOR LOST TIME.
THIS WORLD OF YOURS, JASON, WITH ITS CRYSTAL BLUE SEAS...ITS CRYSTAL CLEAR SKIES...
I WILL NEVER UNDERSTAND HOW YOU IGNORE IT SO EASILY.

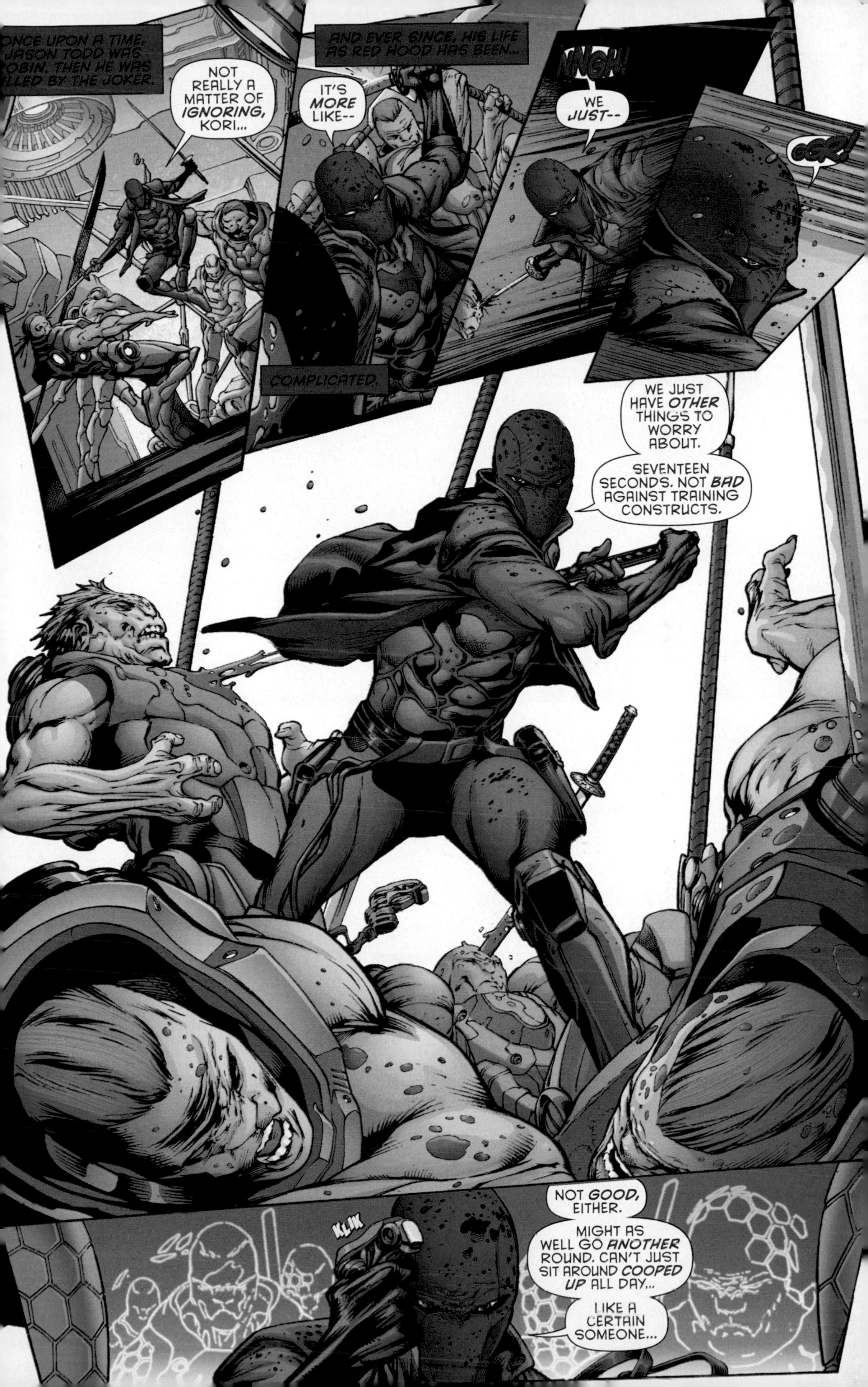
ONCE UPON A TIME, JASON TODD WAS ROBIN. THEN HE WAS KILLED BY THE JOKER.
NOT REALLY A MATTER OF IGNORING, KORI...
AND EVER SINCE, HIS LIFE AS RED HOOD HAS BEEN...
IT'S MORE LIKE--
COMPLICATED.
NNGH!
WE JUST--
GGK!
WE JUST HAVE OTHER THINGS TO WORRY ABOUT.
SEVENTEEN SECONDS. NOT BAD AGAINST TRAINING CONSTRUCTS.
NOT GOOD, EITHER.
KLIK
MIGHT AS WELL GO ANOTHER ROUND. CAN'T JUST SIT AROUND COOPED UP ALL DAY...
LIKE A CERTAIN SOMEONE...

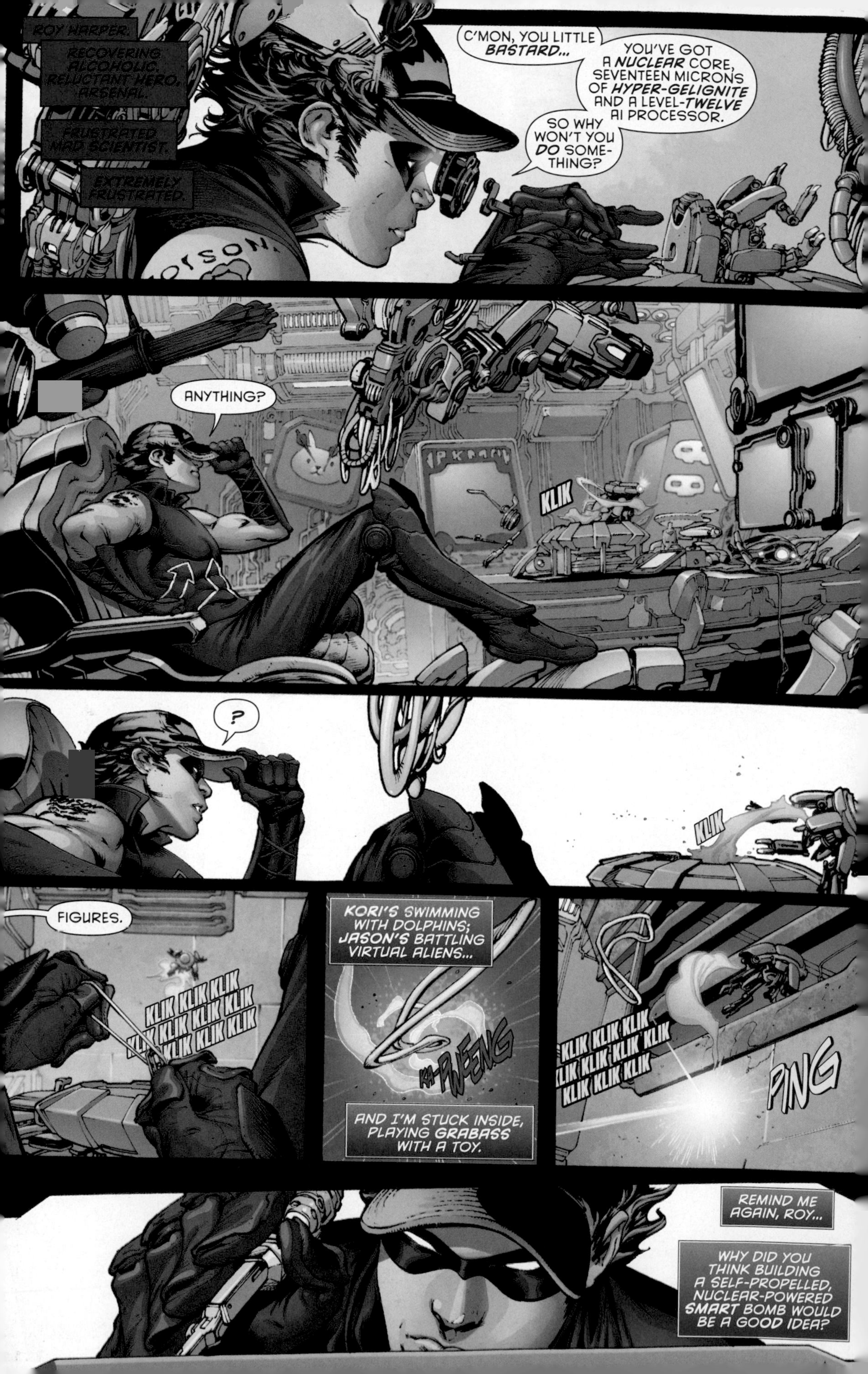

ROY HARPER.
RECOVERING ALCOHOLIC. RELUCTANT HERO. ARSENAL.
FRUSTRATED MAD SCIENTIST.
EXTREMELY FRUSTRATED.
C'MON, YOU LITTLE BASTARD...
YOU'VE GOT A NUCLEAR CORE, SEVENTEEN MICRONS OF HYPER-GELIGNITE AND A LEVEL-TWELVE AI PROCESSOR.
SO WHY WON'T YOU DO SOME-THING?
ANYTHING?
KLIK
?
KLIK
FIGURES.
KLIK KLIK KLIK KLIK KLIK KLIK KLIK KLIK KLIK KLIK KLIK KLIK
KORI'S SWIMMING WITH DOLPHINS; JASON'S BATTLING VIRTUAL ALIENS...
KA-PWENG
AND I'M STUCK INSIDE, PLAYING GRABASS WITH A TOY.
KLIK KLIK KLIK KLIK KLIK KLIK KLIK KLIK KLIK KLIK KLIK
PING
REMIND ME AGAIN, ROY...
WHY DID YOU THINK BUILDING A SELF-PROPELLED, NUCLEAR-POWERED SMART BOMB WOULD BE A GOOD IDEA?

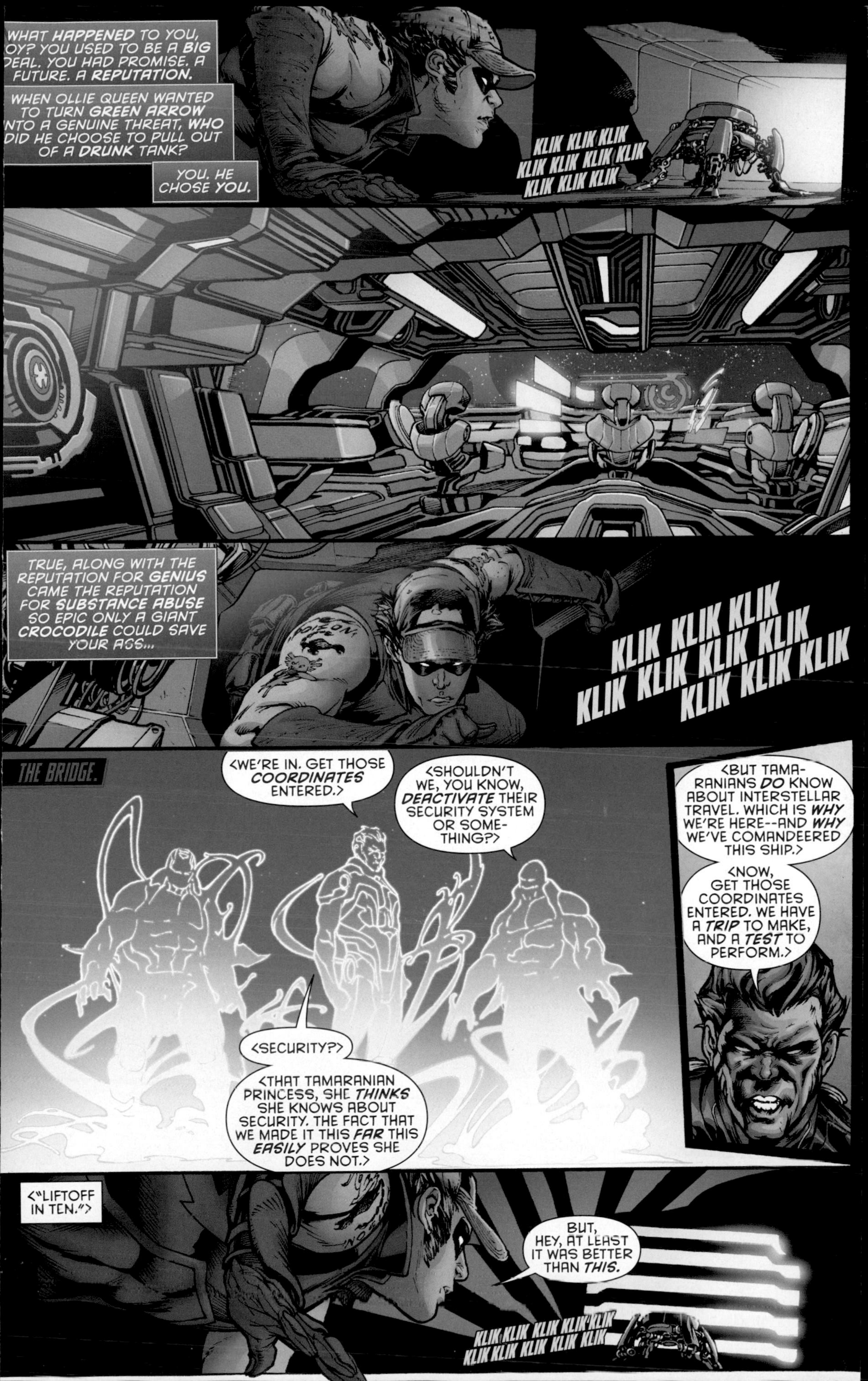

WHAT HAPPENED TO YOU, ROY? YOU USED TO BE A BIG DEAL. YOU HAD PROMISE. A FUTURE. A REPUTATION.
WHEN OLLIE QUEEN WANTED TO TURN GREEN ARROW INTO A GENUINE THREAT, WHO DID HE CHOOSE TO PULL OUT OF A DRUNK TANK?
YOU. HE CHOSE YOU.
KLIK KLIK KLIK KLIK KLIK KLIK KLIK KLIK KLIK KLIK
TRUE, ALONG WITH THE REPUTATION FOR GENIUS CAME THE REPUTATION FOR SUBSTANCE ABUSE SO EPIC ONLY A GIANT CROCODILE COULD SAVE YOUR ASS...
KLIK KLIK KLIK KLIK KLIK KLIK KLIK KLIK KLIK KLIK
THE BRIDGE.
<WE'RE IN. GET THOSE COORDINATES ENTERED.>
<SHOULDN'T WE, YOU KNOW, DEACTIVATE THEIR SECURITY SYSTEM OR SOMETHING?>
<SECURITY?>
<THAT TAMARANIAN PRINCESS, SHE THINKS SHE KNOWS ABOUT SECURITY. THE FACT THAT WE MADE IT THIS FAR THIS EASILY PROVES SHE DOES NOT.>
<BUT TAMARANIANS DO KNOW ABOUT INTERSTELLAR TRAVEL. WHICH IS WHY WE'RE HERE--AND WHY WE'VE COMANDEERED THIS SHIP.>
<NOW, GET THOSE COORDINATES ENTERED. WE HAVE A TRIP TO MAKE, AND A TEST TO PERFORM.>
<"LIFTOFF IN TEN.">
BUT, HEY, AT LEAST IT WAS BETTER THAN THIS.
KLIK KLIK KLIK KLIK KLIK KLIK KLIK KLIK KLIK KLIK

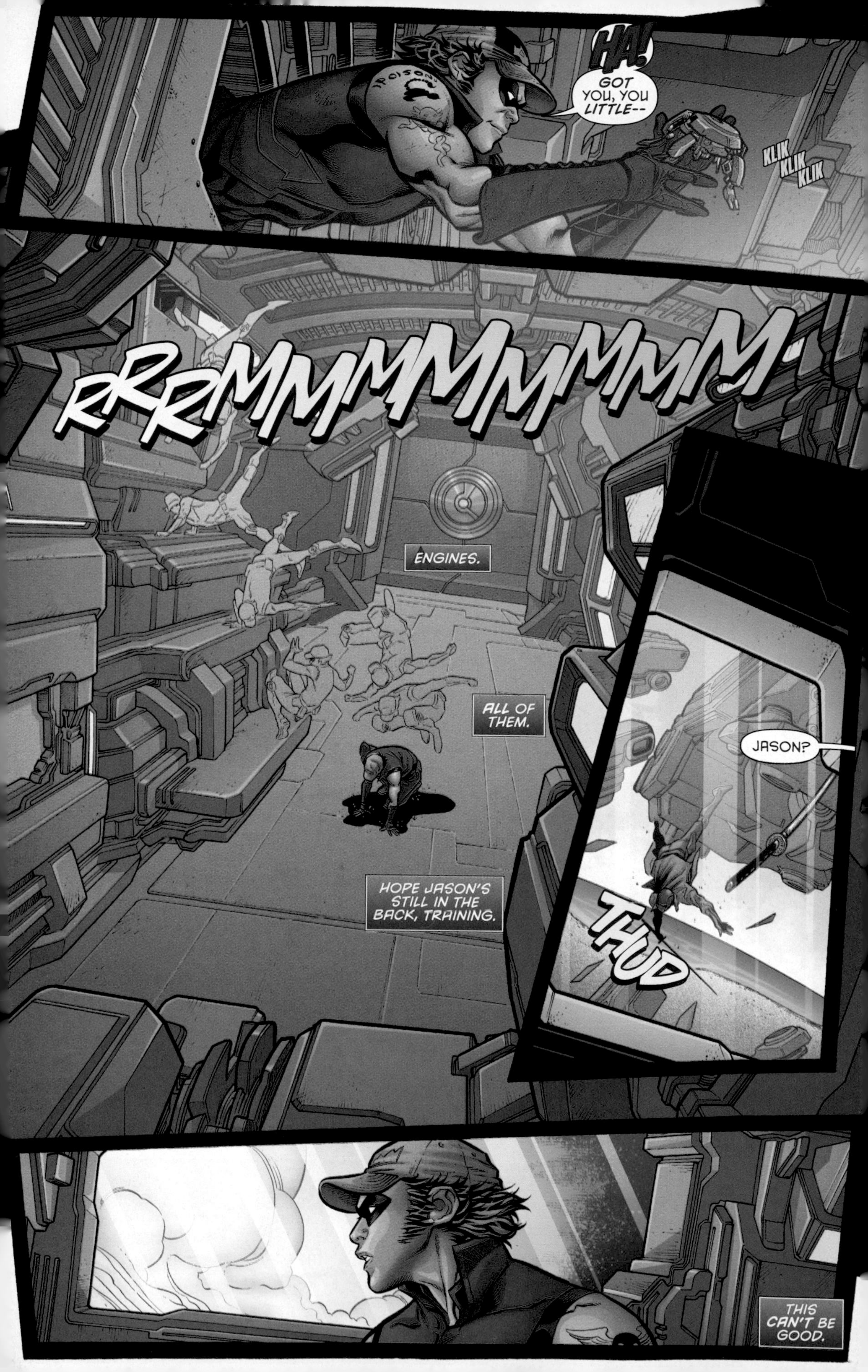
HA!
GOT YOU, YOU LITTLE--
KLIK KLIK KLIK
RRRMMMMMMMMMM
ENGINES.
ALL OF THEM.
HOPE JASON'S STILL IN THE BACK, TRAINING.
JASON?
THUD
THIS CAN'T BE GOOD.

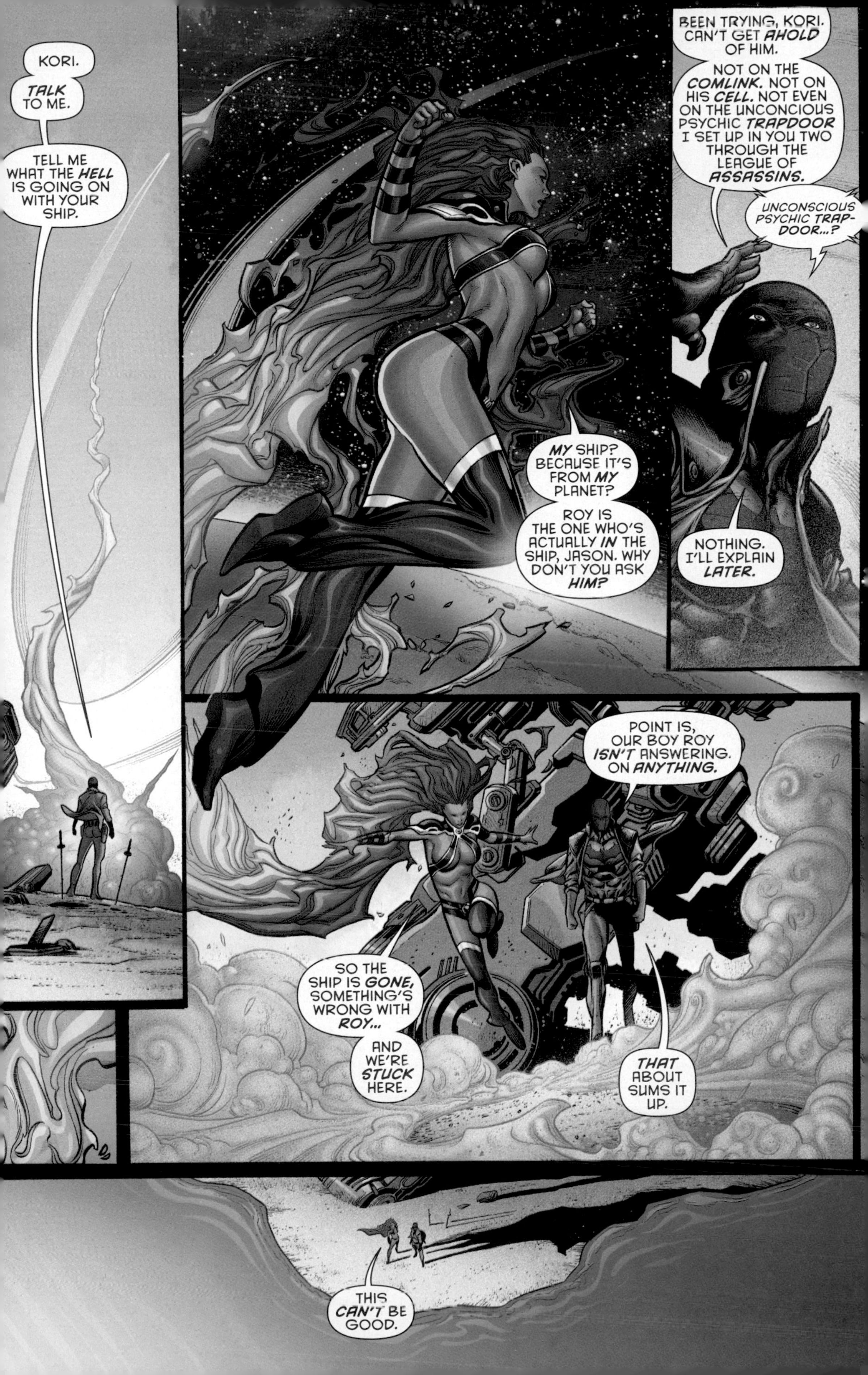

KORI.
TALK TO ME.
TELL ME WHAT THE HELL IS GOING ON WITH YOUR SHIP.
MY SHIP? BECAUSE IT'S FROM MY PLANET?
ROY IS THE ONE WHO'S ACTUALLY IN THE SHIP, JASON. WHY DON'T YOU ASK HIM?
BEEN TRYING, KORI. CAN'T GET AHOLD OF HIM.
NOT ON THE COMLINK. NOT ON HIS CELL. NOT EVEN ON THE UNCONCIOUS PSYCHIC TRAPDOOR I SET UP IN YOU TWO THROUGH THE LEAGUE OF ASSASSINS.
UNCONSCIOUS PSYCHIC TRAP-DOOR...?
NOTHING. I'LL EXPLAIN LATER.
POINT IS, OUR BOY ROY ISN'T ANSWERING. ON ANYTHING.
SO THE SHIP IS GONE, SOMETHING'S WRONG WITH ROY...
AND WE'RE STUCK HERE.
THAT ABOUT SUMS IT UP.
THIS CAN'T BE GOOD.

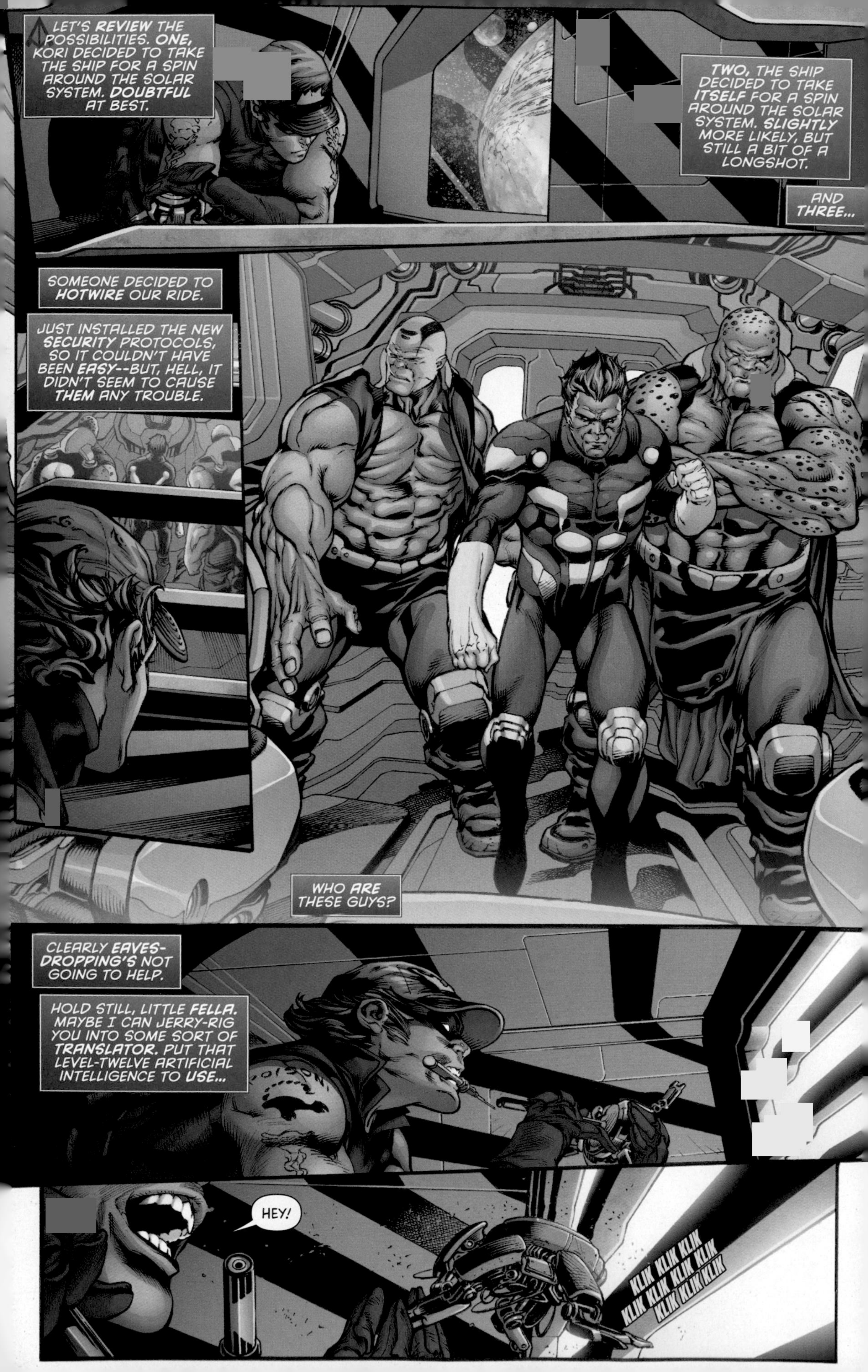

LET'S REVIEW THE POSSIBILITIES. ONE, KORI DECIDED TO TAKE THE SHIP FOR A SPIN AROUND THE SOLAR SYSTEM. DOUBTFUL AT BEST.
TWO, THE SHIP DECIDED TO TAKE ITSELF FOR A SPIN AROUND THE SOLAR SYSTEM. SLIGHTLY MORE LIKELY, BUT STILL A BIT OF A LONGSHOT.
AND THREE...
SOMEONE DECIDED TO HOTWIRE OUR RIDE.
JUST INSTALLED THE NEW SECURITY PROTOCOLS, SO IT COULDN'T HAVE BEEN EASY--BUT, HELL, IT DIDN'T SEEM TO CAUSE THEM ANY TROUBLE.
WHO ARE THESE GUYS?
CLEARLY EAVES-DROPPING'S NOT GOING TO HELP.
HOLD STILL, LITTLE FELLA. MAYBE I CAN JERRY-RIG YOU INTO SOME SORT OF TRANSLATOR. PUT THAT LEVEL-TWELVE ARTIFICIAL INTELLIGENCE TO USE...
HEY!
KLIK KLIK KLIK KLIK KLIK KLIK KLIK KLIK KLIK KLIK KLIK

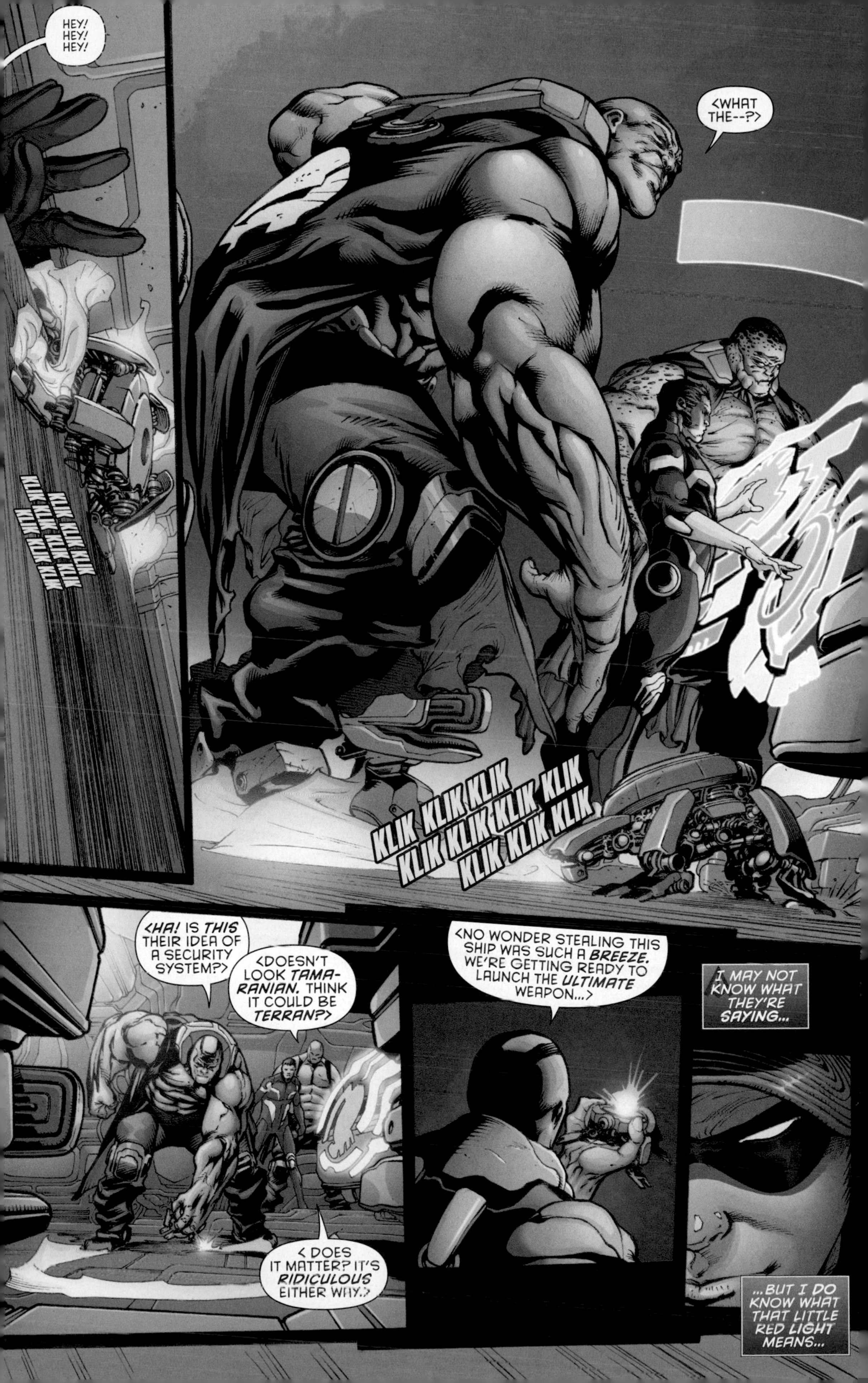
HEY! HEY! HEY!
KLIK KLIK KLIK KLIK KLIK KLIK KLIK KLIK KLIK KLIK
<WHAT THE--?>
KLIK KLIK KLIK KLIK KLIK KLIK KLIK KLIK KLIK KLIK
<HA! IS THIS THEIR IDEA OF A SECURITY SYSTEM?>
<DOESN'T LOOK TAMARANIAN. THINK IT COULD BE TERRAN?>
< DOES IT MATTER? IT'S RIDICULOUS EITHER WAY.>
<NO WONDER STEALING THIS SHIP WAS SUCH A BREEZE. WE'RE GETTING READY TO LAUNCH THE ULTIMATE WEAPON...>
I MAY NOT KNOW WHAT THEY'RE SAYING...
...BUT I DO KNOW WHAT THAT LITTLE RED LIGHT MEANS...

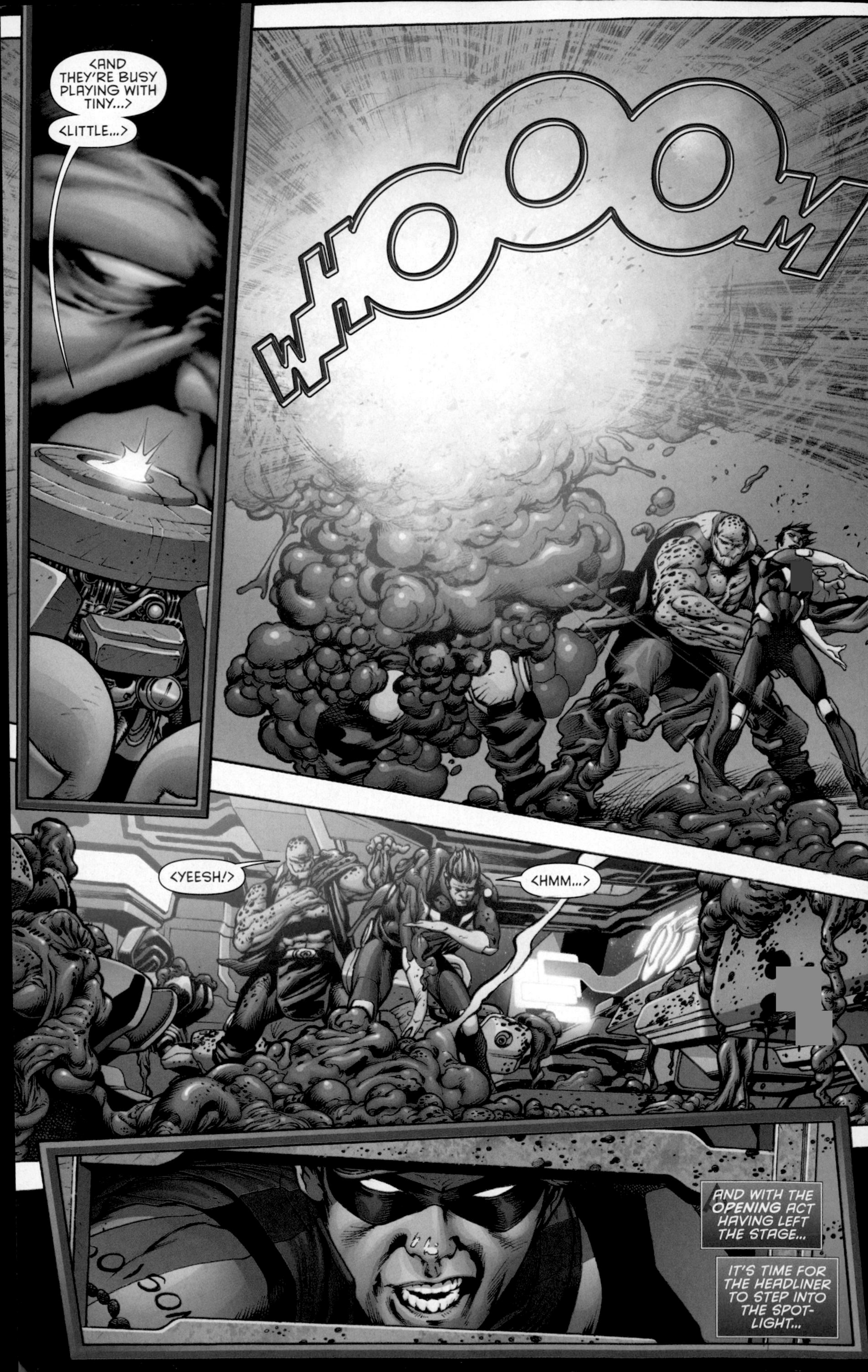
<AND THEY'RE BUSY PLAYING WITH TINY...>
<LITTLE...>
WHOOOOM
<YEESH!>
<HMM...>
AND WITH THE OPENING ACT HAVING LEFT THE STAGE...
IT'S TIME FOR THE HEADLINER TO STEP INTO THE SPOT-LIGHT...

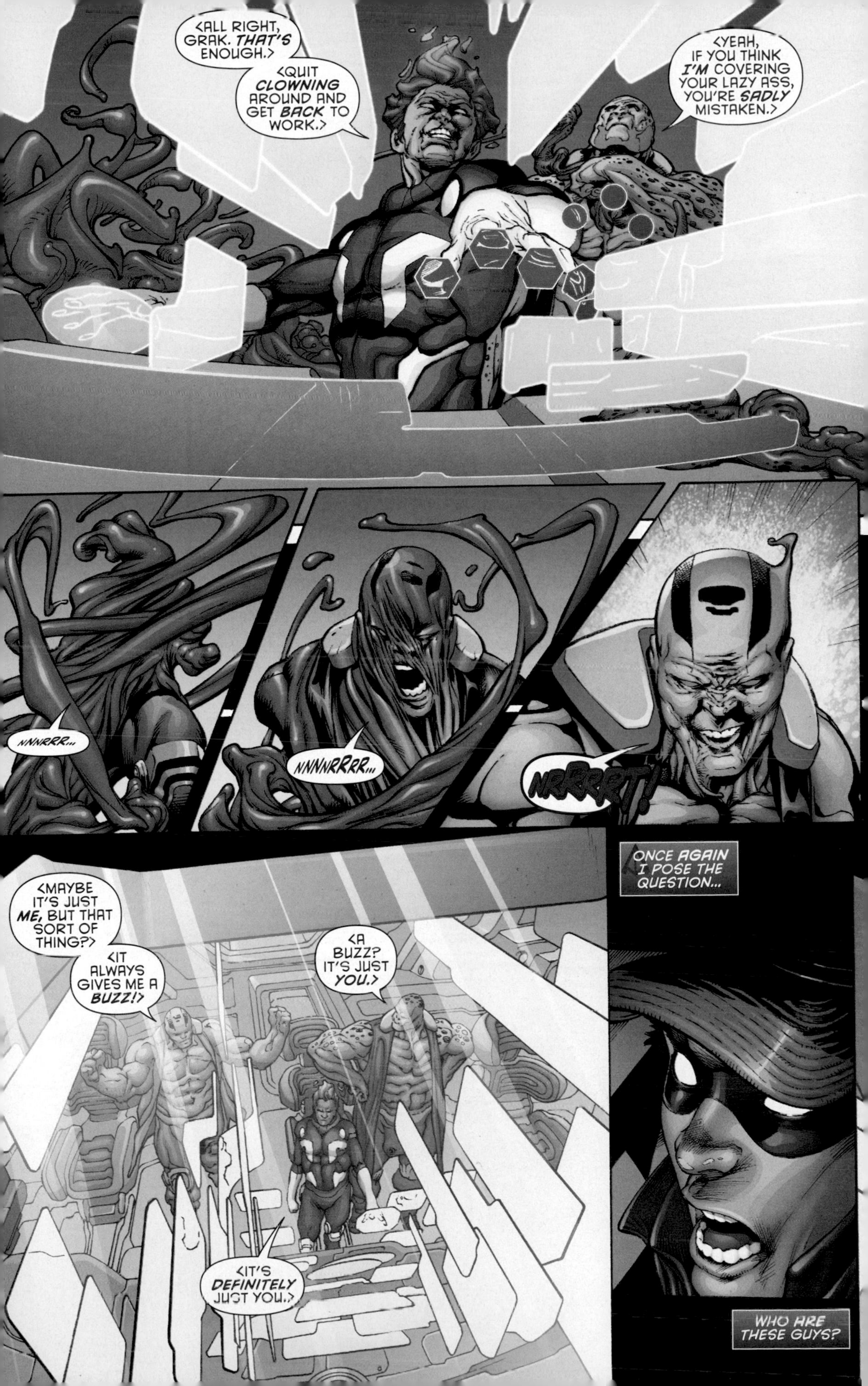
<ALL RIGHT, GRAK. THAT'S ENOUGH.>
<QUIT CLOWNING AROUND AND GET BACK TO WORK.>
<YEAH, IF YOU THINK I'M COVERING YOUR LAZY ASS, YOU'RE SADLY MISTAKEN.>
NNNRRR...
NNNNRRRR...
NRRRRT!
<MAYBE IT'S JUST ME, BUT THAT SORT OF THING?>
<IT ALWAYS GIVES ME A BUZZ!>
<A BUZZ? IT'S JUST YOU.>
<IT'S DEFINITELY JUST YOU.>
ONCE AGAIN I POSE THE QUESTION...
WHO ARE THESE GUYS?

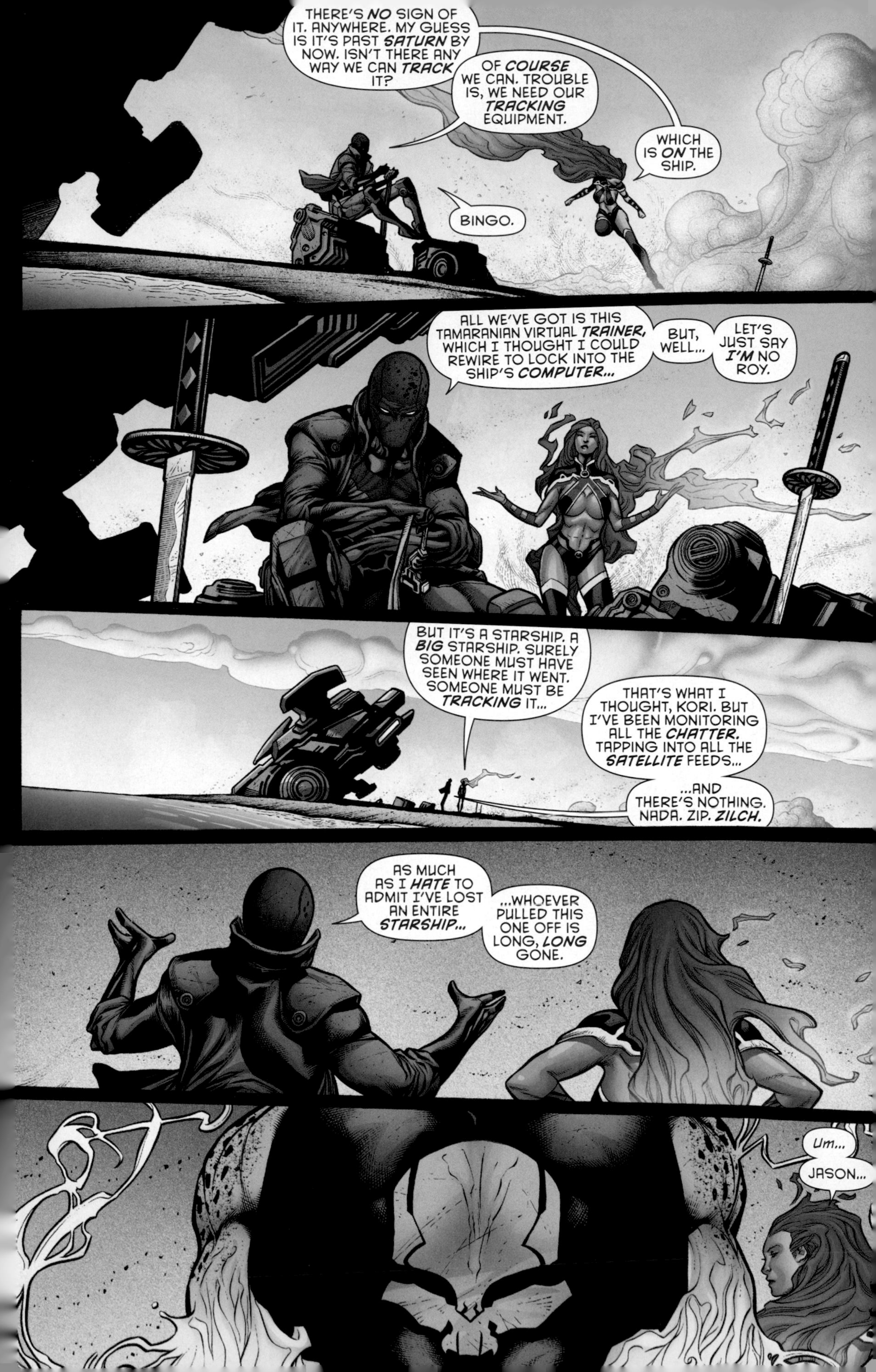
THERE'S NO SIGN OF IT. ANYWHERE. MY GUESS IS IT'S PAST SATURN BY NOW. ISN'T THERE ANY WAY WE CAN TRACK IT?
OF COURSE WE CAN. TROUBLE IS, WE NEED OUR TRACKING EQUIPMENT.
WHICH IS ON THE SHIP.
BINGO.
ALL WE'VE GOT IS THIS TAMARANIAN VIRTUAL TRAINER, WHICH I THOUGHT I COULD REWIRE TO LOCK INTO THE SHIP'S COMPUTER...
BUT, WELL...
LET'S JUST SAY I'M NO ROY.
BUT IT'S A STARSHIP. A BIG STARSHIP. SURELY SOMEONE MUST HAVE SEEN WHERE IT WENT. SOMEONE MUST BE TRACKING IT...
THAT'S WHAT I THOUGHT, KORI. BUT I'VE BEEN MONITORING ALL THE CHATTER. TAPPING INTO ALL THE SATELLITE FEEDS...
...AND THERE'S NOTHING. NADA. ZIP. ZILCH.
AS MUCH AS I HATE TO ADMIT I'VE LOST AN ENTIRE STARSHIP...
...WHOEVER PULLED THIS ONE OFF IS LONG, LONG GONE.
Um...
JASON...

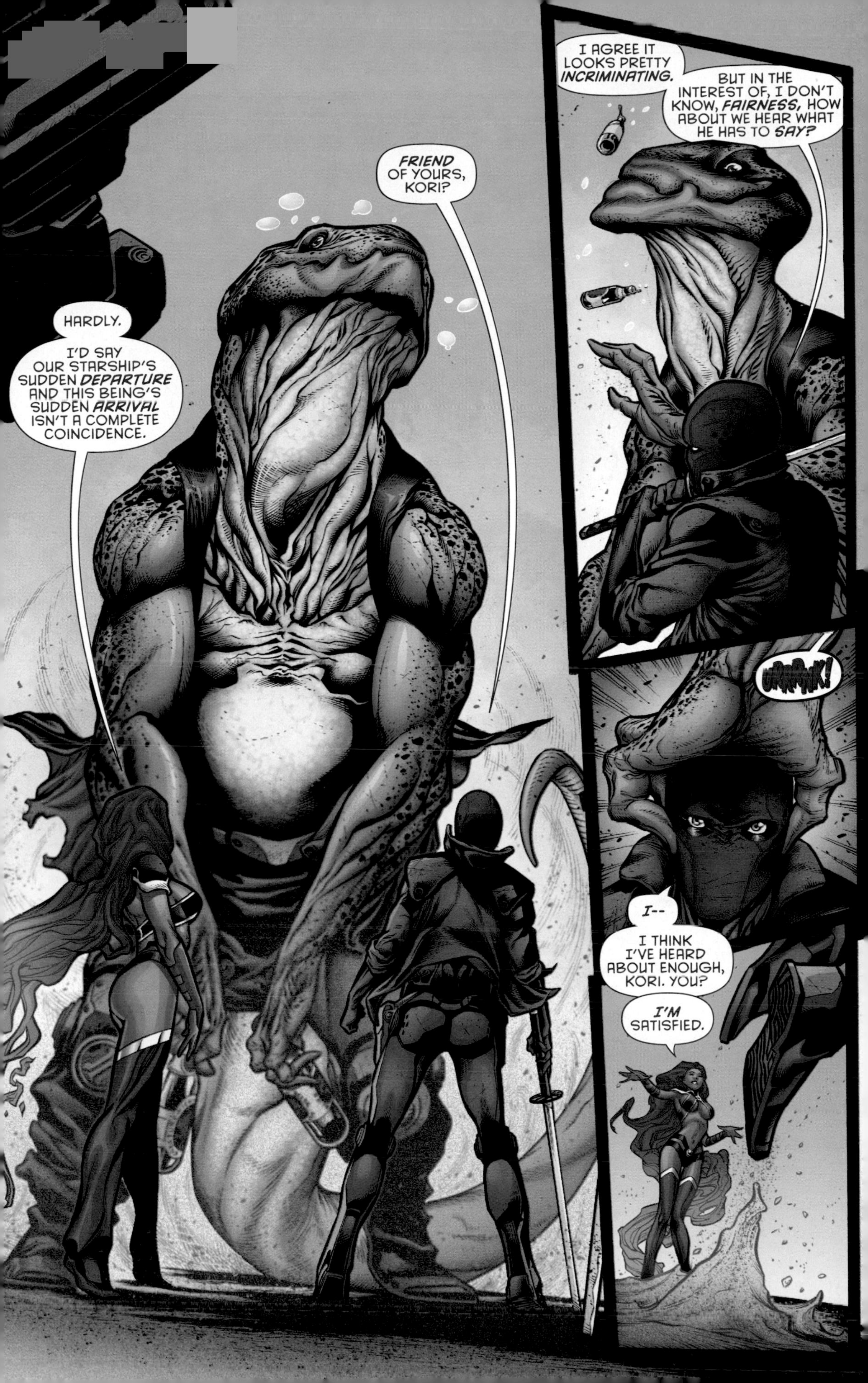
FRIEND OF YOURS, KORI?
HARDLY.
I'D SAY OUR STARSHIP'S SUDDEN DEPARTURE AND THIS BEING'S SUDDEN ARRIVAL ISN'T A COMPLETE COINCIDENCE.
I AGREE IT LOOKS PRETTY INCRIMINATING.
BUT IN THE INTEREST OF, I DON'T KNOW, FAIRNESS, HOW ABOUT WE HEAR WHAT HE HAS TO SAY?
URRRNK!
I--
I THINK I'VE HEARD ABOUT ENOUGH, KORI. YOU?
I'M SATISFIED.

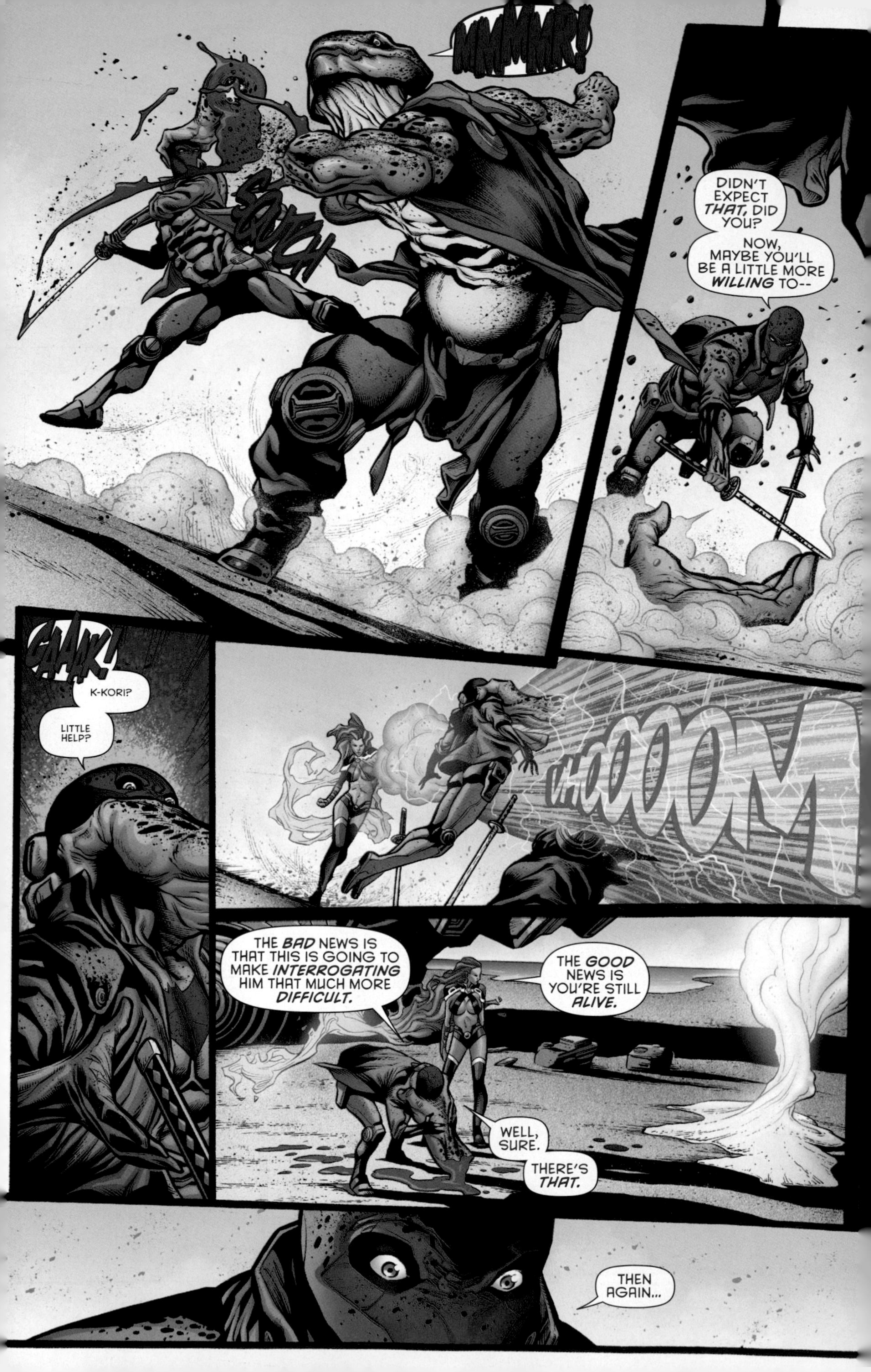
MMMMR!
SQUTCH
DIDN'T EXPECT THAT, DID YOU?
NOW, MAYBE YOU'LL BE A LITTLE MORE WILLING TO--
GAAAK!
K-KORI?
LITTLE HELP?
CHOOOOM
THE BAD NEWS IS THAT THIS IS GOING TO MAKE INTERROGATING HIM THAT MUCH MORE DIFFICULT.
THE GOOD NEWS IS YOU'RE STILL ALIVE.
WELL, SURE.
THERE'S THAT.
THEN AGAIN...

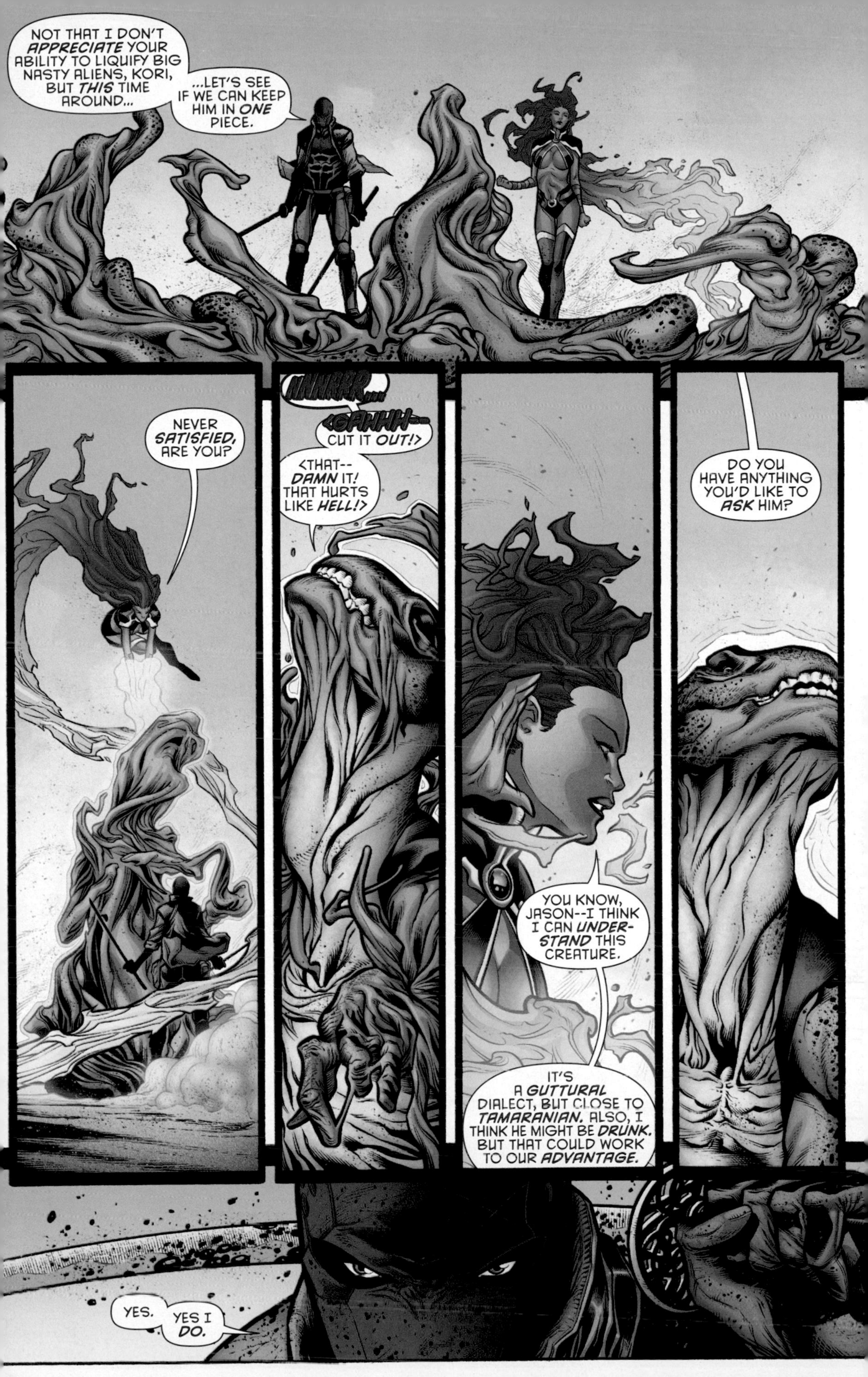
NOT THAT I DON'T APPRECIATE YOUR ABILITY TO LIQUIFY BIG NASTY ALIENS, KORI, BUT THIS TIME AROUND...
...LET'S SEE IF WE CAN KEEP HIM IN ONE PIECE.
NEVER SATISFIED, ARE YOU?
NNNRRR...
<GAHHH-- CUT IT OUT!>
<THAT-- DAMN IT! THAT HURTS LIKE HELL!>
YOU KNOW, JASON--I THINK I CAN UNDERSTAND THIS CREATURE.
IT'S A GUTTURAL DIALECT, BUT CLOSE TO TAMARANIAN. ALSO, I THINK HE MIGHT BE DRUNK. BUT THAT COULD WORK TO OUR ADVANTAGE.
DO YOU HAVE ANYTHING YOU'D LIKE TO ASK HIM?
YES.
YES I DO.

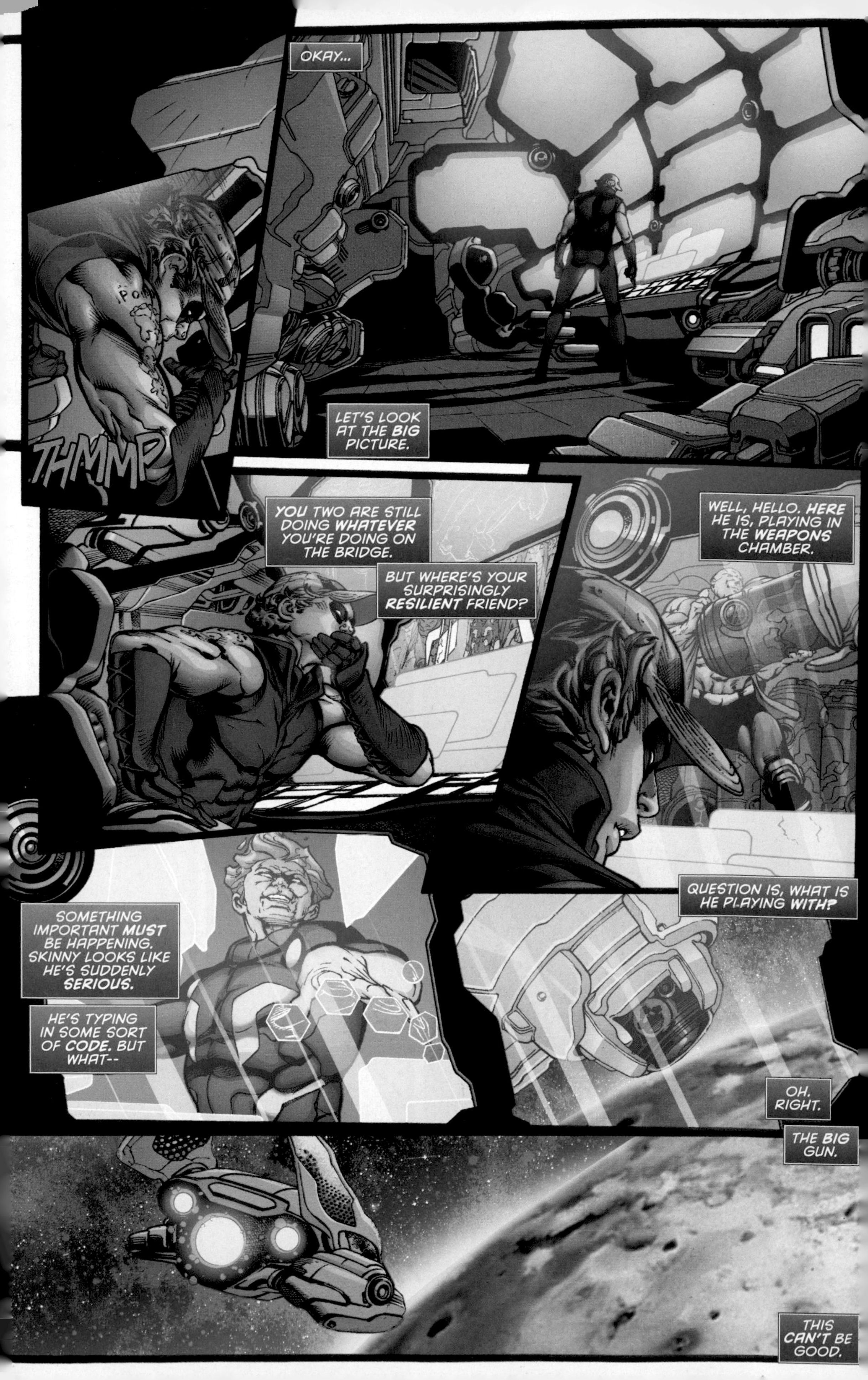
THMMP
OKAY...
LET'S LOOK AT THE BIG PICTURE.
YOU TWO ARE STILL DOING WHATEVER YOU'RE DOING ON THE BRIDGE.
BUT WHERE'S YOUR SURPRISINGLY RESILIENT FRIEND?
WELL, HELLO. HERE HE IS, PLAYING IN THE WEAPONS CHAMBER.
QUESTION IS, WHAT IS HE PLAYING WITH?
SOMETHING IMPORTANT MUST BE HAPPENING. SKINNY LOOKS LIKE HE'S SUDDENLY SERIOUS.
HE'S TYPING IN SOME SORT OF CODE. BUT WHAT--
OH. RIGHT.
THE BIG GUN.
THIS CAN'T BE GOOD.

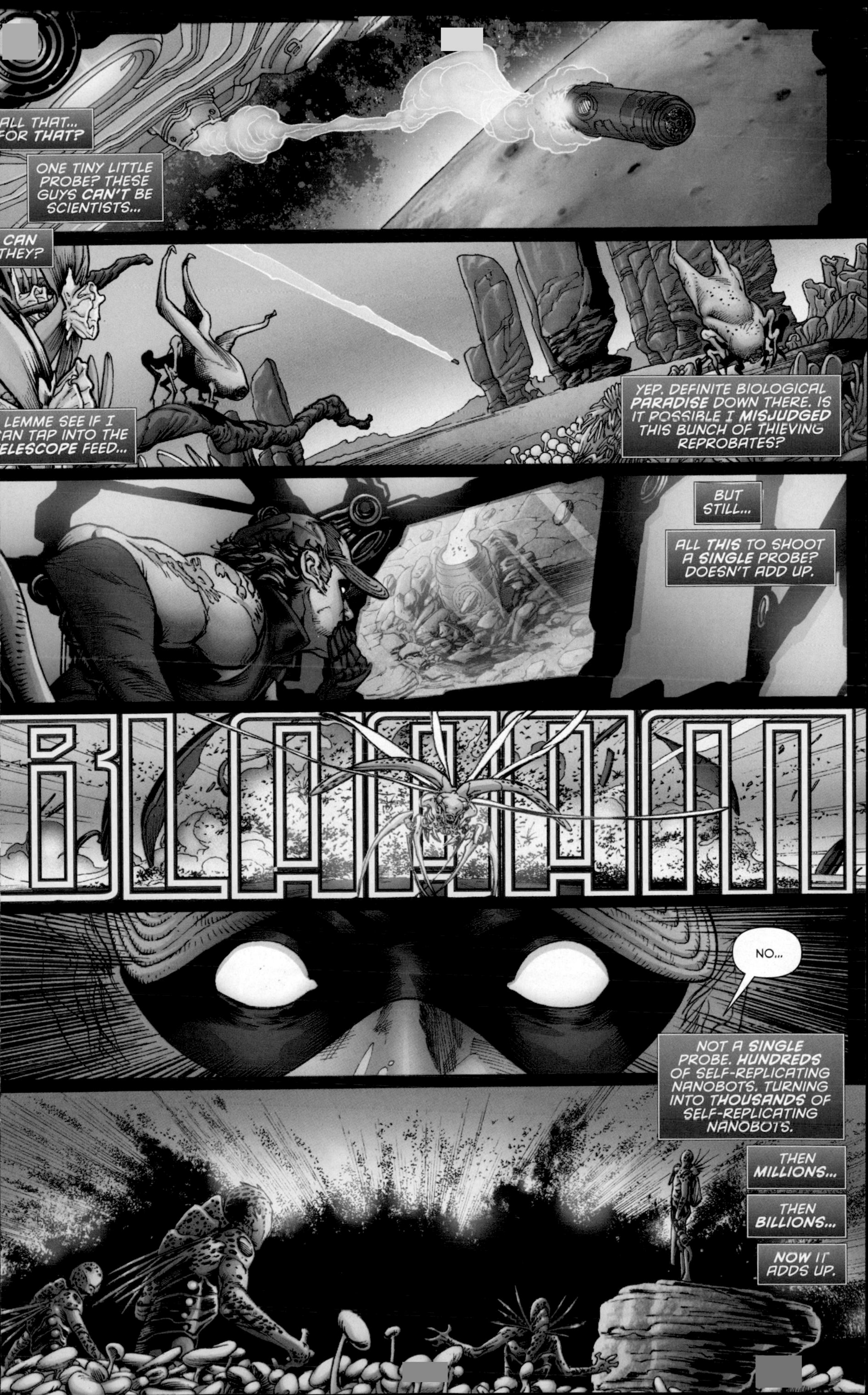

ALL THAT... FOR THAT?
ONE TINY LITTLE PROBE? THESE GUYS CAN'T BE SCIENTISTS...
CAN THEY?
LEMME SEE IF I CAN TAP INTO THE TELESCOPE FEED...
YEP. DEFINITE BIOLOGICAL PARADISE DOWN THERE. IS IT POSSIBLE I MISJUDGED THIS BUNCH OF THIEVING REPROBATES?
BUT STILL...
ALL THIS TO SHOOT A SINGLE PROBE? DOESN'T ADD UP.
NO...
NOT A SINGLE PROBE. HUNDREDS OF SELF-REPLICATING NANOBOTS, TURNING INTO THOUSANDS OF SELF-REPLICATING NANOBOTS.
THEN MILLIONS...
THEN BILLIONS...
NOW IT ADDS UP.

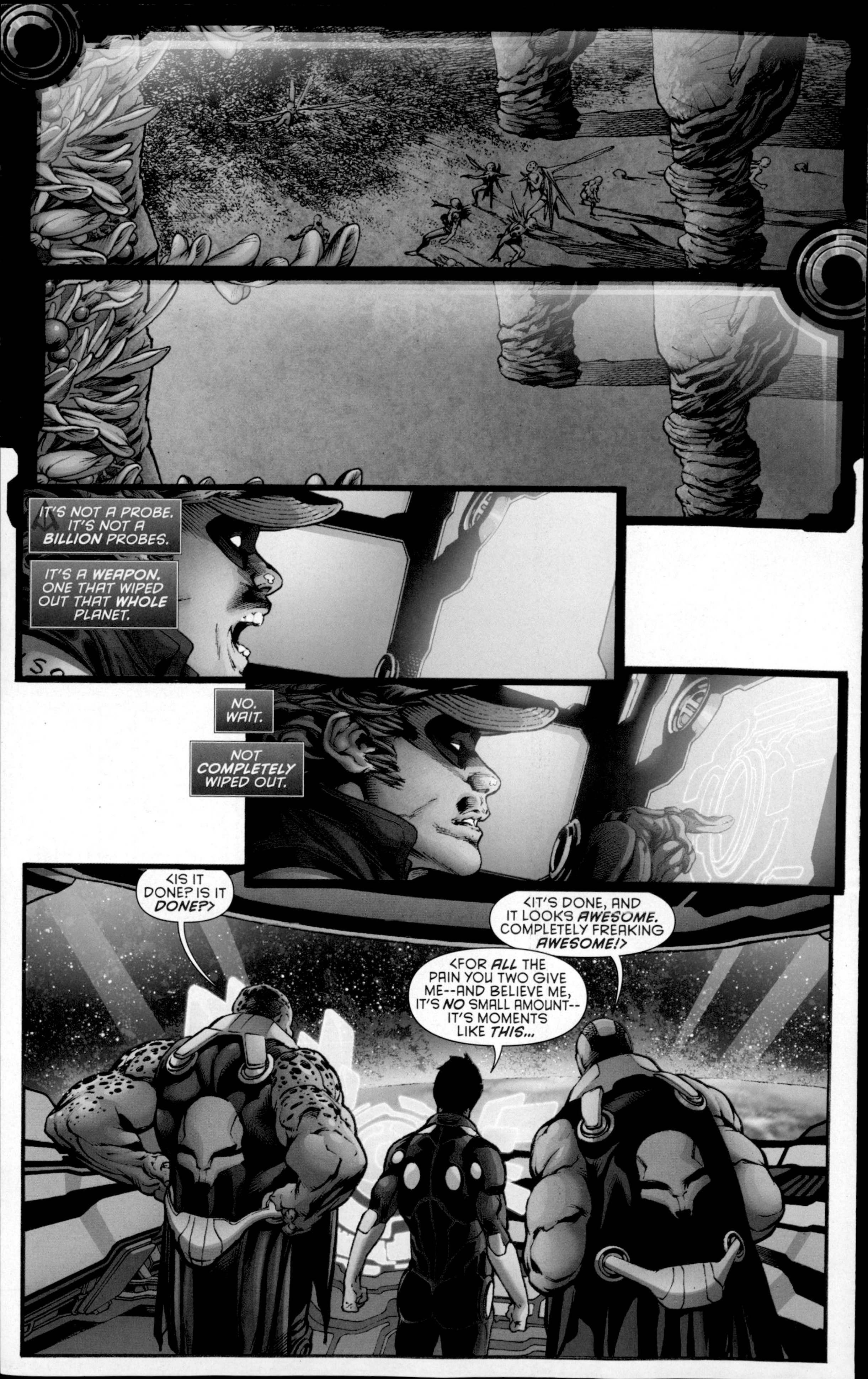
IT'S NOT A PROBE. IT'S NOT A BILLION PROBES.
IT'S A WEAPON. ONE THAT WIPED OUT THAT WHOLE PLANET.
NO. WAIT.
NOT COMPLETELY WIPED OUT.
<IS IT DONE? IS IT DONE?>
<IT'S DONE, AND IT LOOKS AWESOME. COMPLETELY FREAKING AWESOME!>
<FOR ALL THE PAIN YOU TWO GIVE ME--AND BELIEVE ME, IT'S NO SMALL AMOUNT--IT'S MOMENTS LIKE THIS...

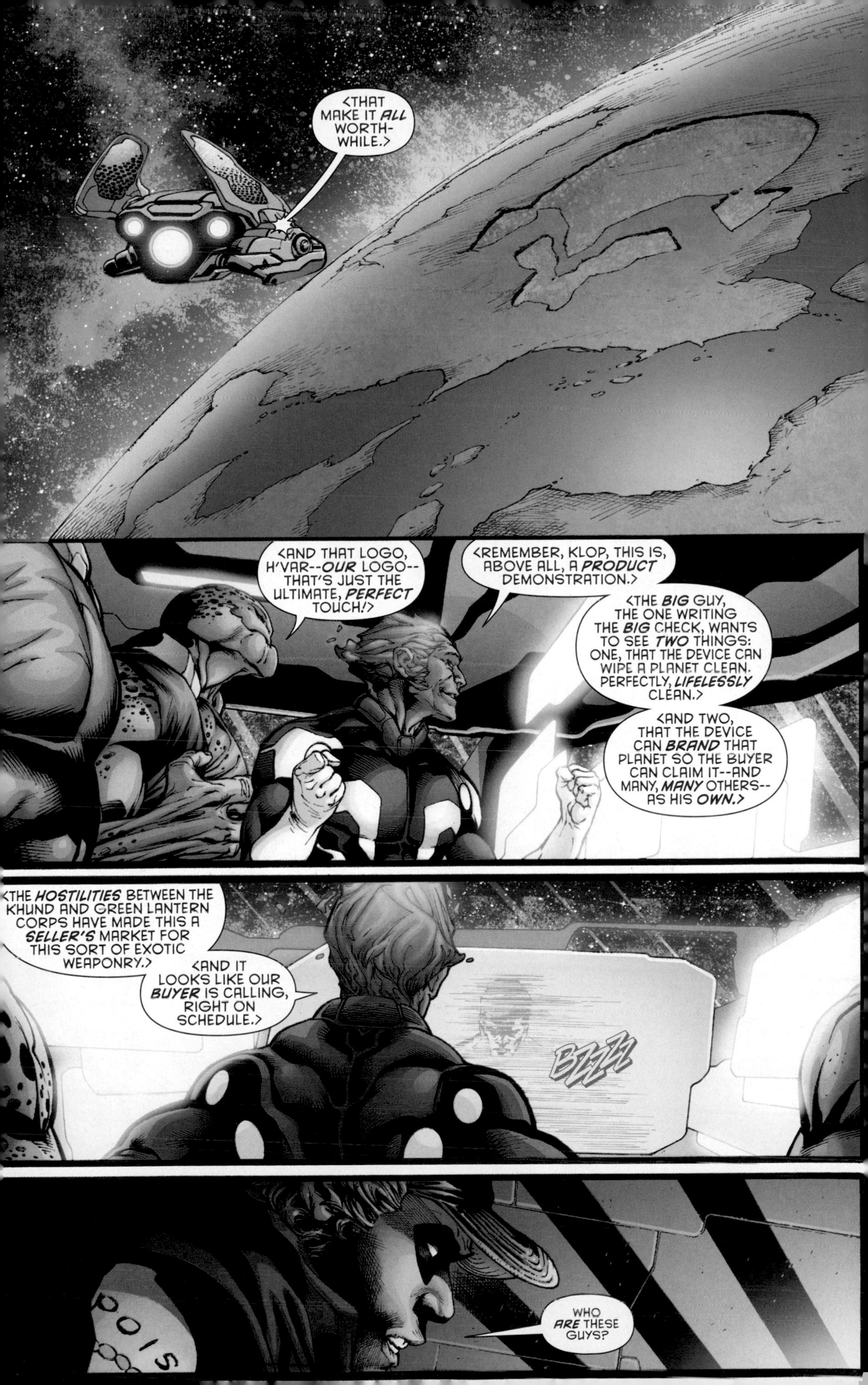
<THAT MAKE IT ALL WORTH-WHILE.>
<AND THAT LOGO, H'VAR--OUR LOGO--THAT'S JUST THE ULTIMATE, PERFECT TOUCH!>
<REMEMBER, KLOP, THIS IS, ABOVE ALL, A PRODUCT DEMONSTRATION.>
<THE BIG GUY, THE ONE WRITING THE BIG CHECK, WANTS TO SEE TWO THINGS: ONE, THAT THE DEVICE CAN WIPE A PLANET CLEAN. PERFECTLY, LIFELESSLY CLEAN.>
<AND TWO, THAT THE DEVICE CAN BRAND THAT PLANET SO THE BUYER CAN CLAIM IT--AND MANY, MANY OTHERS--AS HIS OWN.>
<THE HOSTILITIES BETWEEN THE KHUND AND GREEN LANTERN CORPS HAVE MADE THIS A SELLER'S MARKET FOR THIS SORT OF EXOTIC WEAPONRY.>
<AND IT LOOKS LIKE OUR BUYER IS CALLING, RIGHT ON SCHEDULE.>
BZZZZ
WHO ARE THESE GUYS?

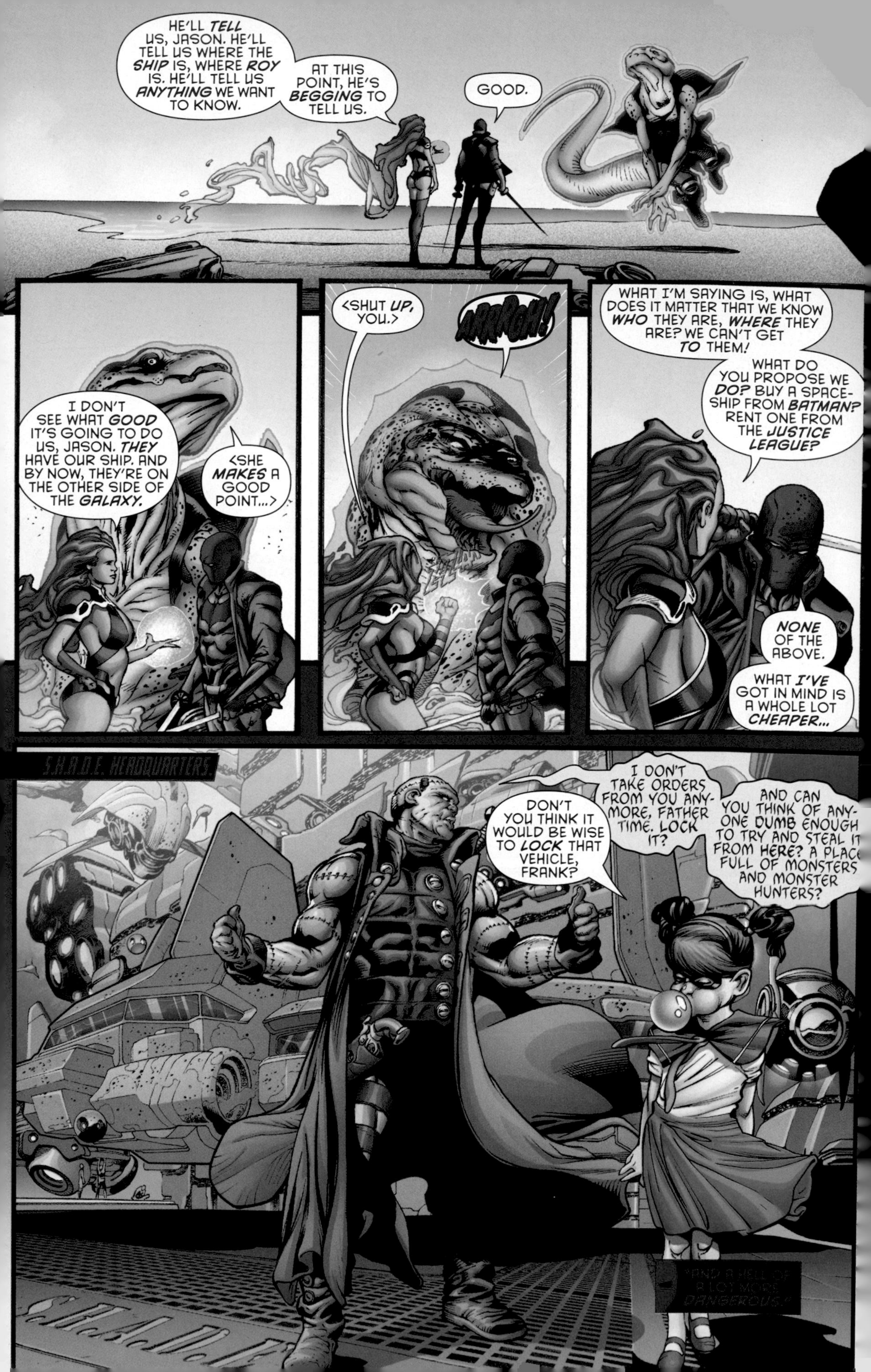
HE'LL TELL US, JASON. HE'LL TELL US WHERE THE SHIP IS, WHERE ROY IS. HE'LL TELL US ANYTHING WE WANT TO KNOW.
AT THIS POINT, HE'S BEGGING TO TELL US.
GOOD.
I DON'T SEE WHAT GOOD IT'S GOING TO DO US, JASON. THEY HAVE OUR SHIP. AND BY NOW, THEY'RE ON THE OTHER SIDE OF THE GALAXY.
<SHE MAKES A GOOD POINT...>
<SHUT UP, YOU.>
AHRRGH!
WHAT I'M SAYING IS, WHAT DOES IT MATTER THAT WE KNOW WHO THEY ARE, WHERE THEY ARE? WE CAN'T GET TO THEM!
WHAT DO YOU PROPOSE WE DO? BUY A SPACESHIP FROM BATMAN? RENT ONE FROM THE JUSTICE LEAGUE?
NONE OF THE ABOVE.
WHAT I'VE GOT IN MIND IS A WHOLE LOT CHEAPER...
S.H.A.D.E. HEADQUARTERS.
DON'T YOU THINK IT WOULD BE WISE TO LOCK THAT VEHICLE, FRANK?
I DON'T TAKE ORDERS FROM YOU ANYMORE, FATHER TIME. LOCK IT?
AND CAN YOU THINK OF ANYONE DUMB ENOUGH TO TRY AND STEAL IT FROM HERE? A PLACE FULL OF MONSTERS AND MONSTER HUNTERS?
"AND A HELL OF A LOT MORE DANGEROUS."

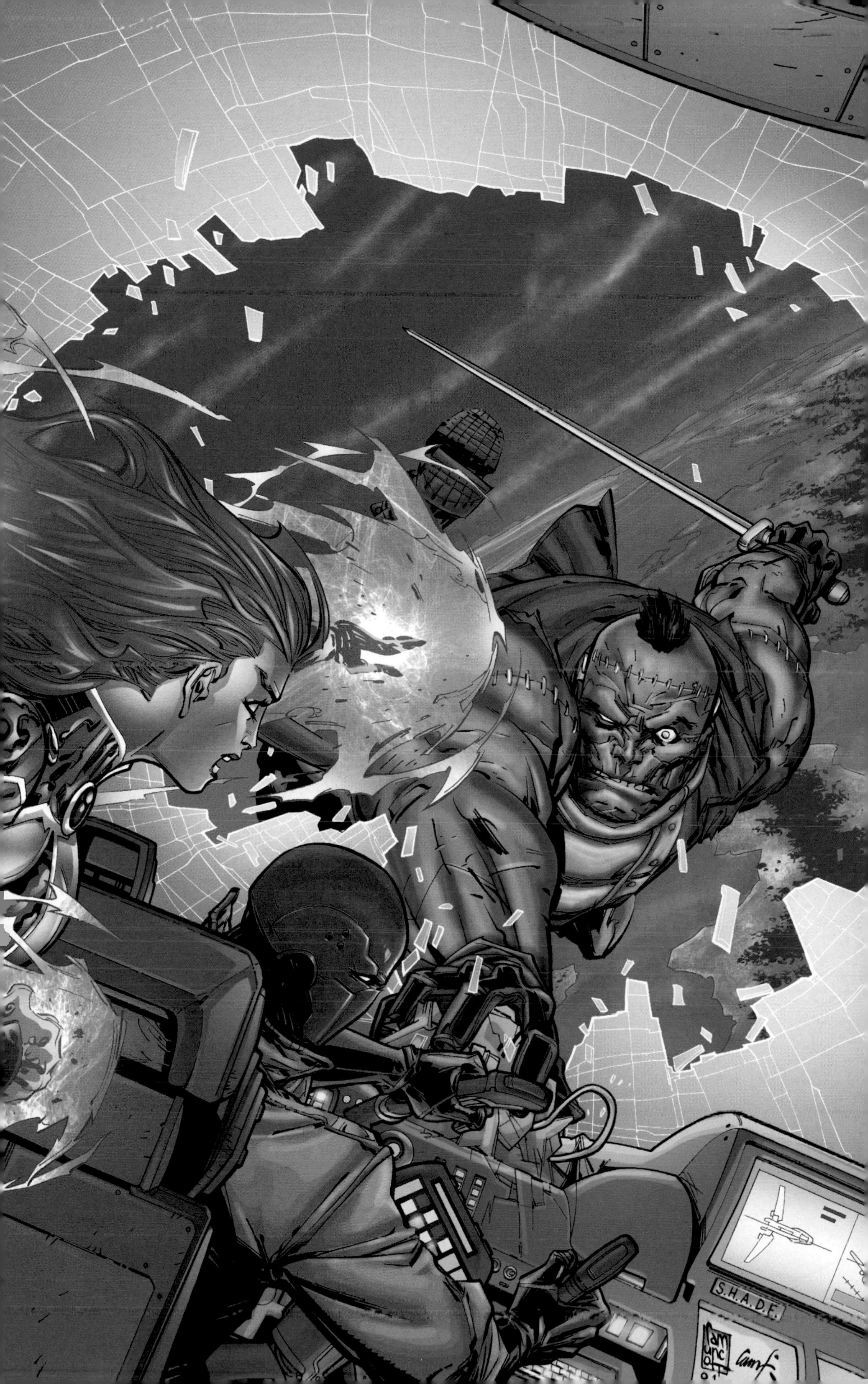
S.H.A.D.E.

THE BIG PICTURE: PART TWO

WILL PFEIFER writer RAFAEL SANDOVAL RB SILVA pencillers PAUL NEARY, WAYNE FAUCHER and JORDI TARRAGONA inkers MATT YACKEY and HIFI colorists TAYLOR ESPOSITO letterer cover art by GIUSEPPE CAMUNCOLI, CAM SMITH and PETE PANTAZIS

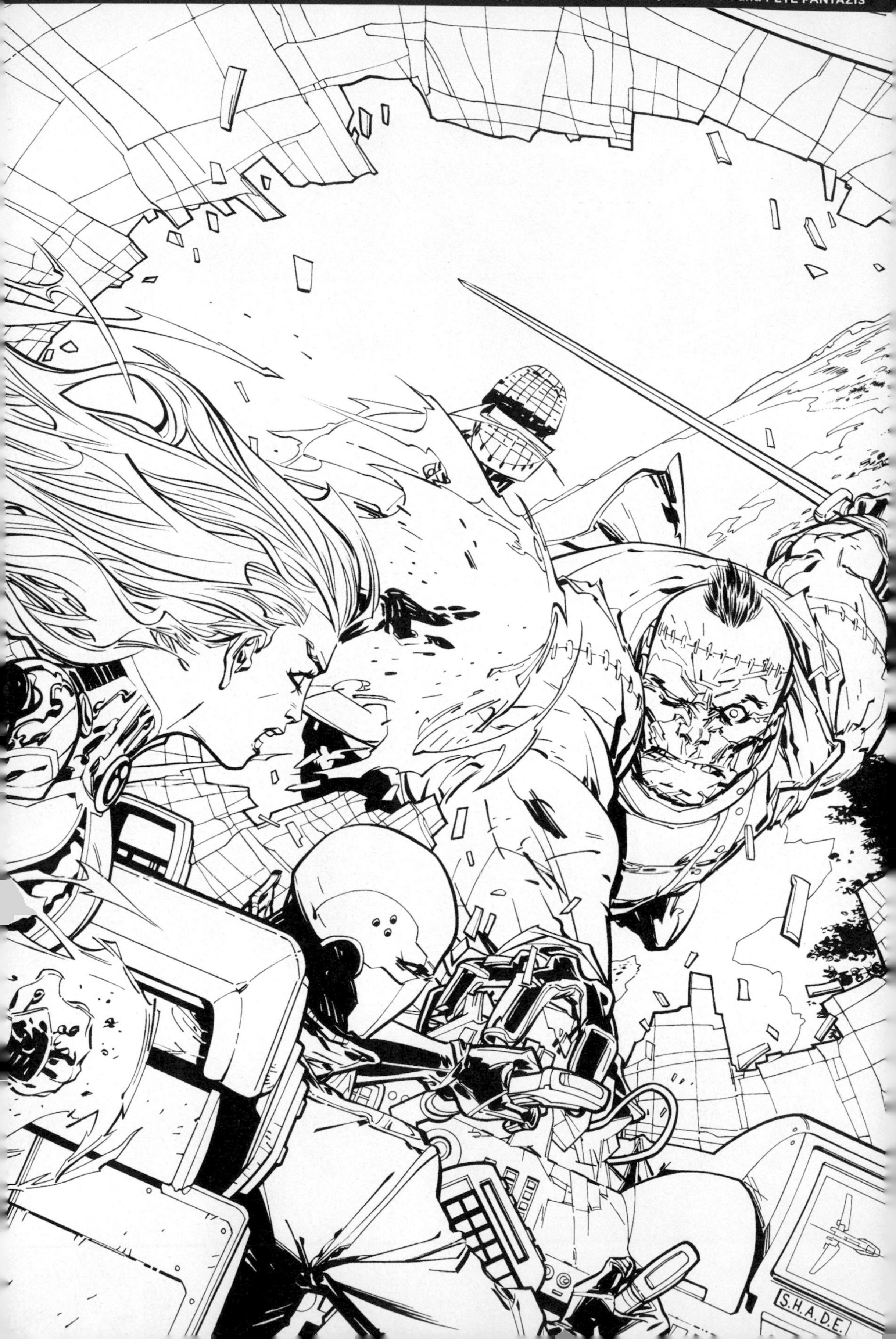
S.H.A.D.E.

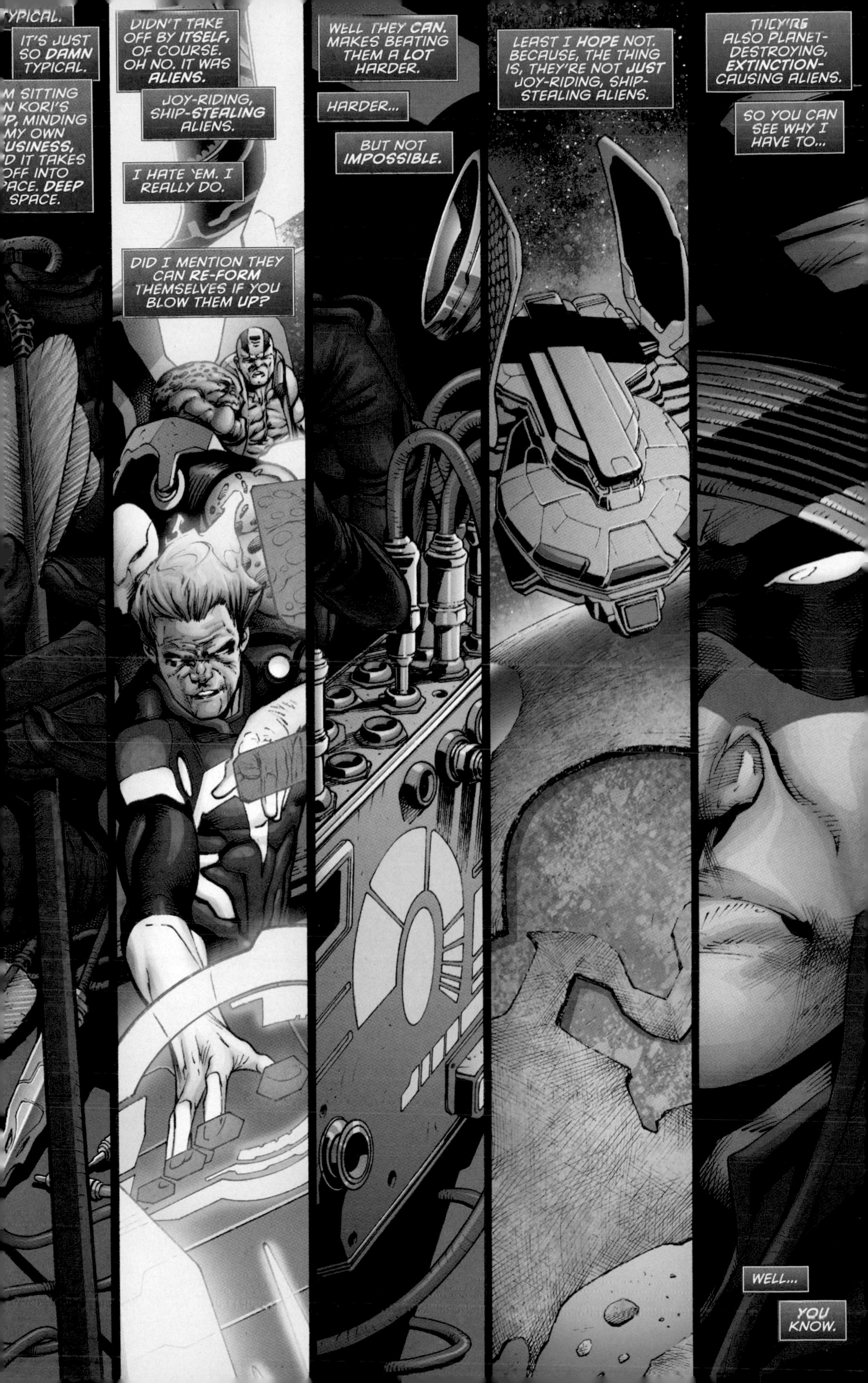

YPICAL.
IT'S JUST SO DAMN TYPICAL.
M SITTING N KORI'S P, MINDING MY OWN USINESS, D IT TAKES OFF INTO PACE. DEEP SPACE.
DIDN'T TAKE OFF BY ITSELF, OF COURSE. OH NO. IT WAS ALIENS.
JOY-RIDING, SHIP-STEALING ALIENS.
I HATE 'EM. I REALLY DO.
DID I MENTION THEY CAN RE-FORM THEMSELVES IF YOU BLOW THEM UP?
WELL THEY CAN. MAKES BEATING THEM A LOT HARDER.
HARDER...
BUT NOT IMPOSSIBLE.
LEAST I HOPE NOT. BECAUSE, THE THING IS, THEY'RE NOT JUST JOY-RIDING, SHIP-STEALING ALIENS.
THEY'RE ALSO PLANET-DESTROYING, EXTINCTION-CAUSING ALIENS.
SO YOU CAN SEE WHY I HAVE TO...
WELL...
YOU KNOW.

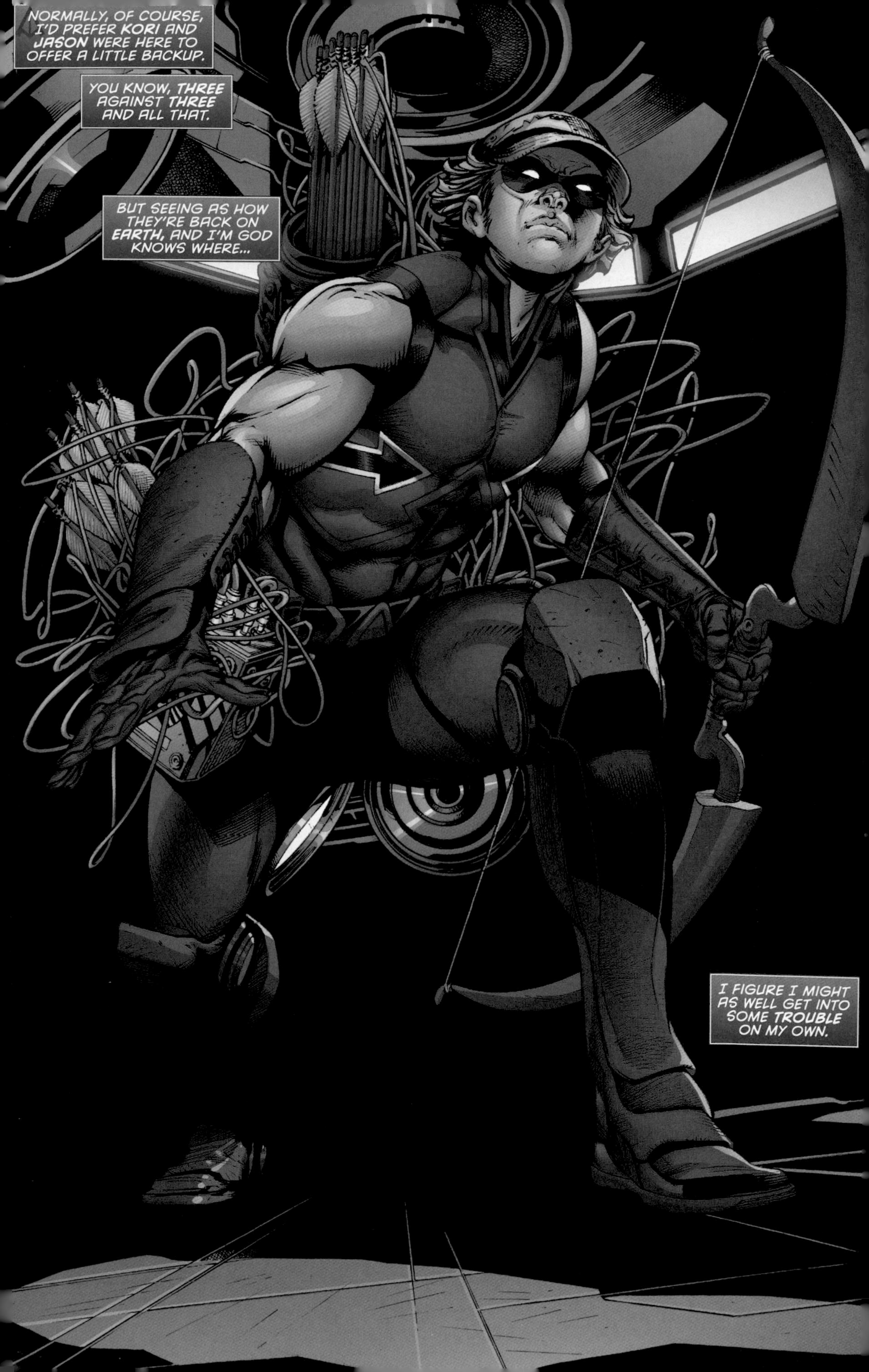
NORMALLY, OF COURSE, I'D PREFER KORI AND JASON WERE HERE TO OFFER A LITTLE BACKUP.
YOU KNOW, THREE AGAINST THREE AND ALL THAT.
BUT SEEING AS HOW THEY'RE BACK ON EARTH, AND I'M GOD KNOWS WHERE...
I FIGURE I MIGHT AS WELL GET INTO SOME TROUBLE ON MY OWN.

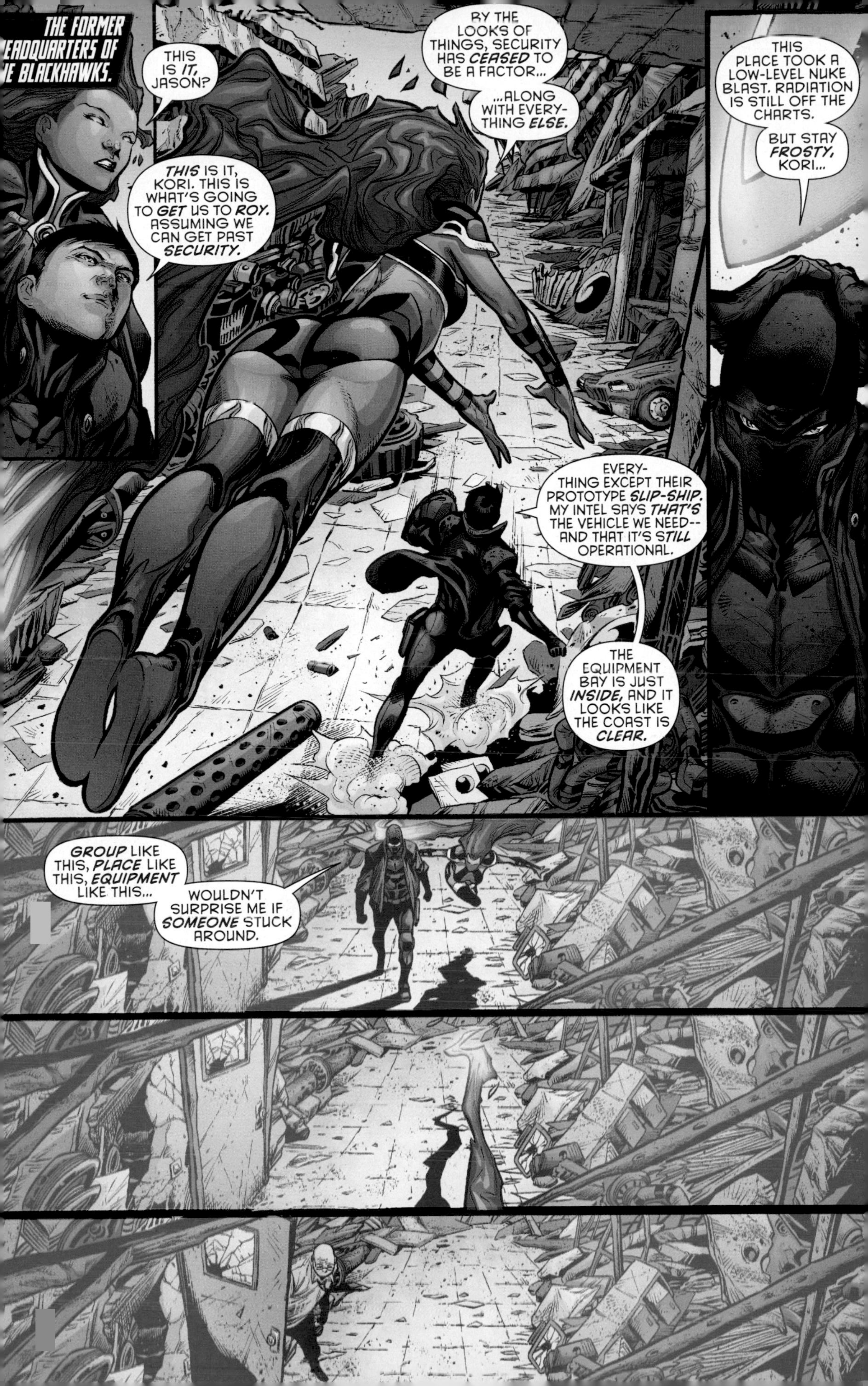
THE FORMER HEADQUARTERS OF THE BLACKHAWKS.
THIS IS IT, JASON?
THIS IS IT, KORI. THIS IS WHAT'S GOING TO GET US TO ROY. ASSUMING WE CAN GET PAST SECURITY.
BY THE LOOKS OF THINGS, SECURITY HAS CEASED TO BE A FACTOR...
...ALONG WITH EVERYTHING ELSE.
THIS PLACE TOOK A LOW-LEVEL NUKE BLAST. RADIATION IS STILL OFF THE CHARTS.
BUT STAY FROSTY, KORI...
EVERYTHING EXCEPT THEIR PROTOTYPE SLIP-SHIP. MY INTEL SAYS THAT'S THE VEHICLE WE NEED--AND THAT IT'S STILL OPERATIONAL.
THE EQUIPMENT BAY IS JUST INSIDE, AND IT LOOKS LIKE THE COAST IS CLEAR.
GROUP LIKE THIS, PLACE LIKE THIS, EQUIPMENT LIKE THIS...
WOULDN'T SURPRISE ME IF SOMEONE STUCK AROUND.

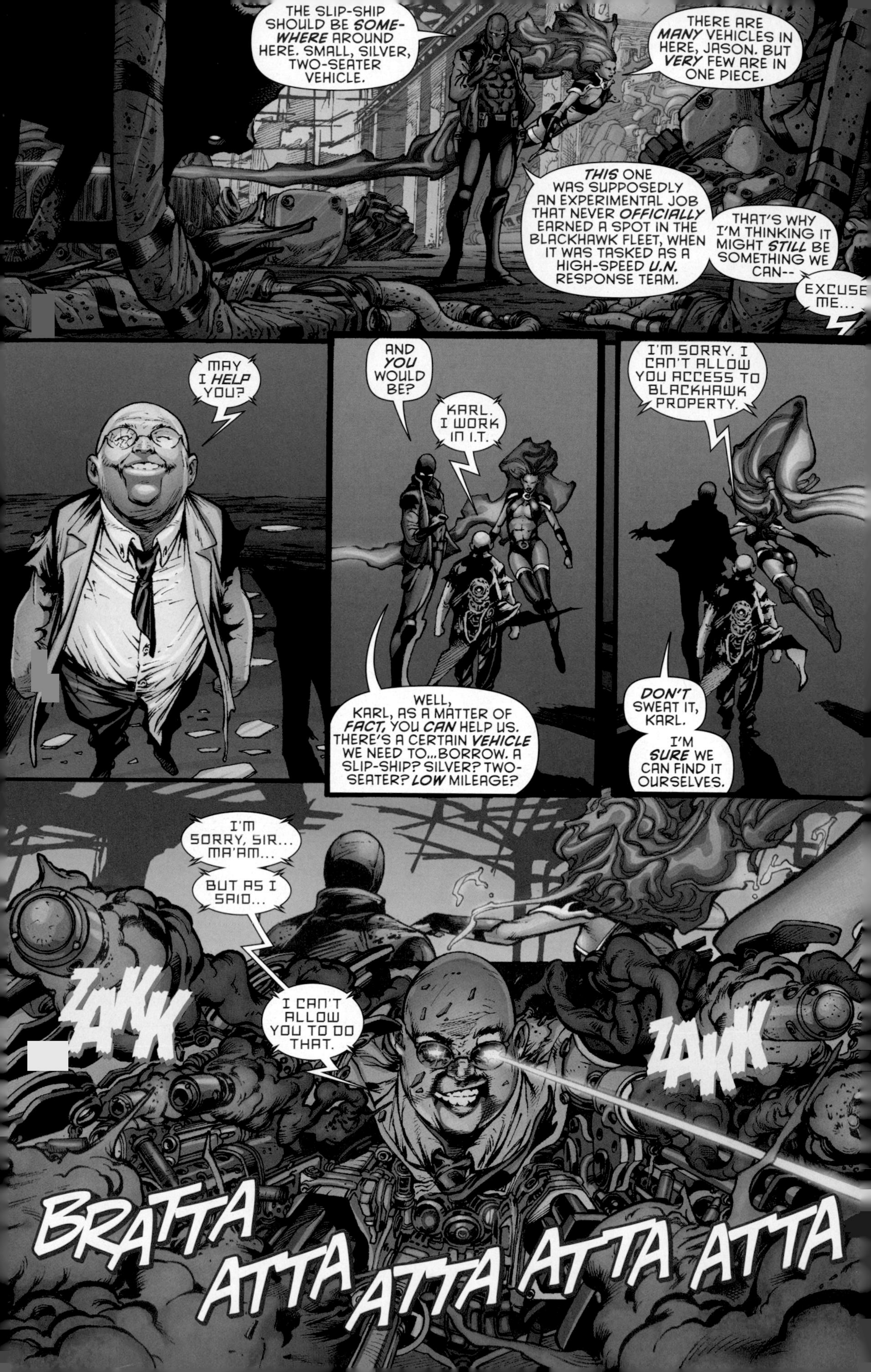
THE SLIP-SHIP SHOULD BE SOME-WHERE AROUND HERE. SMALL, SILVER, TWO-SEATER VEHICLE.
THERE ARE MANY VEHICLES IN HERE, JASON. BUT VERY FEW ARE IN ONE PIECE.
THIS ONE WAS SUPPOSEDLY AN EXPERIMENTAL JOB THAT NEVER OFFICIALLY EARNED A SPOT IN THE BLACKHAWK FLEET, WHEN IT WAS TASKED AS A HIGH-SPEED U.N. RESPONSE TEAM.
THAT'S WHY I'M THINKING IT MIGHT STILL BE SOMETHING WE CAN--
EXCUSE ME...
MAY I HELP YOU?
AND YOU WOULD BE?
KARL. I WORK IN I.T.
WELL, KARL, AS A MATTER OF FACT, YOU CAN HELP US. THERE'S A CERTAIN VEHICLE WE NEED TO...BORROW. A SLIP-SHIP? SILVER? TWO-SEATER? LOW MILEAGE?
I'M SORRY. I CAN'T ALLOW YOU ACCESS TO BLACKHAWK PROPERTY.
DON'T SWEAT IT, KARL.
I'M SURE WE CAN FIND IT OURSELVES.
I'M SORRY, SIR... MA'AM...
BUT AS I SAID...
I CAN'T ALLOW YOU TO DO THAT.
ZAKK
ZAKK
BRATTA ATTA ATTA ATTA ATTA

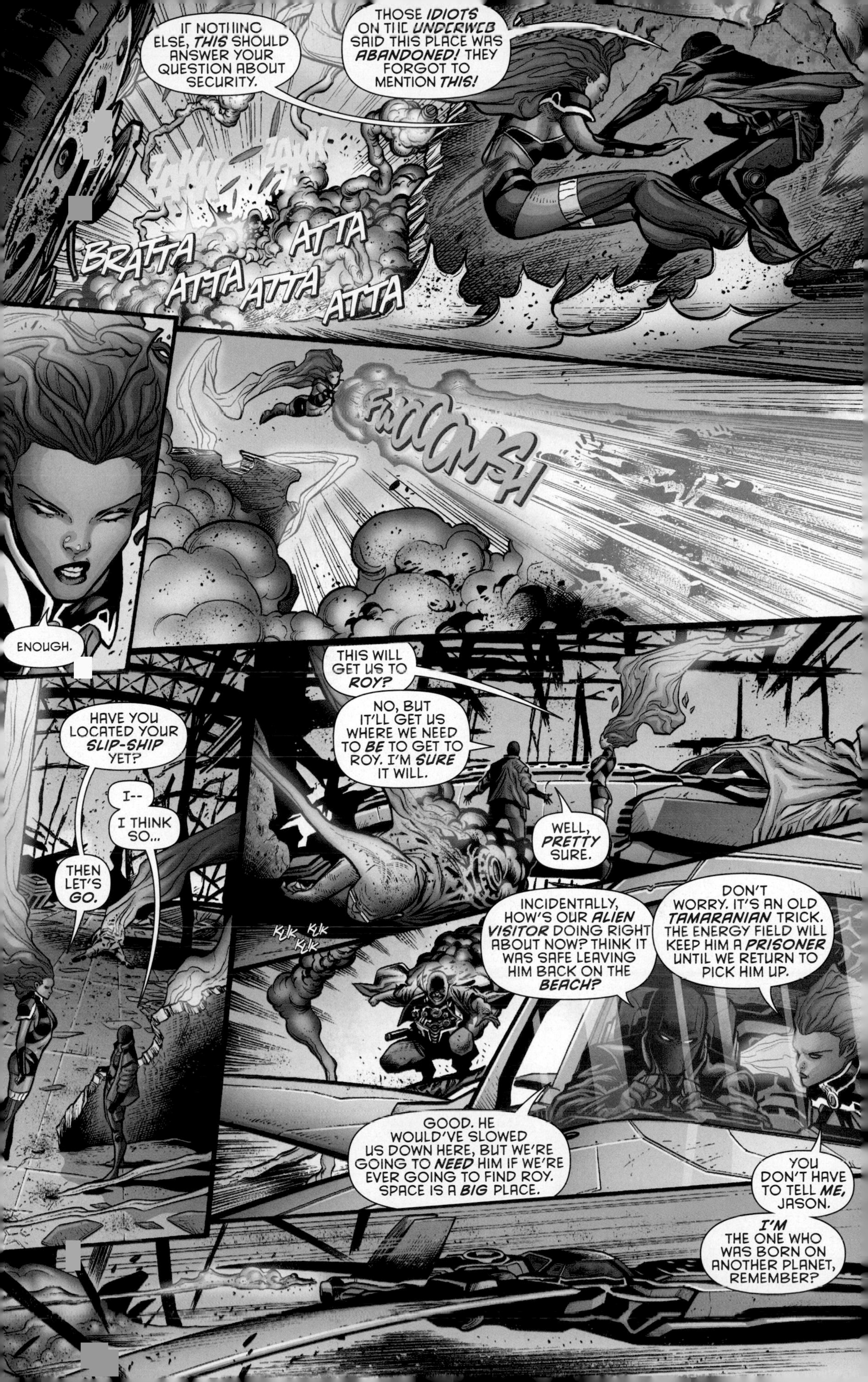
IF NOTHING ELSE, THIS SHOULD ANSWER YOUR QUESTION ABOUT SECURITY.
THOSE IDIOTS ON THE UNDERWEB SAID THIS PLACE WAS ABANDONED! THEY FORGOT TO MENTION THIS!
BRATTA ATTA ATTA ATTA ATTA
FWOOOMSH
ENOUGH.
THIS WILL GET US TO ROY?
NO, BUT IT'LL GET US WHERE WE NEED TO BE TO GET TO ROY. I'M SURE IT WILL.
WELL, PRETTY SURE.
HAVE YOU LOCATED YOUR SLIP-SHIP YET?
I--
I THINK SO...
THEN LET'S GO.
KLIK KLIK KLIK
INCIDENTALLY, HOW'S OUR ALIEN VISITOR DOING RIGHT ABOUT NOW? THINK IT WAS SAFE LEAVING HIM BACK ON THE BEACH?
DON'T WORRY. IT'S AN OLD TAMARANIAN TRICK. THE ENERGY FIELD WILL KEEP HIM A PRISONER UNTIL WE RETURN TO PICK HIM UP.
GOOD. HE WOULD'VE SLOWED US DOWN HERE, BUT WE'RE GOING TO NEED HIM IF WE'RE EVER GOING TO FIND ROY. SPACE IS A BIG PLACE.
YOU DON'T HAVE TO TELL ME, JASON.
I'M THE ONE WHO WAS BORN ON ANOTHER PLANET, REMEMBER?

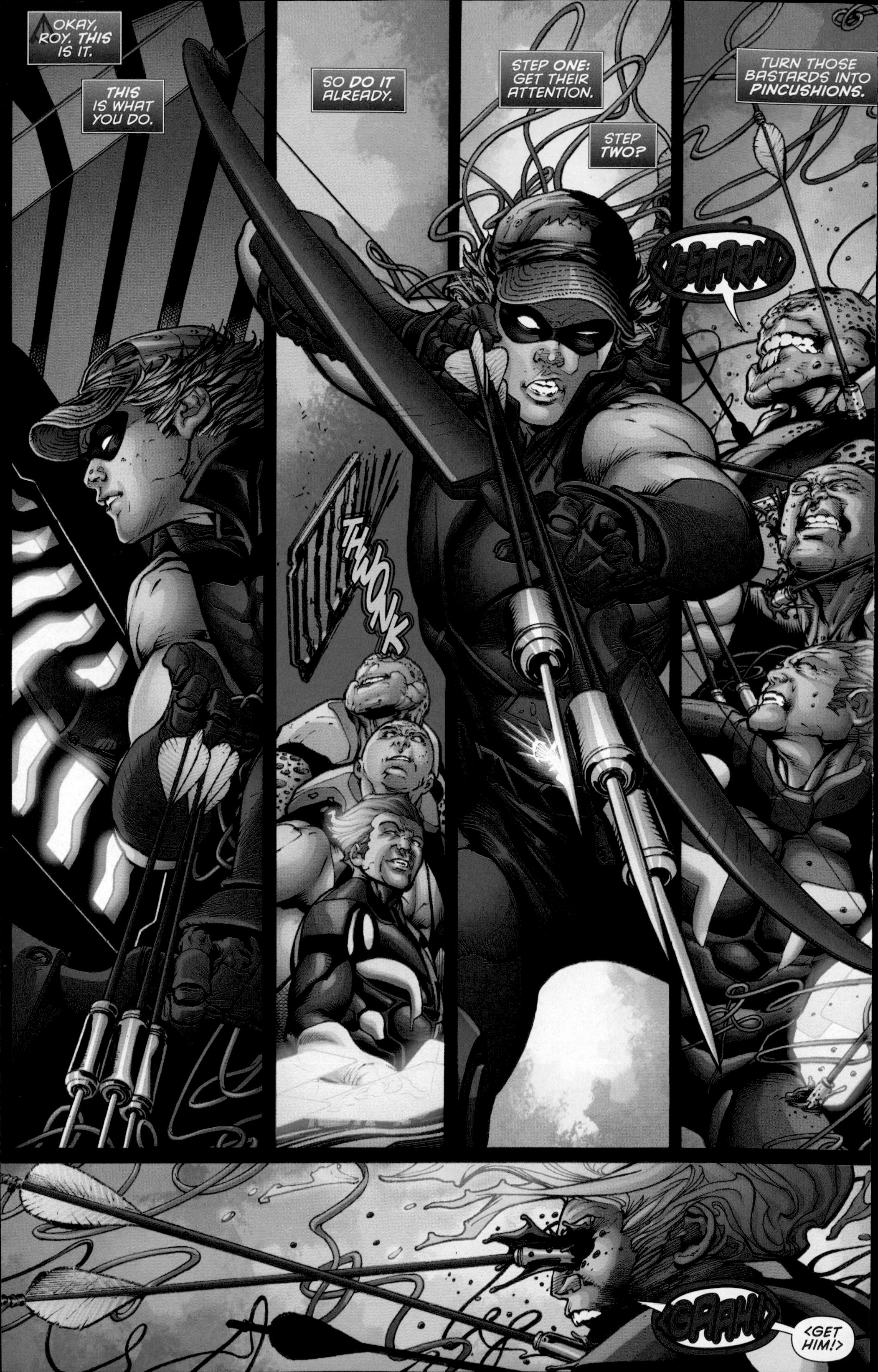
OKAY, ROY. THIS IS IT.
THIS IS WHAT YOU DO.
SO DO IT ALREADY.
STEP ONE: GET THEIR ATTENTION.
STEP TWO?
TURN THOSE BASTARDS INTO PINCUSHIONS.
THWONK
<GET HIM!>

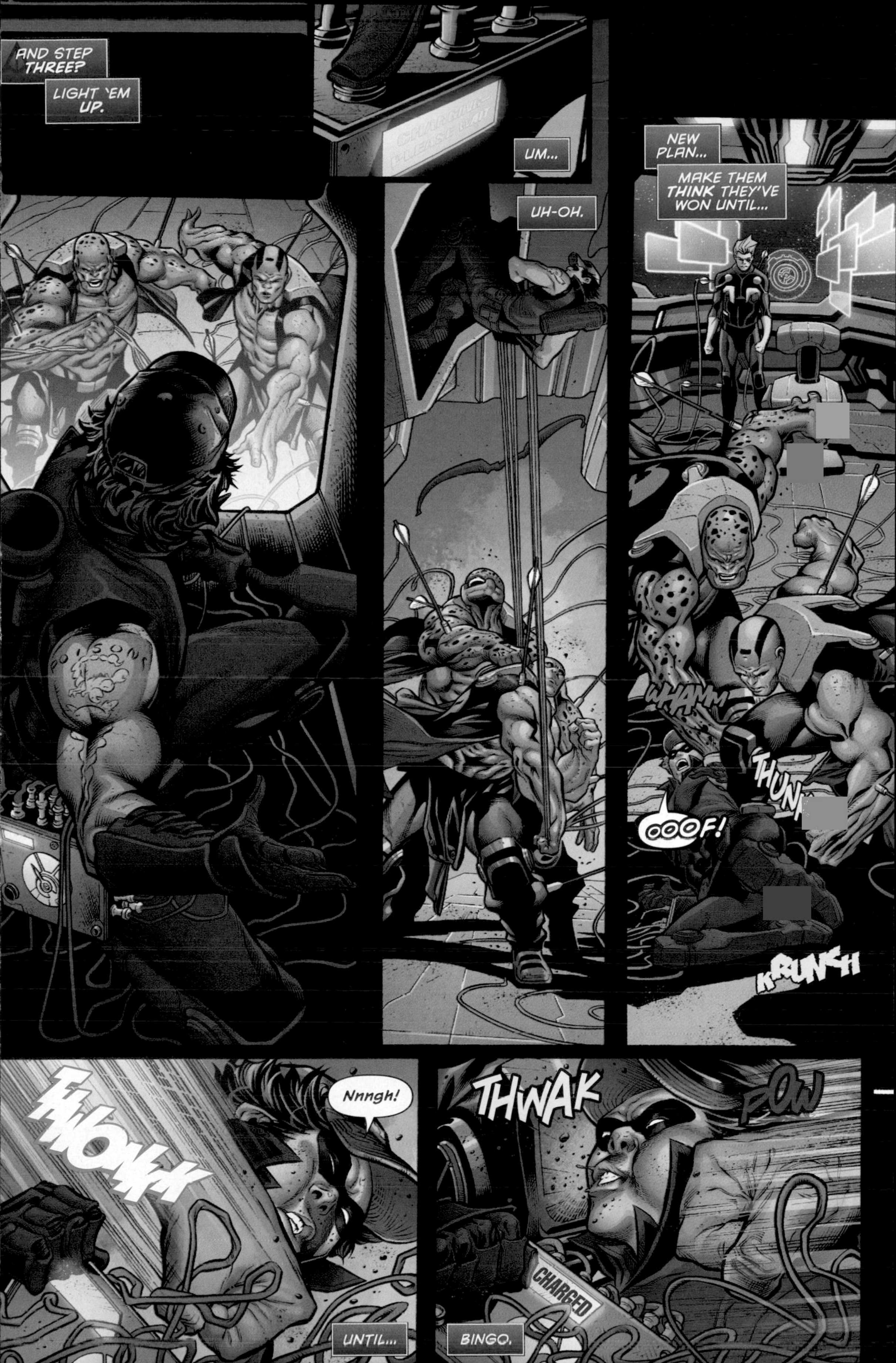
AND STEP THREE?
LIGHT 'EM UP.
UM...
UH-OH.
NEW PLAN...
MAKE THEM THINK THEY'VE WON UNTIL...
WHAMM
THUNK
OOOF!
KRUNCH
Nnngh!
UNTIL...
THWAK
POW
CHARGED
BINGO.

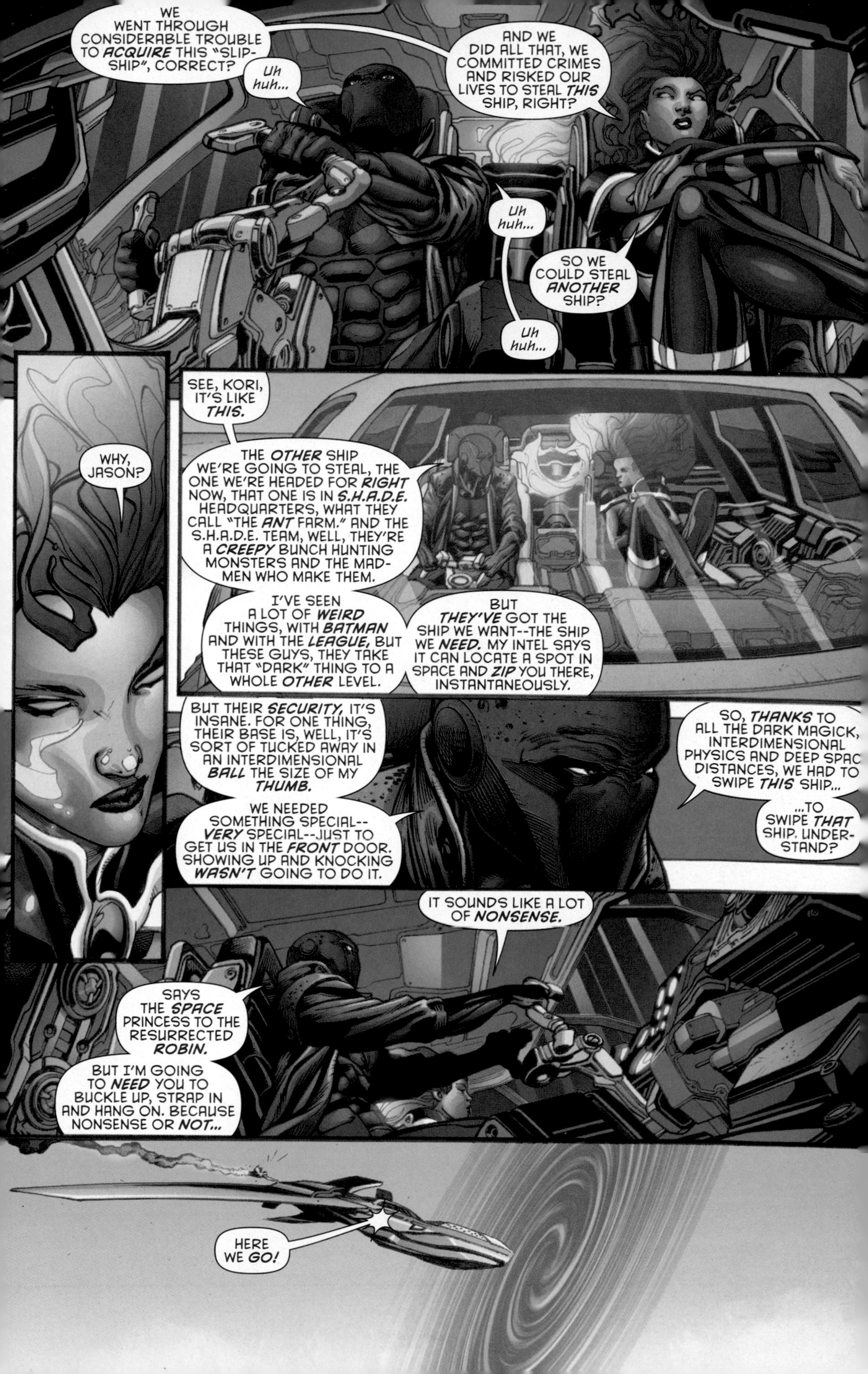
WE WENT THROUGH CONSIDERABLE TROUBLE TO ACQUIRE THIS "SLIP-SHIP", CORRECT?
UH HUH...
AND WE DID ALL THAT, WE COMMITTED CRIMES AND RISKED OUR LIVES TO STEAL THIS SHIP, RIGHT?
UH HUH...
SO WE COULD STEAL ANOTHER SHIP?
UH HUH...
WHY, JASON?
SEE, KORI, IT'S LIKE THIS.
THE OTHER SHIP WE'RE GOING TO STEAL, THE ONE WE'RE HEADED FOR RIGHT NOW, THAT ONE IS IN S.H.A.D.E. HEADQUARTERS, WHAT THEY CALL "THE ANT FARM." AND THE S.H.A.D.E. TEAM, WELL, THEY'RE A CREEPY BUNCH HUNTING MONSTERS AND THE MAD-MEN WHO MAKE THEM.
I'VE SEEN A LOT OF WEIRD THINGS, WITH BATMAN AND WITH THE LEAGUE, BUT THESE GUYS, THEY TAKE THAT "DARK" THING TO A WHOLE OTHER LEVEL.
BUT THEY'VE GOT THE SHIP WE WANT--THE SHIP WE NEED. MY INTEL SAYS IT CAN LOCATE A SPOT IN SPACE AND ZIP YOU THERE, INSTANTANEOUSLY.
BUT THEIR SECURITY, IT'S INSANE. FOR ONE THING, THEIR BASE IS, WELL, IT'S SORT OF TUCKED AWAY IN AN INTERDIMENSIONAL BALL THE SIZE OF MY THUMB.
WE NEEDED SOMETHING SPECIAL--VERY SPECIAL--JUST TO GET US IN THE FRONT DOOR. SHOWING UP AND KNOCKING WASN'T GOING TO DO IT.
SO, THANKS TO ALL THE DARK MAGICK, INTERDIMENSIONAL PHYSICS AND DEEP SPAC DISTANCES, WE HAD TO SWIPE THIS SHIP...
...TO SWIPE THAT SHIP. UNDER-STAND?
IT SOUNDS LIKE A LOT OF NONSENSE.
SAYS THE SPACE PRINCESS TO THE RESURRECTED ROBIN.
BUT I'M GOING TO NEED YOU TO BUCKLE UP, STRAP IN AND HANG ON. BECAUSE NONSENSE OR NOT...
HERE WE GO!

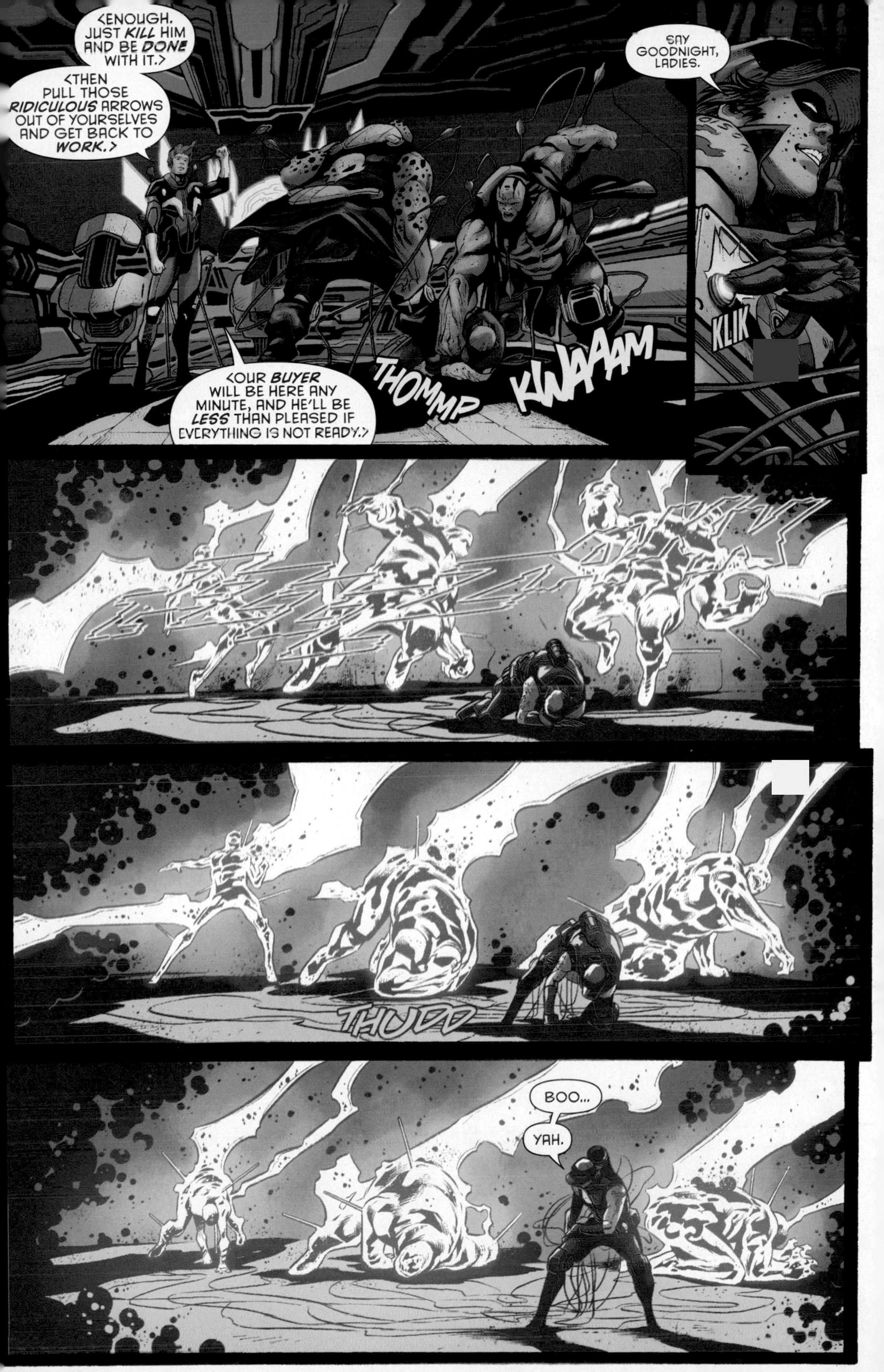
<ENOUGH. JUST KILL HIM AND BE DONE WITH IT.>
<THEN PULL THOSE RIDICULOUS ARROWS OUT OF YOURSELVES AND GET BACK TO WORK.>
<OUR BUYER WILL BE HERE ANY MINUTE, AND HE'LL BE LESS THAN PLEASED IF EVERYTHING IS NOT READY.>
THOMMP
KWAAAM
SAY GOODNIGHT, LADIES.
KLIK
THUDD
BOO...
YAH.

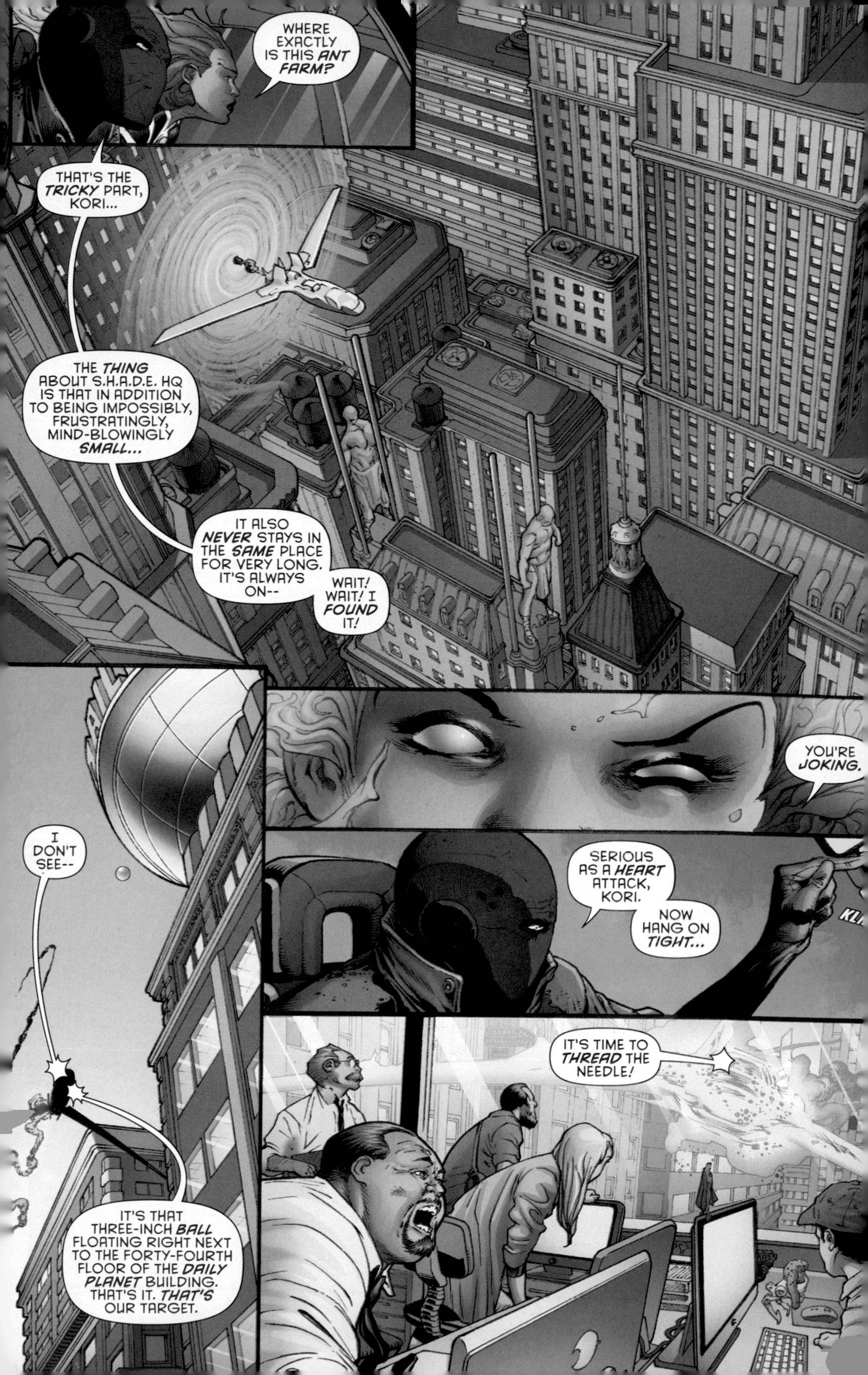
WHERE EXACTLY IS THIS ANT FARM?
THAT'S THE TRICKY PART, KORI...
THE THING ABOUT S.H.A.D.E. HQ IS THAT IN ADDITION TO BEING IMPOSSIBLY, FRUSTRATINGLY, MIND-BLOWINGLY SMALL...
IT ALSO NEVER STAYS IN THE SAME PLACE FOR VERY LONG. IT'S ALWAYS ON--
WAIT! WAIT! I FOUND IT!
I DON'T SEE--
IT'S THAT THREE-INCH BALL FLOATING RIGHT NEXT TO THE FORTY-FOURTH FLOOR OF THE DAILY PLANET BUILDING. THAT'S IT. THAT'S OUR TARGET.
YOU'RE JOKING.
SERIOUS AS A HEART ATTACK, KORI.
NOW HANG ON TIGHT...
IT'S TIME TO THREAD THE NEEDLE!

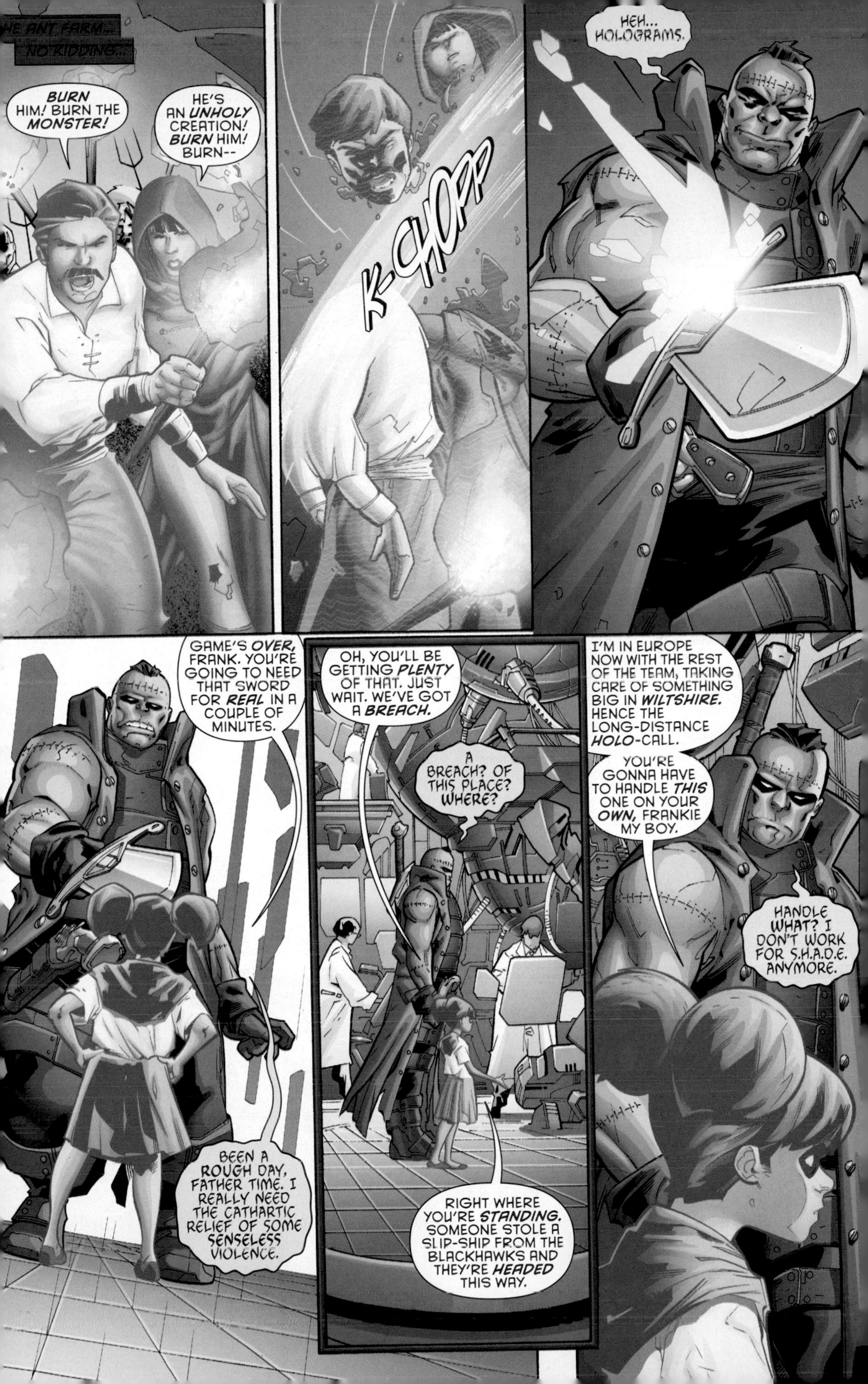

HE ANT FARM... NO KIDDING...
BURN HIM! BURN THE MONSTER!
HE'S AN UNHOLY CREATION! BURN HIM! BURN--
K-CHOPP
HEH... HOLOGRAMS.
GAME'S OVER, FRANK. YOU'RE GOING TO NEED THAT SWORD FOR REAL IN A COUPLE OF MINUTES.
BEEN A ROUGH DAY, FATHER TIME. I REALLY NEED THE CATHARTIC RELIEF OF SOME SENSELESS VIOLENCE.
OH, YOU'LL BE GETTING PLENTY OF THAT. JUST WAIT. WE'VE GOT A BREACH.
A BREACH? OF THIS PLACE? WHERE?
RIGHT WHERE YOU'RE STANDING. SOMEONE STOLE A SLIP-SHIP FROM THE BLACKHAWKS AND THEY'RE HEADED THIS WAY.
I'M IN EUROPE NOW WITH THE REST OF THE TEAM, TAKING CARE OF SOMETHING BIG IN WILTSHIRE. HENCE THE LONG-DISTANCE HOLO-CALL.
YOU'RE GONNA HAVE TO HANDLE THIS ONE ON YOUR OWN, FRANKIE MY BOY.
HANDLE WHAT? I DON'T WORK FOR S.H.A.D.E. ANYMORE.

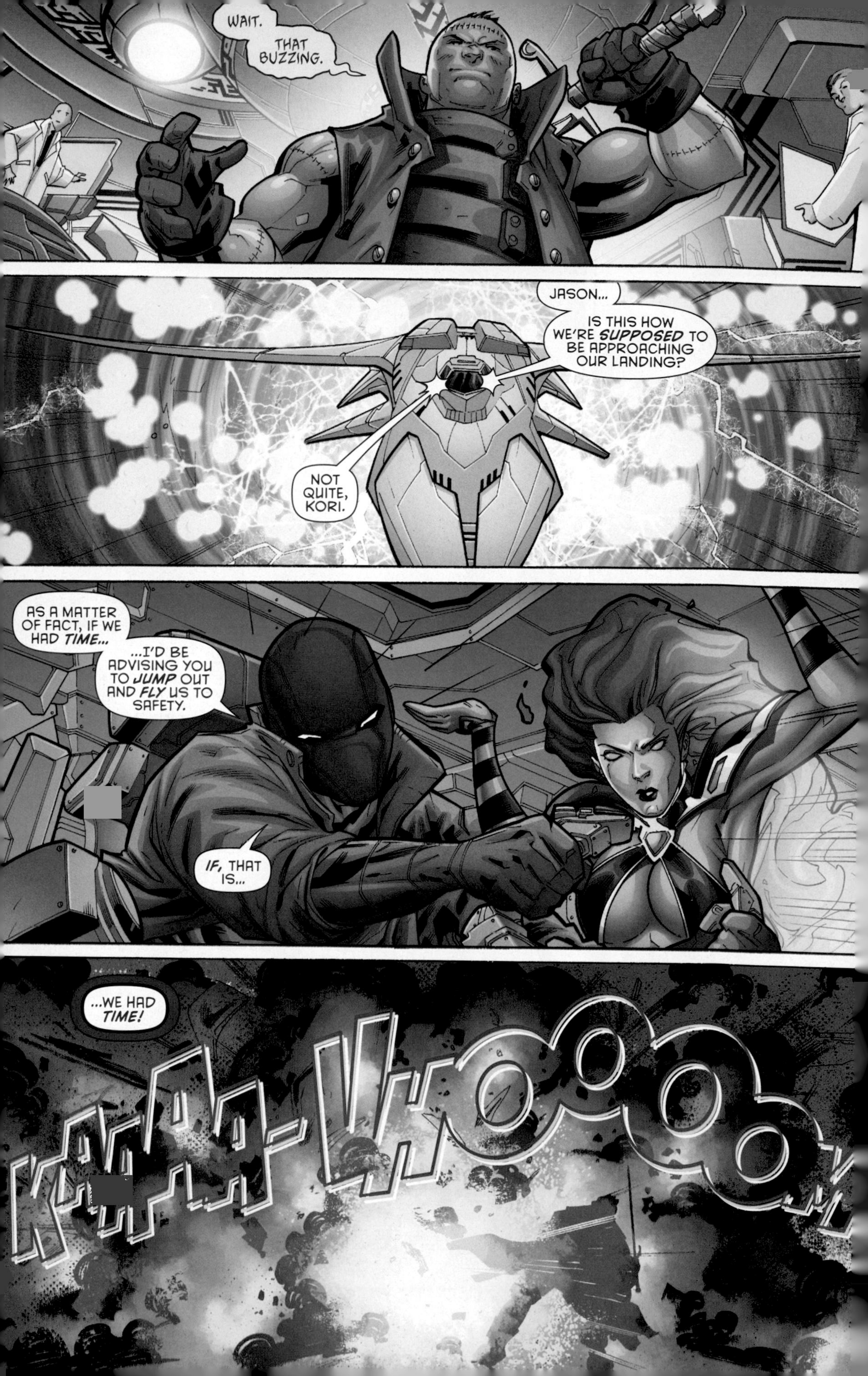
WAIT.
THAT BUZZING.
JASON...
IS THIS HOW WE'RE *SUPPOSED* TO BE APPROACHING OUR LANDING?
NOT QUITE, KORI.
AS A MATTER OF FACT, IF WE HAD *TIME...*
...I'D BE ADVISING YOU TO *JUMP* OUT AND *FLY* US TO SAFETY.
IF, THAT IS...
...WE HAD *TIME!*

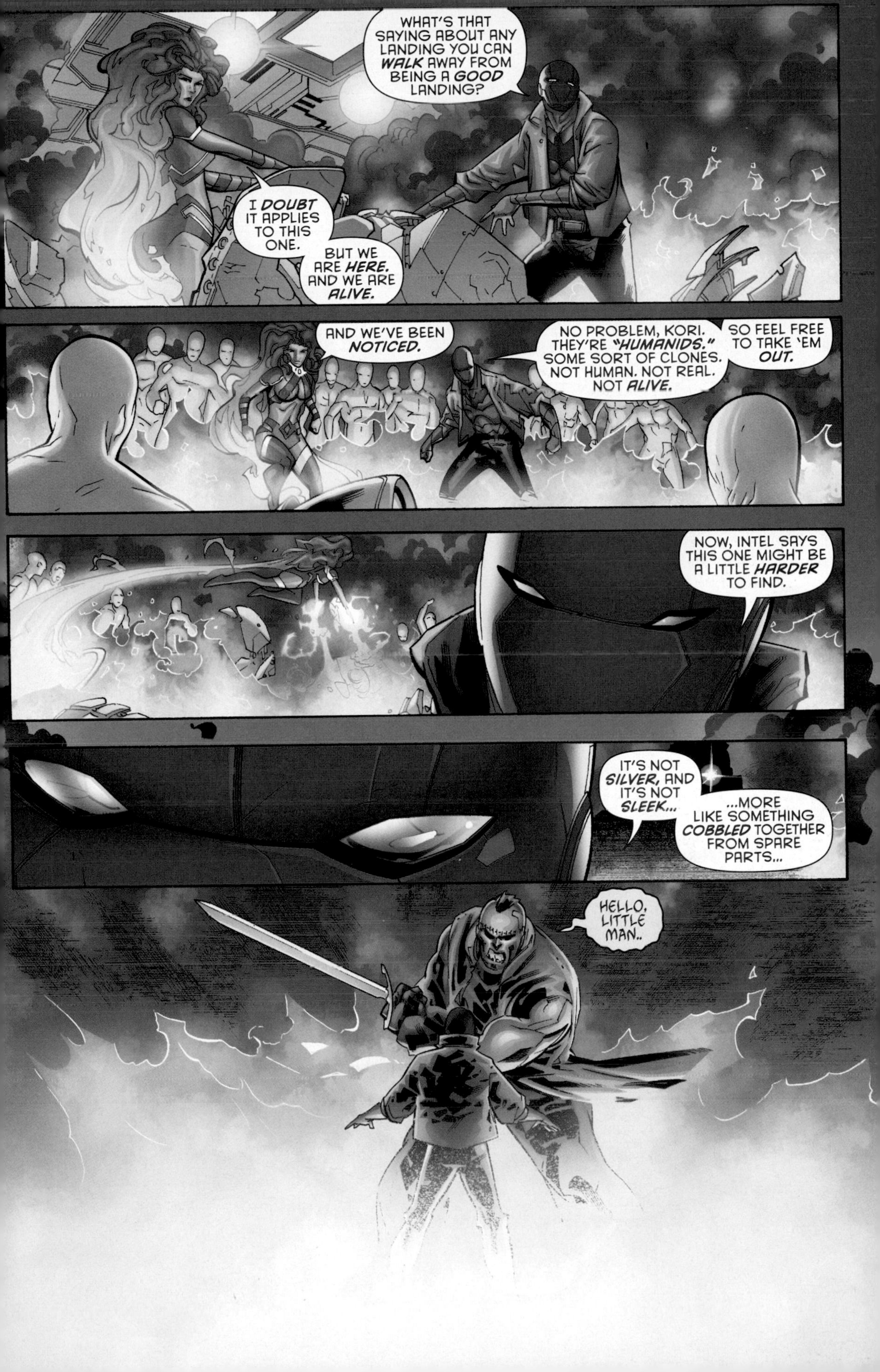
WHAT'S THAT SAYING ABOUT ANY LANDING YOU CAN WALK AWAY FROM BEING A GOOD LANDING?
I DOUBT IT APPLIES TO THIS ONE.
BUT WE ARE HERE. AND WE ARE ALIVE.
AND WE'VE BEEN NOTICED.
NO PROBLEM, KORI. THEY'RE "HUMANIDS." SOME SORT OF CLONES. NOT HUMAN. NOT REAL. NOT ALIVE.
SO FEEL FREE TO TAKE 'EM OUT.
NOW, INTEL SAYS THIS ONE MIGHT BE A LITTLE HARDER TO FIND.
IT'S NOT SILVER, AND IT'S NOT SLEEK...
...MORE LIKE SOMETHING COBBLED TOGETHER FROM SPARE PARTS...
HELLO, LITTLE MAN..

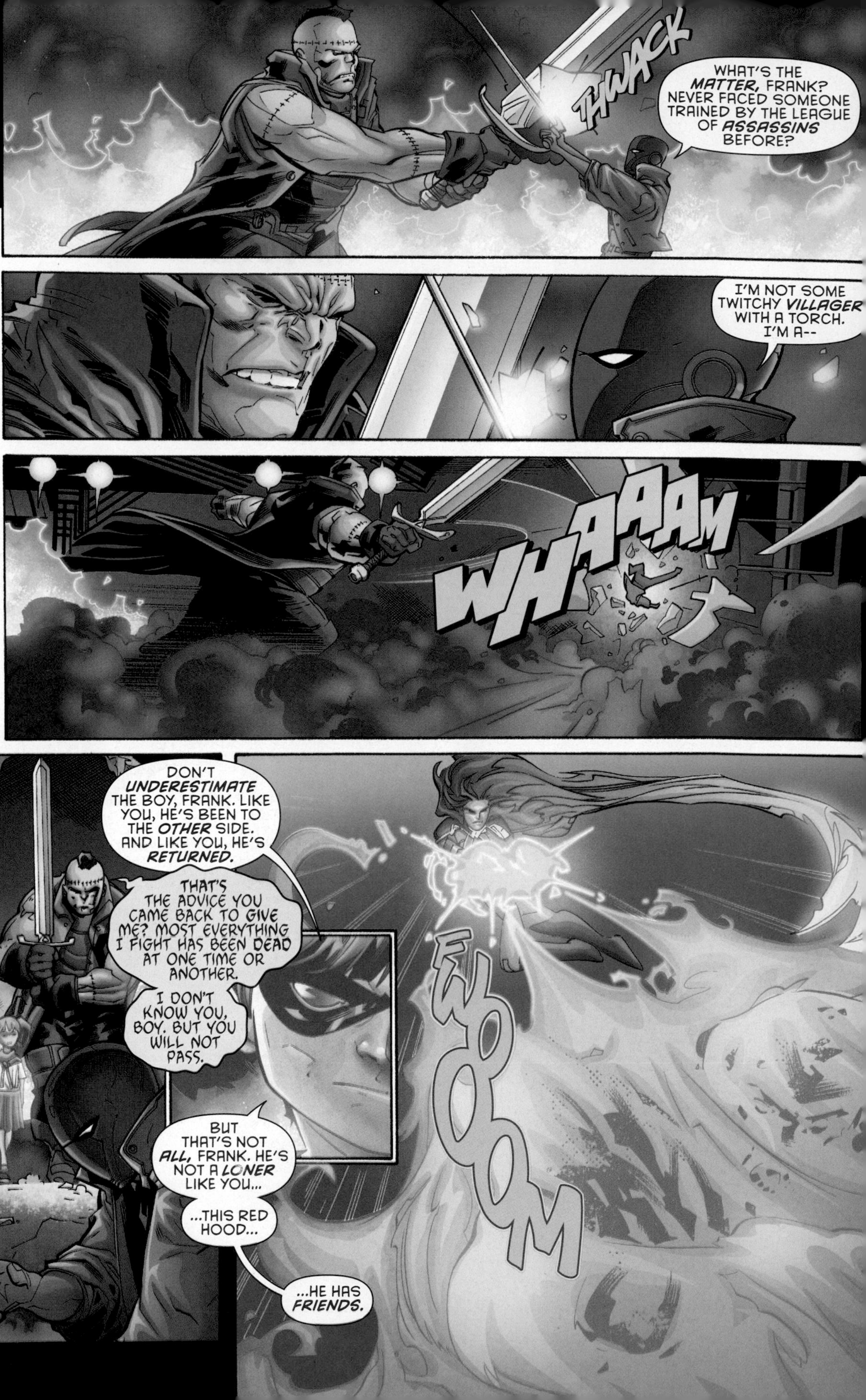
THWACK
WHAT'S THE MATTER, FRANK? NEVER FACED SOMEONE TRAINED BY THE LEAGUE OF ASSASSINS BEFORE?
I'M NOT SOME TWITCHY VILLAGER WITH A TORCH. I'M A--
WHAAAAM
DON'T UNDERESTIMATE THE BOY, FRANK. LIKE YOU, HE'S BEEN TO THE OTHER SIDE. AND LIKE YOU, HE'S RETURNED.
THAT'S THE ADVICE YOU CAME BACK TO GIVE ME? MOST EVERYTHING I FIGHT HAS BEEN DEAD AT ONE TIME OR ANOTHER.
I DON'T KNOW YOU, BOY. BUT YOU WILL NOT PASS.
BUT THAT'S NOT ALL, FRANK. HE'S NOT A LONER LIKE YOU...
...THIS RED HOOD...
...HE HAS FRIENDS.
FWOOOOM

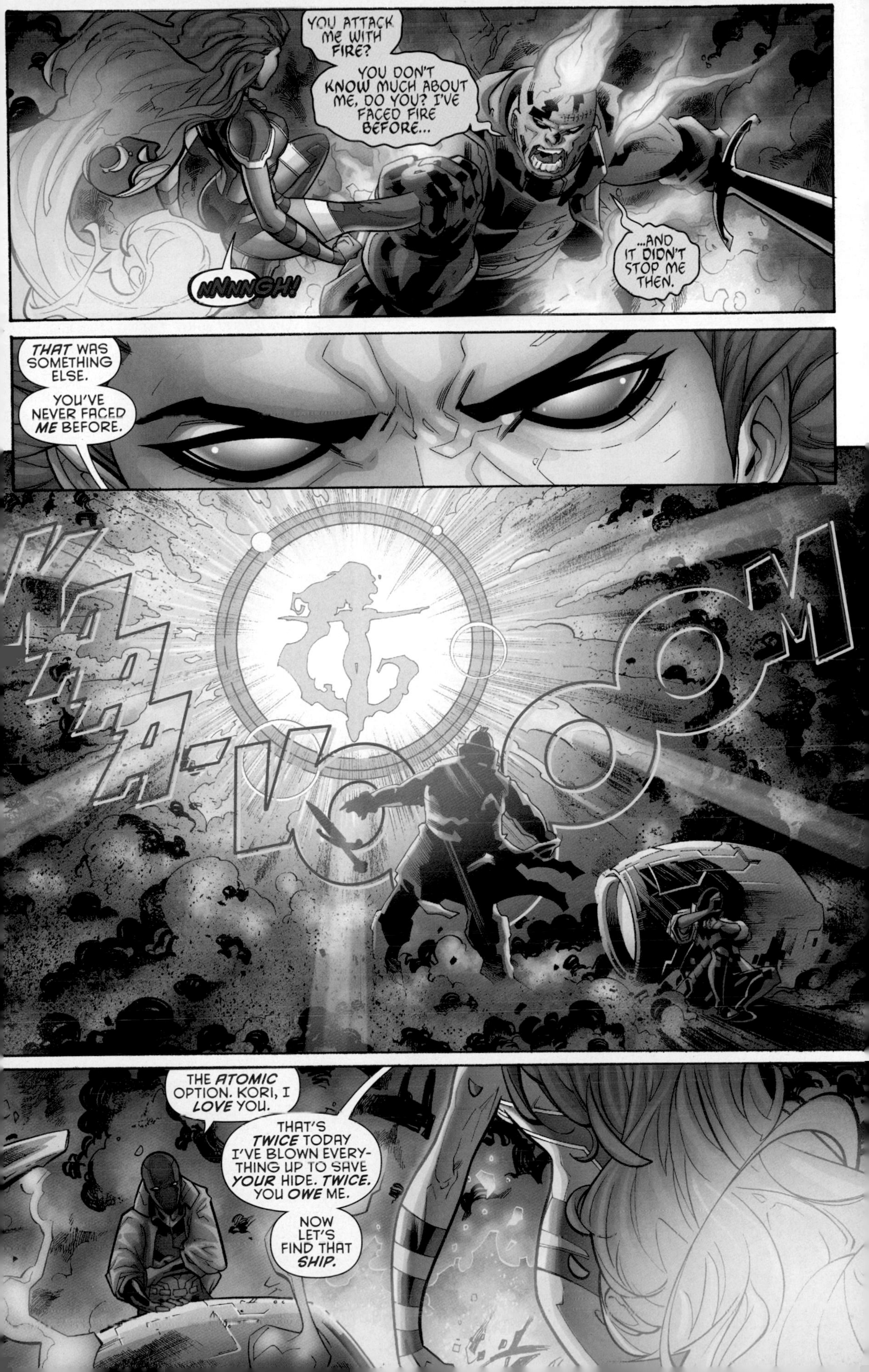
YOU ATTACK ME WITH FIRE?
YOU DON'T KNOW MUCH ABOUT ME, DO YOU? I'VE FACED FIRE BEFORE...
NNNNGH!
...AND IT DIDN'T STOP ME THEN.
THAT WAS SOMETHING ELSE.
YOU'VE NEVER FACED ME BEFORE.
KA-VOOOOM
THE ATOMIC OPTION. KORI, I LOVE YOU.
THAT'S TWICE TODAY I'VE BLOWN EVERY-THING UP TO SAVE YOUR HIDE. TWICE. YOU OWE ME.
NOW LET'S FIND THAT SHIP.

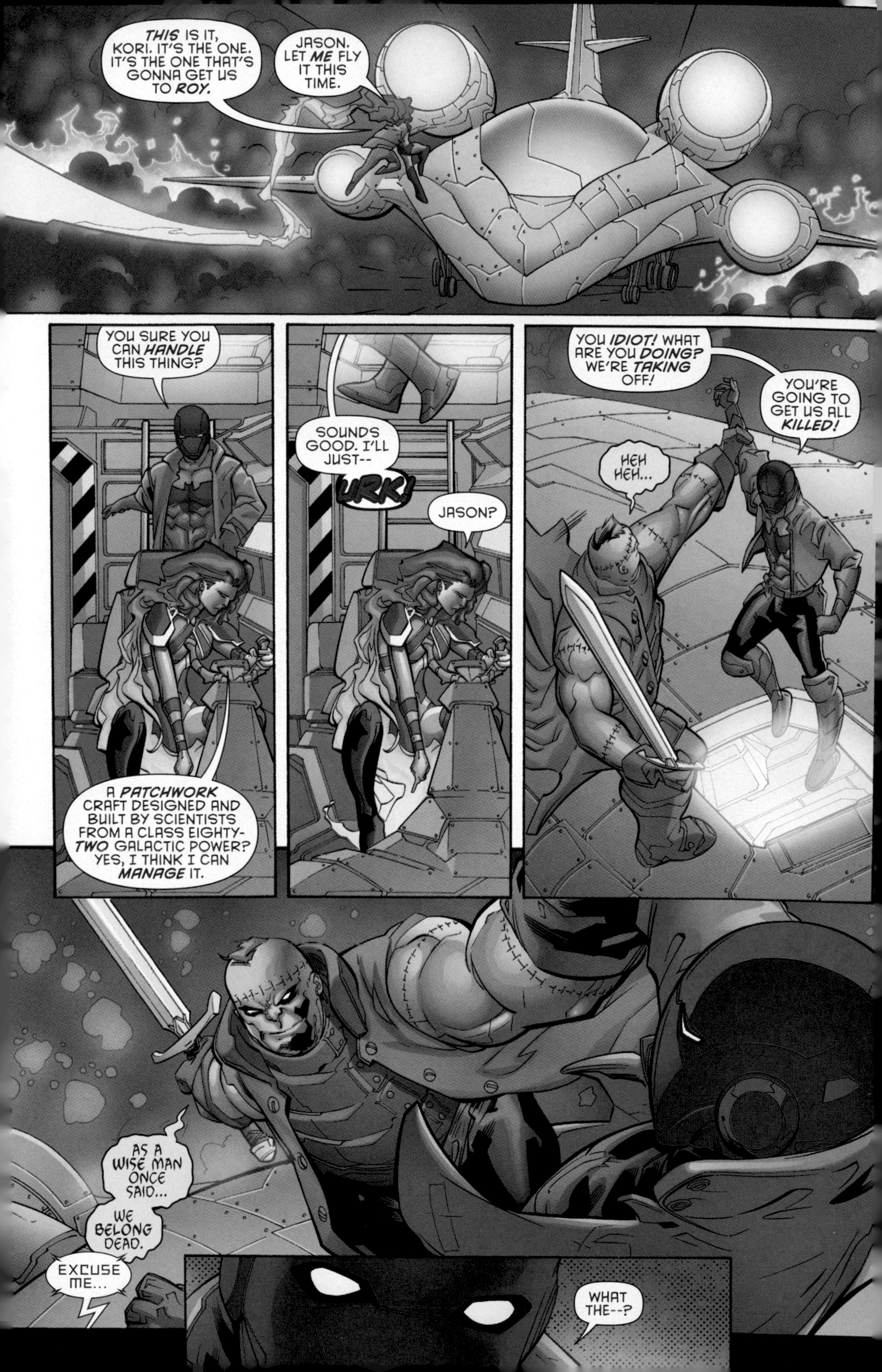

THIS IS IT, KORI. IT'S THE ONE. IT'S THE ONE THAT'S GONNA GET US TO ROY.
JASON. LET ME FLY IT THIS TIME.
YOU SURE YOU CAN HANDLE THIS THING?
A PATCHWORK CRAFT DESIGNED AND BUILT BY SCIENTISTS FROM A CLASS EIGHTY-TWO GALACTIC POWER? YES, I THINK I CAN MANAGE IT.
SOUNDS GOOD. I'LL JUST--
URK!
JASON?
YOU IDIOT! WHAT ARE YOU DOING? WE'RE TAKING OFF!
YOU'RE GOING TO GET US ALL KILLED!
HEH HEH...
AS A WISE MAN ONCE SAID...
WE BELONG DEAD.
EXCUSE ME...
WHAT THE--?

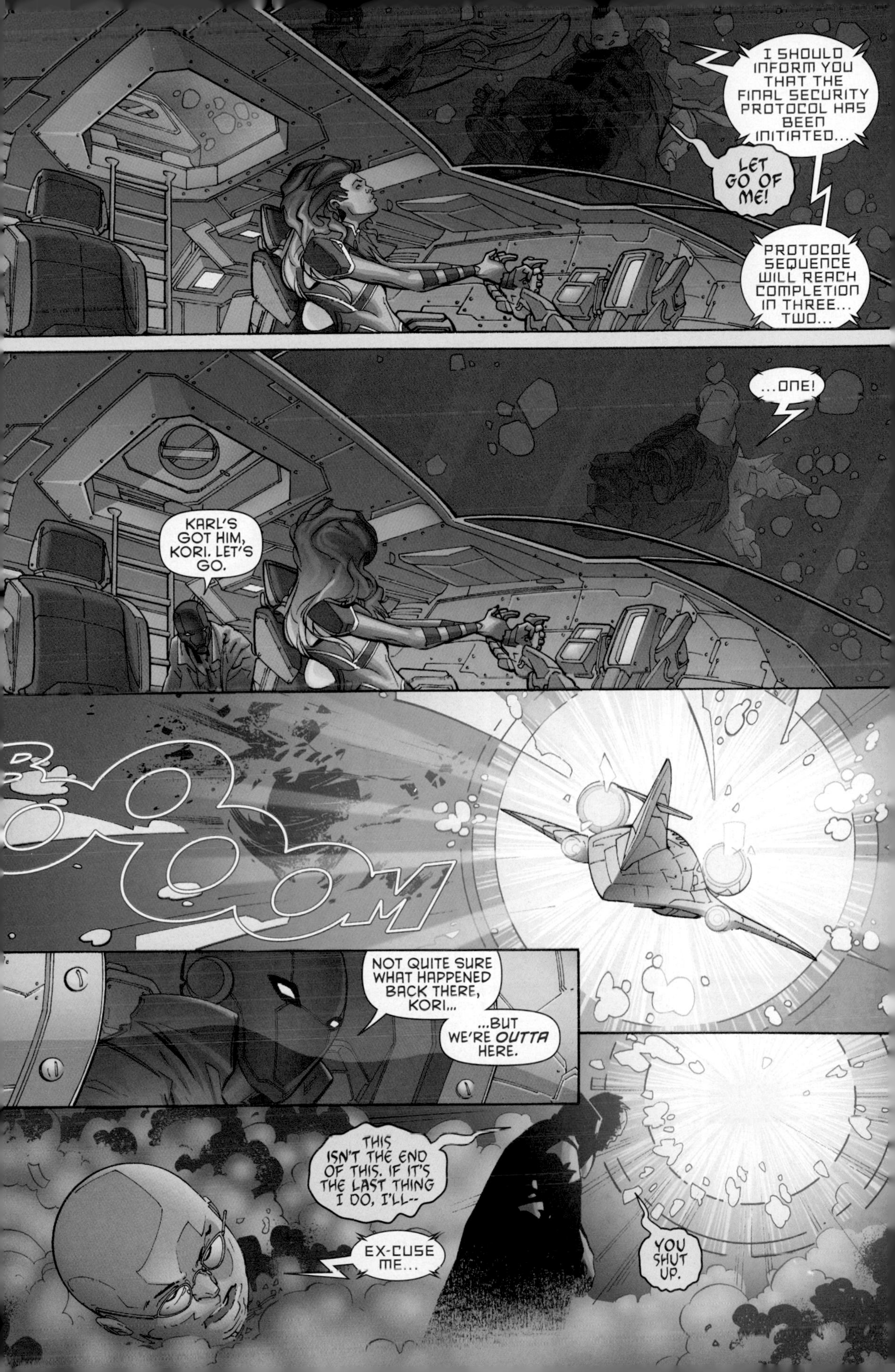
I SHOULD INFORM YOU THAT THE FINAL SECURITY PROTOCOL HAS BEEN INITIATED...
LET GO OF ME!
PROTOCOL SEQUENCE WILL REACH COMPLETION IN THREE... TWO...
...ONE!
KARL'S GOT HIM, KORI. LET'S GO.
BOOOM
NOT QUITE SURE WHAT HAPPENED BACK THERE, KORI...
...BUT WE'RE OUTTA HERE.
THIS ISN'T THE END OF THIS. IF IT'S THE LAST THING I DO, I'LL--
EX-CUSE ME...
YOU SHUT UP.

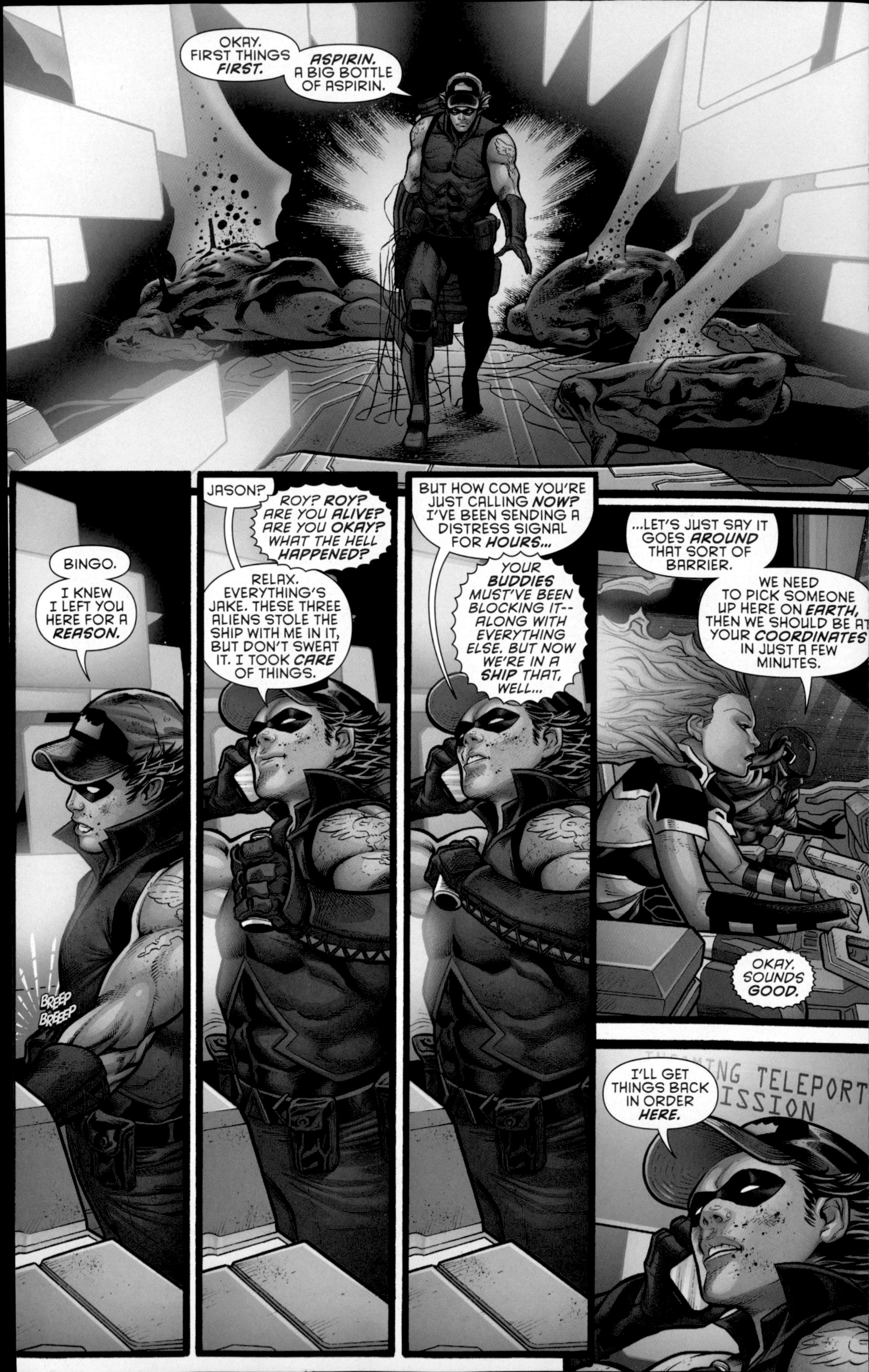
OKAY. FIRST THINGS FIRST.
ASPIRIN. A BIG BOTTLE OF ASPIRIN.
BREEP BREEEP
BINGO.
I KNEW I LEFT YOU HERE FOR A REASON.
JASON?
ROY? ROY? ARE YOU ALIVE? ARE YOU OKAY? WHAT THE HELL HAPPENED?
RELAX. EVERYTHING'S JAKE. THESE THREE ALIENS STOLE THE SHIP WITH ME IN IT, BUT DON'T SWEAT IT. I TOOK CARE OF THINGS.
BUT HOW COME YOU'RE JUST CALLING NOW? I'VE BEEN SENDING A DISTRESS SIGNAL FOR HOURS...
YOUR BUDDIES MUST'VE BEEN BLOCKING IT--ALONG WITH EVERYTHING ELSE. BUT NOW WE'RE IN A SHIP THAT, WELL...
...LET'S JUST SAY IT GOES AROUND THAT SORT OF BARRIER.
WE NEED TO PICK SOMEONE UP HERE ON EARTH, THEN WE SHOULD BE AT YOUR COORDINATES IN JUST A FEW MINUTES.
OKAY. SOUNDS GOOD.
I'LL GET THINGS BACK IN ORDER HERE.

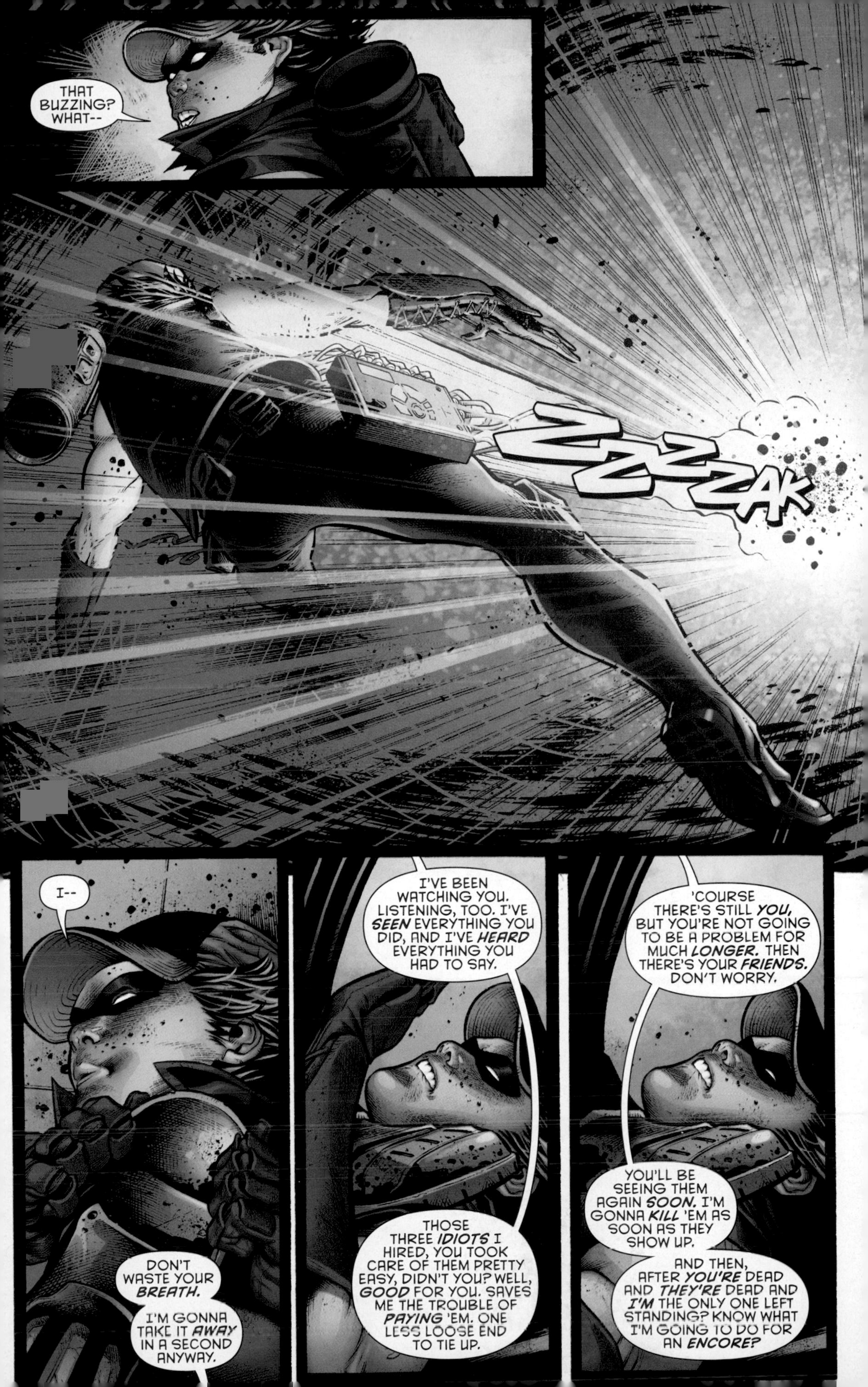
THAT BUZZING? WHAT--
ZZZZZAK
I--
DON'T WASTE YOUR BREATH.
I'M GONNA TAKE IT AWAY IN A SECOND ANYWAY.
I'VE BEEN WATCHING YOU. LISTENING, TOO. I'VE SEEN EVERYTHING YOU DID, AND I'VE HEARD EVERYTHING YOU HAD TO SAY.
THOSE THREE IDIOTS I HIRED, YOU TOOK CARE OF THEM PRETTY EASY, DIDN'T YOU? WELL, GOOD FOR YOU. SAVES ME THE TROUBLE OF PAYING 'EM. ONE LESS LOOSE END TO TIE UP.
'COURSE THERE'S STILL YOU, BUT YOU'RE NOT GOING TO BE A PROBLEM FOR MUCH LONGER. THEN THERE'S YOUR FRIENDS. DON'T WORRY.
YOU'LL BE SEEING THEM AGAIN SOON. I'M GONNA KILL 'EM AS SOON AS THEY SHOW UP.
AND THEN, AFTER YOU'RE DEAD AND THEY'RE DEAD AND I'M THE ONLY ONE LEFT STANDING? KNOW WHAT I'M GOING TO DO FOR AN ENCORE?

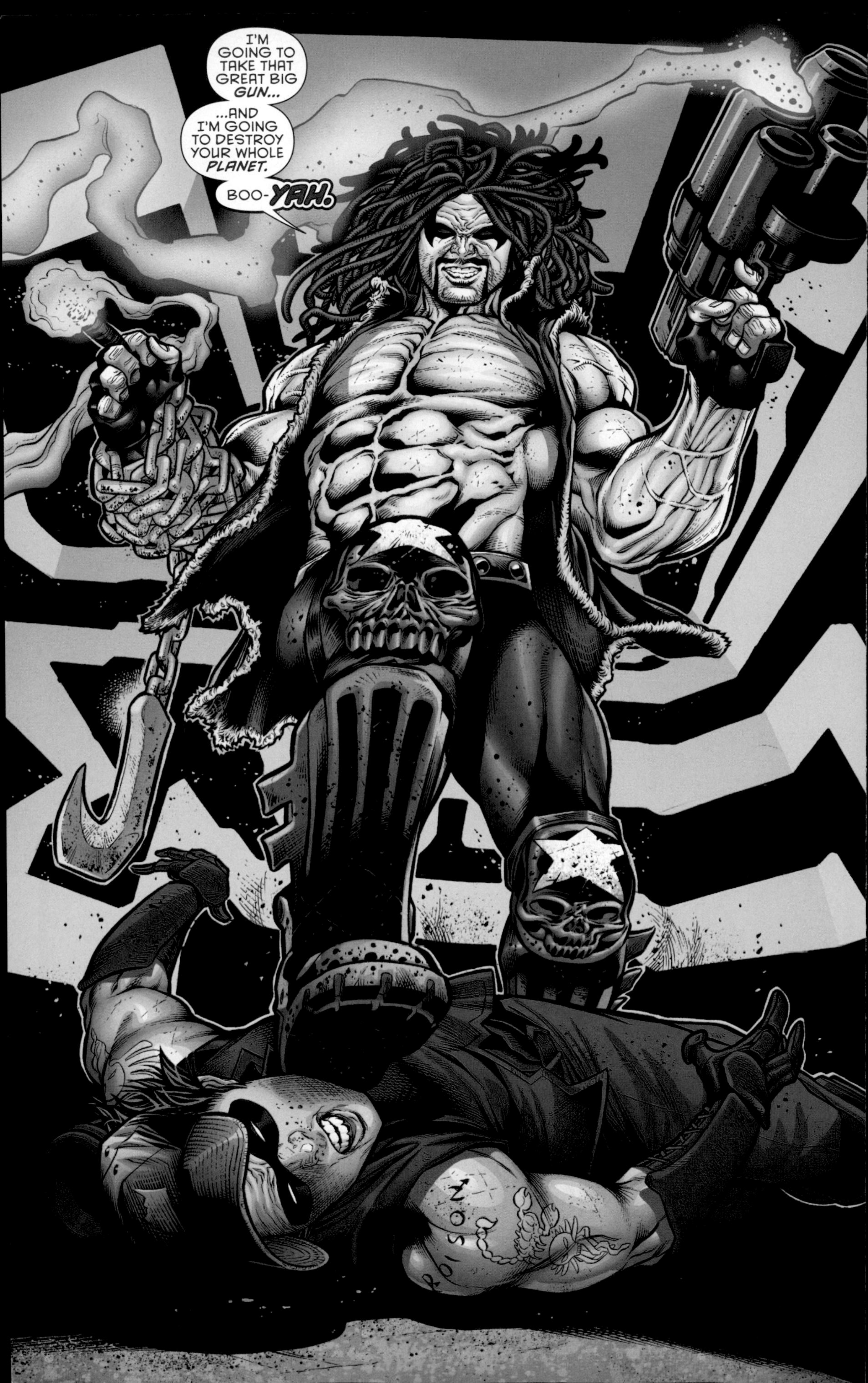

I'M GOING TO TAKE THAT GREAT BIG GUN...
...AND I'M GOING TO DESTROY YOUR WHOLE PLANET.
BOO-YAH.

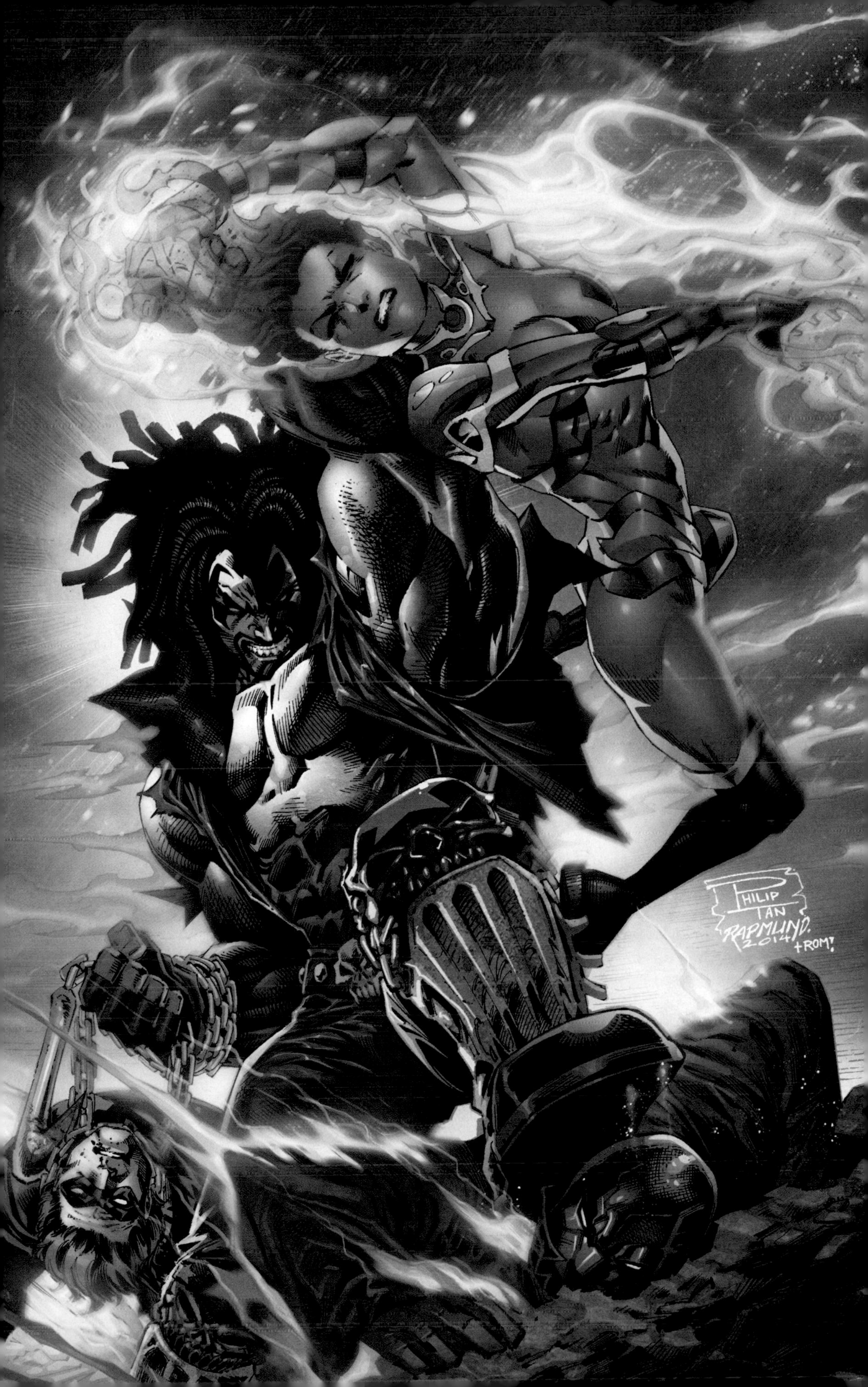
PHILIP TAN
RAPMUND.
2014
+ROM!

THE BIG PICTURE: CONCLUSION

WILL PFEIFER writer RAFAEL SANDOVAL and RB SILVA pencillers PAUL NEARY, WAYNE FAUCHER and JORDI TARRAGONA inkers MATT YACKEY colorist TAYLOR ESPOSITO letterer cover art by PHILIP TAN, NORM RAPMUND and ROMULO FAJARDO, JR.

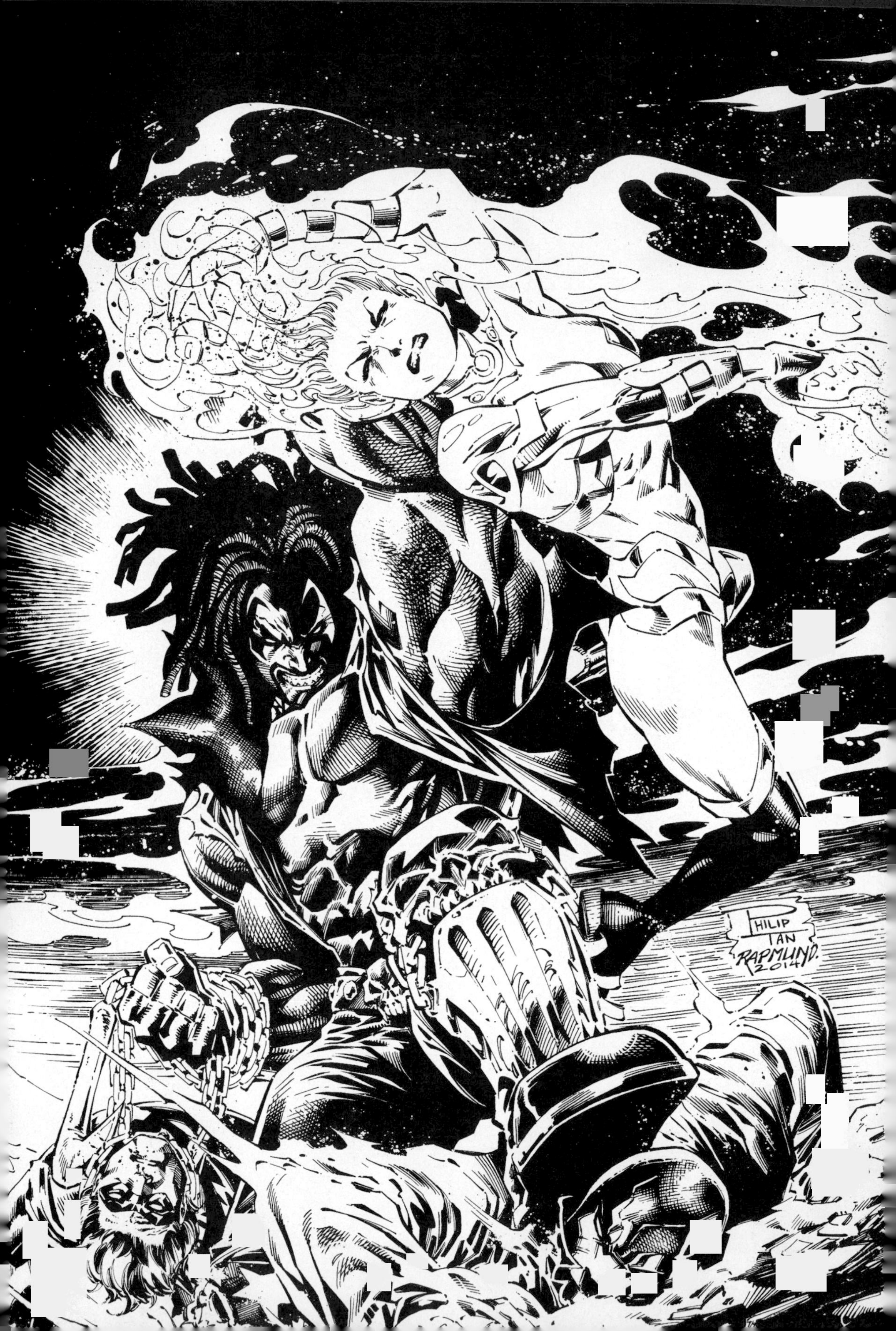
PHILIP TAN
RAPMUND. 2014

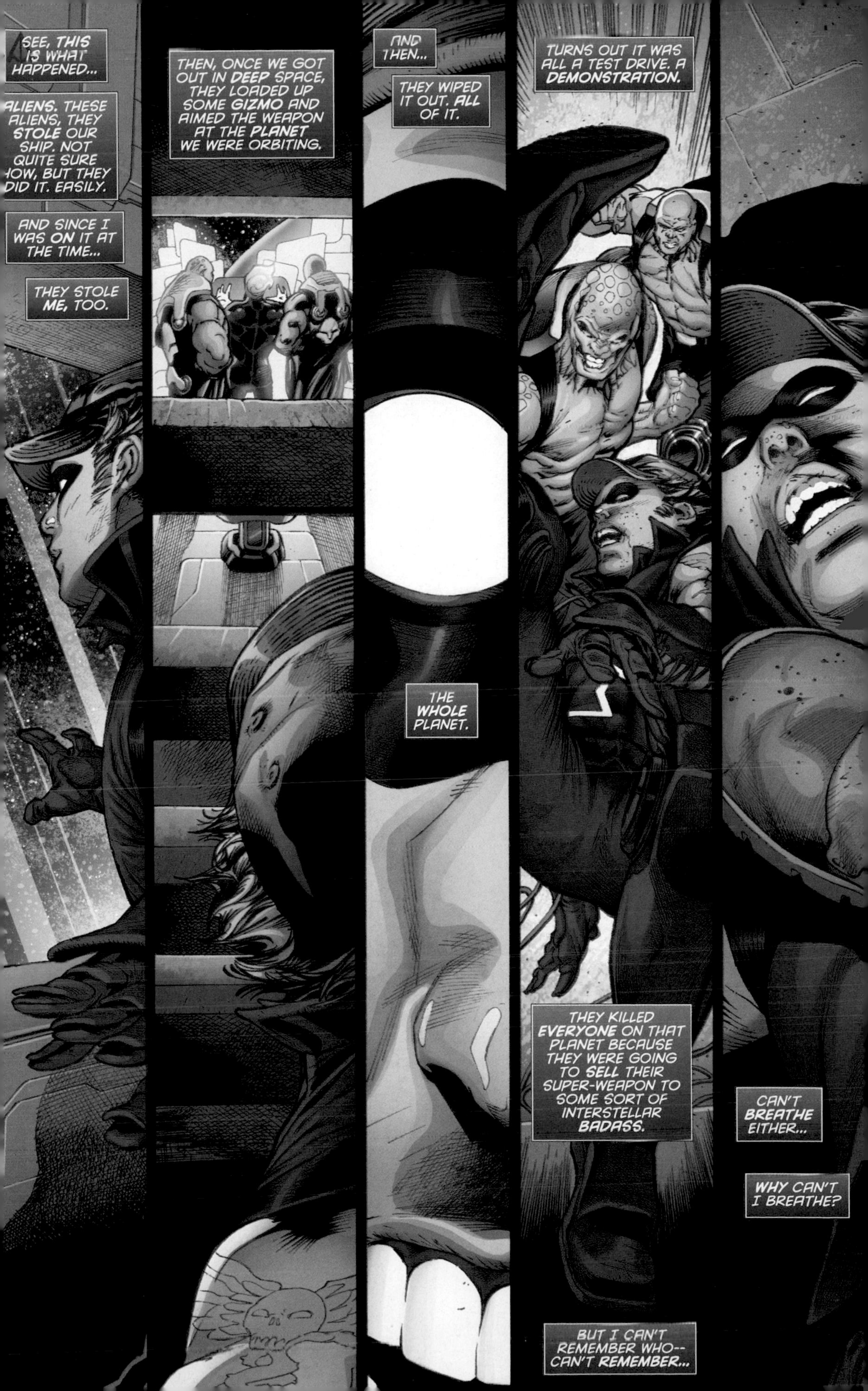
SEE, THIS IS WHAT HAPPENED...
ALIENS. THESE ALIENS, THEY STOLE OUR SHIP. NOT QUITE SURE HOW, BUT THEY DID IT. EASILY.
AND SINCE I WAS ON IT AT THE TIME...
THEY STOLE ME, TOO.
THEN, ONCE WE GOT OUT IN DEEP SPACE, THEY LOADED UP SOME GIZMO AND AIMED THE WEAPON AT THE PLANET WE WERE ORBITING.
AND THEN...
THEY WIPED IT OUT. ALL OF IT.
THE WHOLE PLANET.
TURNS OUT IT WAS ALL A TEST DRIVE. A DEMONSTRATION.
THEY KILLED EVERYONE ON THAT PLANET BECAUSE THEY WERE GOING TO SELL THEIR SUPER-WEAPON TO SOME SORT OF INTERSTELLAR BADASS.
BUT I CAN'T REMEMBER WHO-- CAN'T REMEMBER...
CAN'T BREATHE EITHER...
WHY CAN'T I BREATHE?

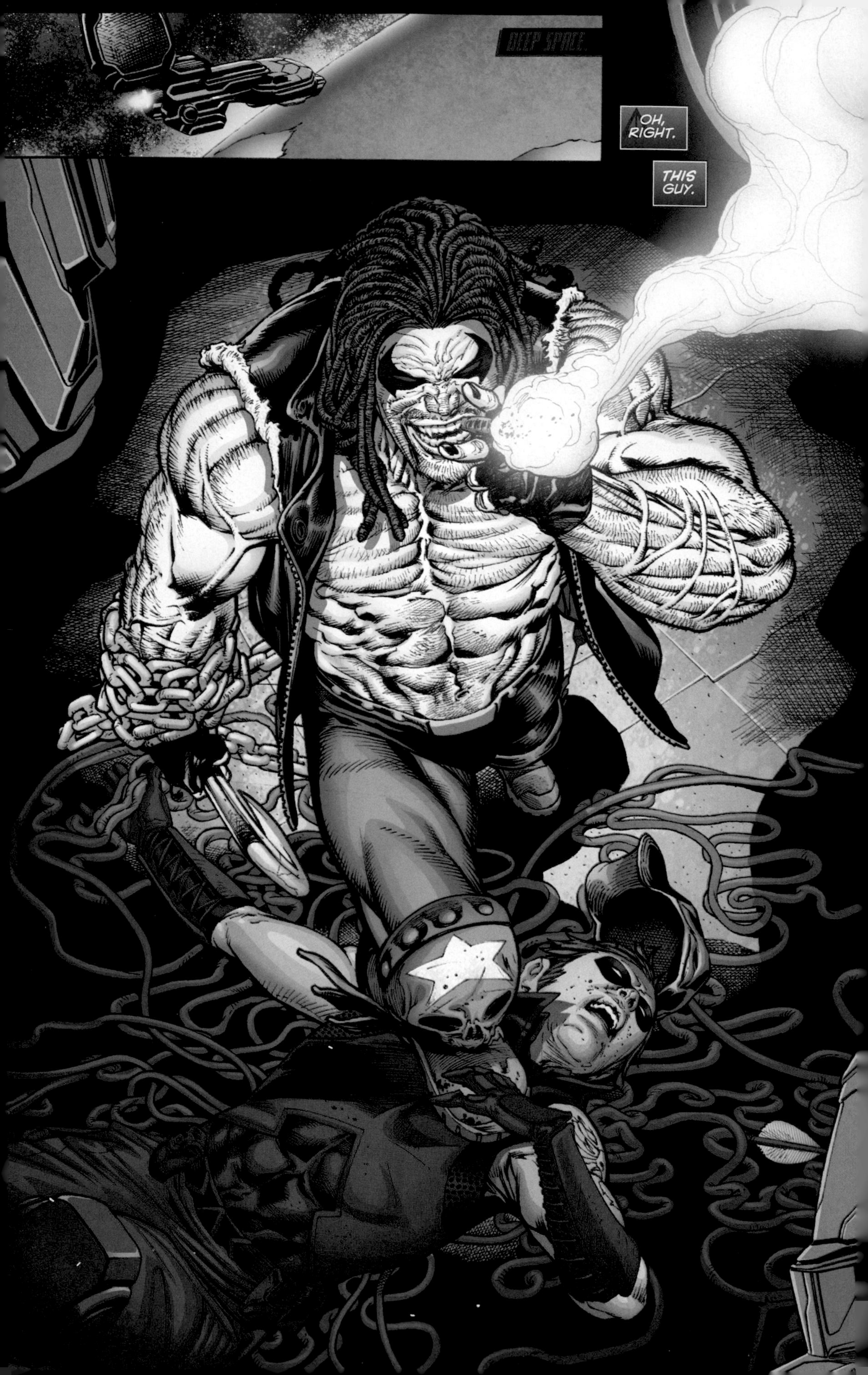
DEEP SPACE.
OH, RIGHT.
THIS GUY.

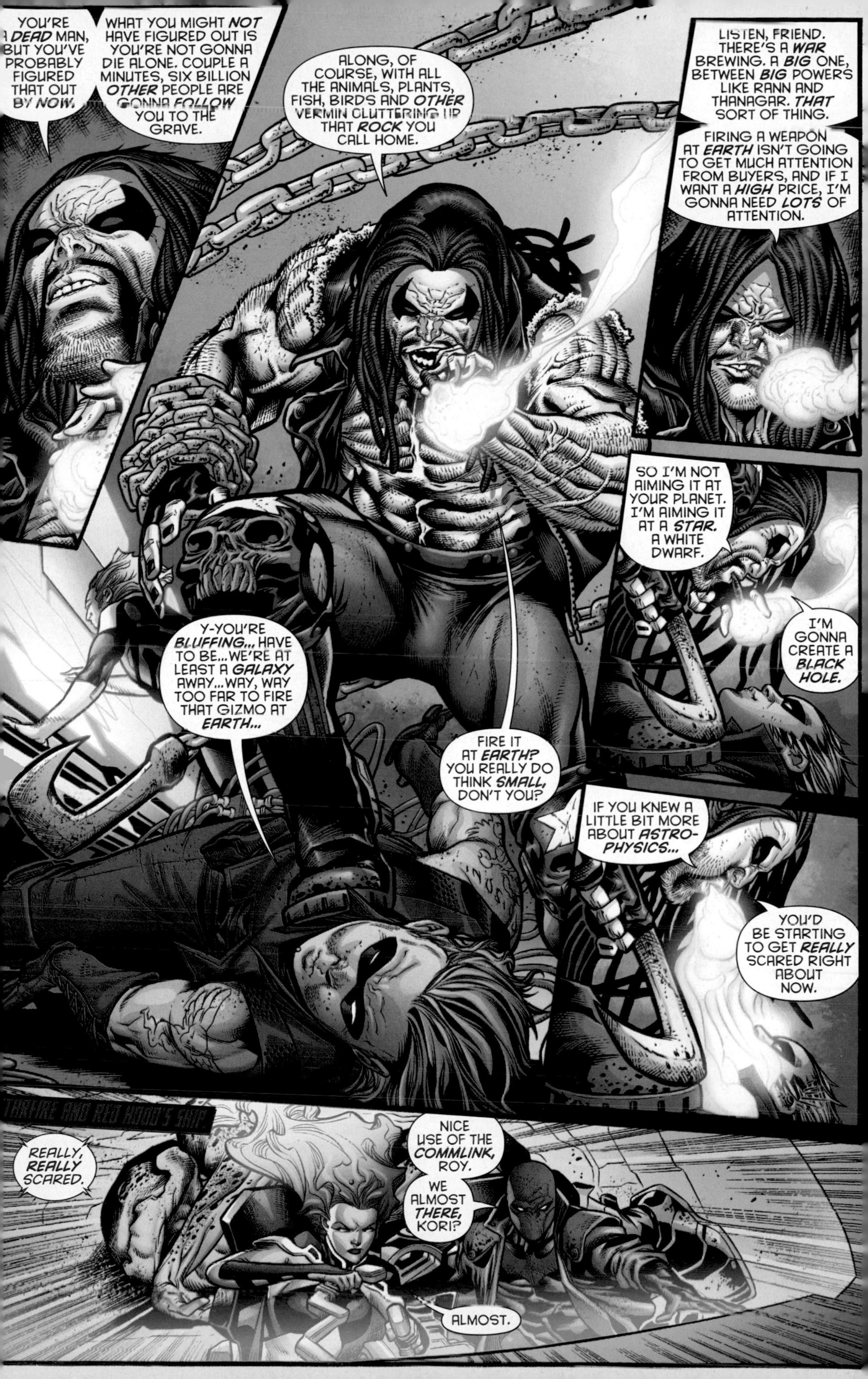
YOU'RE A DEAD MAN, BUT YOU'VE PROBABLY FIGURED THAT OUT BY NOW.
WHAT YOU MIGHT NOT HAVE FIGURED OUT IS YOU'RE NOT GONNA DIE ALONE. COUPLE A MINUTES, SIX BILLION OTHER PEOPLE ARE GONNA FOLLOW YOU TO THE GRAVE.
ALONG, OF COURSE, WITH ALL THE ANIMALS, PLANTS, FISH, BIRDS AND OTHER VERMIN CLUTTERING UP THAT ROCK YOU CALL HOME.
LISTEN, FRIEND. THERE'S A WAR BREWING. A BIG ONE, BETWEEN BIG POWERS LIKE RANN AND THANAGAR. THAT SORT OF THING.
FIRING A WEAPON AT EARTH ISN'T GOING TO GET MUCH ATTENTION FROM BUYERS, AND IF I WANT A HIGH PRICE, I'M GONNA NEED LOTS OF ATTENTION.
Y-YOU'RE BLUFFING... HAVE TO BE... WE'RE AT LEAST A GALAXY AWAY... WAY, WAY TOO FAR TO FIRE THAT GIZMO AT EARTH...
FIRE IT AT EARTH? YOU REALLY DO THINK SMALL, DON'T YOU?
SO I'M NOT AIMING IT AT YOUR PLANET. I'M AIMING IT AT A STAR. A WHITE DWARF.
I'M GONNA CREATE A BLACK HOLE.
IF YOU KNEW A LITTLE BIT MORE ABOUT ASTROPHYSICS...
YOU'D BE STARTING TO GET REALLY SCARED RIGHT ABOUT NOW.
TARFIRE AND RED HOOD'S SHIP
REALLY, REALLY SCARED.
NICE USE OF THE COMMLINK, ROY.
WE ALMOST THERE, KORI?
ALMOST.

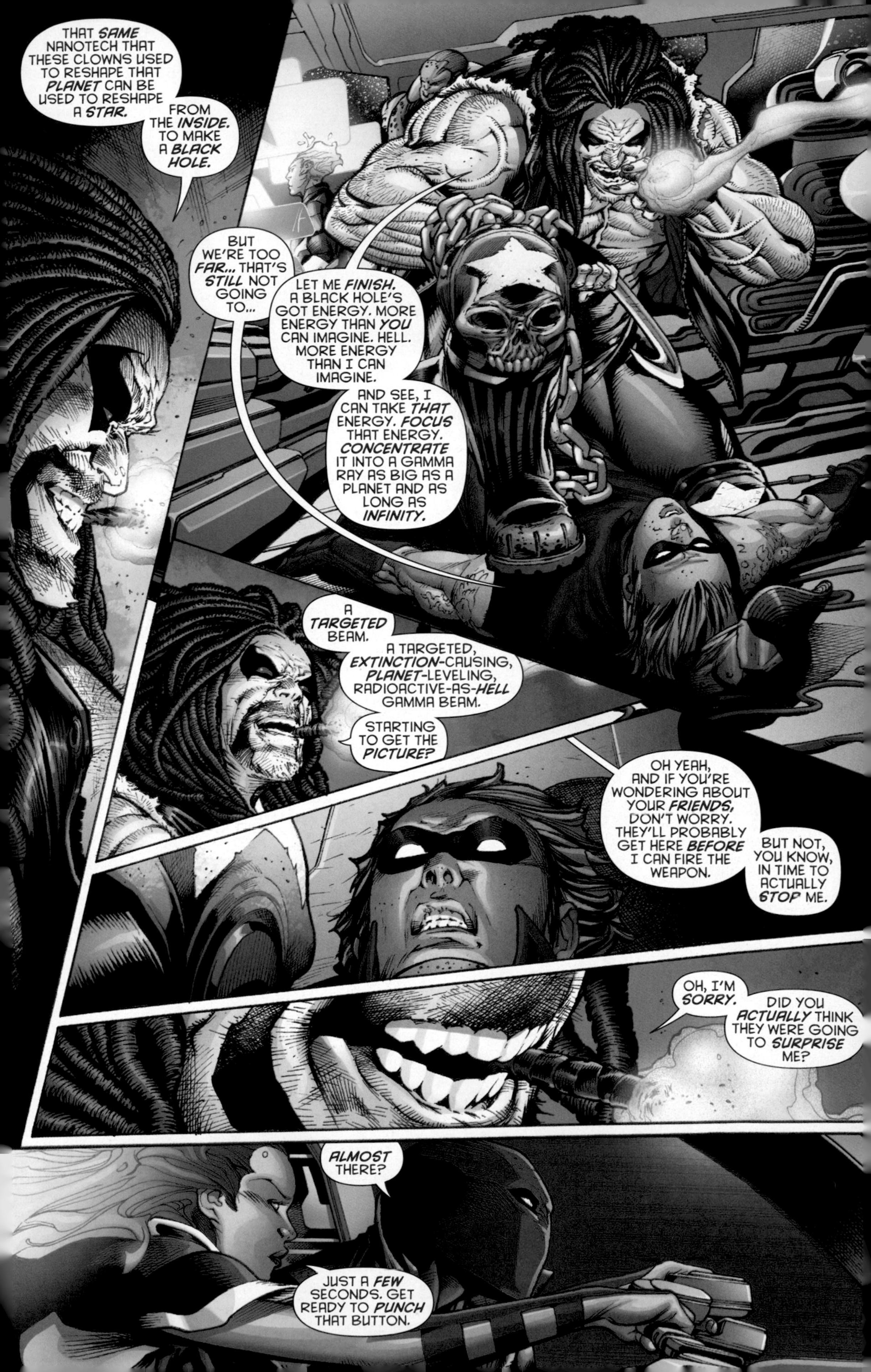
THAT SAME NANOTECH THAT THESE CLOWNS USED TO RESHAPE THAT PLANET CAN BE USED TO RESHAPE A STAR.
FROM THE INSIDE. TO MAKE A BLACK HOLE.
BUT WE'RE TOO FAR... THAT'S STILL NOT GOING TO...
LET ME FINISH. A BLACK HOLE'S GOT ENERGY. MORE ENERGY THAN YOU CAN IMAGINE. HELL. MORE ENERGY THAN I CAN IMAGINE.
AND SEE, I CAN TAKE THAT ENERGY. FOCUS THAT ENERGY. CONCENTRATE IT INTO A GAMMA RAY AS BIG AS A PLANET AND AS LONG AS INFINITY.
A TARGETED BEAM.
A TARGETED, EXTINCTION-CAUSING, PLANET-LEVELING, RADIOACTIVE-AS-HELL GAMMA BEAM.
STARTING TO GET THE PICTURE?
OH YEAH, AND IF YOU'RE WONDERING ABOUT YOUR FRIENDS, DON'T WORRY. THEY'LL PROBABLY GET HERE BEFORE I CAN FIRE THE WEAPON.
BUT NOT, YOU KNOW, IN TIME TO ACTUALLY STOP ME.
OH, I'M SORRY.
DID YOU ACTUALLY THINK THEY WERE GOING TO SURPRISE ME?
ALMOST THERE?
JUST A FEW SECONDS. GET READY TO PUNCH THAT BUTTON.

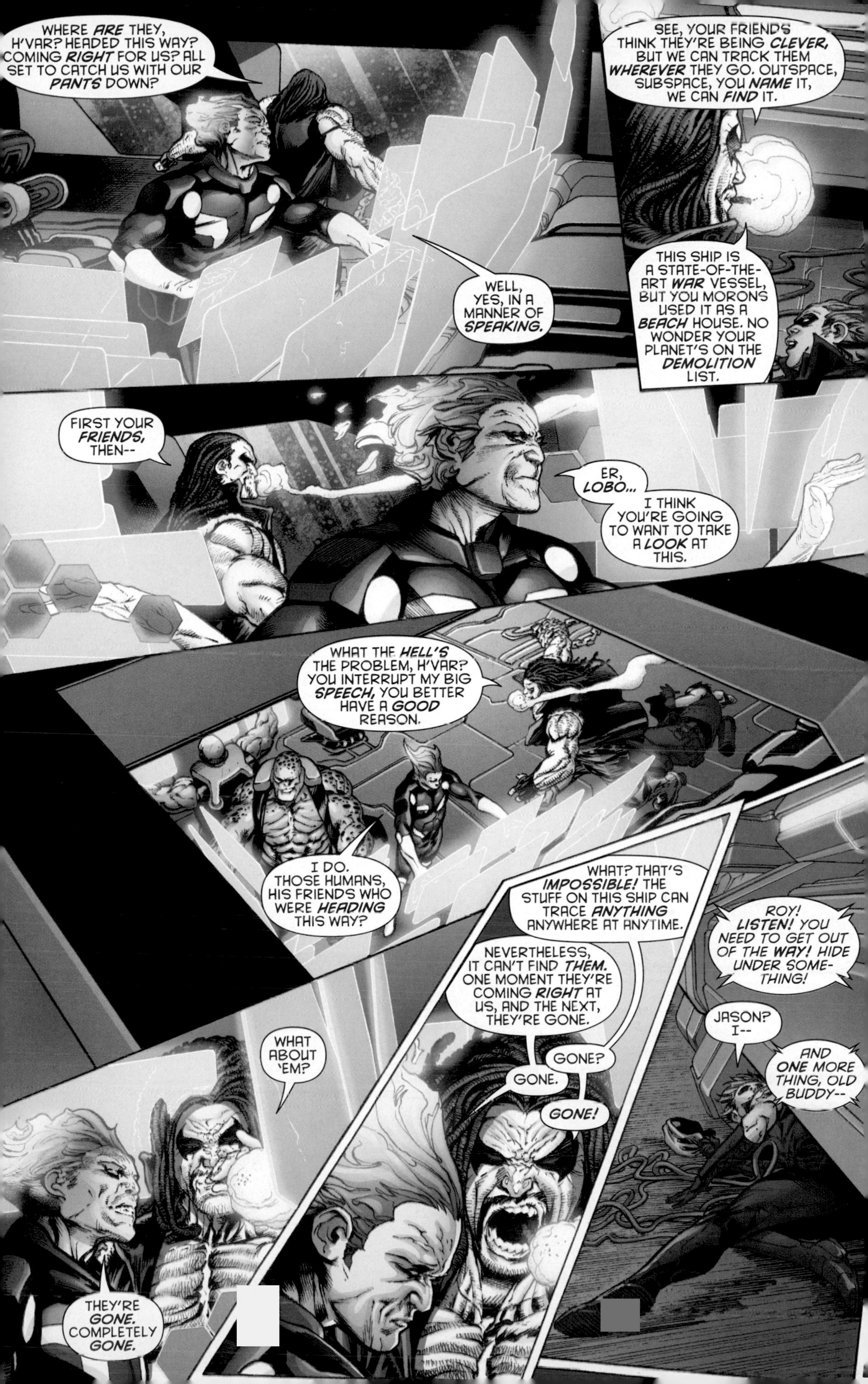
WHERE ARE THEY, H'VAR? HEADED THIS WAY? COMING RIGHT FOR US? ALL SET TO CATCH US WITH OUR PANTS DOWN?
WELL, YES, IN A MANNER OF SPEAKING.
SEE, YOUR FRIENDS THINK THEY'RE BEING CLEVER, BUT WE CAN TRACK THEM WHEREVER THEY GO. OUTSPACE, SUBSPACE, YOU NAME IT, WE CAN FIND IT.
THIS SHIP IS A STATE-OF-THE-ART WAR VESSEL, BUT YOU MORONS USED IT AS A BEACH HOUSE. NO WONDER YOUR PLANET'S ON THE DEMOLITION LIST.
FIRST YOUR FRIENDS, THEN--
ER, LOBO...
I THINK YOU'RE GOING TO WANT TO TAKE A LOOK AT THIS.
WHAT THE HELL'S THE PROBLEM, H'VAR? YOU INTERRUPT MY BIG SPEECH, YOU BETTER HAVE A GOOD REASON.
I DO. THOSE HUMANS, HIS FRIENDS WHO WERE HEADING THIS WAY?
WHAT ABOUT 'EM?
THEY'RE GONE. COMPLETELY GONE.
WHAT? THAT'S IMPOSSIBLE! THE STUFF ON THIS SHIP CAN TRACE ANYTHING ANYWHERE AT ANYTIME.
NEVERTHELESS, IT CAN'T FIND THEM. ONE MOMENT THEY'RE COMING RIGHT AT US, AND THE NEXT, THEY'RE GONE.
GONE?
GONE.
GONE!
ROY! LISTEN! YOU NEED TO GET OUT OF THE WAY! HIDE UNDER SOME-THING!
JASON? I--
AND ONE MORE THING, OLD BUDDY--

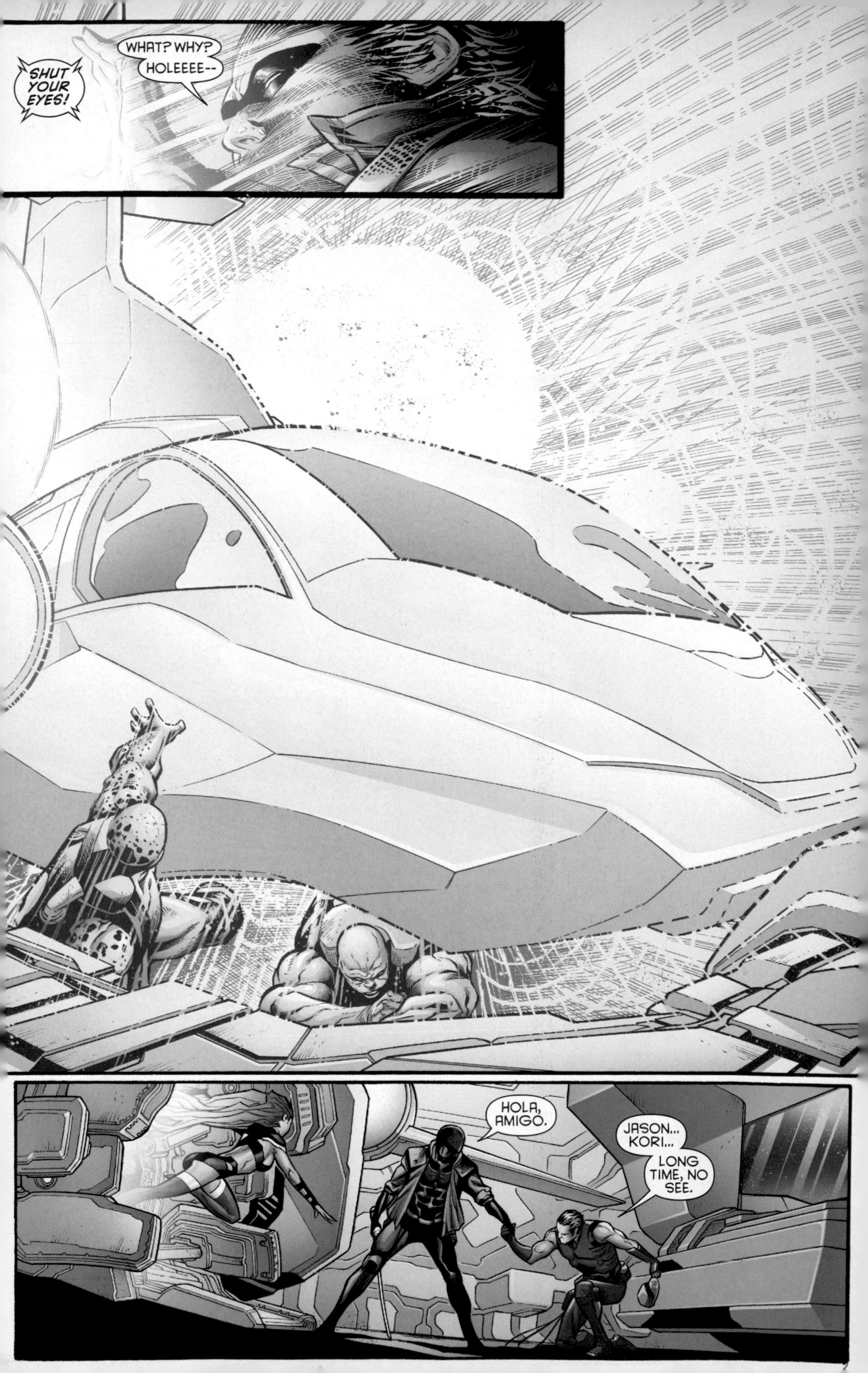
SHUT YOUR EYES!
WHAT? WHY?
HOLEEEE--
HOLA, AMIGO.
JASON... KORI...
LONG TIME, NO SEE.

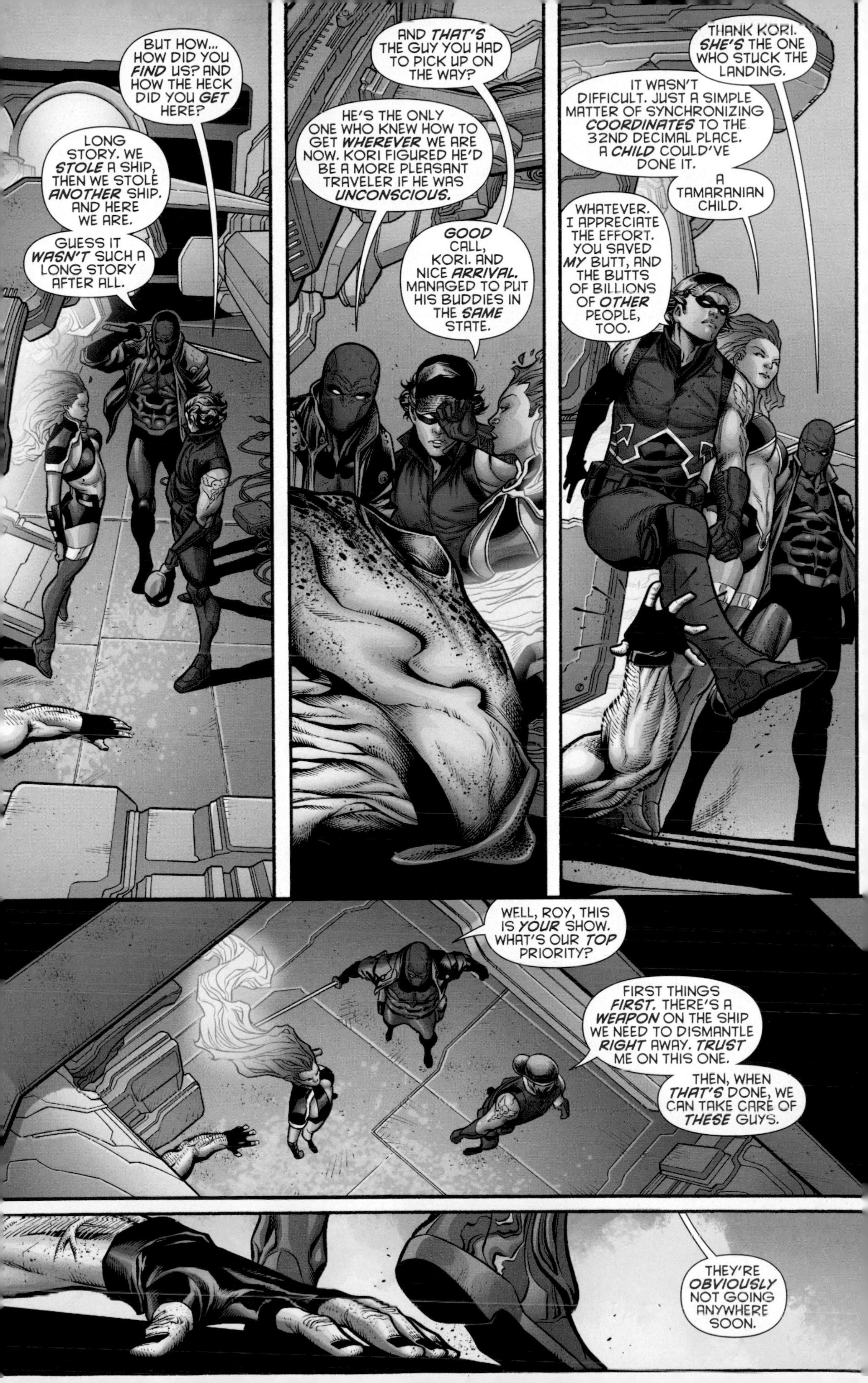
BUT HOW... HOW DID YOU FIND US? AND HOW THE HECK DID YOU GET HERE?
LONG STORY. WE STOLE A SHIP, THEN WE STOLE ANOTHER SHIP. AND HERE WE ARE.
GUESS IT WASN'T SUCH A LONG STORY AFTER ALL.
AND THAT'S THE GUY YOU HAD TO PICK UP ON THE WAY?
HE'S THE ONLY ONE WHO KNEW HOW TO GET WHEREVER WE ARE NOW. KORI FIGURED HE'D BE A MORE PLEASANT TRAVELER IF HE WAS UNCONSCIOUS.
GOOD CALL, KORI. AND NICE ARRIVAL. MANAGED TO PUT HIS BUDDIES IN THE SAME STATE.
THANK KORI. SHE'S THE ONE WHO STUCK THE LANDING.
IT WASN'T DIFFICULT. JUST A SIMPLE MATTER OF SYNCHRONIZING COORDINATES TO THE 32ND DECIMAL PLACE. A CHILD COULD'VE DONE IT.
A TAMARANIAN CHILD.
WHATEVER. I APPRECIATE THE EFFORT. YOU SAVED MY BUTT, AND THE BUTTS OF BILLIONS OF OTHER PEOPLE, TOO.
WELL, ROY, THIS IS YOUR SHOW. WHAT'S OUR TOP PRIORITY?
FIRST THINGS FIRST. THERE'S A WEAPON ON THE SHIP WE NEED TO DISMANTLE RIGHT AWAY. TRUST ME ON THIS ONE.
THEN, WHEN THAT'S DONE, WE CAN TAKE CARE OF THESE GUYS.
THEY'RE OBVIOUSLY NOT GOING ANYWHERE SOON.

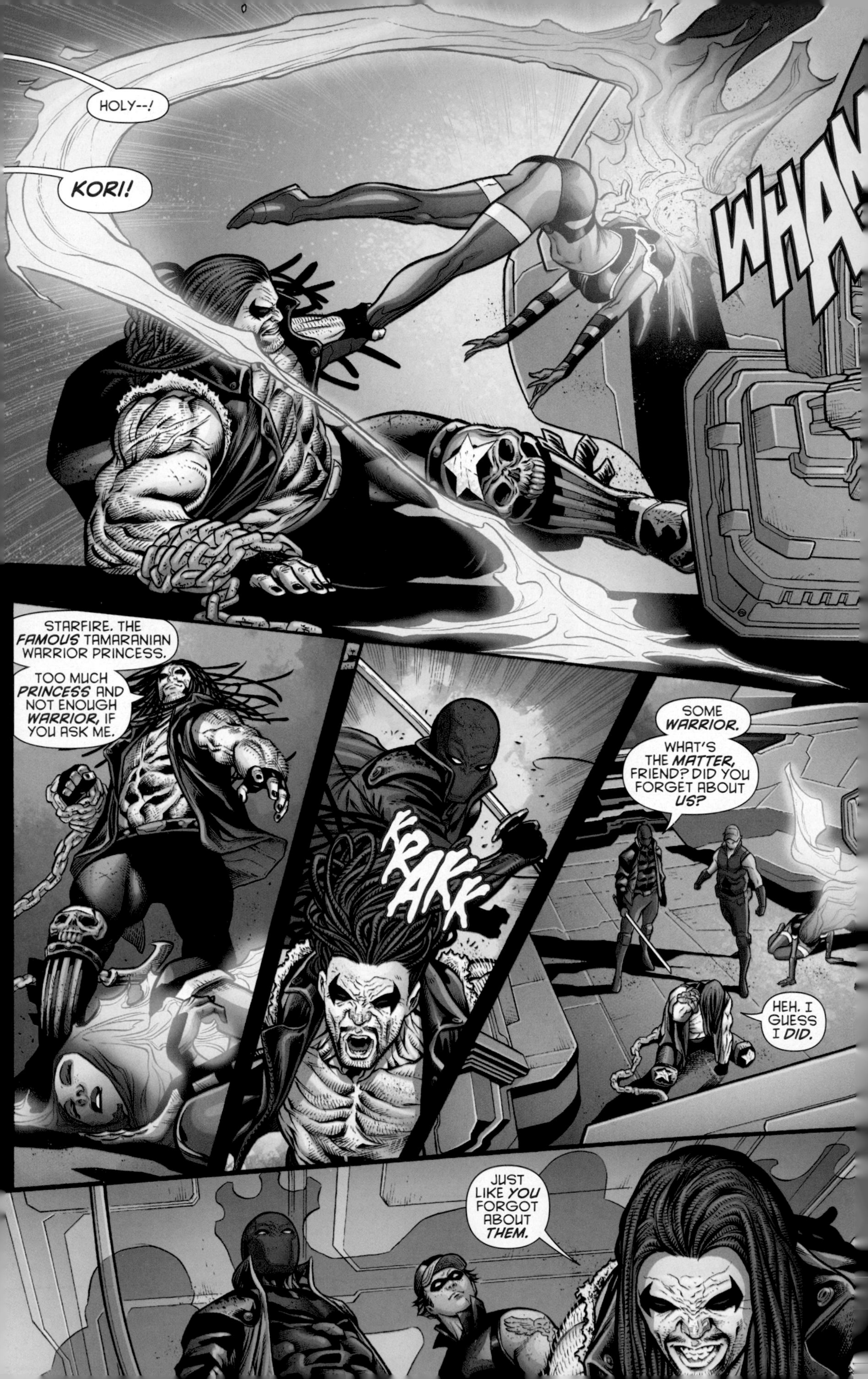
HOLY--!
KORI!
WHAM
STARFIRE. THE FAMOUS TAMARANIAN WARRIOR PRINCESS.
TOO MUCH PRINCESS AND NOT ENOUGH WARRIOR, IF YOU ASK ME.
KRAKK
SOME WARRIOR.
WHAT'S THE MATTER, FRIEND? DID YOU FORGET ABOUT US?
HEH. I GUESS I DID.
JUST LIKE YOU FORGOT ABOUT THEM.

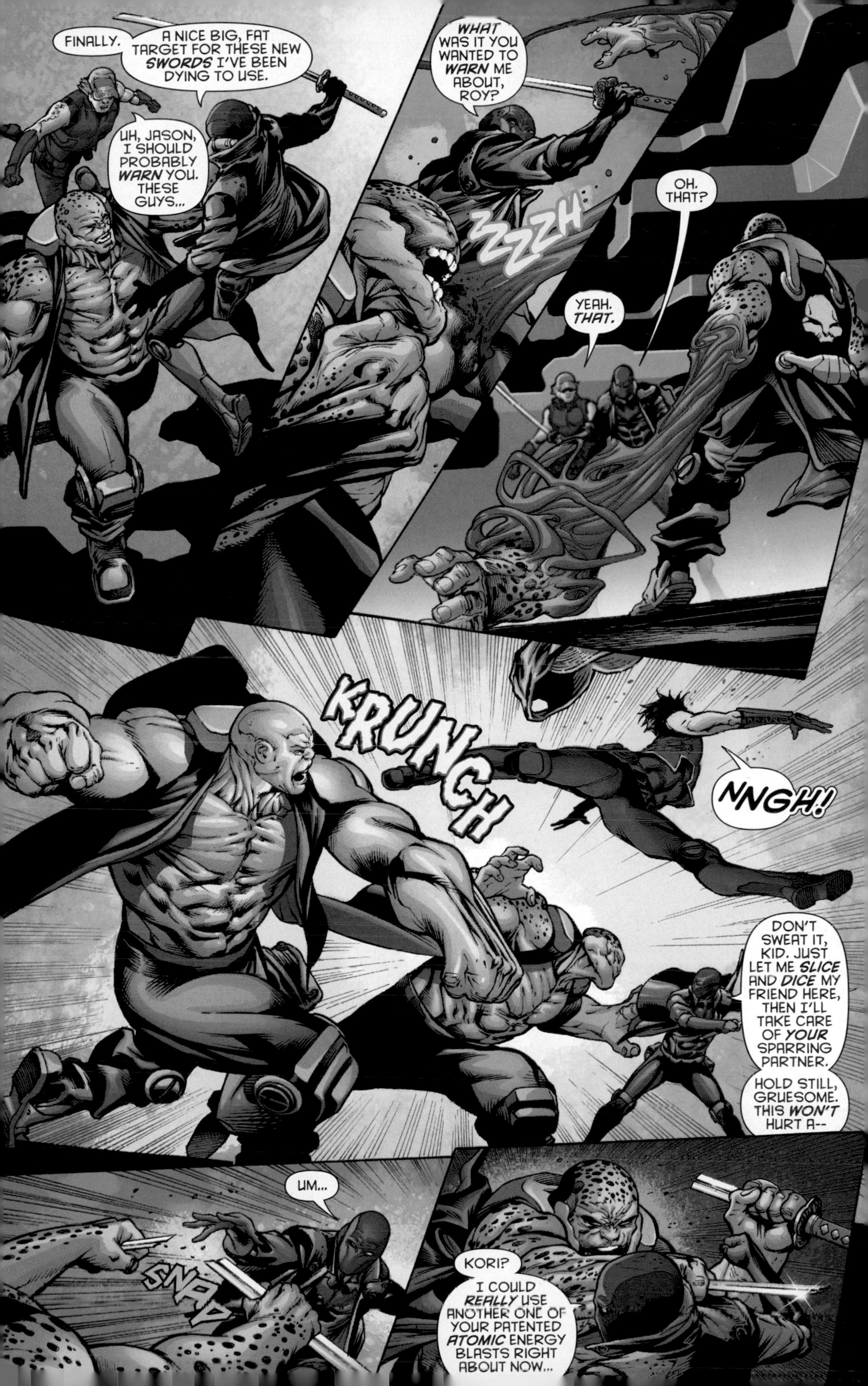

FINALLY.
A NICE BIG, FAT TARGET FOR THESE NEW SWORDS I'VE BEEN DYING TO USE.
UH, JASON, I SHOULD PROBABLY WARN YOU. THESE GUYS...
WHAT WAS IT YOU WANTED TO WARN ME ABOUT, ROY?
ZZZZH
OH. THAT?
YEAH. THAT.
KRUNCH
NNGH!
DON'T SWEAT IT, KID. JUST LET ME SLICE AND DICE MY FRIEND HERE, THEN I'LL TAKE CARE OF YOUR SPARRING PARTNER.
HOLD STILL, GRUESOME. THIS WON'T HURT A--
UM...
SNAP
KORI?
I COULD REALLY USE ANOTHER ONE OF YOUR PATENTED ATOMIC ENERGY BLASTS RIGHT ABOUT NOW...

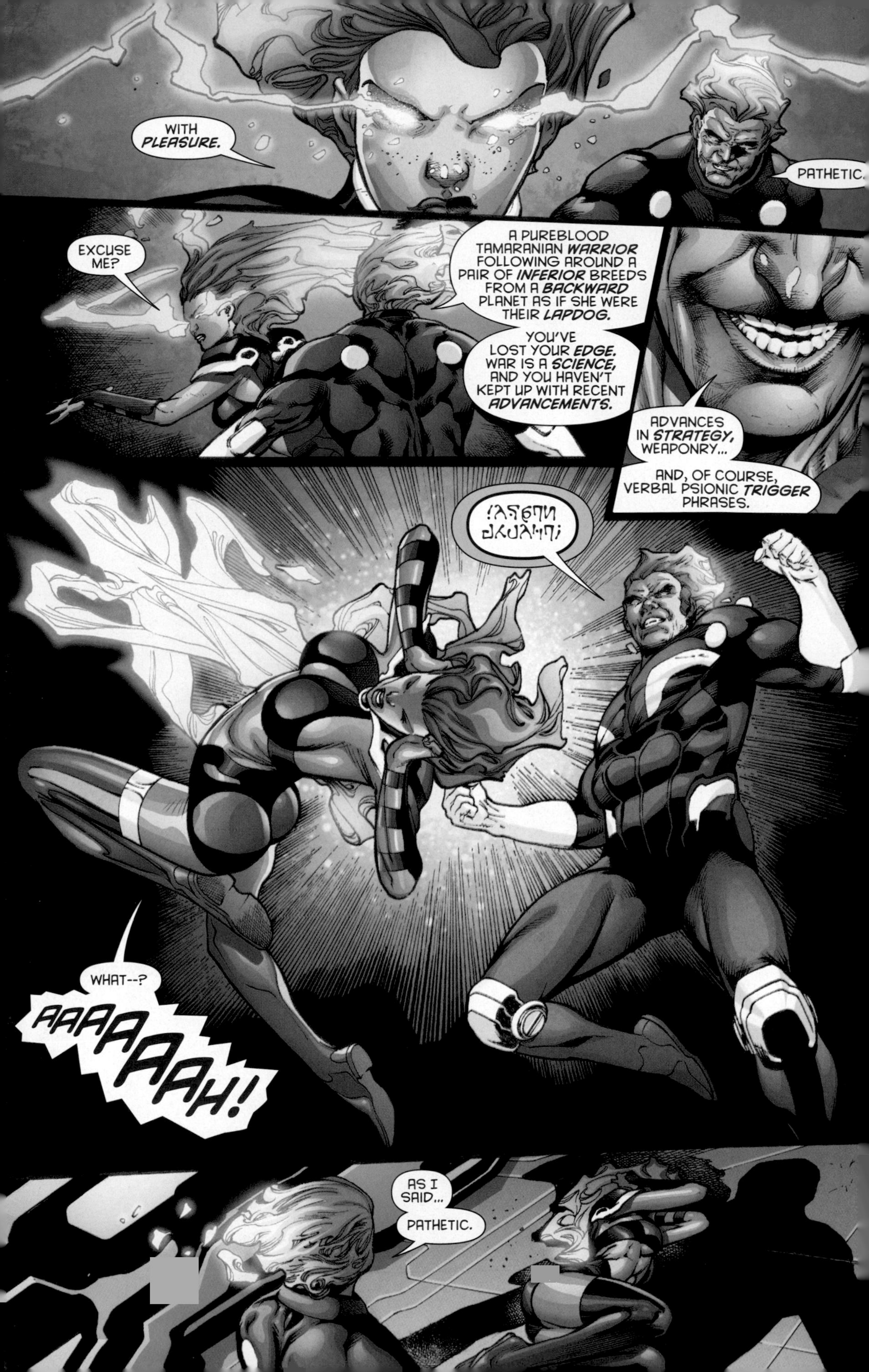
WITH *PLEASURE.*
PATHETIC.
EXCUSE ME?
A PUREBLOOD TAMARANIAN *WARRIOR* FOLLOWING AROUND A PAIR OF *INFERIOR* BREEDS FROM A *BACKWARD* PLANET AS IF SHE WERE THEIR *LAPDOG.*
YOU'VE LOST YOUR *EDGE.* WAR IS A *SCIENCE,* AND YOU HAVEN'T KEPT UP WITH RECENT *ADVANCEMENTS.*
ADVANCES IN *STRATEGY,* WEAPONRY...
AND, OF COURSE, VERBAL PSIONIC *TRIGGER* PHRASES.
WHAT--?
AAAAAAAH!
AS I SAID...
PATHETIC.

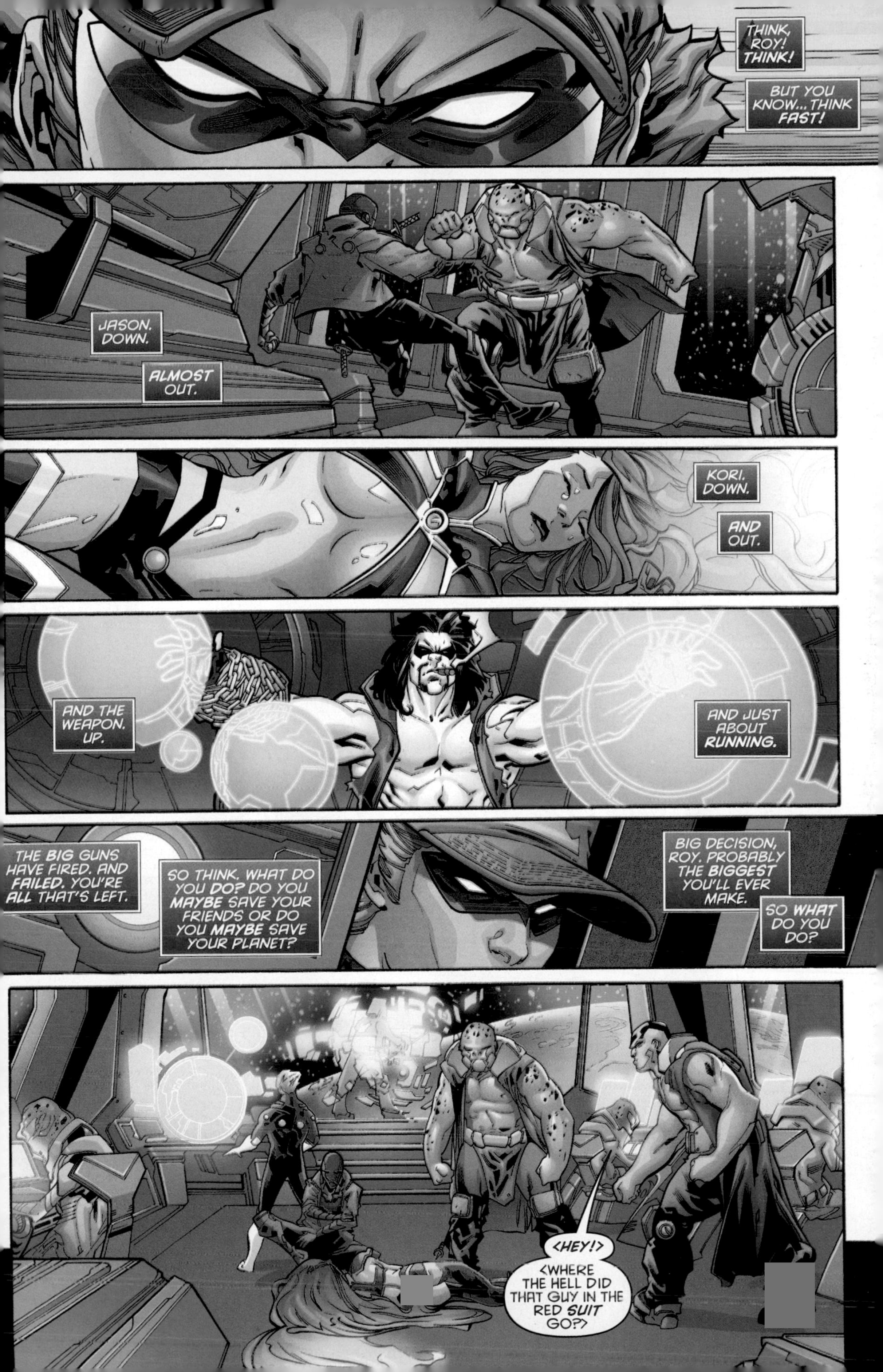

THINK, ROY! THINK!
BUT YOU KNOW... THINK FAST!
JASON. DOWN.
ALMOST OUT.
KORI. DOWN.
AND OUT.
AND THE WEAPON. UP.
AND JUST ABOUT RUNNING.
THE BIG GUNS HAVE FIRED. AND FAILED. YOU'RE ALL THAT'S LEFT.
SO THINK. WHAT DO YOU DO? DO YOU MAYBE SAVE YOUR FRIENDS OR DO YOU MAYBE SAVE YOUR PLANET?
BIG DECISION, ROY. PROBABLY THE BIGGEST YOU'LL EVER MAKE.
SO WHAT DO YOU DO?
<HEY!>
<WHERE THE HELL DID THAT GUY IN THE RED SUIT GO?>

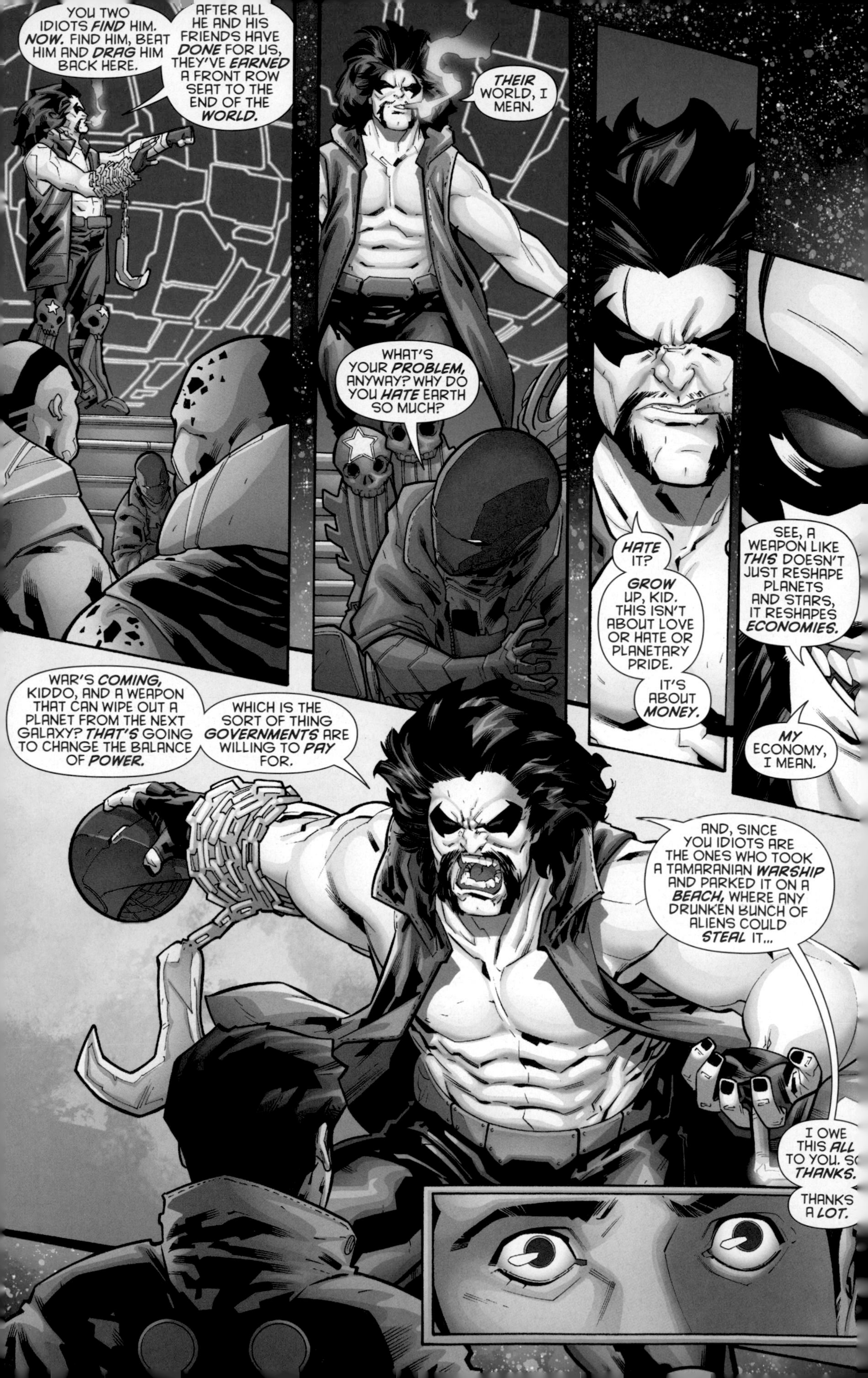
YOU TWO IDIOTS FIND HIM. NOW. FIND HIM, BEAT HIM AND DRAG HIM BACK HERE.
AFTER ALL HE AND HIS FRIENDS HAVE DONE FOR US, THEY'VE EARNED A FRONT ROW SEAT TO THE END OF THE WORLD.
THEIR WORLD, I MEAN.
WHAT'S YOUR PROBLEM, ANYWAY? WHY DO YOU HATE EARTH SO MUCH?
HATE IT?
GROW UP, KID. THIS ISN'T ABOUT LOVE OR HATE OR PLANETARY PRIDE.
IT'S ABOUT MONEY.
SEE, A WEAPON LIKE THIS DOESN'T JUST RESHAPE PLANETS AND STARS, IT RESHAPES ECONOMIES.
MY ECONOMY, I MEAN.
WAR'S COMING, KIDDO, AND A WEAPON THAT CAN WIPE OUT A PLANET FROM THE NEXT GALAXY? THAT'S GOING TO CHANGE THE BALANCE OF POWER.
WHICH IS THE SORT OF THING GOVERNMENTS ARE WILLING TO PAY FOR.
AND, SINCE YOU IDIOTS ARE THE ONES WHO TOOK A TAMARANIAN WARSHIP AND PARKED IT ON A BEACH, WHERE ANY DRUNKEN BUNCH OF ALIENS COULD STEAL IT...
I OWE THIS ALL TO YOU. SO THANKS.
THANKS A LOT.

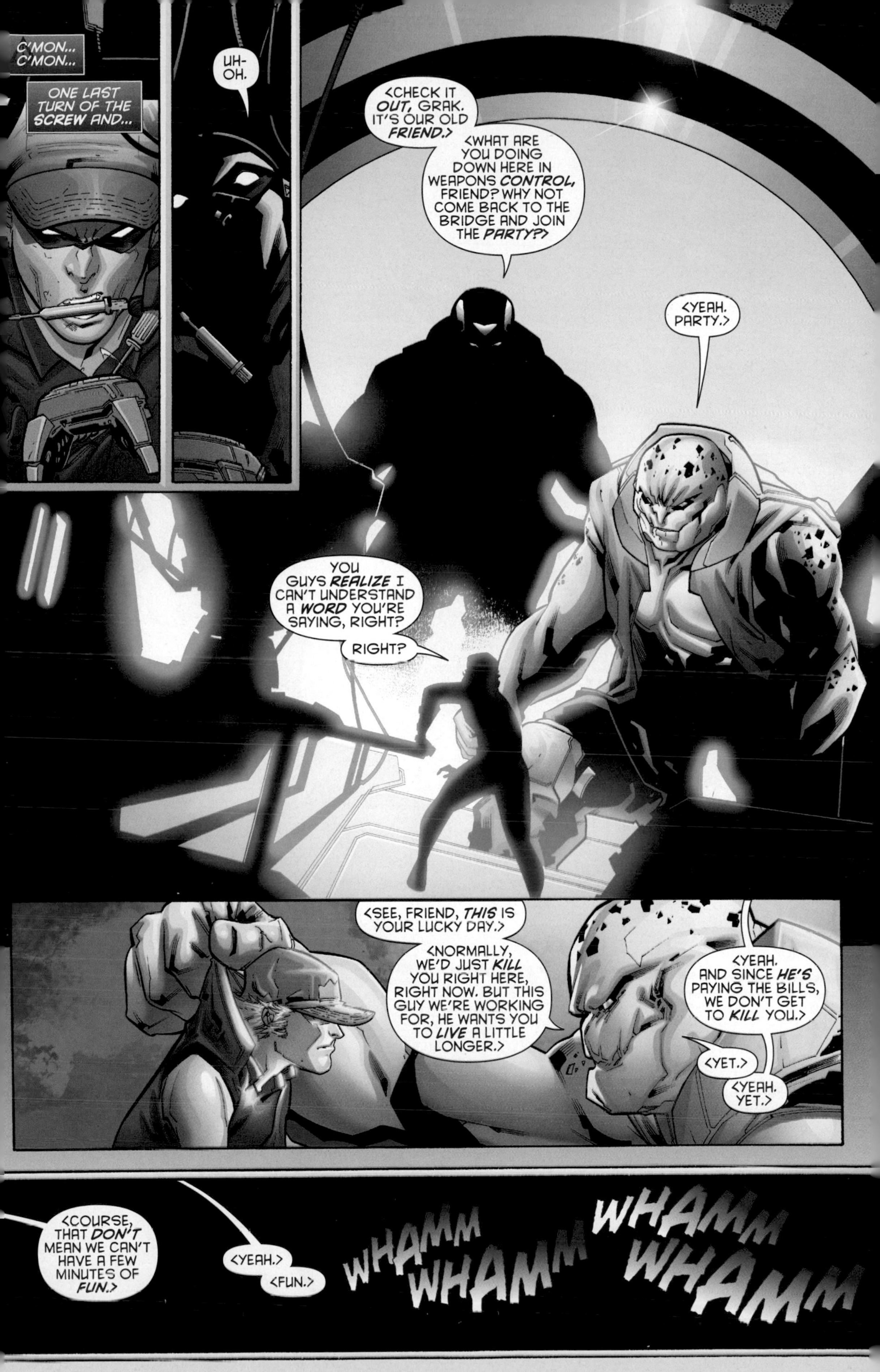
C'MON... C'MON...
ONE LAST TURN OF THE SCREW AND...
UH-OH.
<CHECK IT OUT, GRAK. IT'S OUR OLD FRIEND.>
<WHAT ARE YOU DOING DOWN HERE IN WEAPONS CONTROL, FRIEND? WHY NOT COME BACK TO THE BRIDGE AND JOIN THE PARTY?>
<YEAH. PARTY.>
YOU GUYS REALIZE I CAN'T UNDERSTAND A WORD YOU'RE SAYING, RIGHT?
RIGHT?
<SEE, FRIEND, THIS IS YOUR LUCKY DAY.>
<NORMALLY, WE'D JUST KILL YOU RIGHT HERE, RIGHT NOW. BUT THIS GUY WE'RE WORKING FOR, HE WANTS YOU TO LIVE A LITTLE LONGER.>
<YEAH. AND SINCE HE'S PAYING THE BILLS, WE DON'T GET TO KILL YOU.>
<YET.>
<YEAH. YET.>
<COURSE, THAT DON'T MEAN WE CAN'T HAVE A FEW MINUTES OF FUN.>
<YEAH.>
<FUN.>
WHAMM WHAMM WHAMM WHAMM

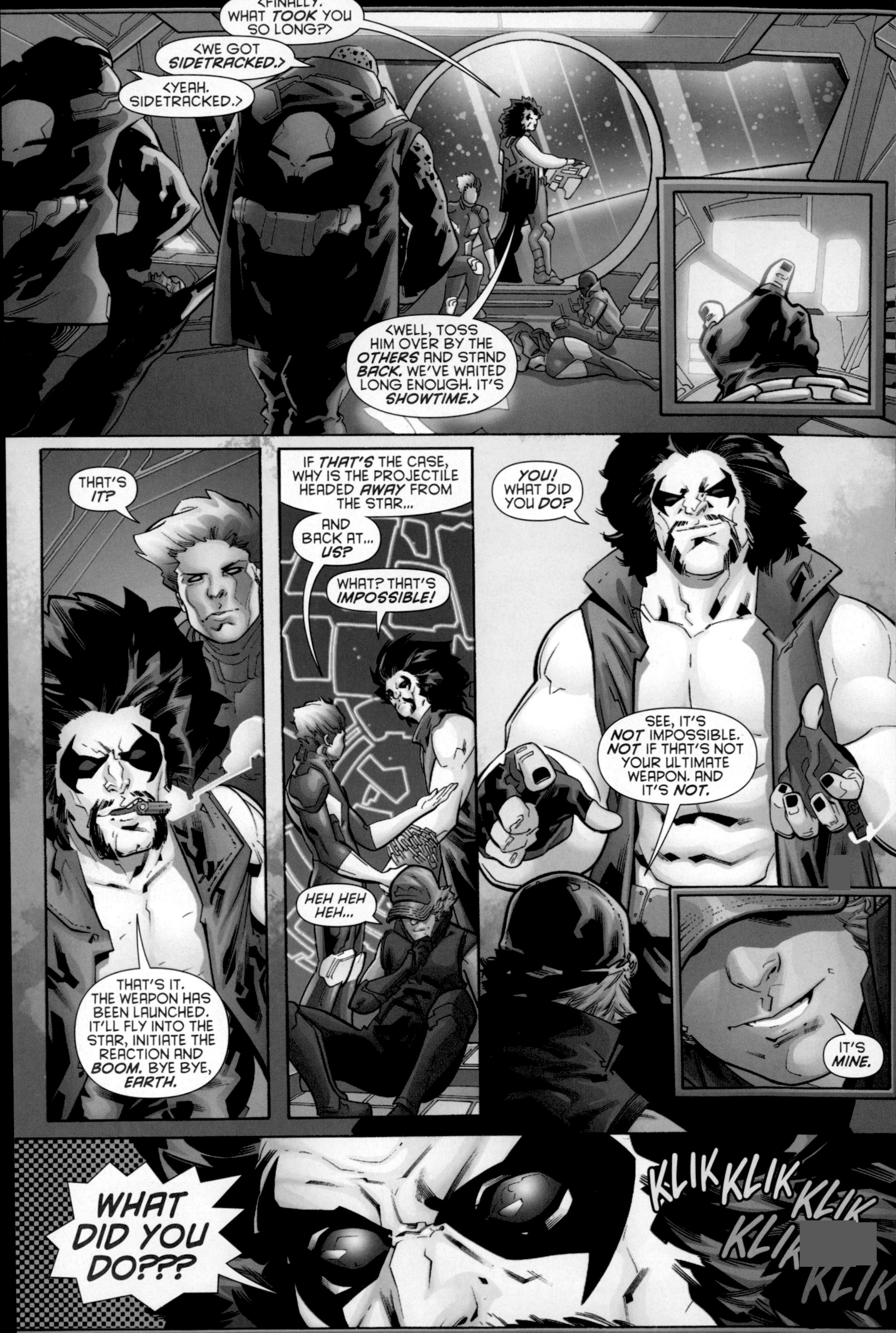

<FINALLY. WHAT TOOK YOU SO LONG?>
<WE GOT SIDETRACKED.>
<YEAH. SIDETRACKED.>
<WELL, TOSS HIM OVER BY THE OTHERS AND STAND BACK. WE'VE WAITED LONG ENOUGH. IT'S SHOWTIME.>
THAT'S IT?
THAT'S IT. THE WEAPON HAS BEEN LAUNCHED. IT'LL FLY INTO THE STAR, INITIATE THE REACTION AND BOOM. BYE BYE, EARTH.
IF THAT'S THE CASE, WHY IS THE PROJECTILE HEADED AWAY FROM THE STAR...
AND BACK AT... US?
WHAT? THAT'S IMPOSSIBLE!
HEH HEH HEH...
YOU! WHAT DID YOU DO?
SEE, IT'S NOT IMPOSSIBLE. NOT IF THAT'S NOT YOUR ULTIMATE WEAPON. AND IT'S NOT.
IT'S MINE.
WHAT DID YOU DO???
K-LIK KLIK KLIK KLIK KLIK

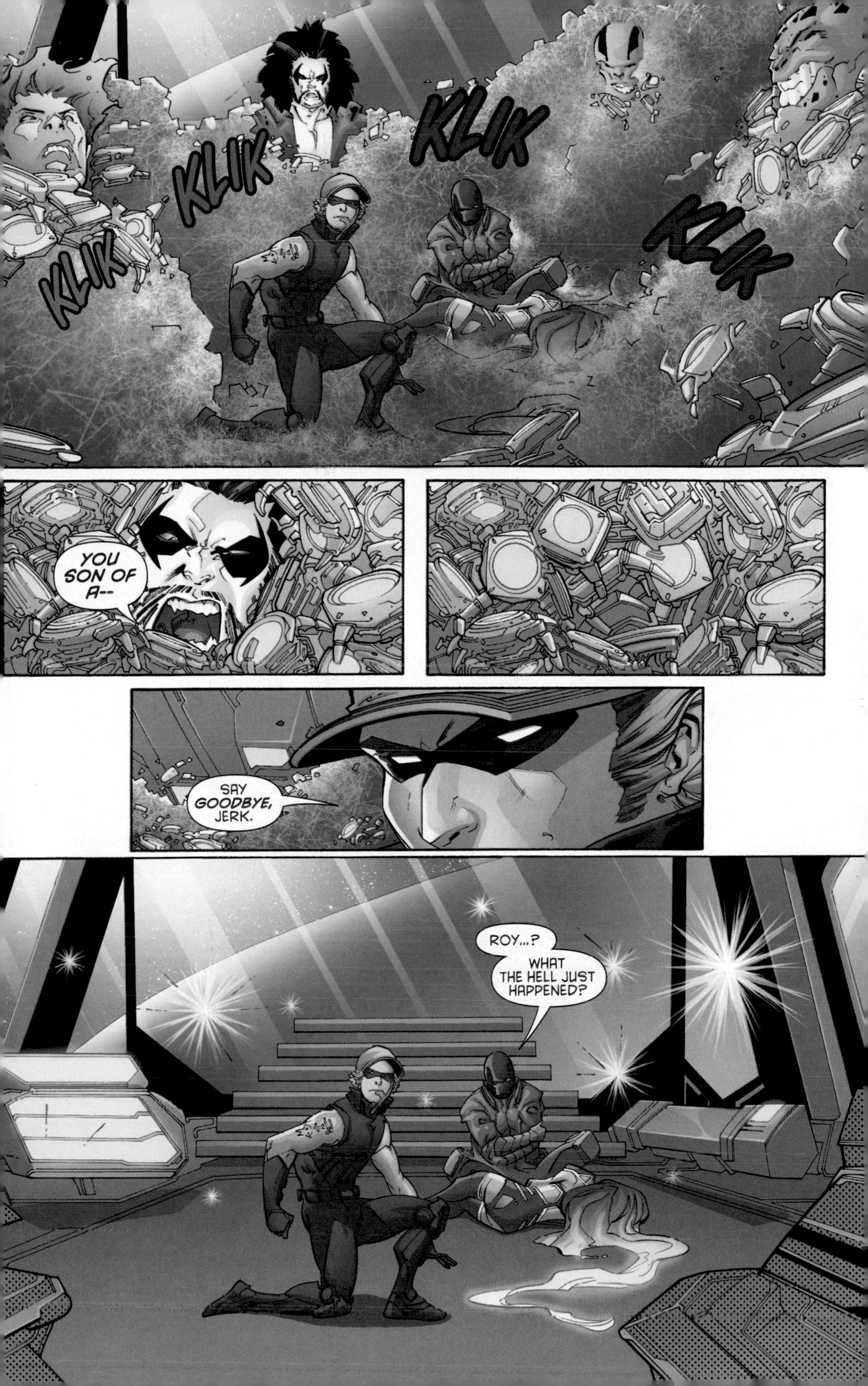
KLIK
KLIK
KLIK
KLIK
YOU SON OF A--
SAY GOODBYE, JERK.
ROY...? WHAT THE HELL JUST HAPPENED?

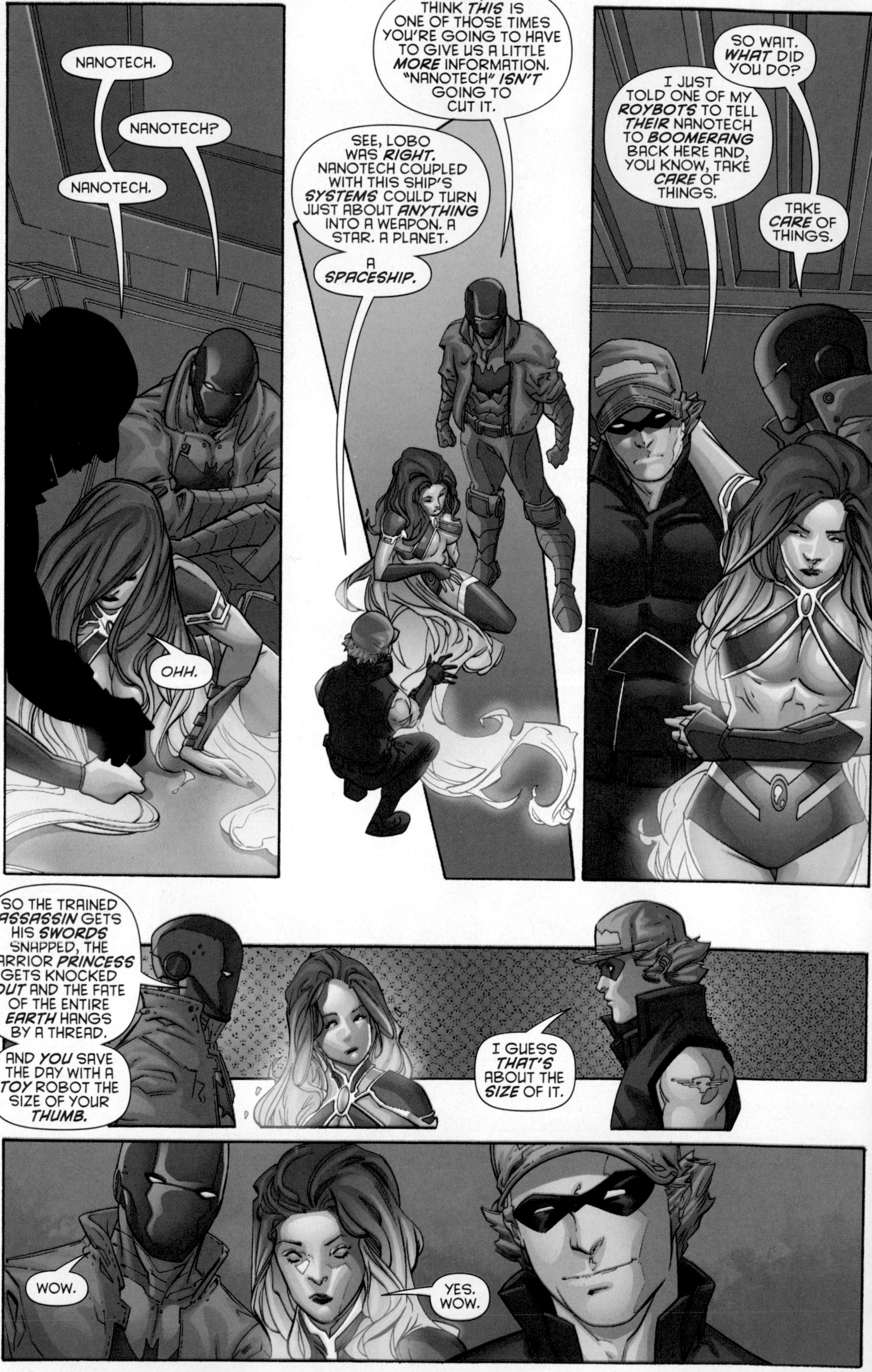
NANOTECH.
NANOTECH?
NANOTECH.
OHH.
ROY, I THINK THIS IS ONE OF THOSE TIMES YOU'RE GOING TO HAVE TO GIVE US A LITTLE MORE INFORMATION. "NANOTECH" ISN'T GOING TO CUT IT.
SEE, LOBO WAS RIGHT. NANOTECH COUPLED WITH THIS SHIP'S SYSTEMS COULD TURN JUST ABOUT ANYTHING INTO A WEAPON. A STAR. A PLANET.
A SPACESHIP.
SO WAIT. WHAT DID YOU DO?
I JUST TOLD ONE OF MY ROYBOTS TO TELL THEIR NANOTECH TO BOOMERANG BACK HERE AND, YOU KNOW, TAKE CARE OF THINGS.
TAKE CARE OF THINGS.
SO THE TRAINED ASSASSIN GETS HIS SWORDS SNAPPED, THE WARRIOR PRINCESS GETS KNOCKED OUT AND THE FATE OF THE ENTIRE EARTH HANGS BY A THREAD.
AND YOU SAVE THE DAY WITH A TOY ROBOT THE SIZE OF YOUR THUMB.
I GUESS THAT'S ABOUT THE SIZE OF IT.
WOW.
YES. WOW.

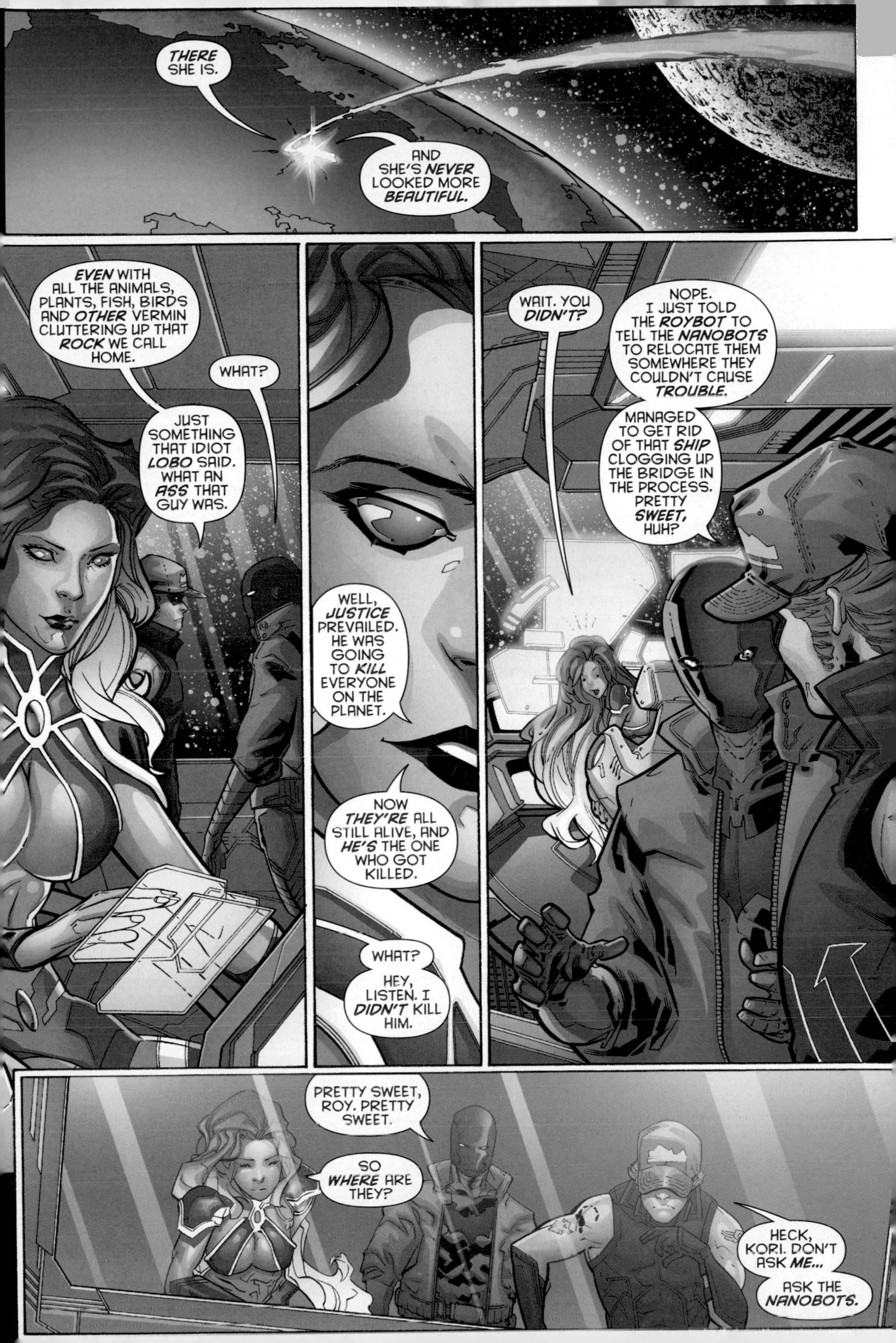

THERE SHE IS.
AND SHE'S NEVER LOOKED MORE BEAUTIFUL.
EVEN WITH ALL THE ANIMALS, PLANTS, FISH, BIRDS AND OTHER VERMIN CLUTTERING UP THAT ROCK WE CALL HOME.
WHAT?
JUST SOMETHING THAT IDIOT LOBO SAID. WHAT AN ASS THAT GUY WAS.
WELL, JUSTICE PREVAILED. HE WAS GOING TO KILL EVERYONE ON THE PLANET.
NOW THEY'RE ALL STILL ALIVE, AND HE'S THE ONE WHO GOT KILLED.
WHAT?
HEY, LISTEN. I DIDN'T KILL HIM.
WAIT. YOU DIDN'T?
NOPE. I JUST TOLD THE ROYBOT TO TELL THE NANOBOTS TO RELOCATE THEM SOMEWHERE THEY COULDN'T CAUSE TROUBLE.
MANAGED TO GET RID OF THAT SHIP CLOGGING UP THE BRIDGE IN THE PROCESS. PRETTY SWEET, HUH?
PRETTY SWEET, ROY. PRETTY SWEET.
SO WHERE ARE THEY?
HECK, KORI. DON'T ASK ME...
ASK THE NANOBOTS.

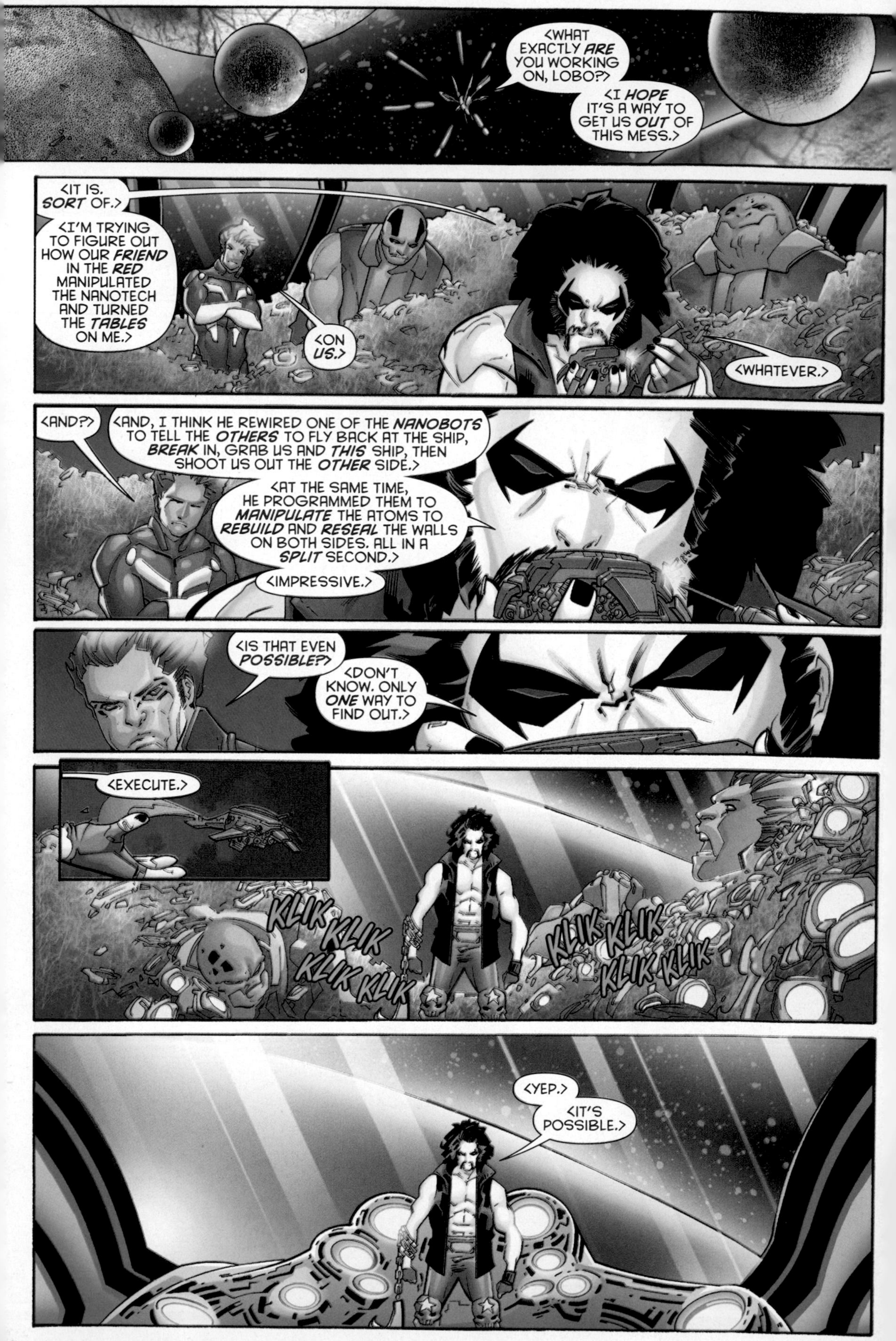
<WHAT EXACTLY ARE YOU WORKING ON, LOBO?>
<I HOPE IT'S A WAY TO GET US OUT OF THIS MESS.>
<IT IS. SORT OF.>
<I'M TRYING TO FIGURE OUT HOW OUR FRIEND IN THE RED MANIPULATED THE NANOTECH AND TURNED THE TABLES ON ME.>
<ON US.>
<WHATEVER.>
<AND?>
<AND, I THINK HE REWIRED ONE OF THE NANOBOTS TO TELL THE OTHERS TO FLY BACK AT THE SHIP, BREAK IN, GRAB US AND THIS SHIP, THEN SHOOT US OUT THE OTHER SIDE.>
<AT THE SAME TIME, HE PROGRAMMED THEM TO MANIPULATE THE ATOMS TO REBUILD AND RESEAL THE WALLS ON BOTH SIDES. ALL IN A SPLIT SECOND.>
<IMPRESSIVE.>
<IS THAT EVEN POSSIBLE?>
<DON'T KNOW. ONLY ONE WAY TO FIND OUT.>
<EXECUTE.>
KLIK KLIK KLIK KLIK
KLIK KLIK KLIK KLIK
<YEP.>
<IT'S POSSIBLE.>

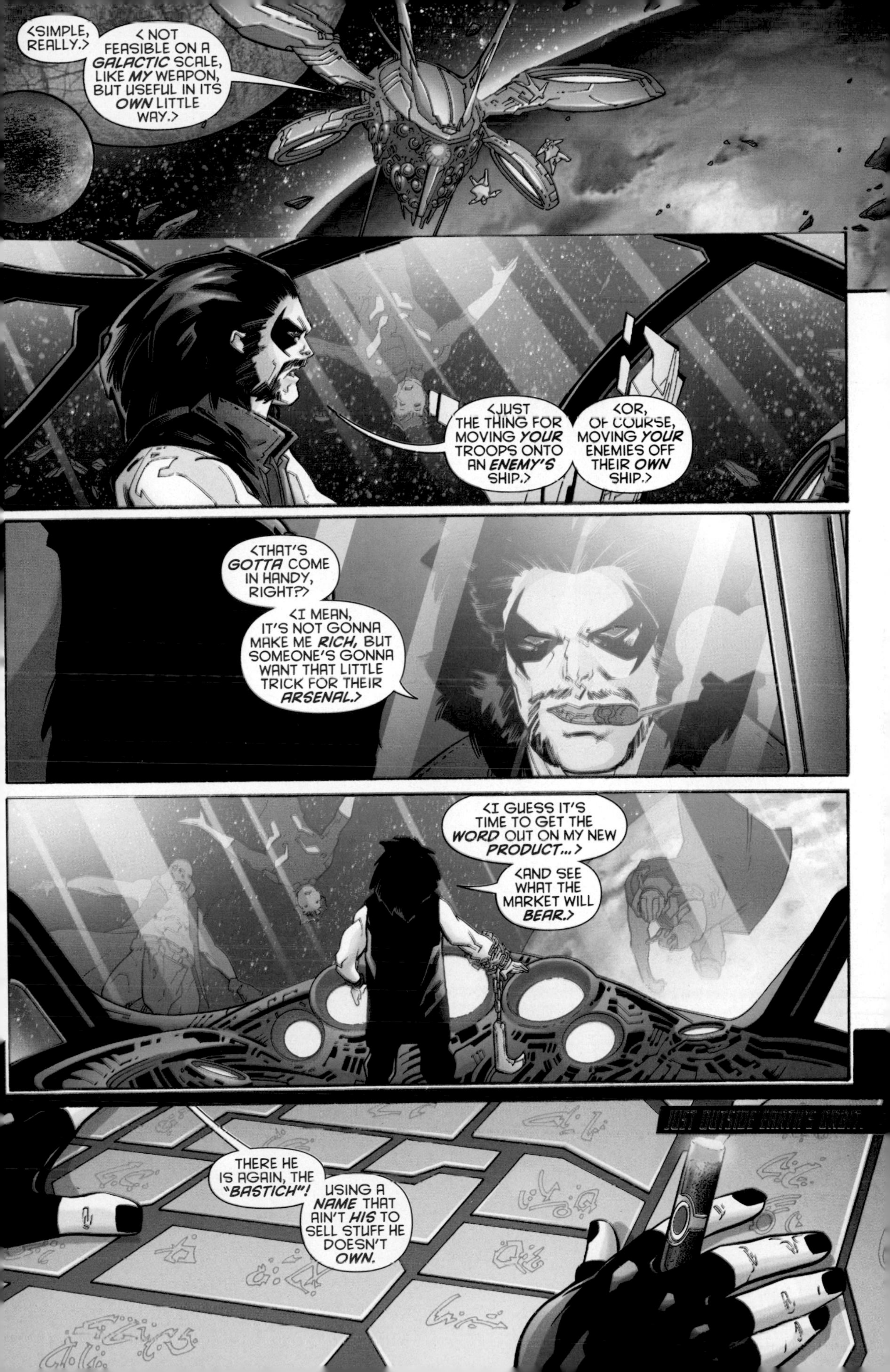

<SIMPLE, REALLY.>
< NOT FEASIBLE ON A GALACTIC SCALE, LIKE MY WEAPON, BUT USEFUL IN ITS OWN LITTLE WAY.>
<JUST THE THING FOR MOVING YOUR TROOPS ONTO AN ENEMY'S SHIP.>
<OR, OF COURSE, MOVING YOUR ENEMIES OFF THEIR OWN SHIP.>
<THAT'S GOTTA COME IN HANDY, RIGHT?>
<I MEAN, IT'S NOT GONNA MAKE ME RICH, BUT SOMEONE'S GONNA WANT THAT LITTLE TRICK FOR THEIR ARSENAL.>
<I GUESS IT'S TIME TO GET THE WORD OUT ON MY NEW PRODUCT...>
<AND SEE WHAT THE MARKET WILL BEAR.>
JUST OUTSIDE EARTH'S ORBIT.
THERE HE IS AGAIN, THE "BASTICH"!
USING A NAME THAT AIN'T HIS TO SELL STUFF HE DOESN'T OWN.

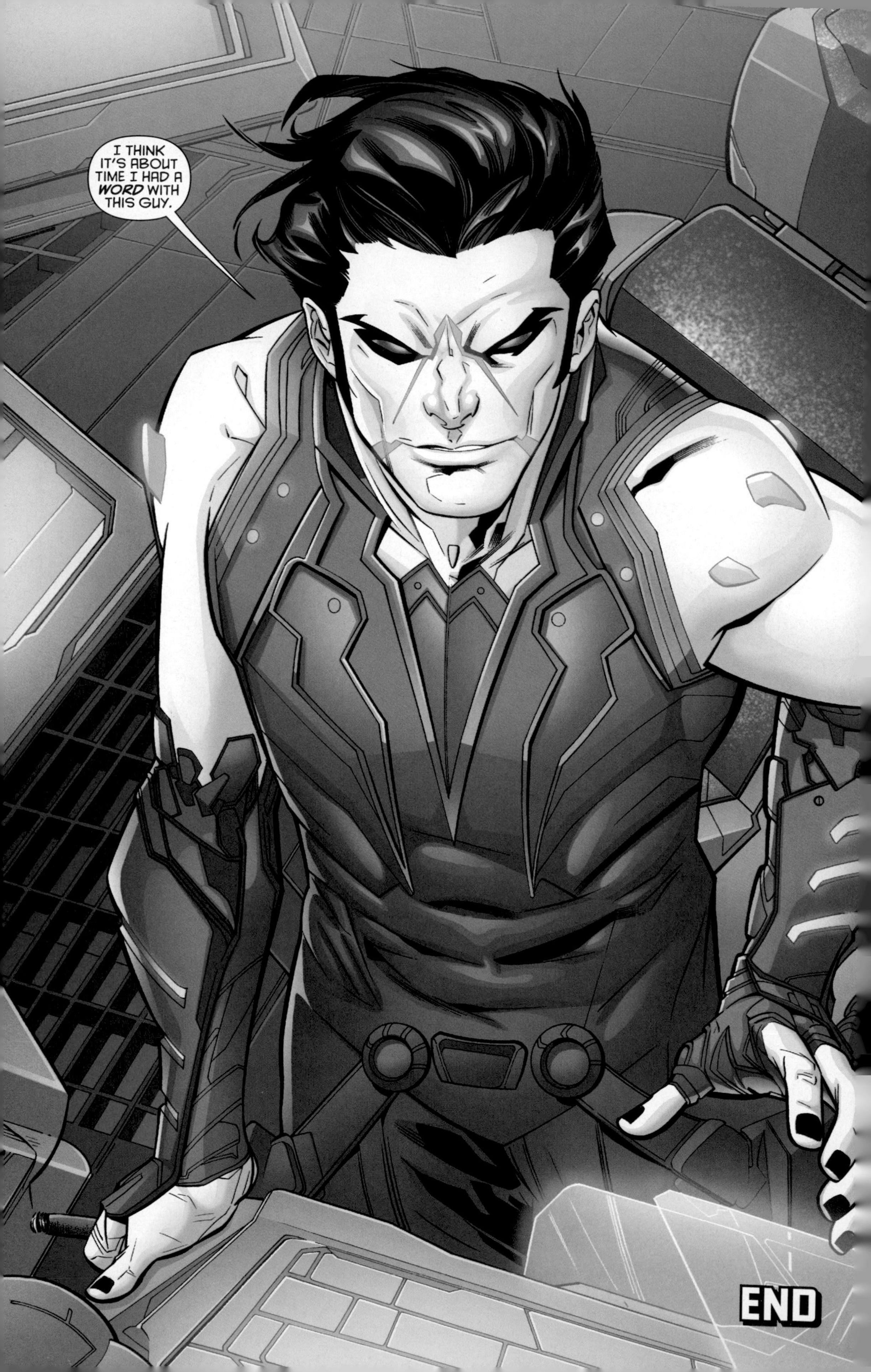
I THINK IT'S ABOUT TIME I HAD A WORD WITH THIS GUY.
END

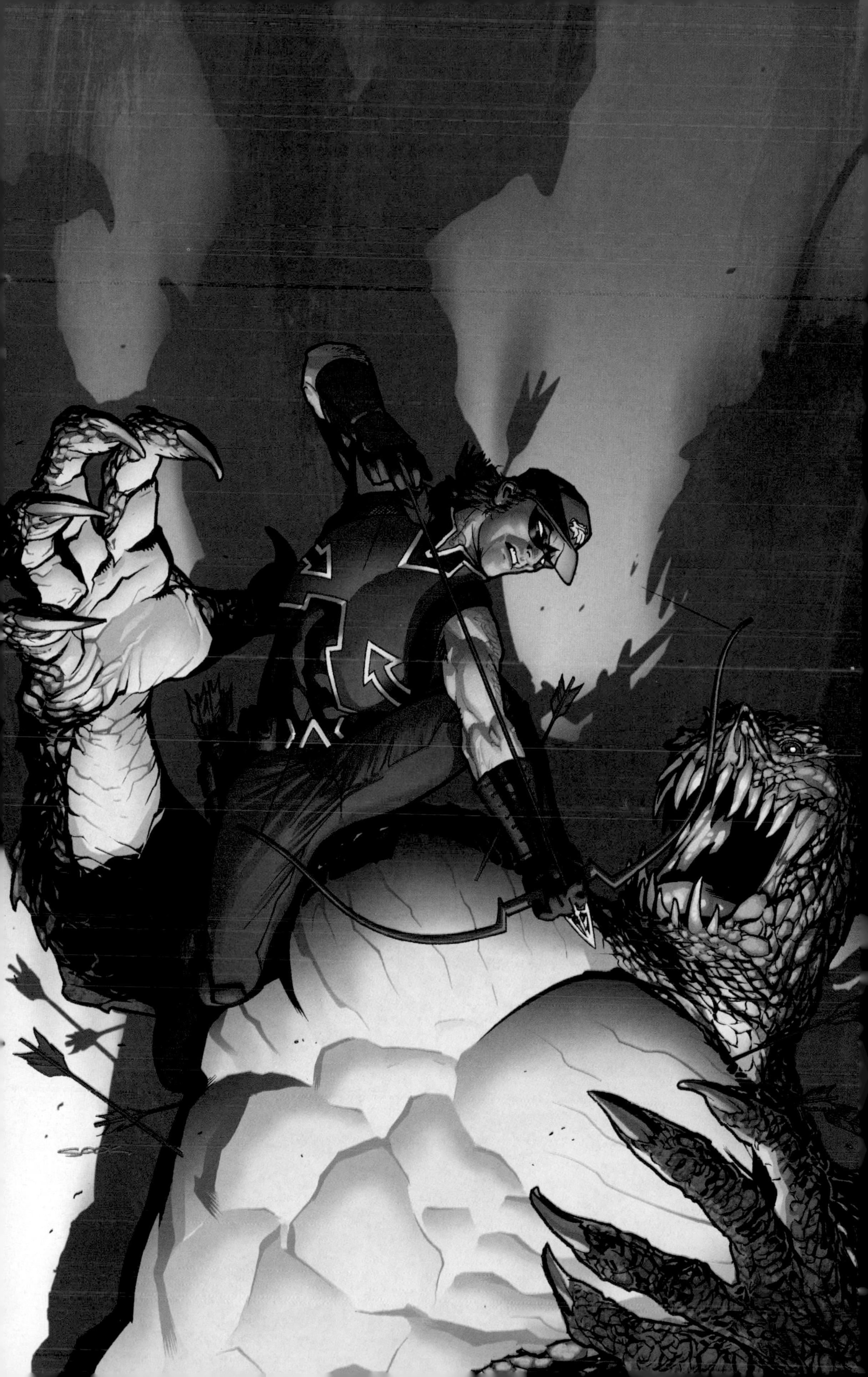

ROY'S NIGHT OUT

JOE KEATINGE writer RICKEN artist PETE PANTAZIS colorist DEZI SIENTY letterer cover art by RYAN SOOK

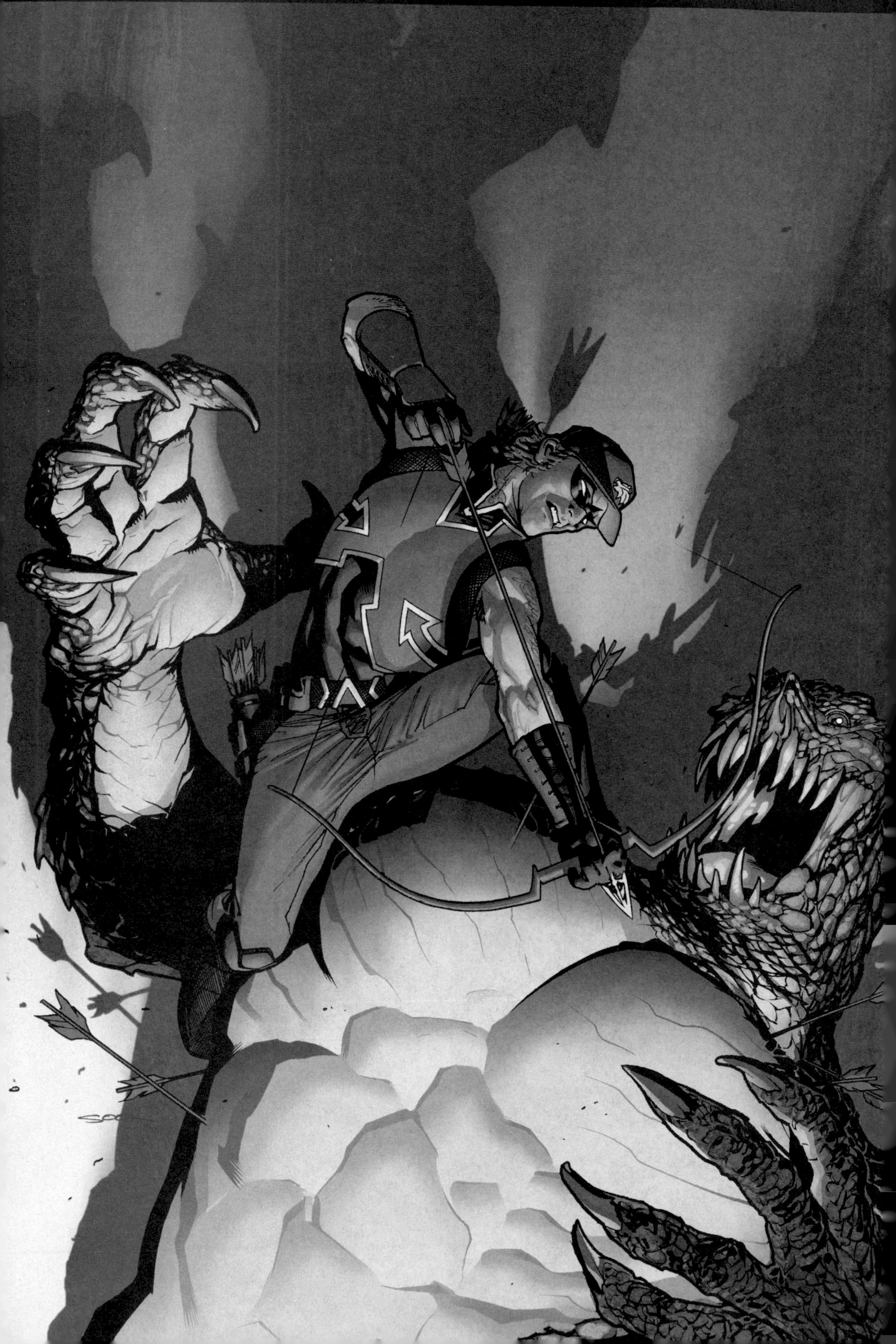

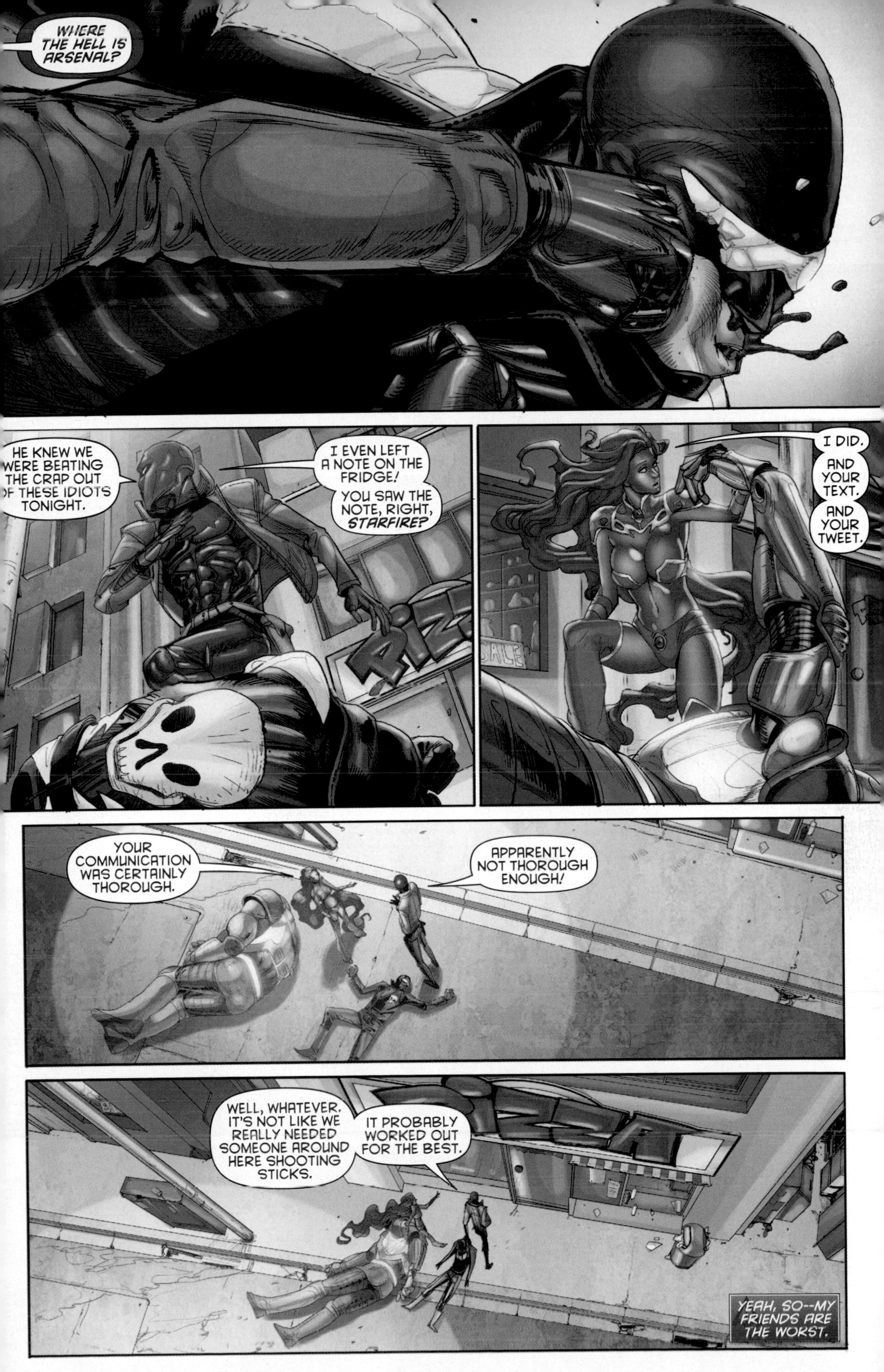
WHERE THE HELL IS ARSENAL?
HE KNEW WE WERE BEATING THE CRAP OUT OF THESE IDIOTS TONIGHT.
I EVEN LEFT A NOTE ON THE FRIDGE!
YOU SAW THE NOTE, RIGHT, STARFIRE?
I DID.
AND YOUR TEXT.
AND YOUR TWEET.
YOUR COMMUNICATION WAS CERTAINLY THOROUGH.
APPARENTLY NOT THOROUGH ENOUGH!
WELL, WHATEVER. IT'S NOT LIKE WE REALLY NEEDED SOMEONE AROUND HERE SHOOTING STICKS.
IT PROBABLY WORKED OUT FOR THE BEST.
YEAH, SO--MY FRIENDS ARE THE WORST.

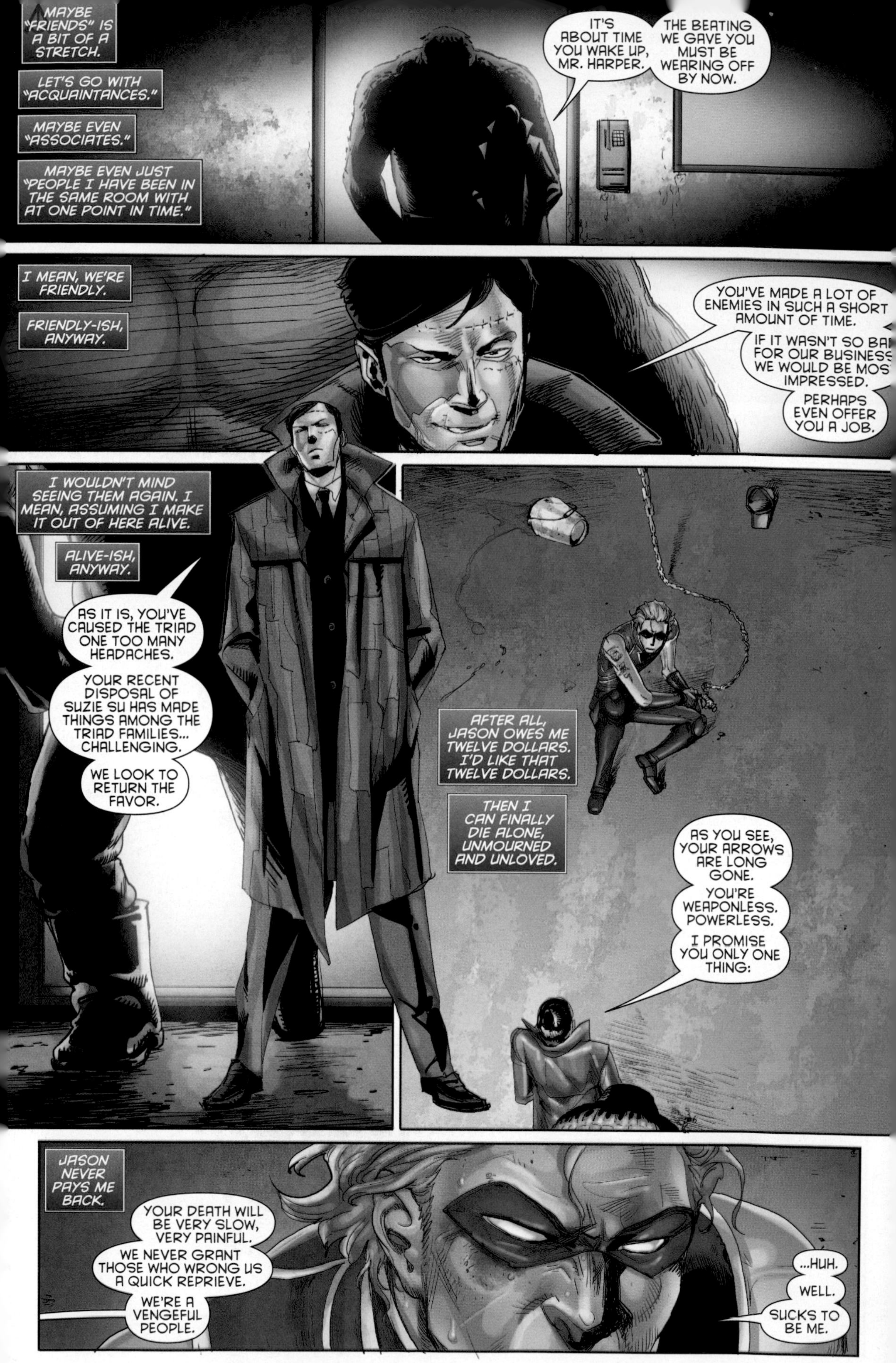

MAYBE "FRIENDS" IS A BIT OF A STRETCH.
LET'S GO WITH "ACQUAINTANCES."
MAYBE EVEN "ASSOCIATES."
MAYBE EVEN JUST "PEOPLE I HAVE BEEN IN THE SAME ROOM WITH AT ONE POINT IN TIME."
IT'S ABOUT TIME YOU WAKE UP, MR. HARPER.
THE BEATING WE GAVE YOU MUST BE WEARING OFF BY NOW.
I MEAN, WE'RE FRIENDLY.
FRIENDLY-ISH, ANYWAY.
YOU'VE MADE A LOT OF ENEMIES IN SUCH A SHORT AMOUNT OF TIME.
IF IT WASN'T SO BA FOR OUR BUSINESS WE WOULD BE MOS IMPRESSED.
PERHAPS EVEN OFFER YOU A JOB.
I WOULDN'T MIND SEEING THEM AGAIN. I MEAN, ASSUMING I MAKE IT OUT OF HERE ALIVE.
ALIVE-ISH, ANYWAY.
AS IT IS, YOU'VE CAUSED THE TRIAD ONE TOO MANY HEADACHES.
YOUR RECENT DISPOSAL OF SUZIE SU HAS MADE THINGS AMONG THE TRIAD FAMILIES... CHALLENGING.
WE LOOK TO RETURN THE FAVOR.
AFTER ALL, JASON OWES ME TWELVE DOLLARS. I'D LIKE THAT TWELVE DOLLARS.
THEN I CAN FINALLY DIE ALONE, UNMOURNED AND UNLOVED.
AS YOU SEE, YOUR ARROWS ARE LONG GONE.
YOU'RE WEAPONLESS. POWERLESS.
I PROMISE YOU ONLY ONE THING:
JASON NEVER PAYS ME BACK.
YOUR DEATH WILL BE VERY SLOW, VERY PAINFUL.
WE NEVER GRANT THOSE WHO WRONG US A QUICK REPRIEVE.
WE'RE A VENGEFUL PEOPLE.
...HUH.
WELL.
SUCKS TO BE ME.

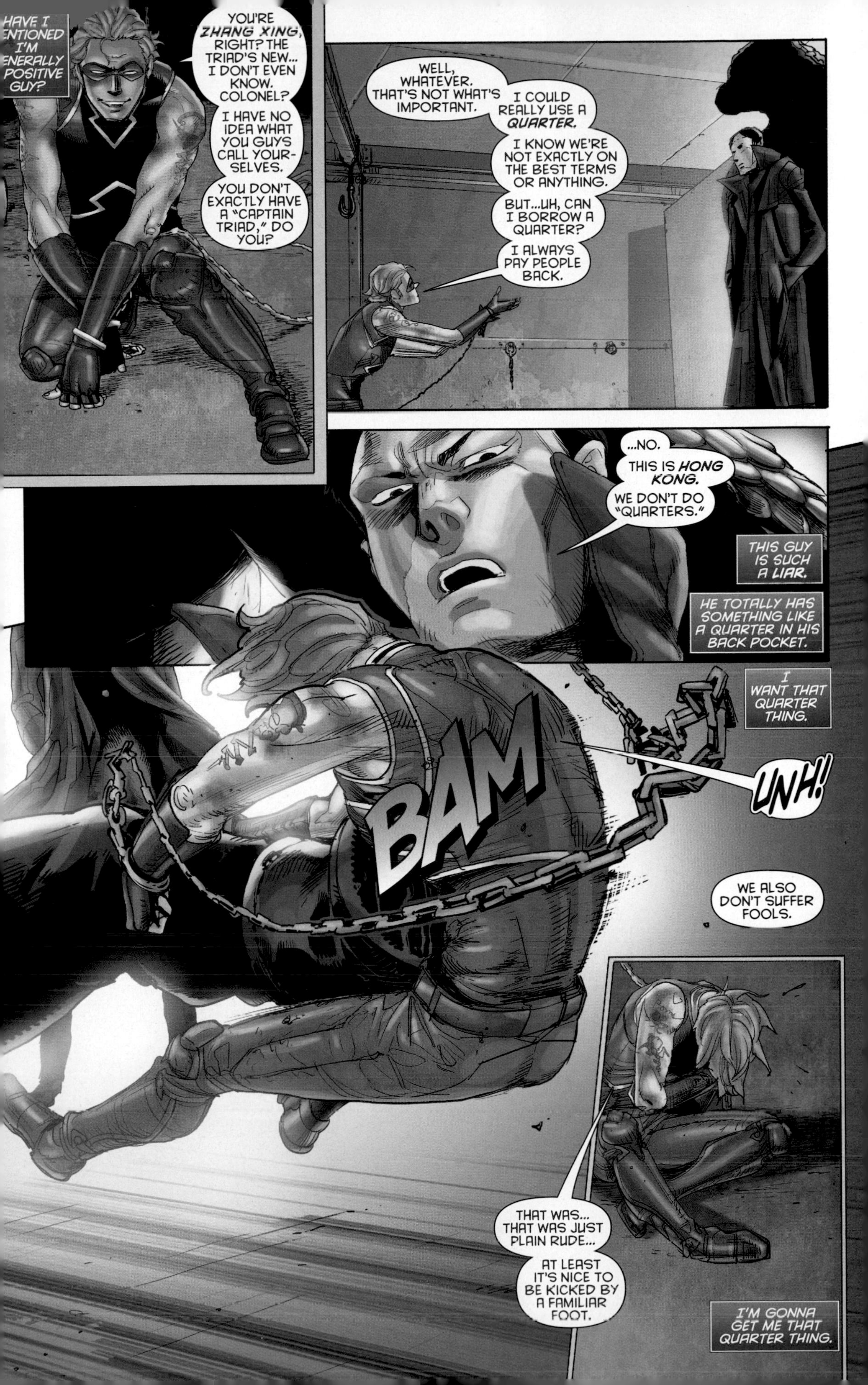
HAVE I ENTIONED I'M ENERALLY POSITIVE GUY?
YOU'RE ZHANG XING, RIGHT? THE TRIAD'S NEW... I DON'T EVEN KNOW. COLONEL?
I HAVE NO IDEA WHAT YOU GUYS CALL YOURSELVES.
YOU DON'T EXACTLY HAVE A "CAPTAIN TRIAD," DO YOU?
WELL, WHATEVER. THAT'S NOT WHAT'S IMPORTANT.
I COULD REALLY USE A QUARTER.
I KNOW WE'RE NOT EXACTLY ON THE BEST TERMS OR ANYTHING.
BUT...UH, CAN I BORROW A QUARTER?
I ALWAYS PAY PEOPLE BACK.
...NO.
THIS IS HONG KONG.
WE DON'T DO "QUARTERS."
THIS GUY IS SUCH A LIAR.
HE TOTALLY HAS SOMETHING LIKE A QUARTER IN HIS BACK POCKET.
I WANT THAT QUARTER THING.
BAM
UNH!
WE ALSO DON'T SUFFER FOOLS.
THAT WAS... THAT WAS JUST PLAIN RUDE...
AT LEAST IT'S NICE TO BE KICKED BY A FAMILIAR FOOT.
I'M GONNA GET ME THAT QUARTER THING.

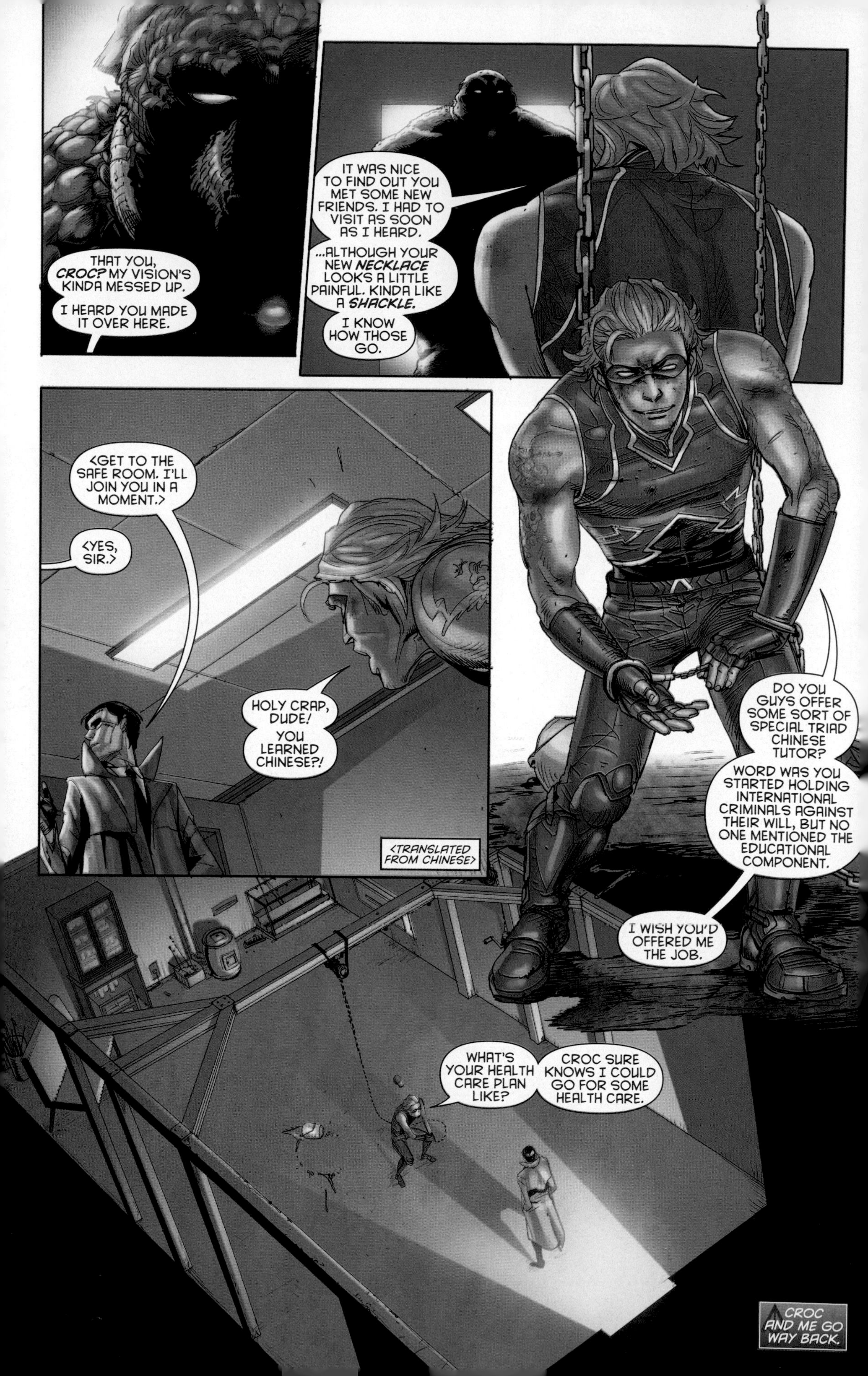
THAT YOU, CROC? MY VISION'S KINDA MESSED UP.
I HEARD YOU MADE IT OVER HERE.
IT WAS NICE TO FIND OUT YOU MET SOME NEW FRIENDS. I HAD TO VISIT AS SOON AS I HEARD.
...ALTHOUGH YOUR NEW NECKLACE LOOKS A LITTLE PAINFUL. KINDA LIKE A SHACKLE.
I KNOW HOW THOSE GO.
<GET TO THE SAFE ROOM. I'LL JOIN YOU IN A MOMENT.>
<YES, SIR.>
HOLY CRAP, DUDE!
YOU LEARNED CHINESE?!
<TRANSLATED FROM CHINESE>
DO YOU GUYS OFFER SOME SORT OF SPECIAL TRIAD CHINESE TUTOR?
WORD WAS YOU STARTED HOLDING INTERNATIONAL CRIMINALS AGAINST THEIR WILL, BUT NO ONE MENTIONED THE EDUCATIONAL COMPONENT.
I WISH YOU'D OFFERED ME THE JOB.
WHAT'S YOUR HEALTH CARE PLAN LIKE?
CROC SURE KNOWS I COULD GO FOR SOME HEALTH CARE.
CROC AND ME GO WAY BACK.

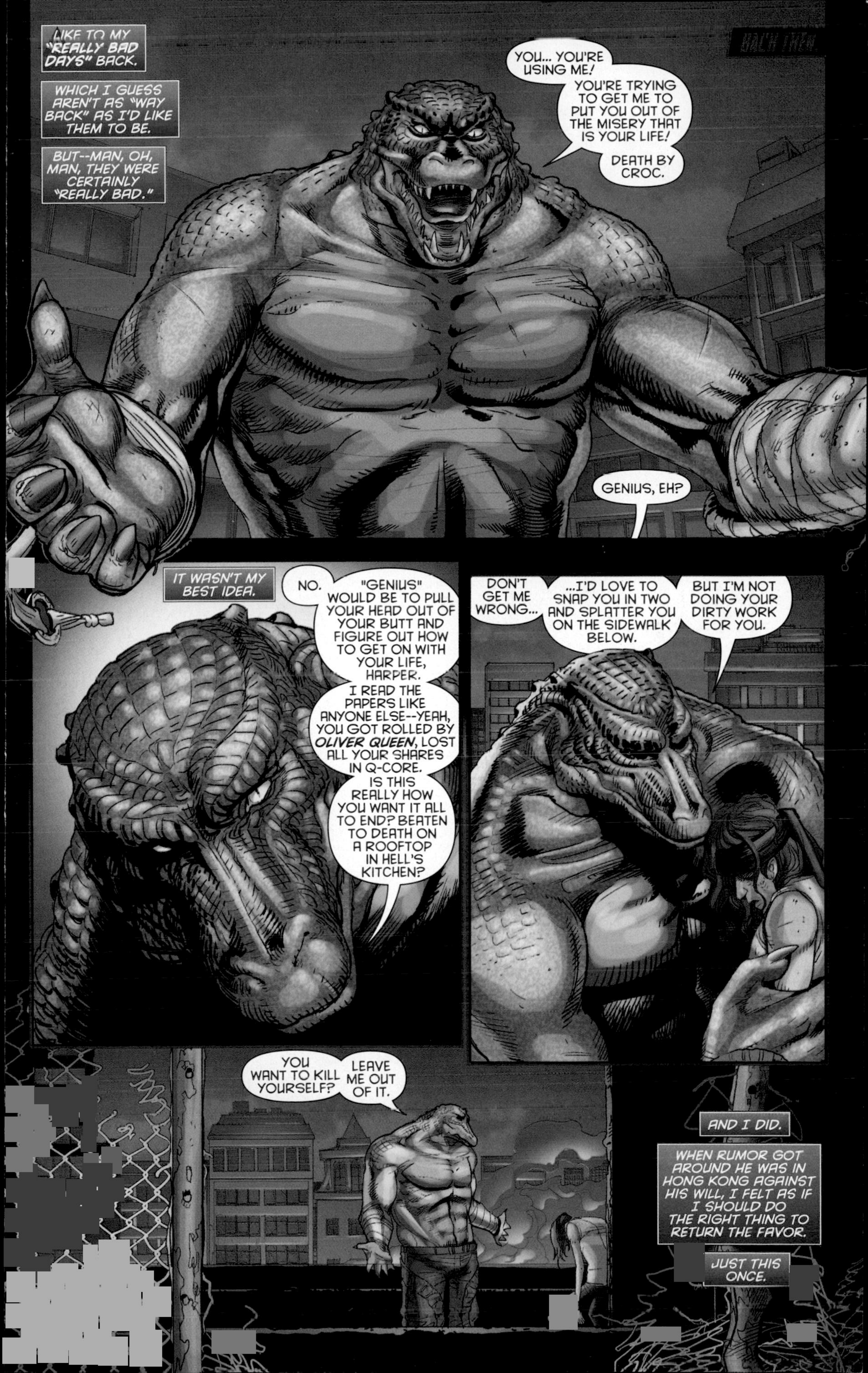
LIKE TO MY "REALLY BAD DAYS" BACK.
WHICH I GUESS AREN'T AS "WAY BACK" AS I'D LIKE THEM TO BE.
BUT--MAN, OH, MAN, THEY WERE CERTAINLY "REALLY BAD."
YOU... YOU'RE USING ME!
YOU'RE TRYING TO GET ME TO PUT YOU OUT OF THE MISERY THAT IS YOUR LIFE!
DEATH BY CROC.
GENIUS, EH?
IT WASN'T MY BEST IDEA.
NO.
"GENIUS" WOULD BE TO PULL YOUR HEAD OUT OF YOUR BUTT AND FIGURE OUT HOW TO GET ON WITH YOUR LIFE, HARPER.
I READ THE PAPERS LIKE ANYONE ELSE--YEAH, YOU GOT ROLLED BY OLIVER QUEEN, LOST ALL YOUR SHARES IN Q-CORE.
IS THIS REALLY HOW YOU WANT IT ALL TO END? BEATEN TO DEATH ON A ROOFTOP IN HELL'S KITCHEN?
DON'T GET ME WRONG...
...I'D LOVE TO SNAP YOU IN TWO AND SPLATTER YOU ON THE SIDEWALK BELOW.
BUT I'M NOT DOING YOUR DIRTY WORK FOR YOU.
YOU WANT TO KILL YOURSELF?
LEAVE ME OUT OF IT.
AND I DID.
WHEN RUMOR GOT AROUND HE WAS IN HONG KONG AGAINST HIS WILL, I FELT AS IF I SHOULD DO THE RIGHT THING TO RETURN THE FAVOR.
JUST THIS ONCE.

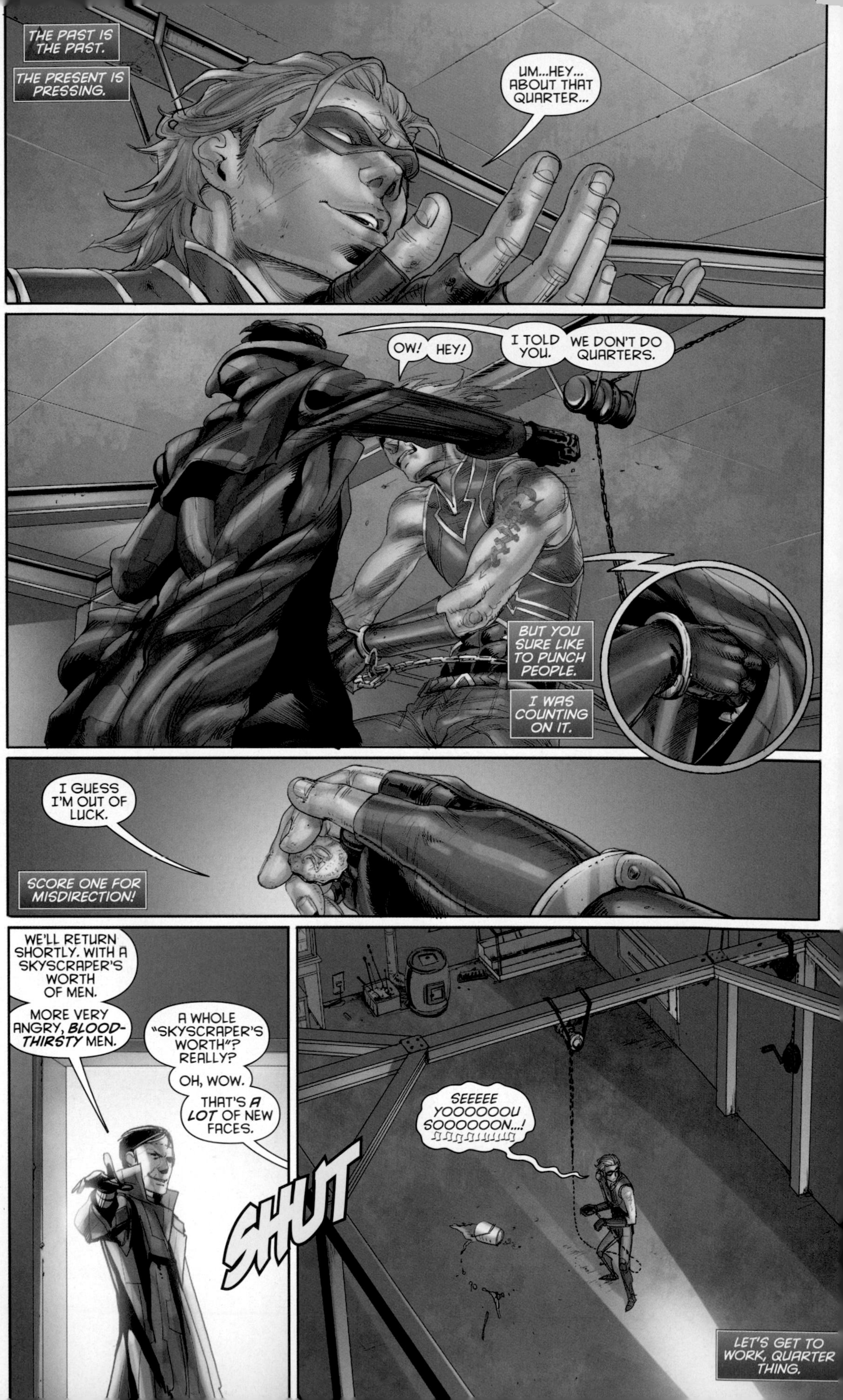

THE PAST IS THE PAST.
THE PRESENT IS PRESSING.
UM...HEY... ABOUT THAT QUARTER...
OW! HEY!
I TOLD YOU.
WE DON'T DO QUARTERS.
BUT YOU SURE LIKE TO PUNCH PEOPLE.
I WAS COUNTING ON IT.
I GUESS I'M OUT OF LUCK.
SCORE ONE FOR MISDIRECTION!
WE'LL RETURN SHORTLY. WITH A SKYSCRAPER'S WORTH OF MEN.
MORE VERY ANGRY, BLOOD-THIRSTY MEN.
A WHOLE "SKYSCRAPER'S WORTH"? REALLY?
OH, WOW.
THAT'S A LOT OF NEW FACES.
SHUT
SEEEEE YOOOOOOU SOOOOOON...!
LET'S GET TO WORK, QUARTER THING.

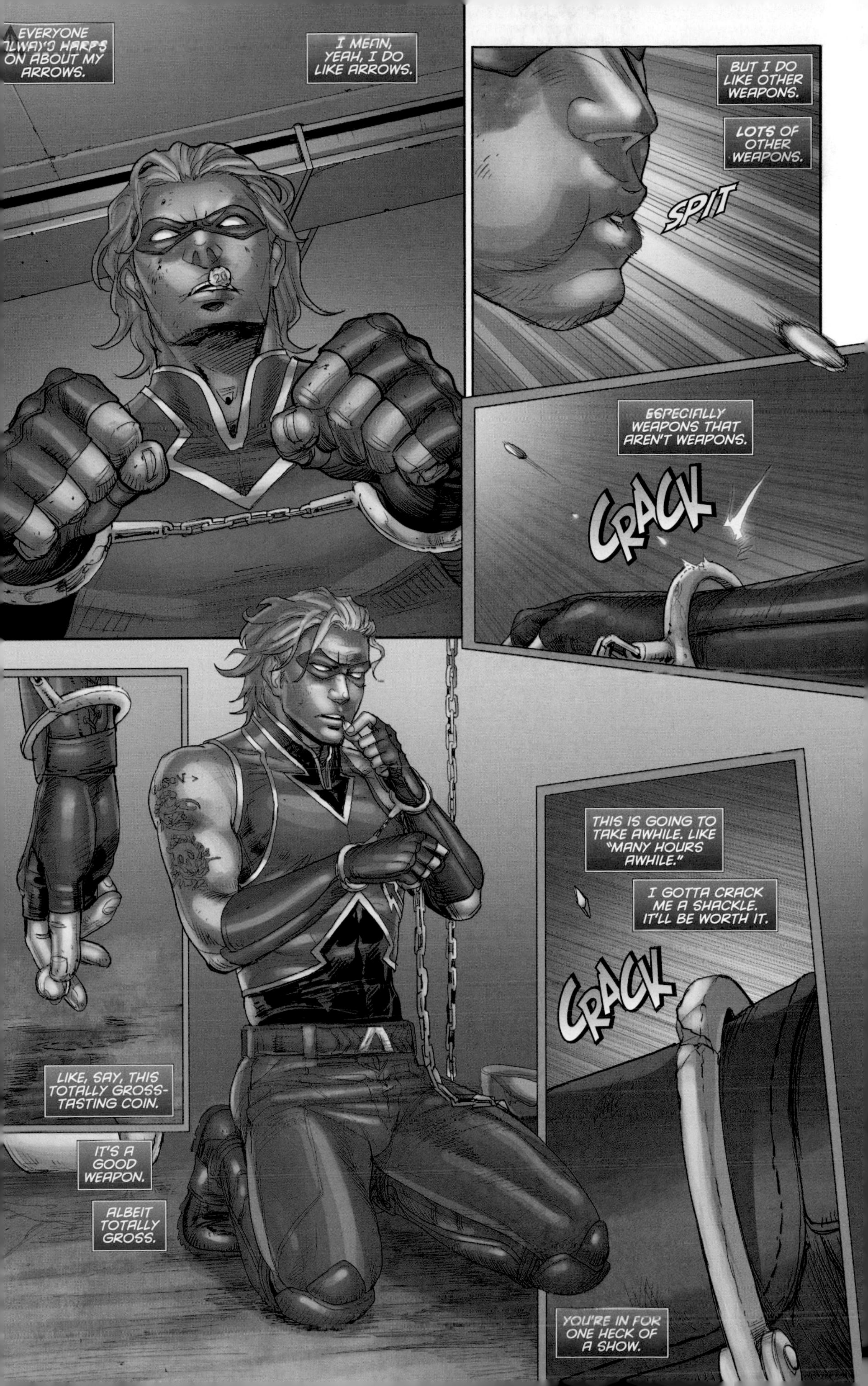
EVERYONE ALWAYS HARPS ON ABOUT MY ARROWS.
I MEAN, YEAH, I DO LIKE ARROWS.
BUT I DO LIKE OTHER WEAPONS.
LOTS OF OTHER WEAPONS.
SPIT
ESPECIALLY WEAPONS THAT AREN'T WEAPONS.
CRACK
LIKE, SAY, THIS TOTALLY GROSS-TASTING COIN.
IT'S A GOOD WEAPON.
ALBEIT TOTALLY GROSS.
THIS IS GOING TO TAKE AWHILE. LIKE "MANY HOURS AWHILE."
I GOTTA CRACK ME A SHACKLE. IT'LL BE WORTH IT.
CRACK
YOU'RE IN FOR ONE HECK OF A SHOW.

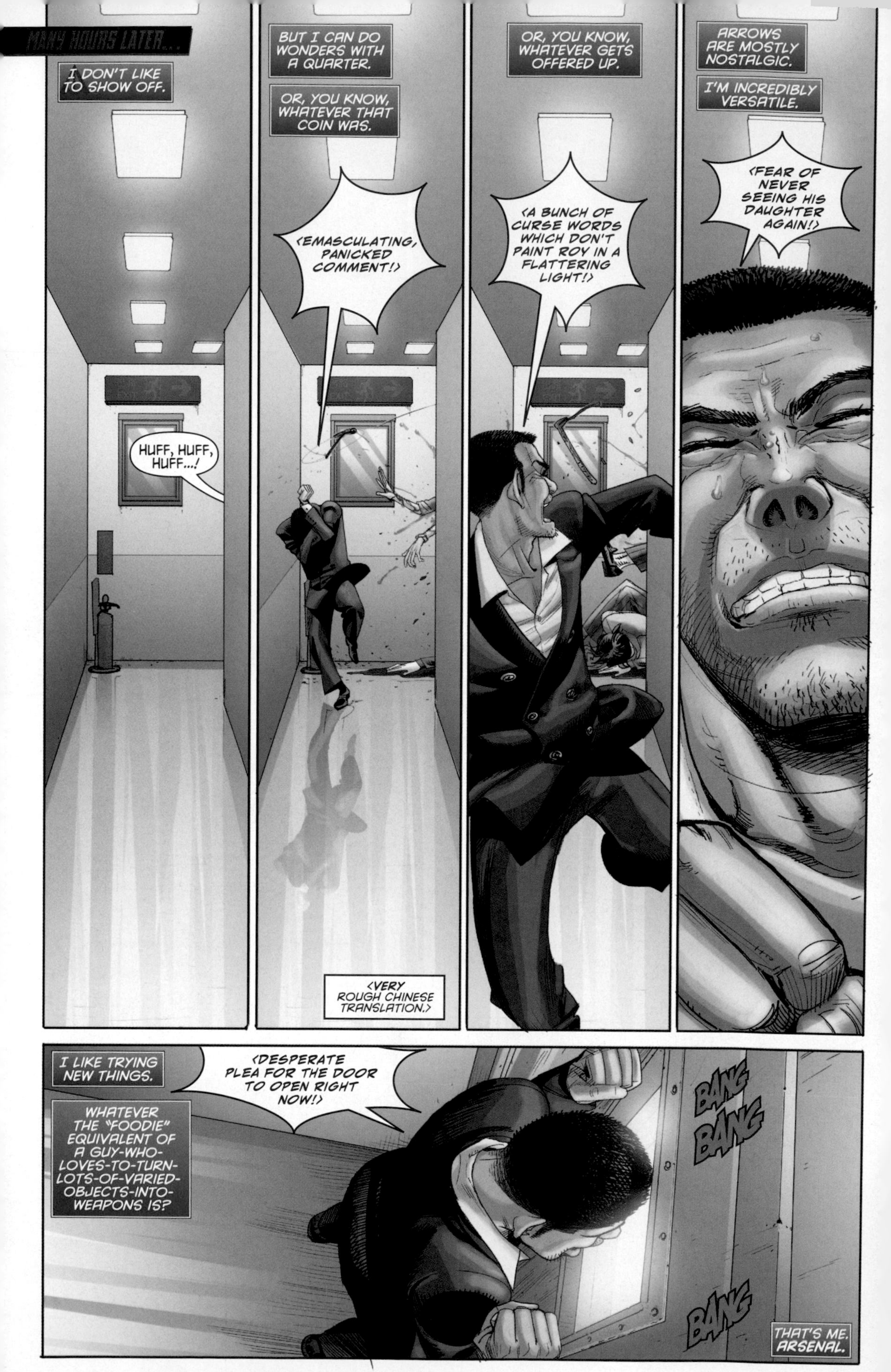

MANY HOURS LATER...
I DON'T LIKE TO SHOW OFF.
HUFF, HUFF, HUFF...!
BUT I CAN DO WONDERS WITH A QUARTER.
OR, YOU KNOW, WHATEVER THAT COIN WAS.
<EMASCULATING, PANICKED COMMENT!>
<VERY ROUGH CHINESE TRANSLATION.>
OR, YOU KNOW, WHATEVER GETS OFFERED UP.
<A BUNCH OF CURSE WORDS WHICH DON'T PAINT ROY IN A FLATTERING LIGHT!>
ARROWS ARE MOSTLY NOSTALGIC.
I'M INCREDIBLY VERSATILE.
<FEAR OF NEVER SEEING HIS DAUGHTER AGAIN!>
I LIKE TRYING NEW THINGS.
WHATEVER THE "FOODIE" EQUIVALENT OF A GUY-WHO-LOVES-TO-TURN-LOTS-OF-VARIED-OBJECTS-INTO-WEAPONS IS?
<DESPERATE PLEA FOR THE DOOR TO OPEN RIGHT NOW!>
BANG
BANG
BANG
THAT'S ME. ARSENAL.

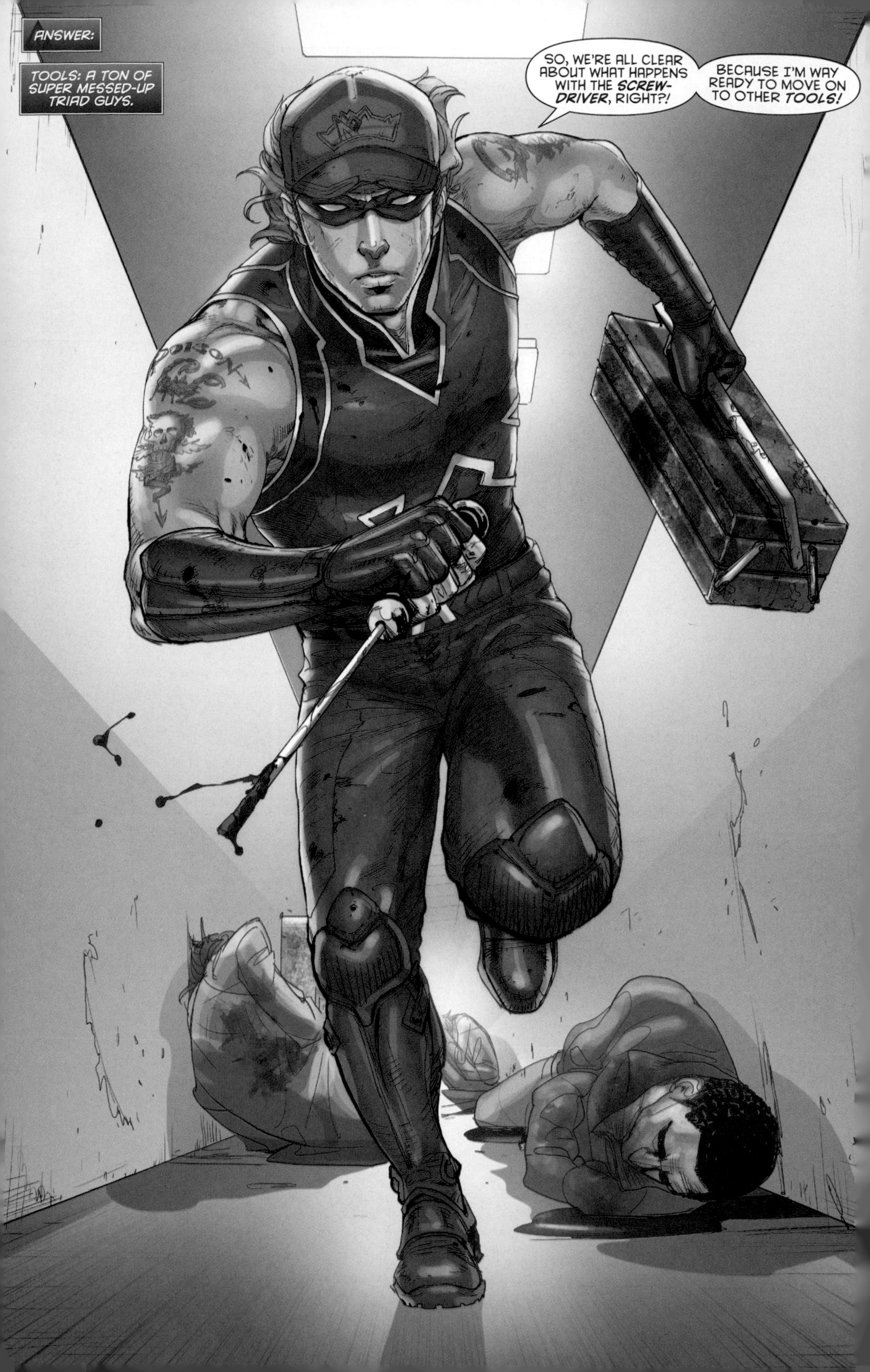
ANSWER:
TOOLS: A TON OF SUPER MESSED-UP TRIAD GUYS.
SO, WE'RE ALL CLEAR ABOUT WHAT HAPPENS WITH THE SCREW-DRIVER, RIGHT?!
BECAUSE I'M WAY READY TO MOVE ON TO OTHER TOOLS!

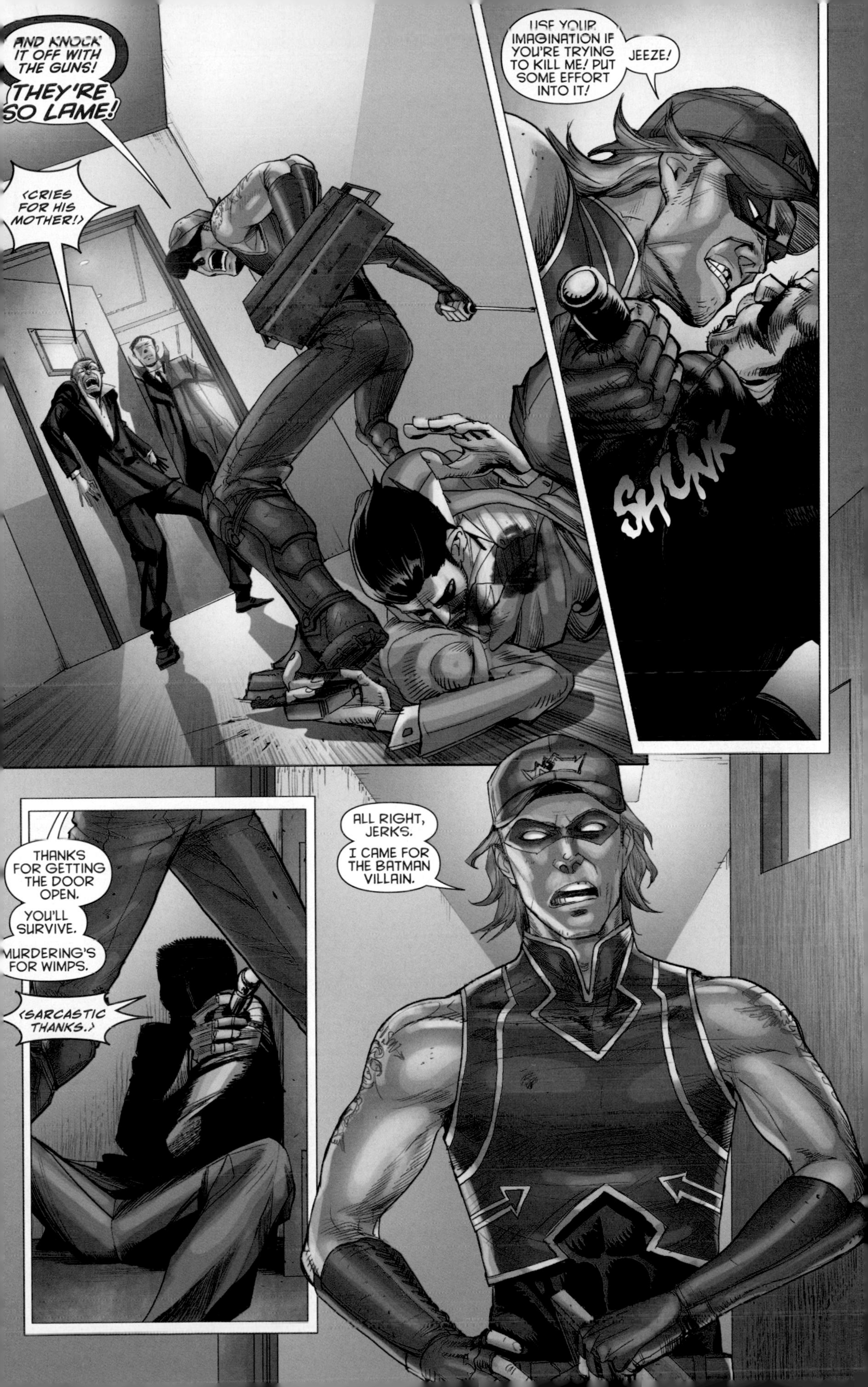
AND KNOCK IT OFF WITH THE GUNS!
THEY'RE SO LAME!
‹CRIES FOR HIS MOTHER!›
USE YOUR IMAGINATION IF YOU'RE TRYING TO KILL ME! PUT SOME EFFORT INTO IT!
JEEZE!
SHUNK
THANKS FOR GETTING THE DOOR OPEN.
YOU'LL SURVIVE.
MURDERING'S FOR WIMPS.
‹SARCASTIC THANKS.›
ALL RIGHT, JERKS.
I CAME FOR THE BATMAN VILLAIN.

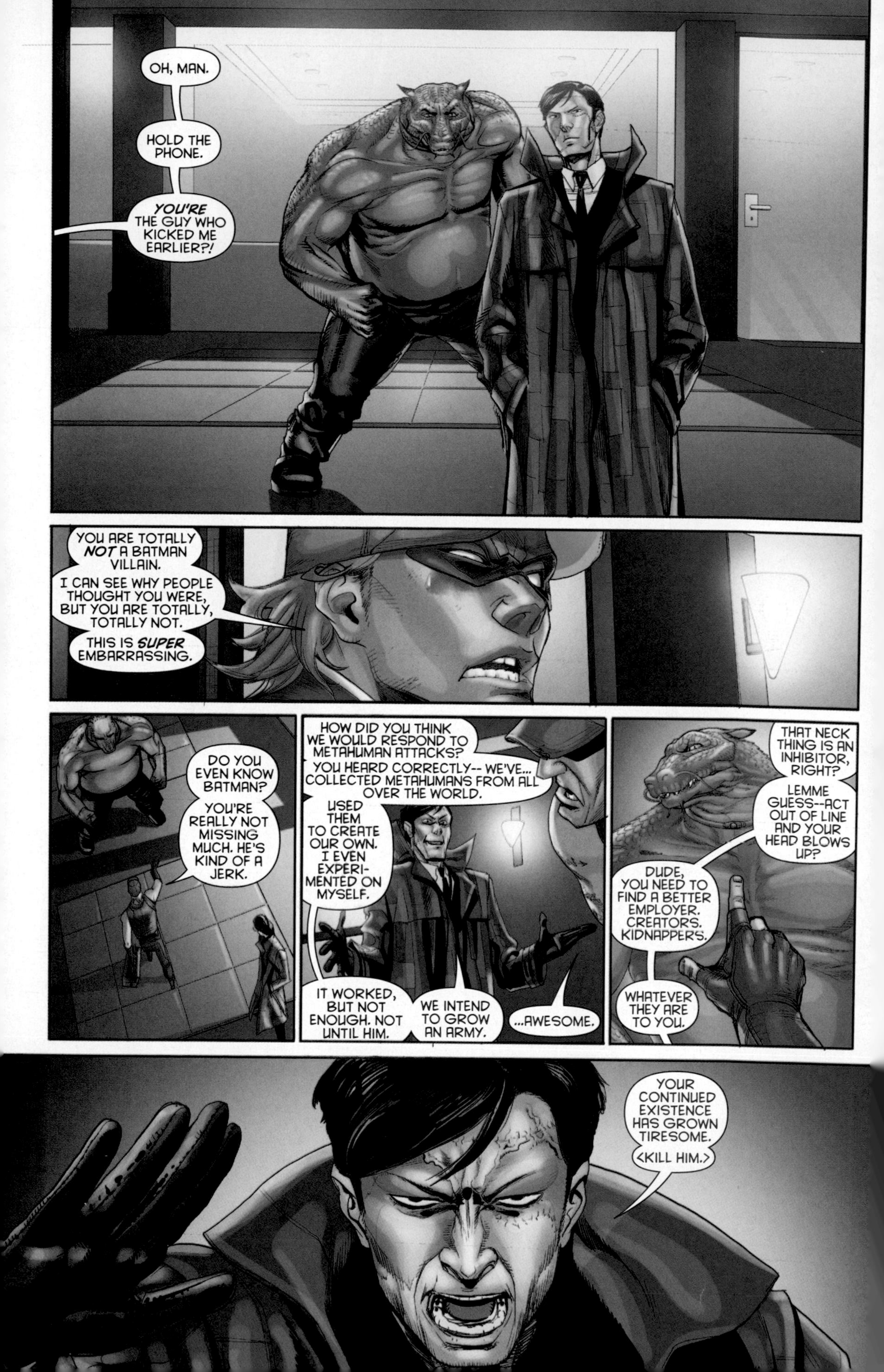
OH, MAN.
HOLD THE PHONE.
YOU'RE THE GUY WHO KICKED ME EARLIER?!
YOU ARE TOTALLY NOT A BATMAN VILLAIN.
I CAN SEE WHY PEOPLE THOUGHT YOU WERE, BUT YOU ARE TOTALLY, TOTALLY NOT.
THIS IS SUPER EMBARRASSING.
DO YOU EVEN KNOW BATMAN?
YOU'RE REALLY NOT MISSING MUCH. HE'S KIND OF A JERK.
HOW DID YOU THINK WE WOULD RESPOND TO METAHUMAN ATTACKS?
YOU HEARD CORRECTLY-- WE'VE... COLLECTED METAHUMANS FROM ALL OVER THE WORLD.
USED THEM TO CREATE OUR OWN. I EVEN EXPERIMENTED ON MYSELF.
IT WORKED, BUT NOT ENOUGH. NOT UNTIL HIM.
WE INTEND TO GROW AN ARMY.
...AWESOME.
THAT NECK THING IS AN INHIBITOR, RIGHT?
LEMME GUESS--ACT OUT OF LINE AND YOUR HEAD BLOWS UP?
DUDE, YOU NEED TO FIND A BETTER EMPLOYER. CREATORS. KIDNAPPERS.
WHATEVER THEY ARE TO YOU.
YOUR CONTINUED EXISTENCE HAS GROWN TIRESOME.
<KILL HIM.>

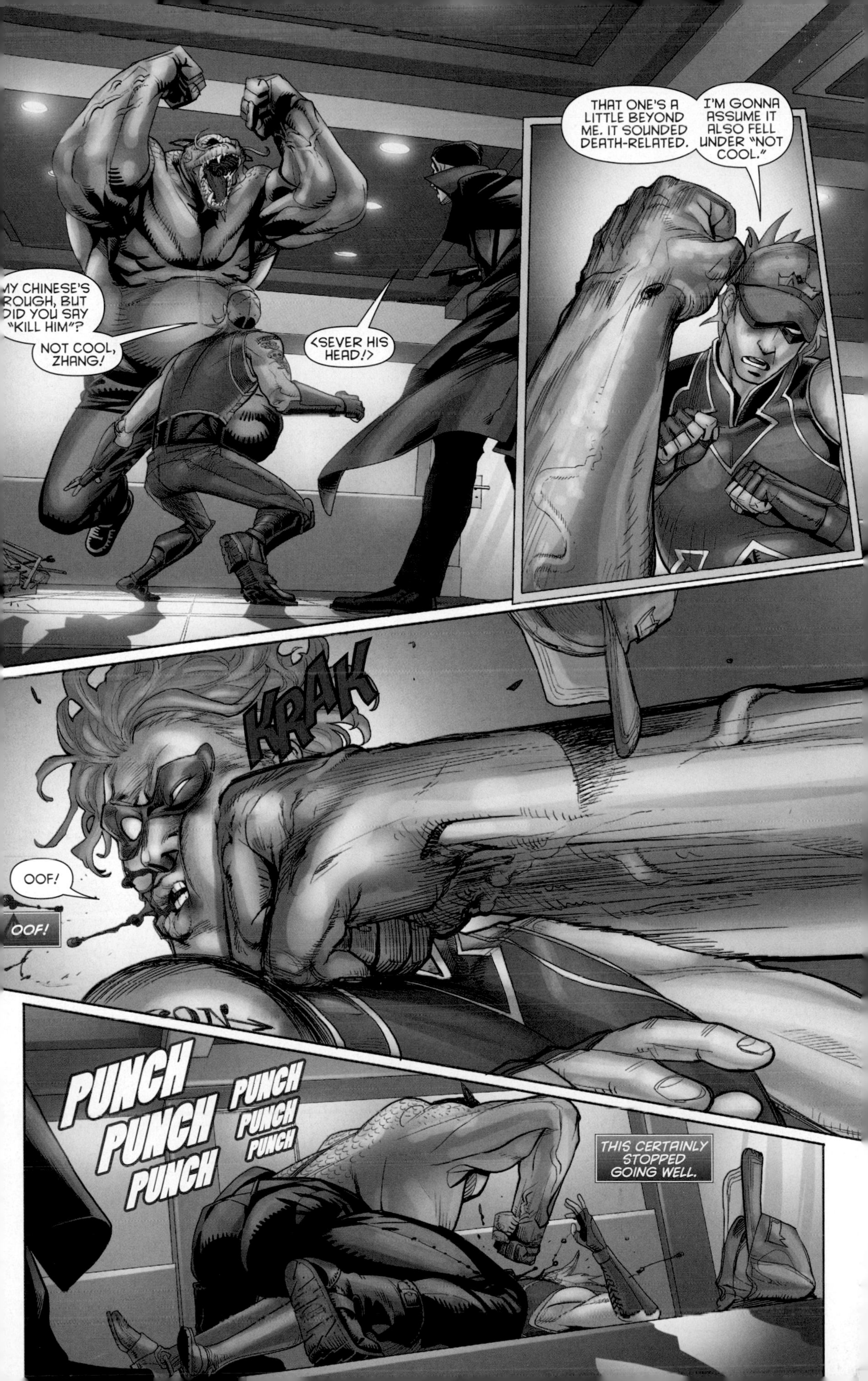
MY CHINESE'S ROUGH, BUT DID YOU SAY "KILL HIM"?
NOT COOL, ZHANG!
<SEVER HIS HEAD!>
THAT ONE'S A LITTLE BEYOND ME. IT SOUNDED DEATH-RELATED.
I'M GONNA ASSUME IT ALSO FELL UNDER "NOT COOL."
KRAK
OOF!
OOF!
PUNCH PUNCH PUNCH
PUNCH PUNCH PUNCH
THIS CERTAINLY STOPPED GOING WELL.

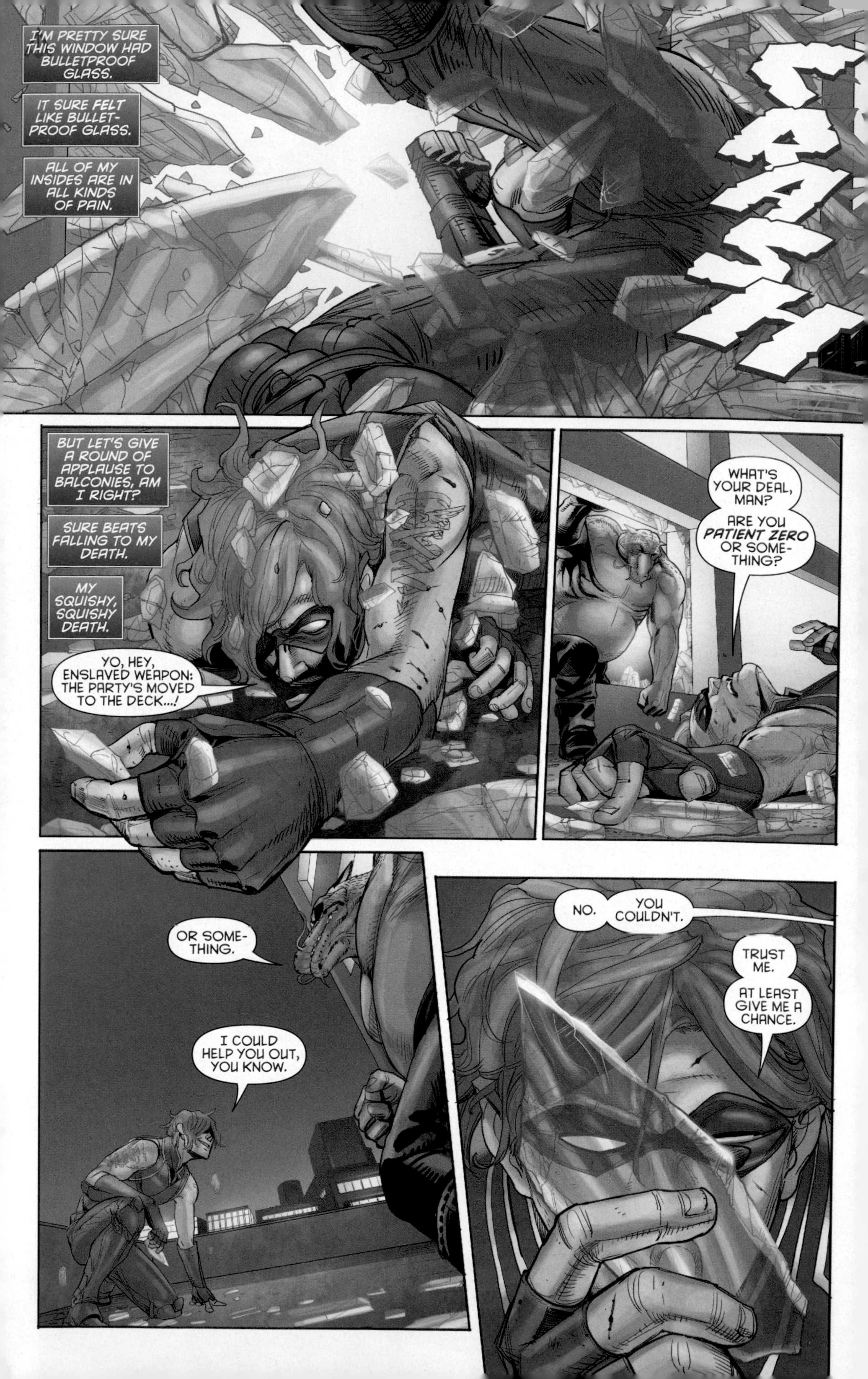
I'M PRETTY SURE THIS WINDOW HAD BULLETPROOF GLASS.
IT SURE FELT LIKE BULLET-PROOF GLASS.
ALL OF MY INSIDES ARE IN ALL KINDS OF PAIN.
CRASH
BUT LET'S GIVE A ROUND OF APPLAUSE TO BALCONIES, AM I RIGHT?
SURE BEATS FALLING TO MY DEATH.
MY SQUISHY, SQUISHY DEATH.
YO, HEY, ENSLAVED WEAPON: THE PARTY'S MOVED TO THE DECK...!
WHAT'S YOUR DEAL, MAN?
ARE YOU PATIENT ZERO OR SOME-THING?
OR SOME-THING.
I COULD HELP YOU OUT, YOU KNOW.
NO.
YOU COULDN'T.
TRUST ME.
AT LEAST GIVE ME A CHANCE.

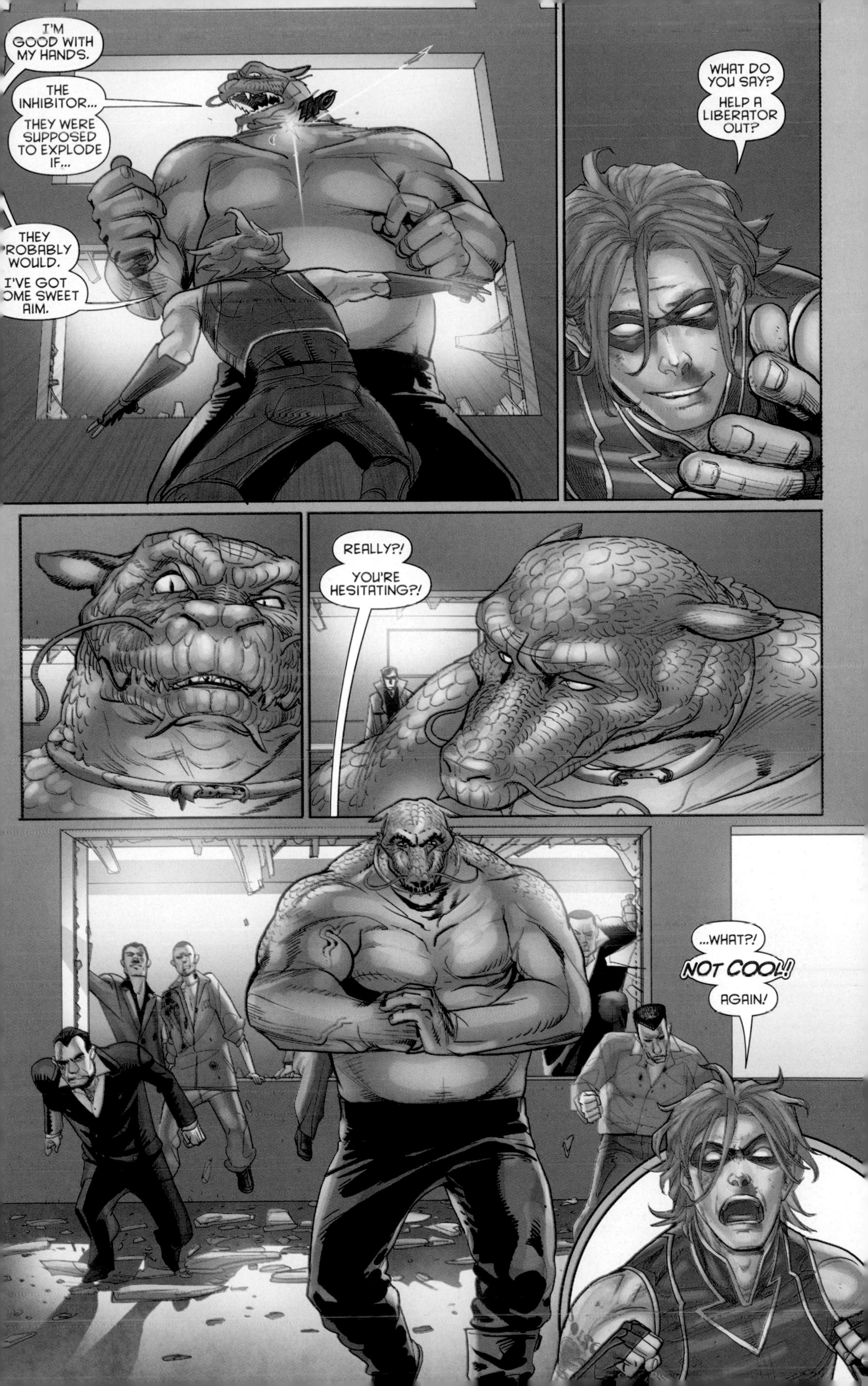
I'M GOOD WITH MY HANDS.
THE INHIBITOR... THEY WERE SUPPOSED TO EXPLODE IF...
THEY PROBABLY WOULD.
I'VE GOT SOME SWEET AIM.
WHAT DO YOU SAY? HELP A LIBERATOR OUT?
REALLY?! YOU'RE HESITATING?!
...WHAT?!
NOT COOL!
AGAIN!

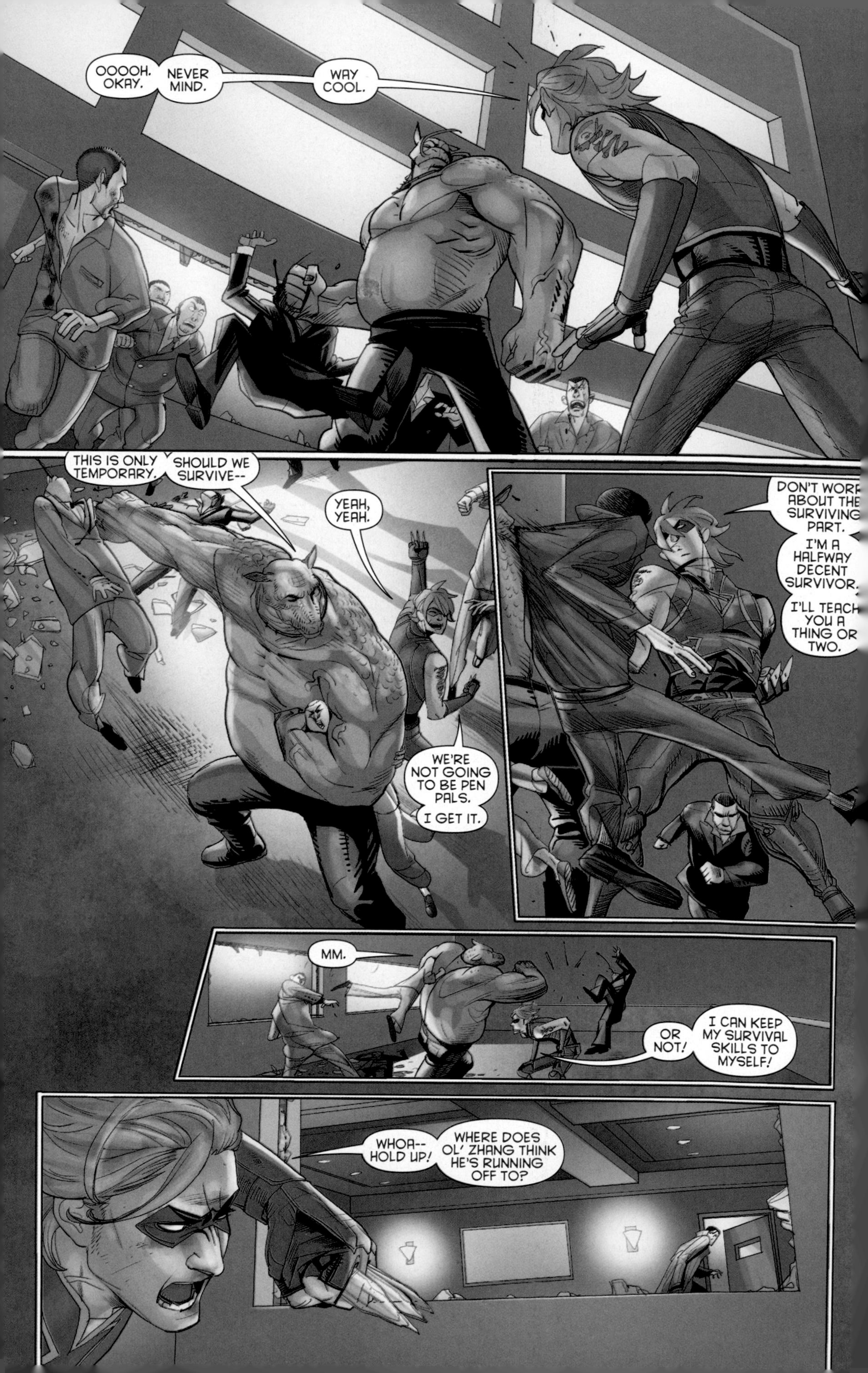
OOOOH. OKAY.
NEVER MIND.
WAY COOL.
THIS IS ONLY TEMPORARY.
SHOULD WE SURVIVE--
YEAH, YEAH.
WE'RE NOT GOING TO BE PEN PALS.
I GET IT.
DON'T WORRY ABOUT THE SURVIVING PART.
I'M A HALFWAY DECENT SURVIVOR.
I'LL TEACH YOU A THING OR TWO.
MM.
OR NOT!
I CAN KEEP MY SURVIVAL SKILLS TO MYSELF!
WHOA-- HOLD UP!
WHERE DOES OL' ZHANG THINK HE'S RUNNING OFF TO?

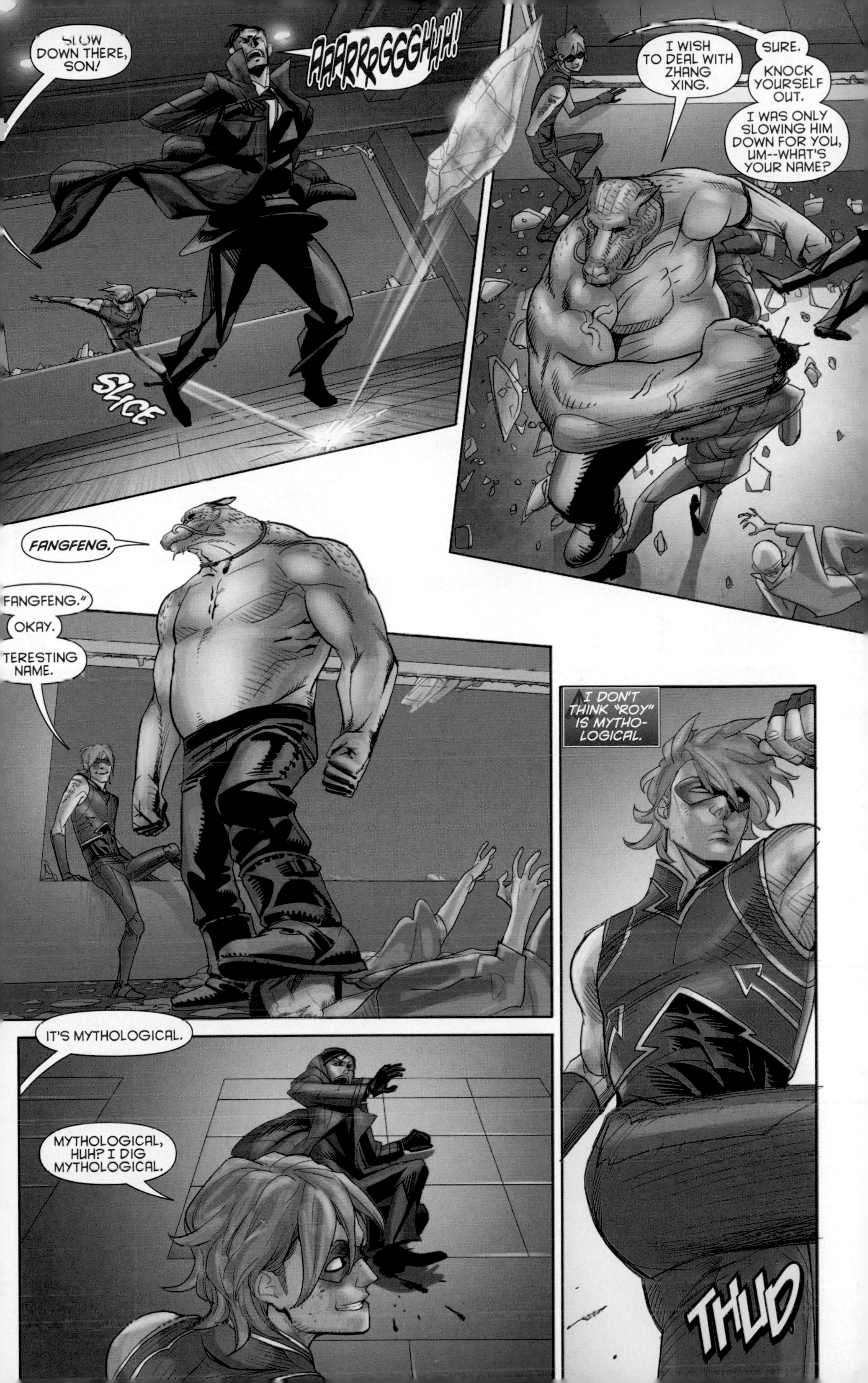
SLOW DOWN THERE, SON!
AAARRRGGGHHH!
SLICE
I WISH TO DEAL WITH ZHANG XING.
SURE.
KNOCK YOURSELF OUT.
I WAS ONLY SLOWING HIM DOWN FOR YOU, UM--WHAT'S YOUR NAME?
FANGFENG.
FANGFENG."
OKAY.
TERESTING NAME.
I DON'T THINK "ROY" IS MYTHOLOGICAL.
IT'S MYTHOLOGICAL.
MYTHOLOGICAL, HUH? I DIG MYTHOLOGICAL.
THUD

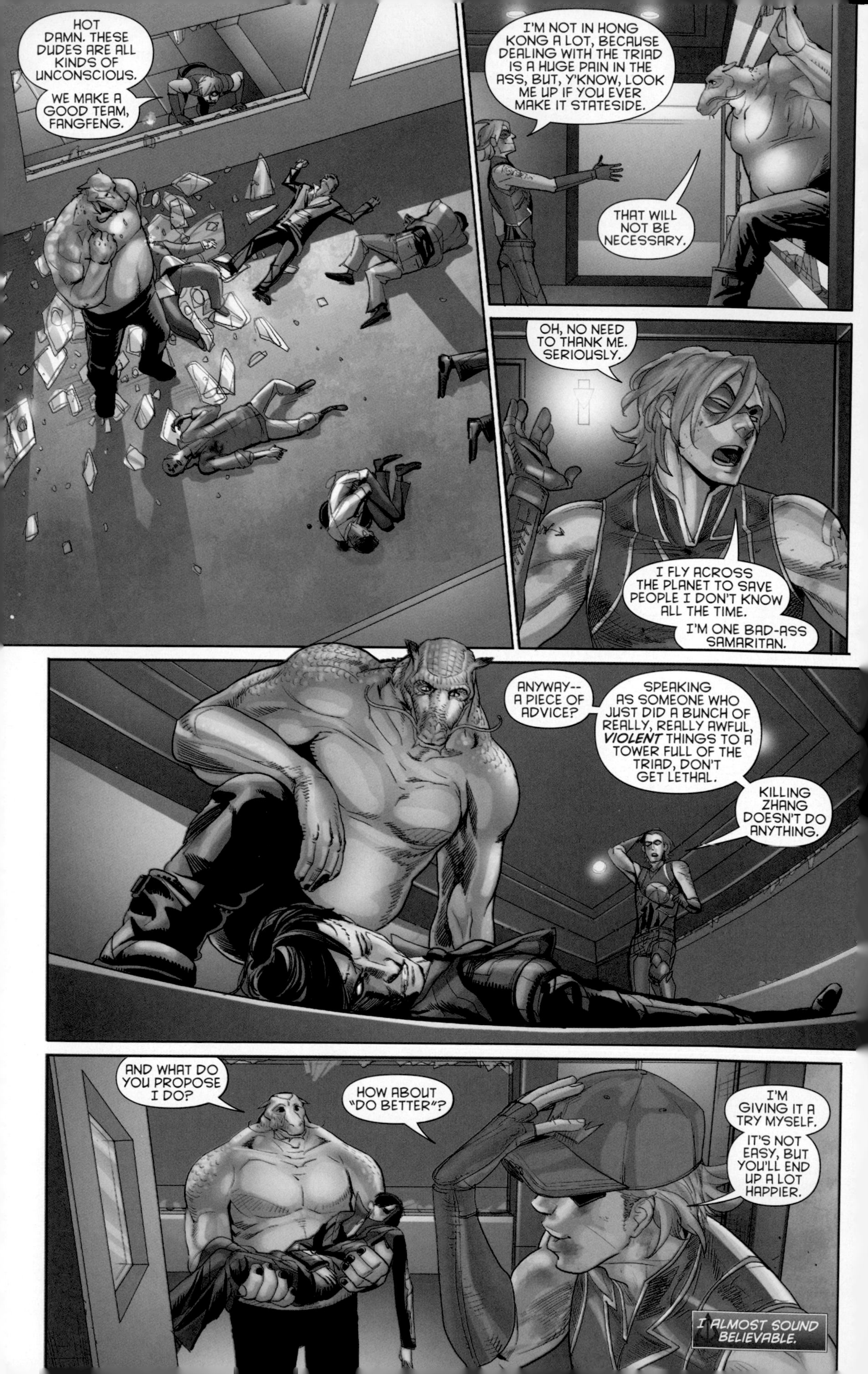
HOT DAMN. THESE DUDES ARE ALL KINDS OF UNCONSCIOUS.
WE MAKE A GOOD TEAM, FANGFENG.
I'M NOT IN HONG KONG A LOT, BECAUSE DEALING WITH THE TRIAD IS A HUGE PAIN IN THE ASS, BUT, Y'KNOW, LOOK ME UP IF YOU EVER MAKE IT STATESIDE.
THAT WILL NOT BE NECESSARY.
OH, NO NEED TO THANK ME. SERIOUSLY.
I FLY ACROSS THE PLANET TO SAVE PEOPLE I DON'T KNOW ALL THE TIME.
I'M ONE BAD-ASS SAMARITAN.
ANYWAY-- A PIECE OF ADVICE?
SPEAKING AS SOMEONE WHO JUST DID A BUNCH OF REALLY, REALLY AWFUL, *VIOLENT* THINGS TO A TOWER FULL OF THE TRIAD, DON'T GET LETHAL.
KILLING ZHANG DOESN'T DO ANYTHING.
AND WHAT DO YOU PROPOSE I DO?
HOW ABOUT "DO BETTER"?
I'M GIVING IT A TRY MYSELF.
IT'S NOT EASY, BUT YOU'LL END UP A LOT HAPPIER.
I ALMOST SOUND BELIEVABLE.

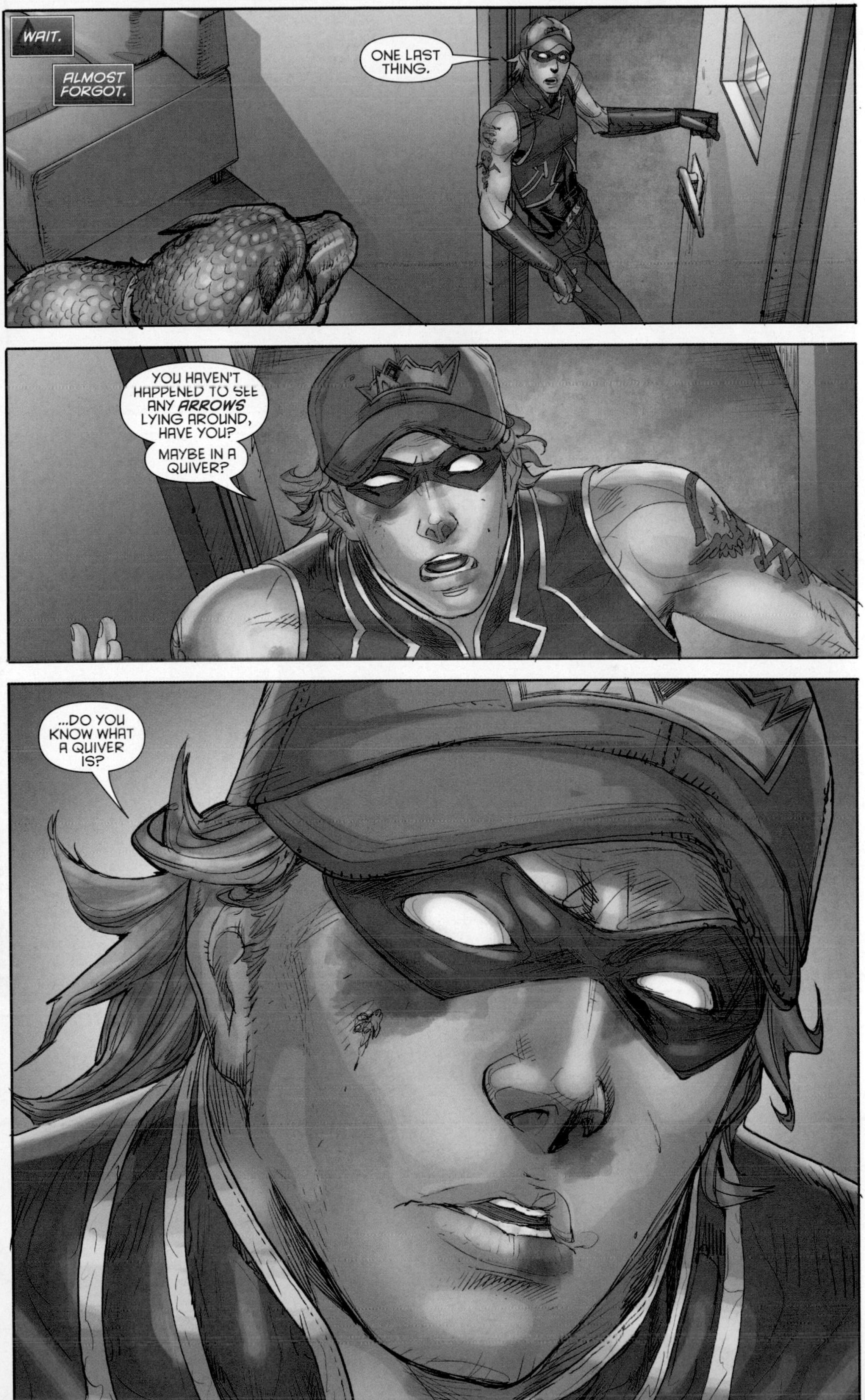
WAIT.
ALMOST FORGOT.
ONE LAST THING.
YOU HAVEN'T HAPPENED TO SEE ANY *ARROWS* LYING AROUND, HAVE YOU?
MAYBE IN A QUIVER?
...DO YOU KNOW WHAT A QUIVER IS?

ABOARD STARFIRE'S SHIP.
...ROY? WHERE HAVE YOU BEEN?
ME?
SAME PLACE I ALWAYS GO.
MY FRIENDS MAY BE THE WORST...
NOWHERE
...BUT, HEY, MAN--SO AM I.
END

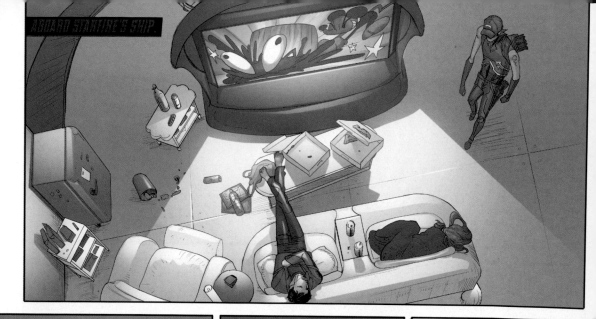

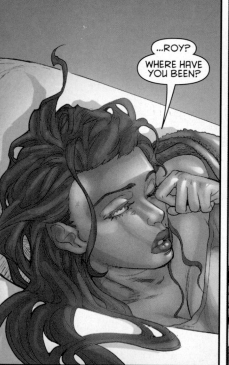

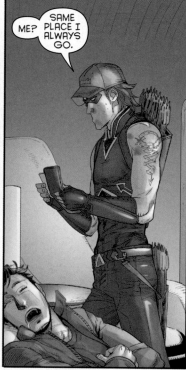

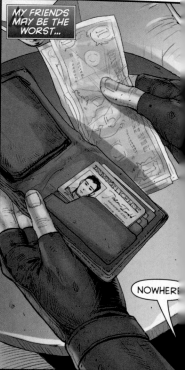

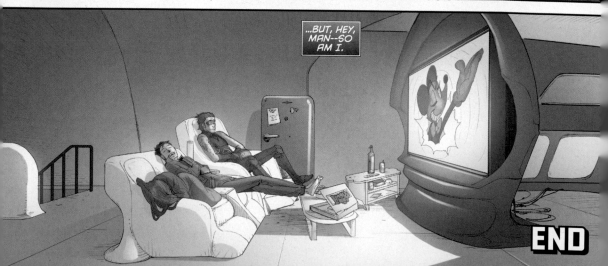

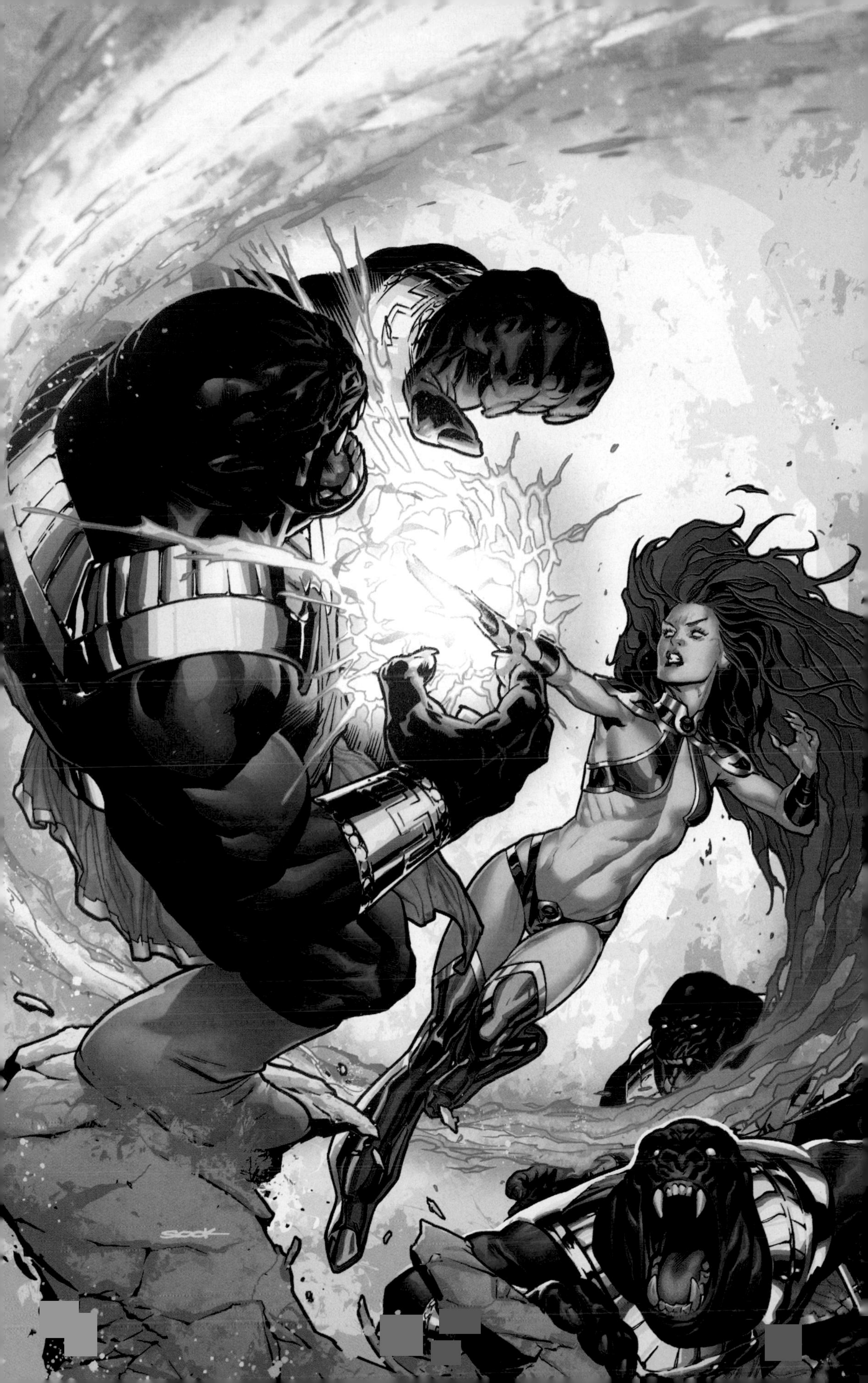

WITHOUT HONOR OR HUMANITY

JOE KEATINGE writer **FEDERICO DALLOCCHIO** artist **ALLEN PASSALAQUA** colorist **TAYLOR ESPOSITO** letterer cover art by **RYAN SOOK**

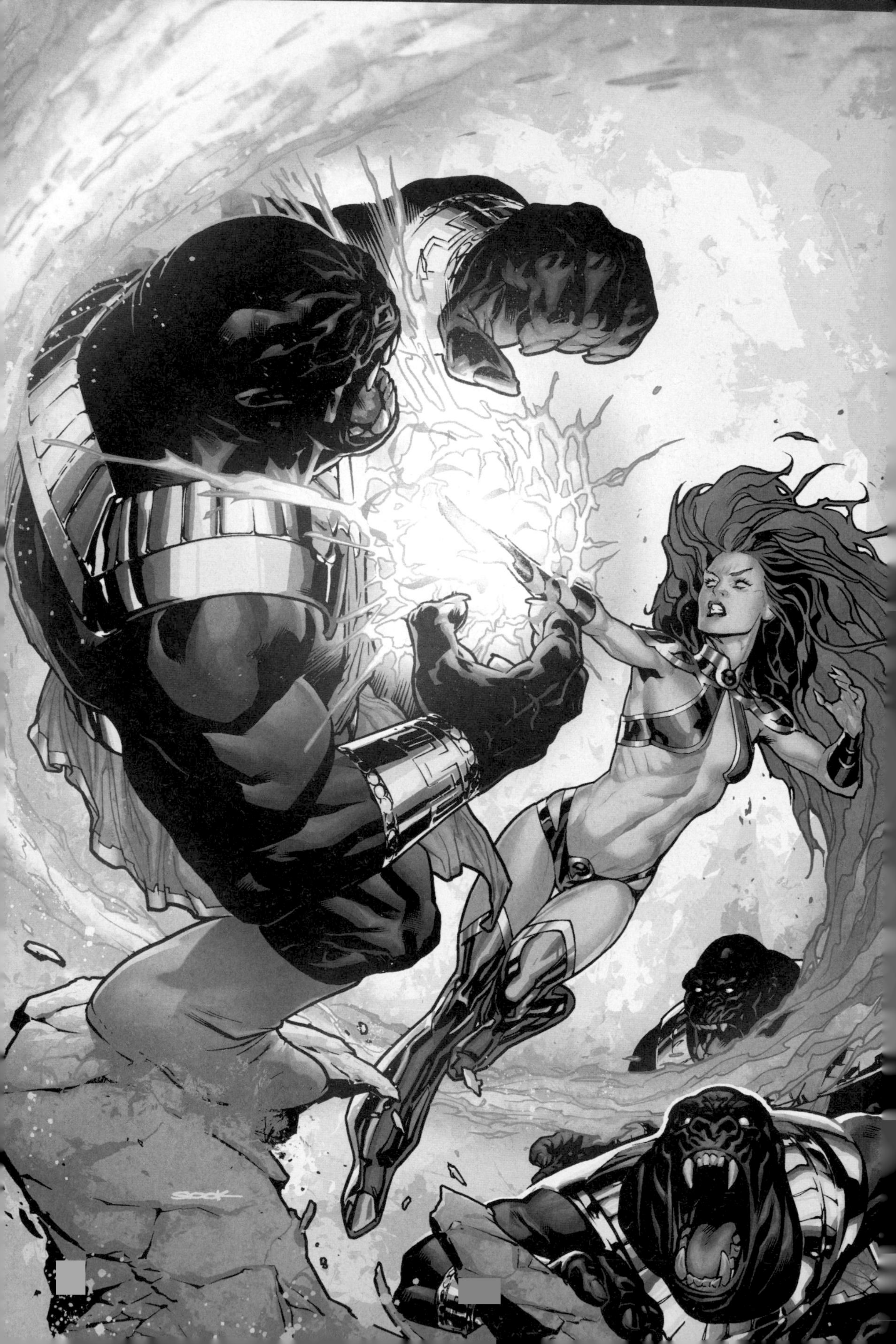
SOOK

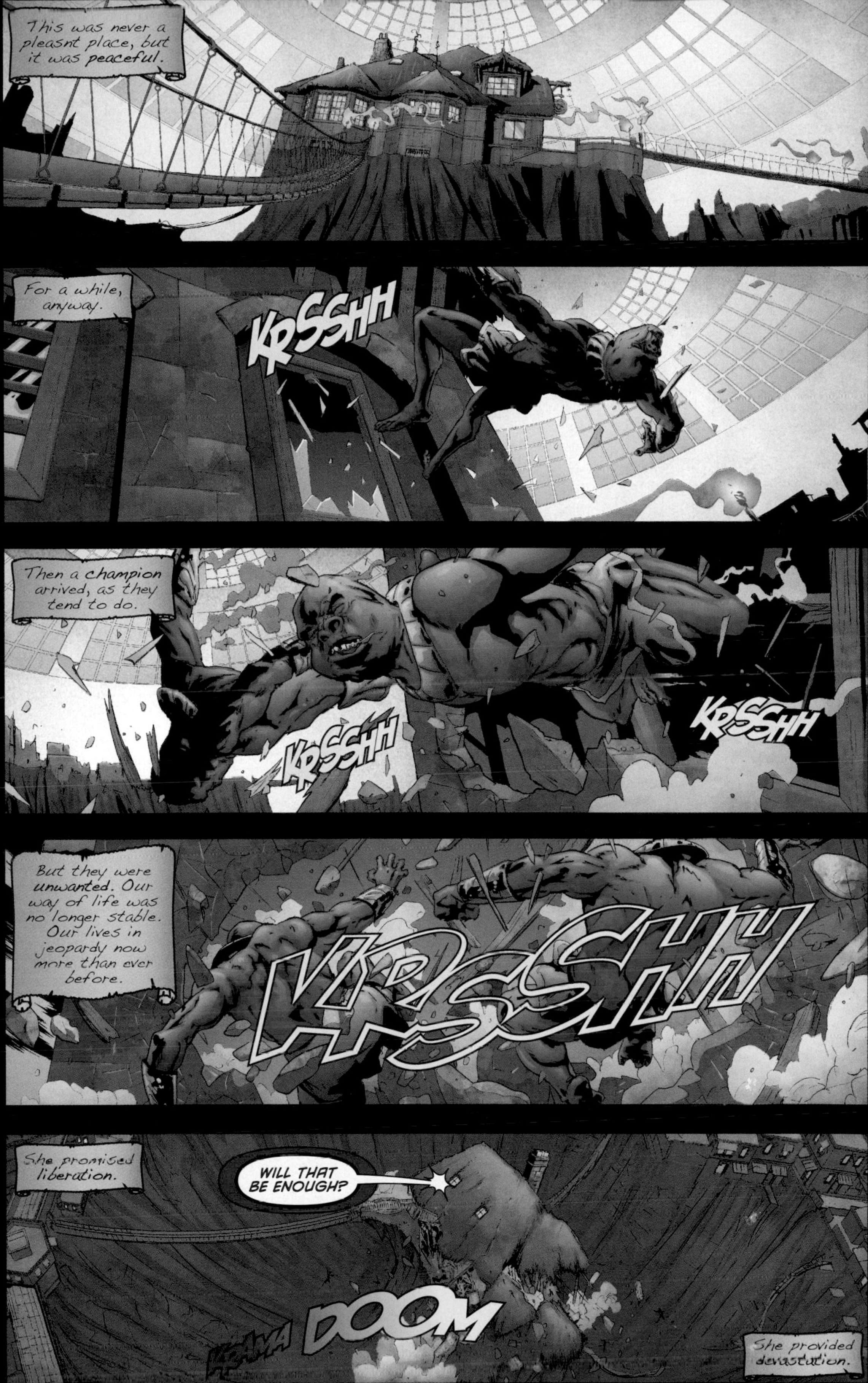
This was never a pleasnt place, but it was peaceful.
For a while, anyway.
KRSSHH
Then a champion arrived, as they tend to do.
KRSSHH
KRSSHH
But they were unwanted. Our way of life was no longer stable. Our lives in jeopardy now more than ever before.
KRSSHH
She promised liberation.
WILL THAT BE ENOUGH?
DOOM
She provided devastation.

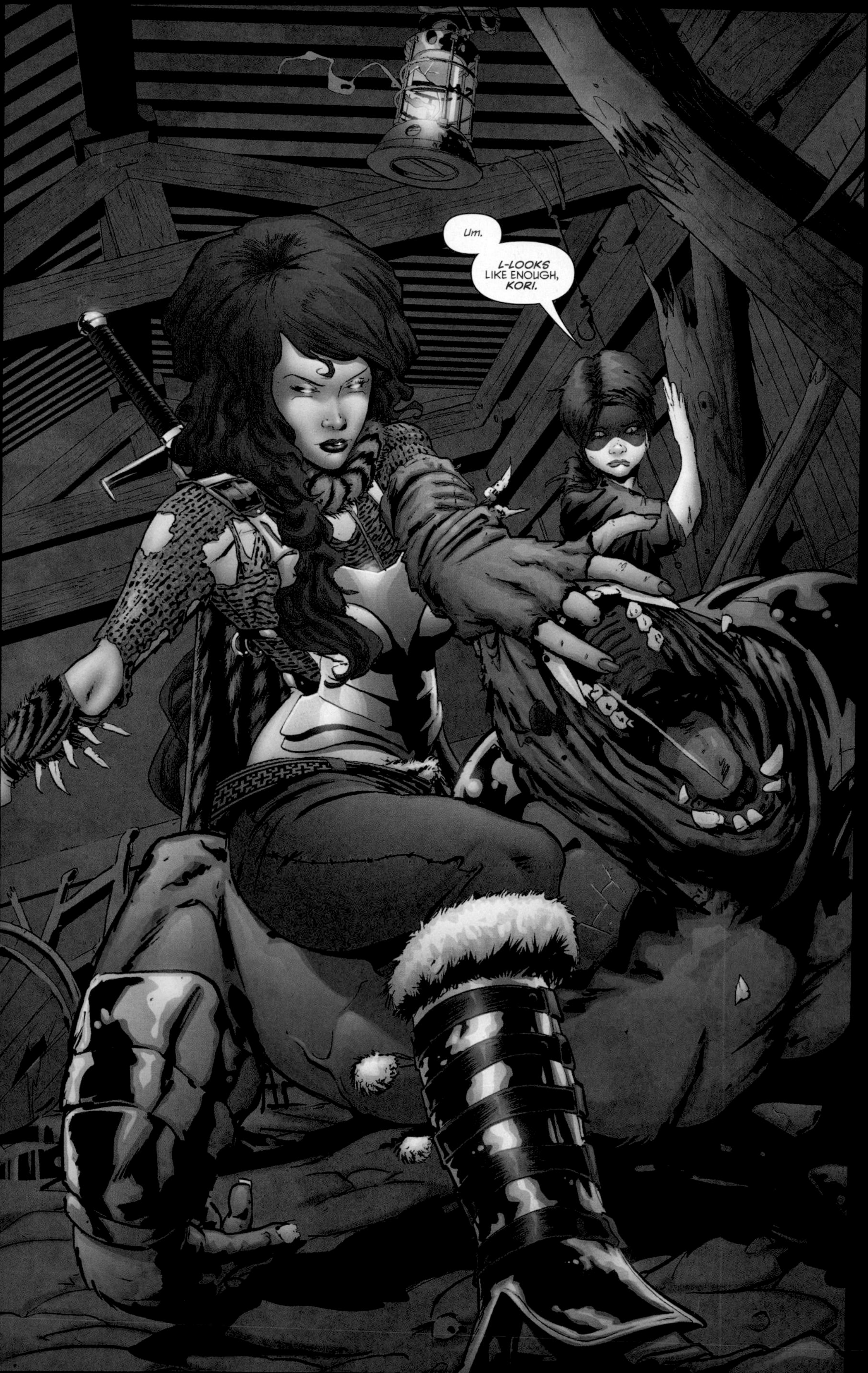
Um.
L-LOOKS LIKE ENOUGH, KORI.

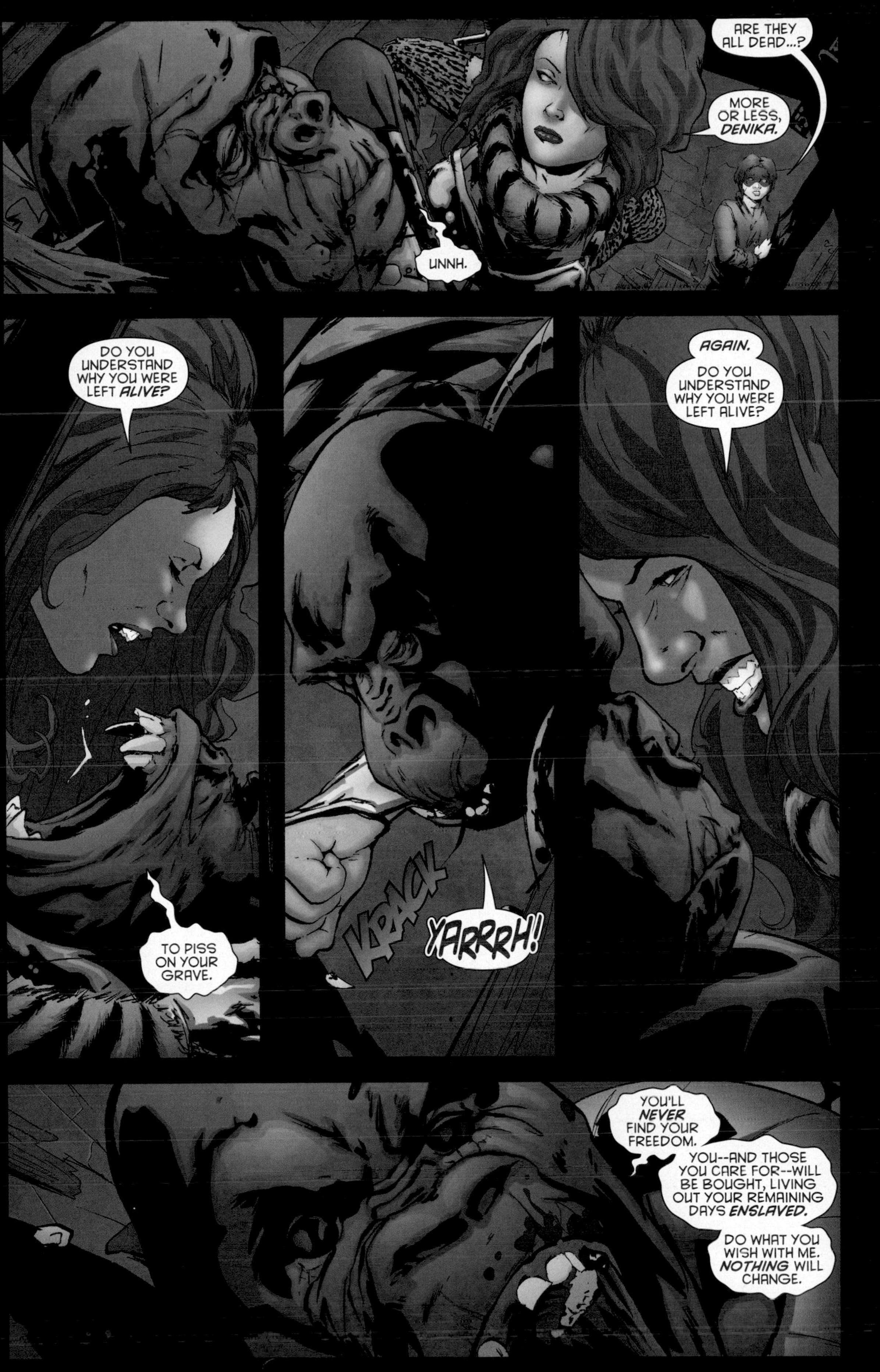
ARE THEY ALL DEAD...?
MORE OR LESS, DENIKA.
UNNH.
DO YOU UNDERSTAND WHY YOU WERE LEFT ALIVE?
TO PISS ON YOUR GRAVE.
KRACK
YARRRH!
AGAIN.
DO YOU UNDERSTAND WHY YOU WERE LEFT ALIVE?
YOU'LL NEVER FIND YOUR FREEDOM.
YOU--AND THOSE YOU CARE FOR--WILL BE BOUGHT, LIVING OUT YOUR REMAINING DAYS ENSLAVED.
DO WHAT YOU WISH WITH ME. NOTHING WILL CHANGE.

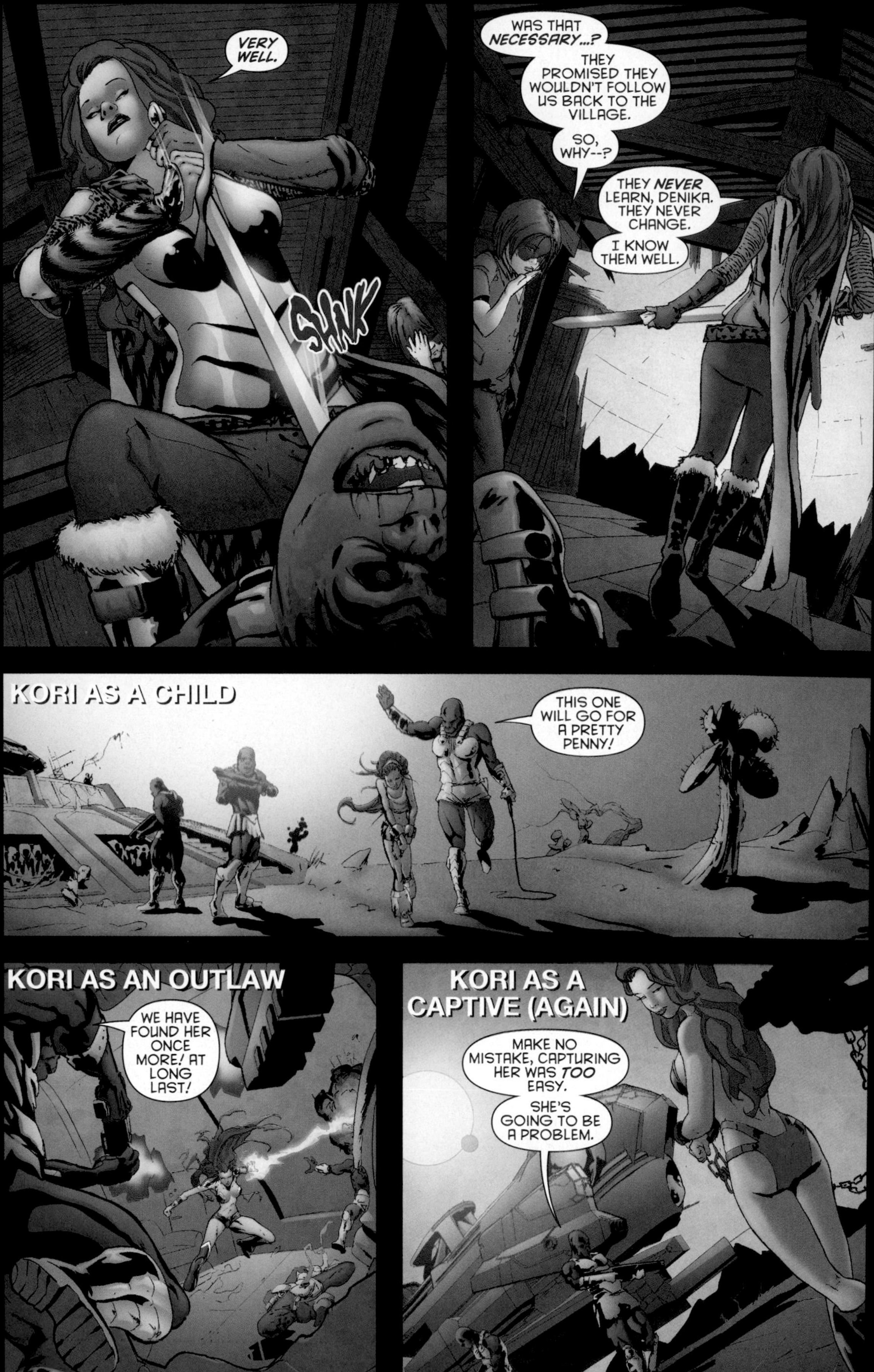
VERY WELL.
SHNK
WAS THAT NECESSARY...?
THEY PROMISED THEY WOULDN'T FOLLOW US BACK TO THE VILLAGE.
SO, WHY--?
THEY NEVER LEARN, DENIKA. THEY NEVER CHANGE.
I KNOW THEM WELL.
KORI AS A CHILD
THIS ONE WILL GO FOR A PRETTY PENNY!
KORI AS AN OUTLAW
WE HAVE FOUND HER ONCE MORE! AT LONG LAST!
KORI AS A CAPTIVE (AGAIN)
MAKE NO MISTAKE, CAPTURING HER WAS TOO EASY.
SHE'S GOING TO BE A PROBLEM.

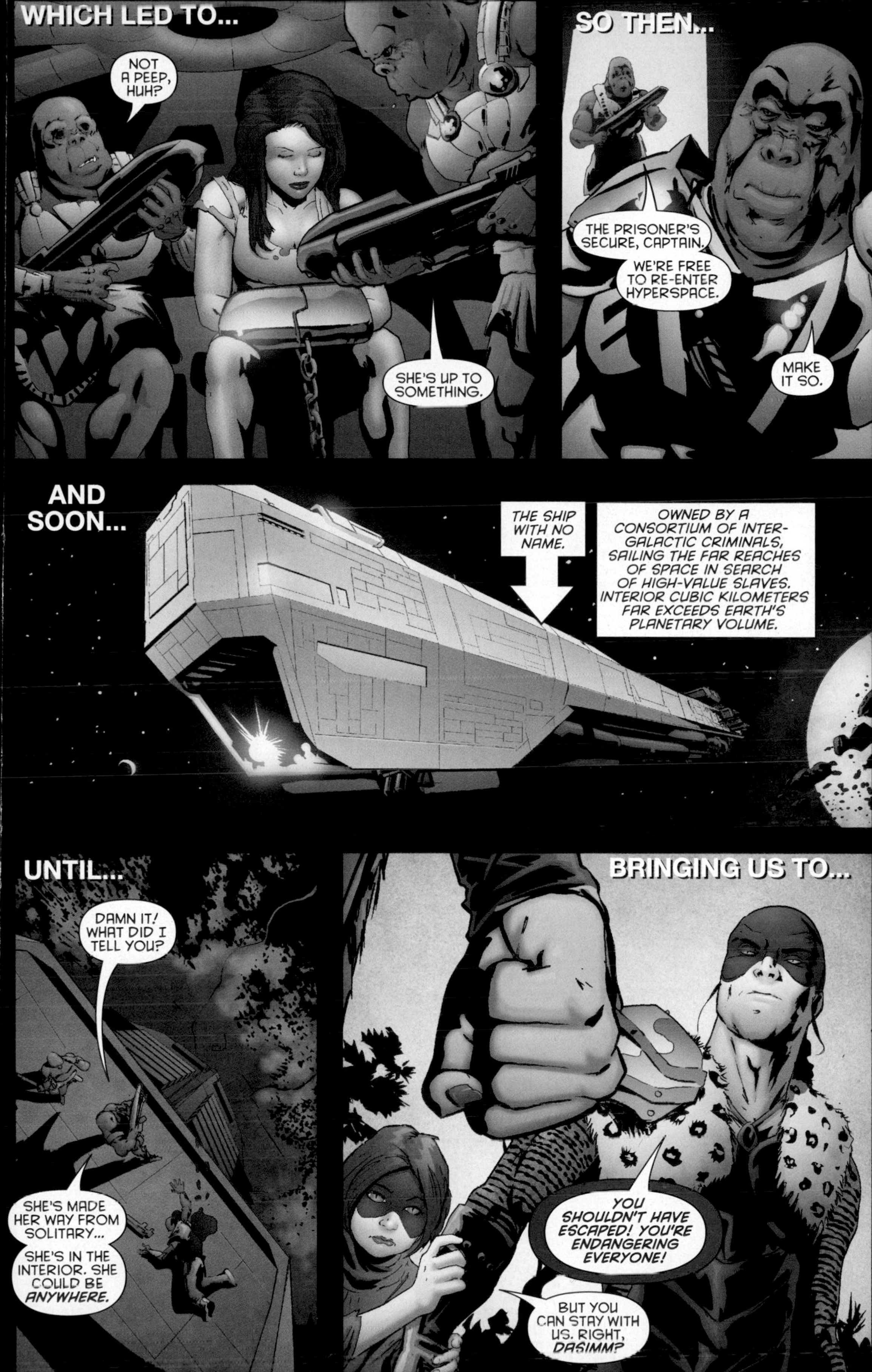
WHICH LED TO...
NOT A PEEP, HUH?
SHE'S UP TO SOMETHING.
SO THEN...
THE PRISONER'S SECURE, CAPTAIN.
WE'RE FREE TO RE-ENTER HYPERSPACE.
MAKE IT SO.
AND SOON...
THE SHIP WITH NO NAME.
OWNED BY A CONSORTIUM OF INTER-GALACTIC CRIMINALS, SAILING THE FAR REACHES OF SPACE IN SEARCH OF HIGH-VALUE SLAVES. INTERIOR CUBIC KILOMETERS FAR EXCEEDS EARTH'S PLANETARY VOLUME.
UNTIL...
DAMN IT! WHAT DID I TELL YOU?
SHE'S MADE HER WAY FROM SOLITARY...
SHE'S IN THE INTERIOR. SHE COULD BE ANYWHERE.
BRINGING US TO...
YOU SHOULDN'T HAVE ESCAPED! YOU'RE ENDANGERING EVERYONE!
BUT YOU CAN STAY WITH US. RIGHT, DASIMM?

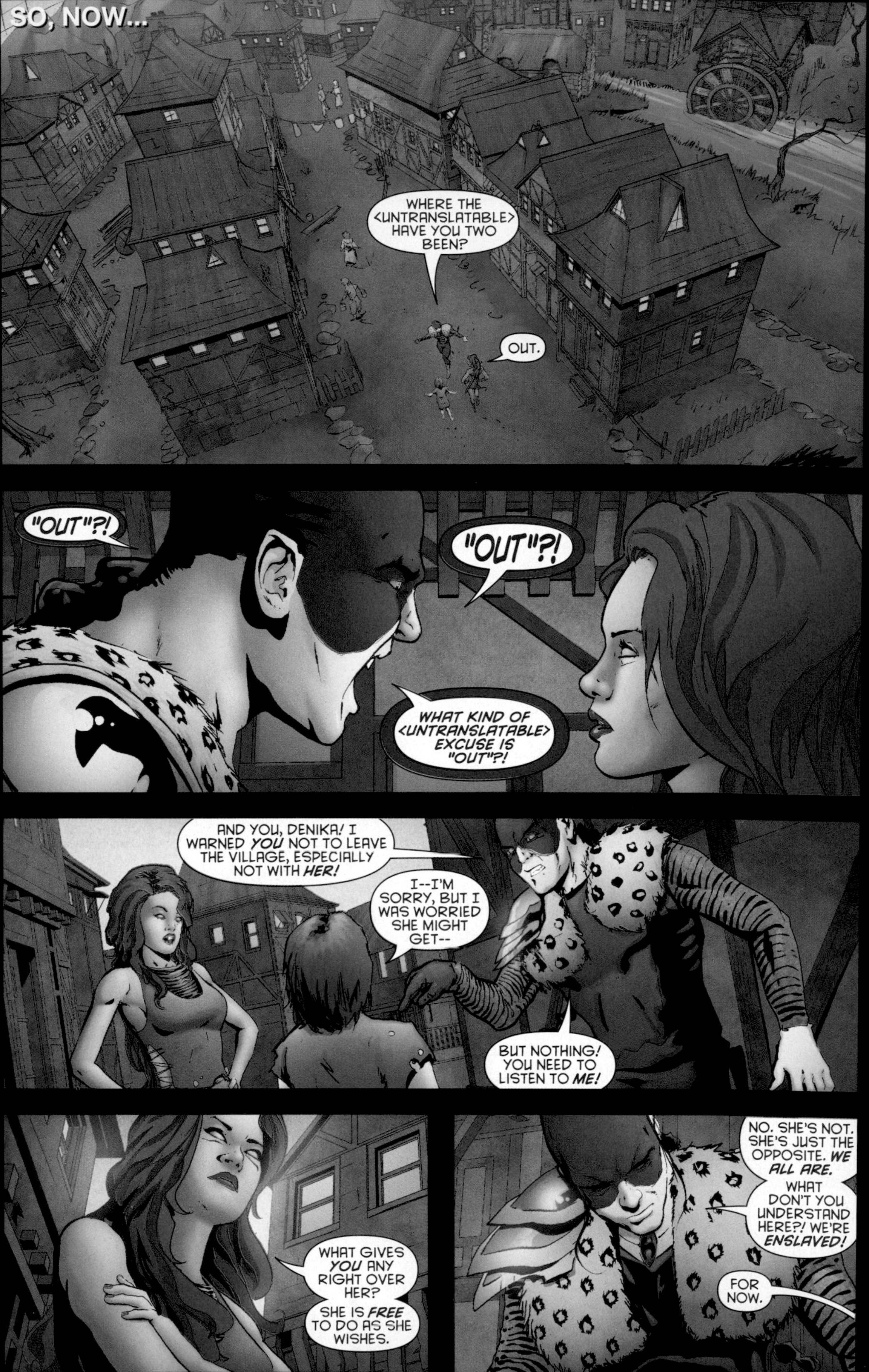
SO, NOW...
WHERE THE <UNTRANSLATABLE> HAVE YOU TWO BEEN?
OUT.
"OUT"?!
"OUT"?!
WHAT KIND OF <UNTRANSLATABLE> EXCUSE IS "OUT"?!
AND YOU, DENIKA! I WARNED YOU NOT TO LEAVE THE VILLAGE, ESPECIALLY NOT WITH HER!
I--I'M SORRY, BUT I WAS WORRIED SHE MIGHT GET--
BUT NOTHING! YOU NEED TO LISTEN TO ME!
WHAT GIVES YOU ANY RIGHT OVER HER?
SHE IS FREE TO DO AS SHE WISHES.
NO. SHE'S NOT. SHE'S JUST THE OPPOSITE. WE ALL ARE.
WHAT DON'T YOU UNDERSTAND HERE?! WE'RE ENSLAVED!
FOR NOW.

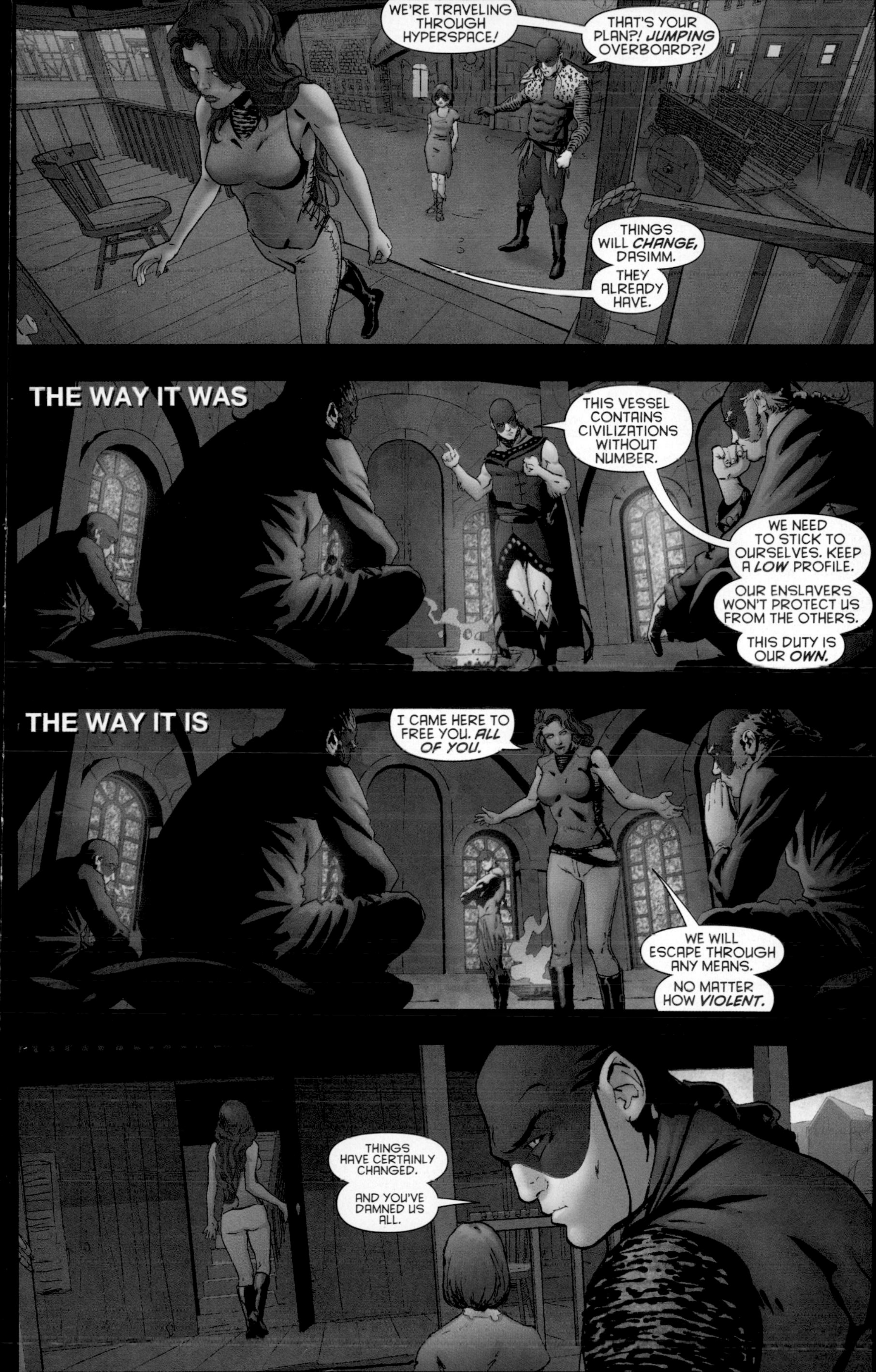
WE'RE TRAVELING THROUGH HYPERSPACE!
THAT'S YOUR PLAN?! JUMPING OVERBOARD?!
THINGS WILL CHANGE, DASIMM.
THEY ALREADY HAVE.
THE WAY IT WAS
THIS VESSEL CONTAINS CIVILIZATIONS WITHOUT NUMBER.
WE NEED TO STICK TO OURSELVES. KEEP A LOW PROFILE.
OUR ENSLAVERS WON'T PROTECT US FROM THE OTHERS.
THIS DUTY IS OUR OWN.
THE WAY IT IS
I CAME HERE TO FREE YOU. ALL OF YOU.
WE WILL ESCAPE THROUGH ANY MEANS.
NO MATTER HOW VIOLENT.
THINGS HAVE CERTAINLY CHANGED.
AND YOU'VE DAMNED US ALL.

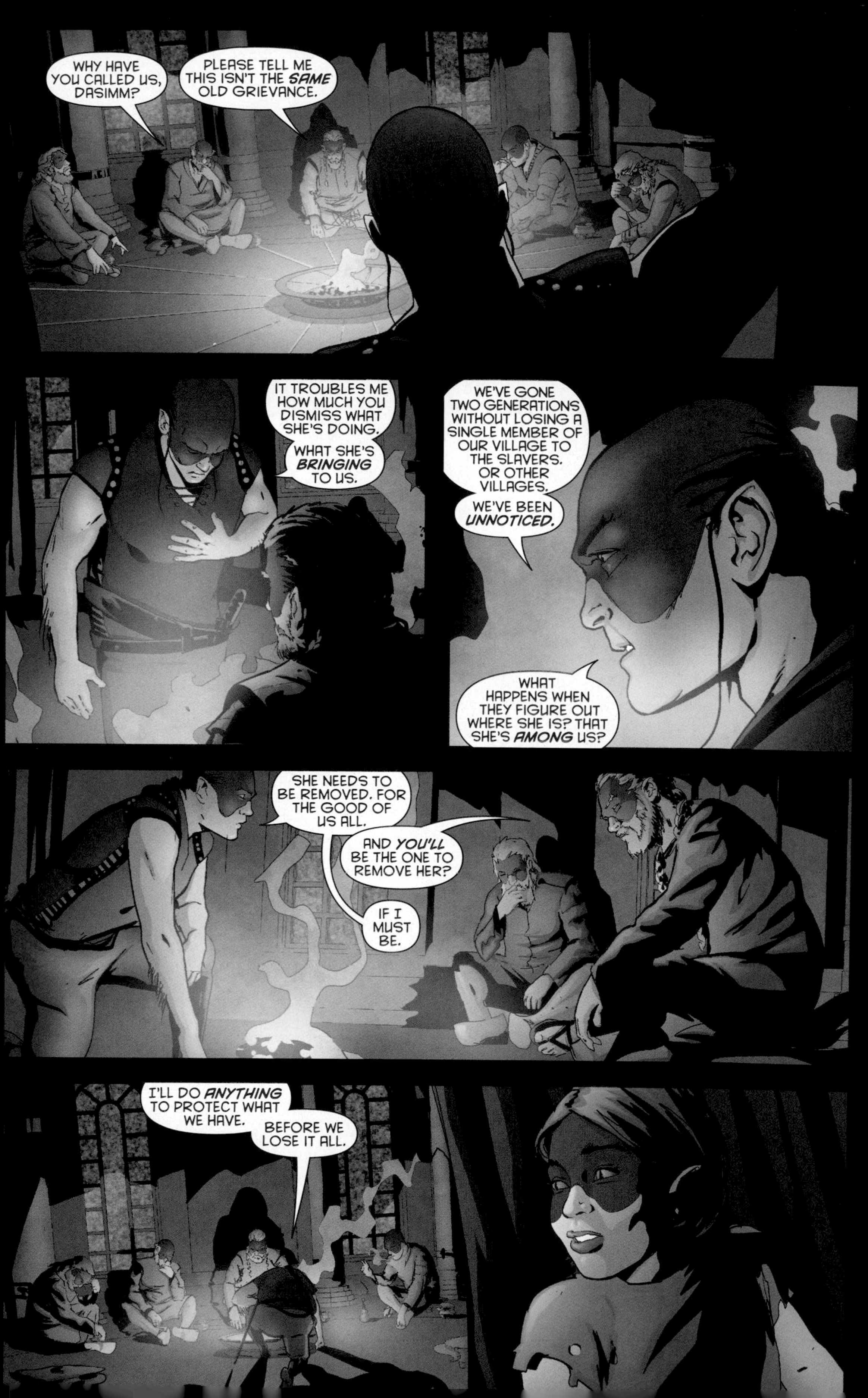
WHY HAVE YOU CALLED US, DASIMM?
PLEASE TELL ME THIS ISN'T THE SAME OLD GRIEVANCE.
IT TROUBLES ME HOW MUCH YOU DISMISS WHAT SHE'S DOING.
WHAT SHE'S BRINGING TO US.
WE'VE GONE TWO GENERATIONS WITHOUT LOSING A SINGLE MEMBER OF OUR VILLAGE TO THE SLAVERS. OR OTHER VILLAGES.
WE'VE BEEN UNNOTICED.
WHAT HAPPENS WHEN THEY FIGURE OUT WHERE SHE IS? THAT SHE'S AMONG US?
SHE NEEDS TO BE REMOVED. FOR THE GOOD OF US ALL.
AND YOU'LL BE THE ONE TO REMOVE HER?
IF I MUST BE.
I'LL DO ANYTHING TO PROTECT WHAT WE HAVE.
BEFORE WE LOSE IT ALL.

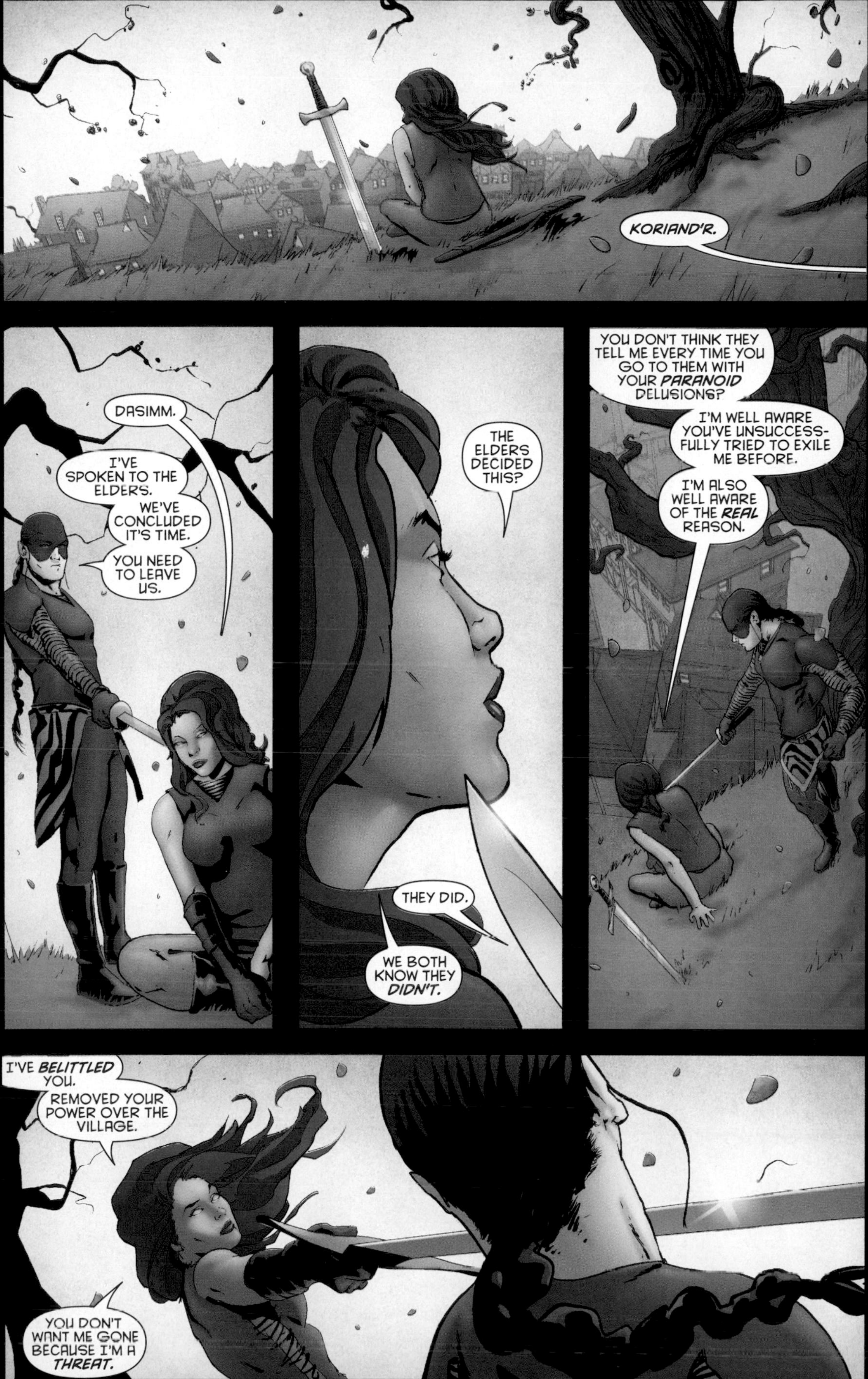
KORIAND'R.
DASIMM.
I'VE SPOKEN TO THE ELDERS.
WE'VE CONCLUDED IT'S TIME.
YOU NEED TO LEAVE US.
THE ELDERS DECIDED THIS?
THEY DID.
WE BOTH KNOW THEY DIDN'T.
YOU DON'T THINK THEY TELL ME EVERY TIME YOU GO TO THEM WITH YOUR PARANOID DELUSIONS?
I'M WELL AWARE YOU'VE UNSUCCESSFULLY TRIED TO EXILE ME BEFORE.
I'M ALSO WELL AWARE OF THE REAL REASON.
I'VE BELITTLED YOU.
REMOVED YOUR POWER OVER THE VILLAGE.
YOU DON'T WANT ME GONE BECAUSE I'M A THREAT.

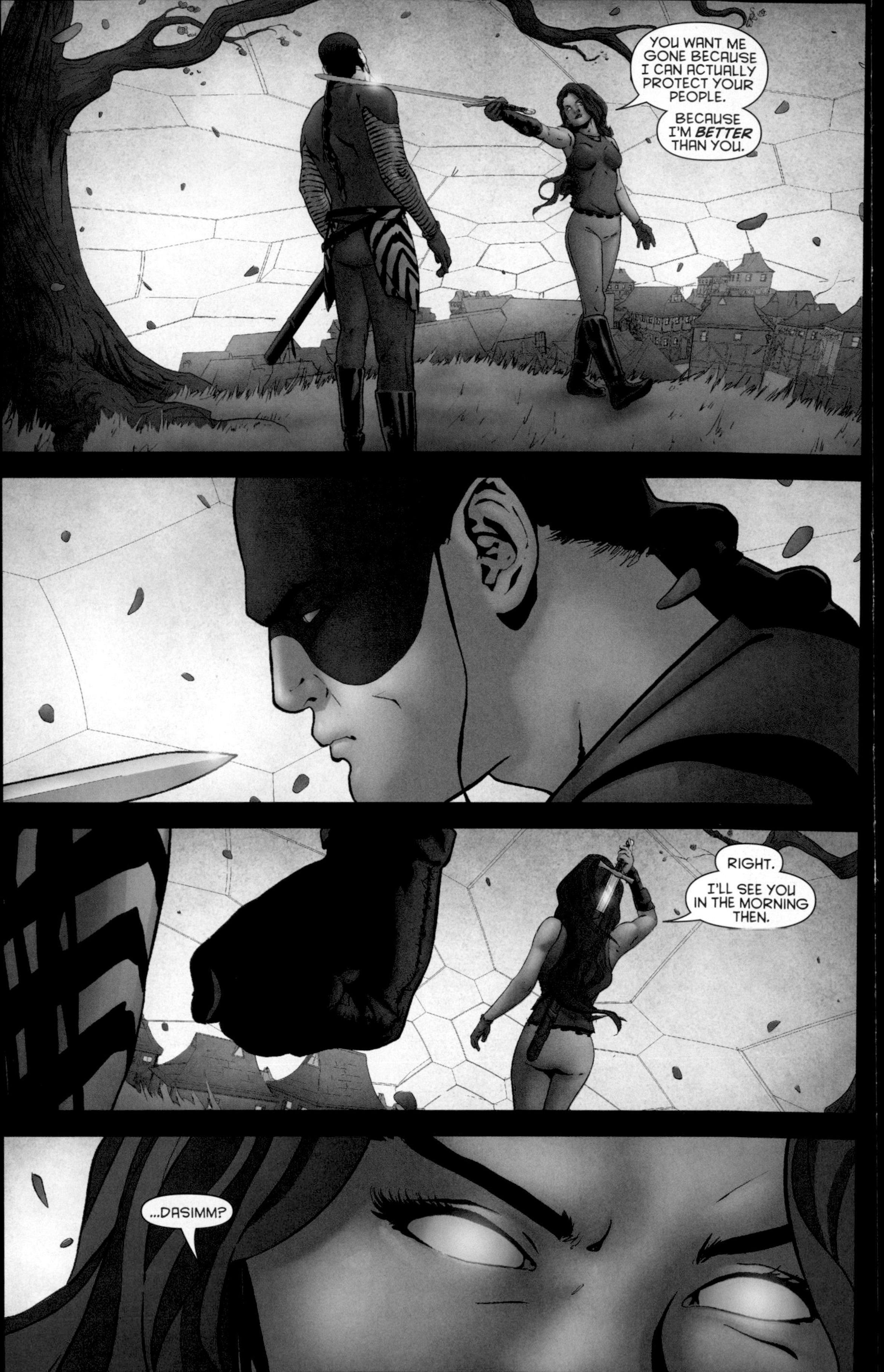
YOU WANT ME GONE BECAUSE I CAN ACTUALLY PROTECT YOUR PEOPLE.
BECAUSE I'M **BETTER** THAN YOU.
RIGHT.
I'LL SEE YOU IN THE MORNING THEN.
...DASIMM?

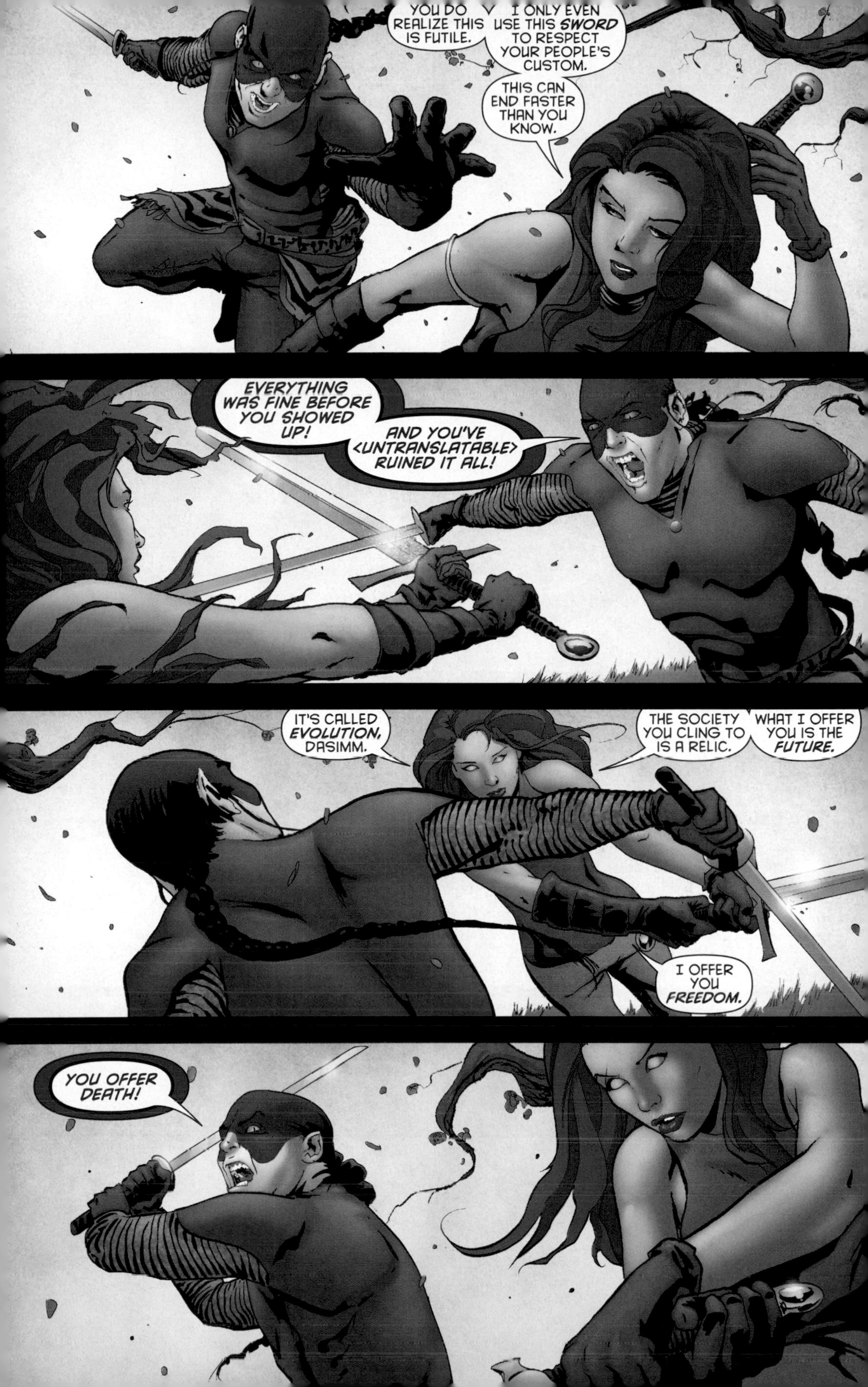
YOU DO REALIZE THIS IS FUTILE.
I ONLY EVEN USE THIS SWORD TO RESPECT YOUR PEOPLE'S CUSTOM.
THIS CAN END FASTER THAN YOU KNOW.
EVERYTHING WAS FINE BEFORE YOU SHOWED UP!
AND YOU'VE <UNTRANSLATABLE> RUINED IT ALL!
IT'S CALLED EVOLUTION, DASIMM.
THE SOCIETY YOU CLING TO IS A RELIC.
WHAT I OFFER YOU IS THE FUTURE.
I OFFER YOU FREEDOM.
YOU OFFER DEATH!

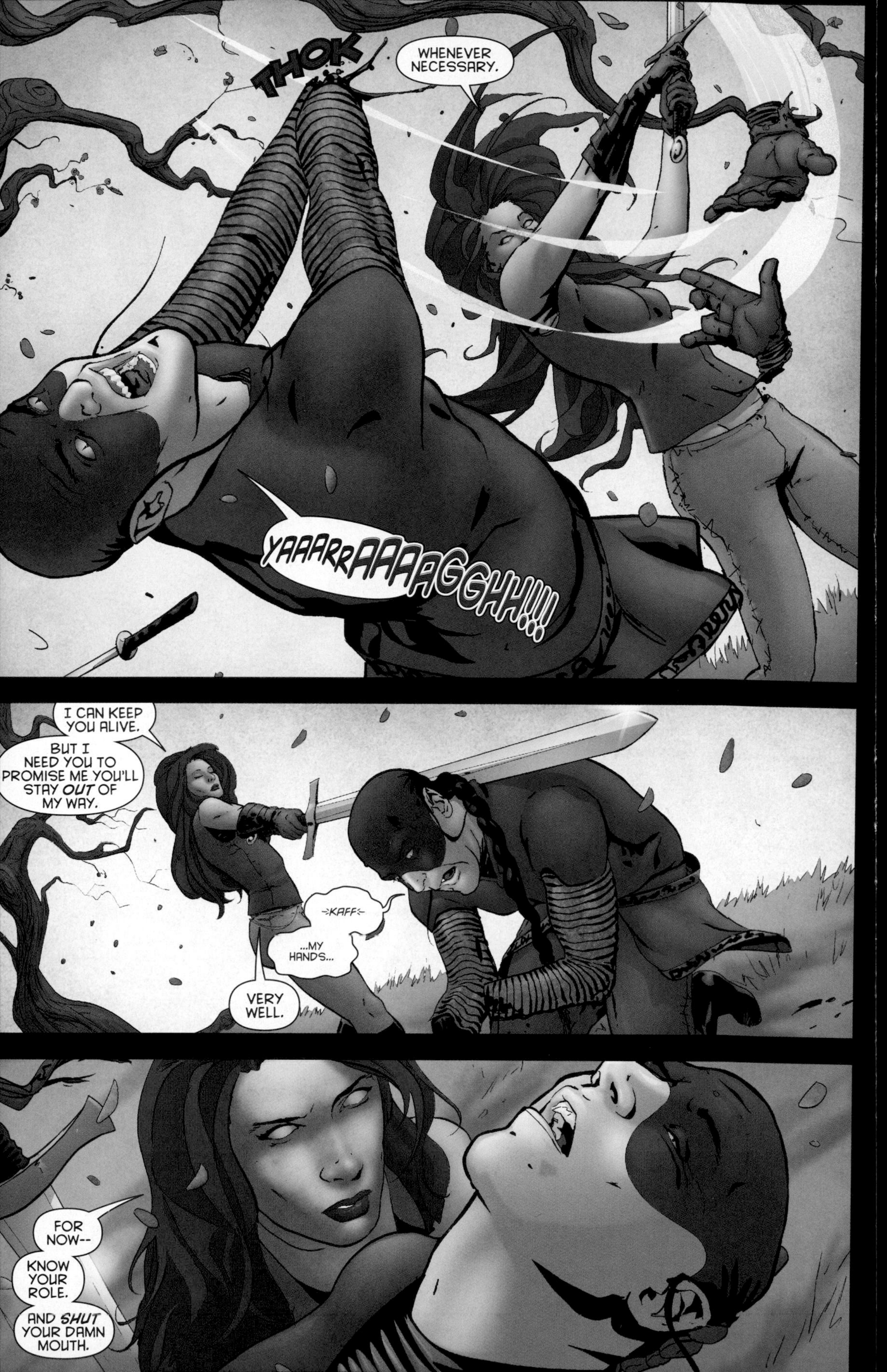
THOK
WHENEVER NECESSARY.
YAAARRAAAAAGGHH!!!!
I CAN KEEP YOU ALIVE.
BUT I NEED YOU TO PROMISE ME YOU'LL STAY OUT OF MY WAY.
KAFF
...MY HANDS...
VERY WELL.
FOR NOW--
KNOW YOUR ROLE.
AND SHUT YOUR DAMN MOUTH.

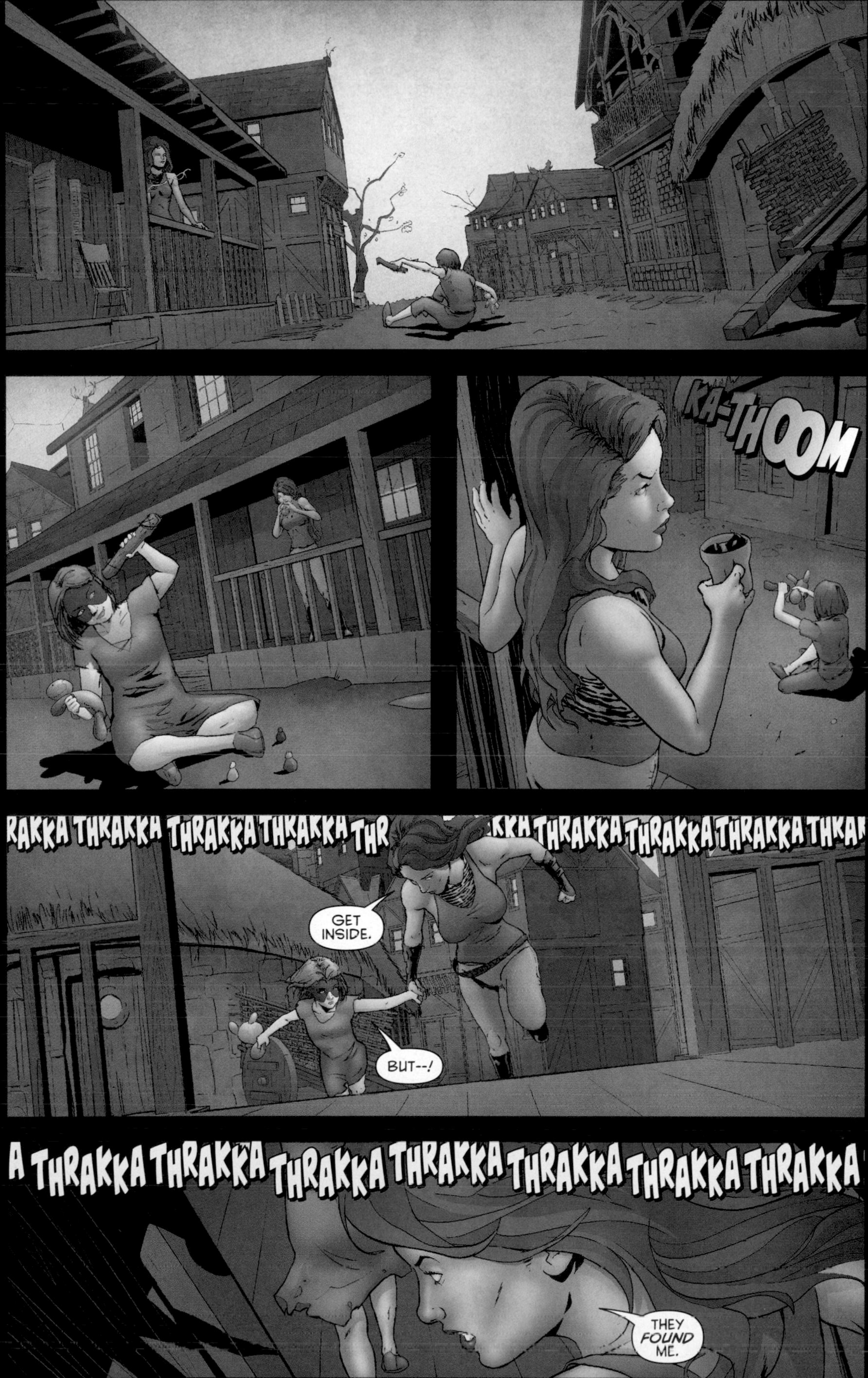
KA-THOOM
RAKKA THRAKKA THRAKKA THRAKKA THR
KKA THRAKKA THRAKKA THRAKKA THRAK
GET INSIDE.
BUT--!
A THRAKKA THRAKKA THRAKKA THRAKKA THRAKKA THRAKKA THRAKKA
THEY *FOUND* ME.

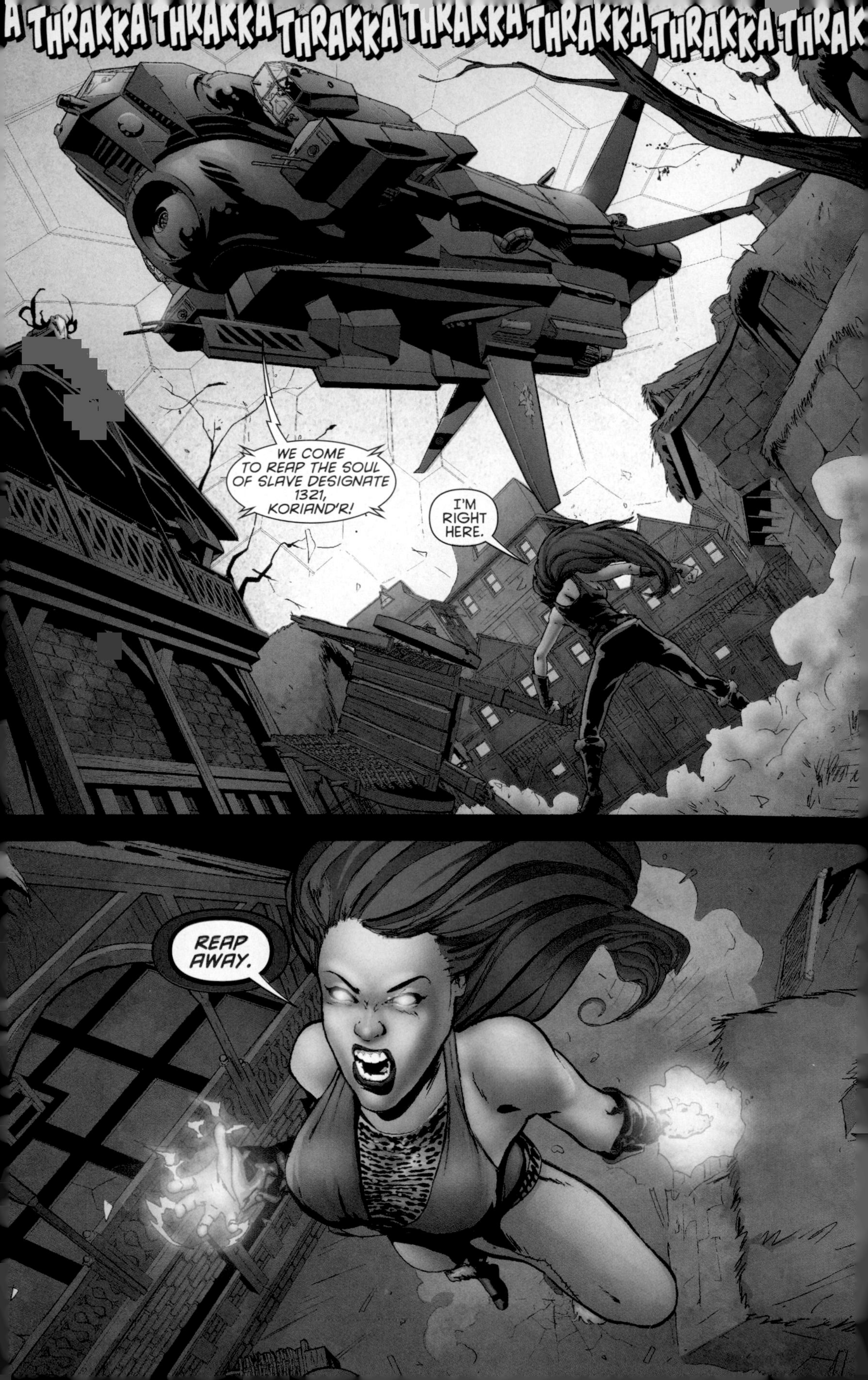
A THRAKKA THRAKKA THRAKKA THRAKKA THRAKKA THRAKKA THRAK
WE COME TO REAP THE SOUL OF SLAVE DESIGNATE 1321, KORIAND'R!
I'M RIGHT HERE.
REAP AWAY.

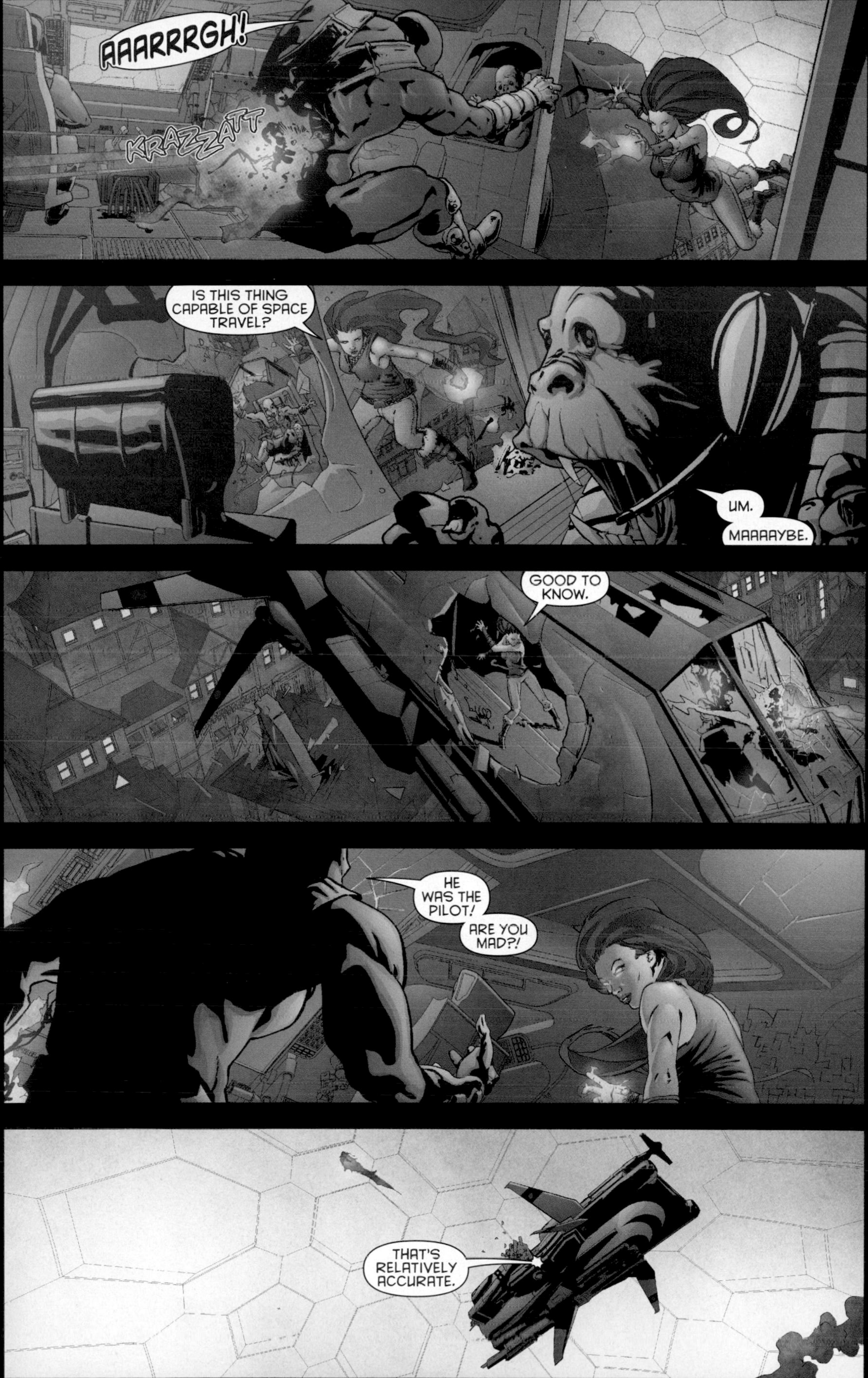
AAARRRGH!
KRAZZATT
IS THIS THING CAPABLE OF SPACE TRAVEL?
UM.
MAAAAYBE.
GOOD TO KNOW.
HE WAS THE PILOT!
ARE YOU MAD?!
THAT'S RELATIVELY ACCURATE.

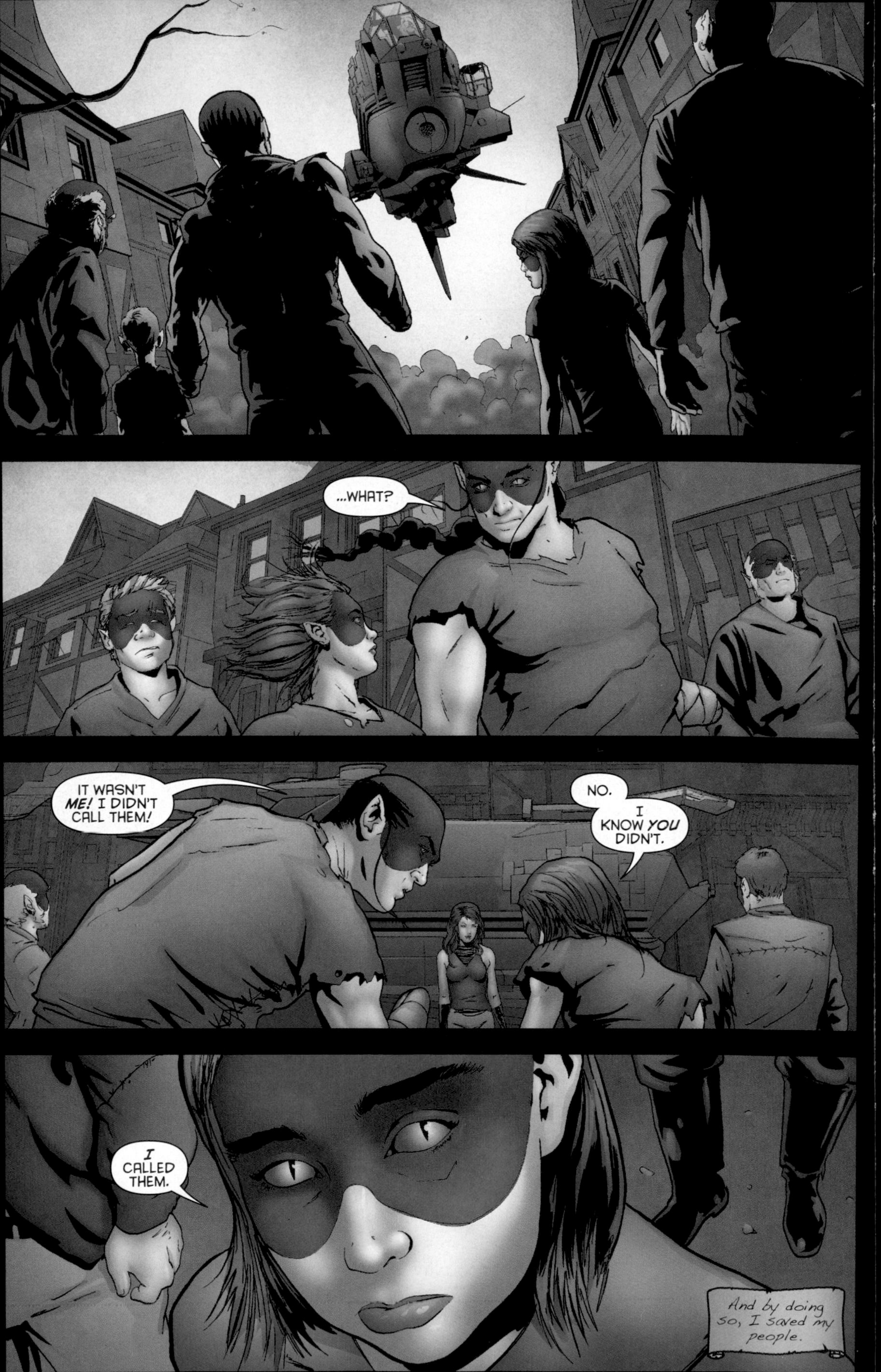
...WHAT?
IT WASN'T ME! I DIDN'T CALL THEM!
NO.
I KNOW YOU DIDN'T.
I CALLED THEM.
And by doing so, I saved my people.

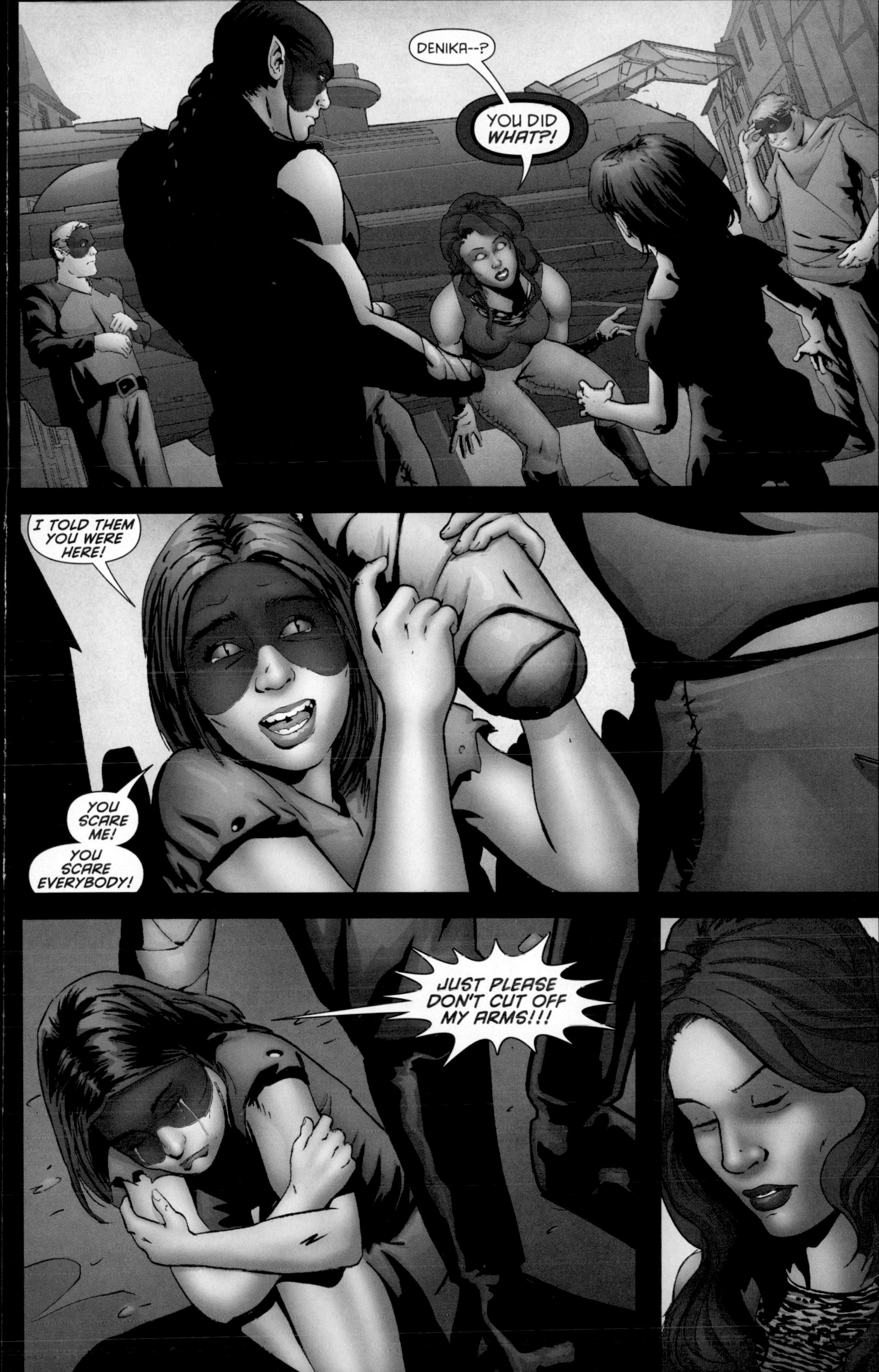
DENIKA--?
YOU DID WHAT?!
I TOLD THEM YOU WERE HERE!
YOU SCARE ME!
YOU SCARE EVERYBODY!
JUST PLEASE DON'T CUT OFF MY ARMS!!!

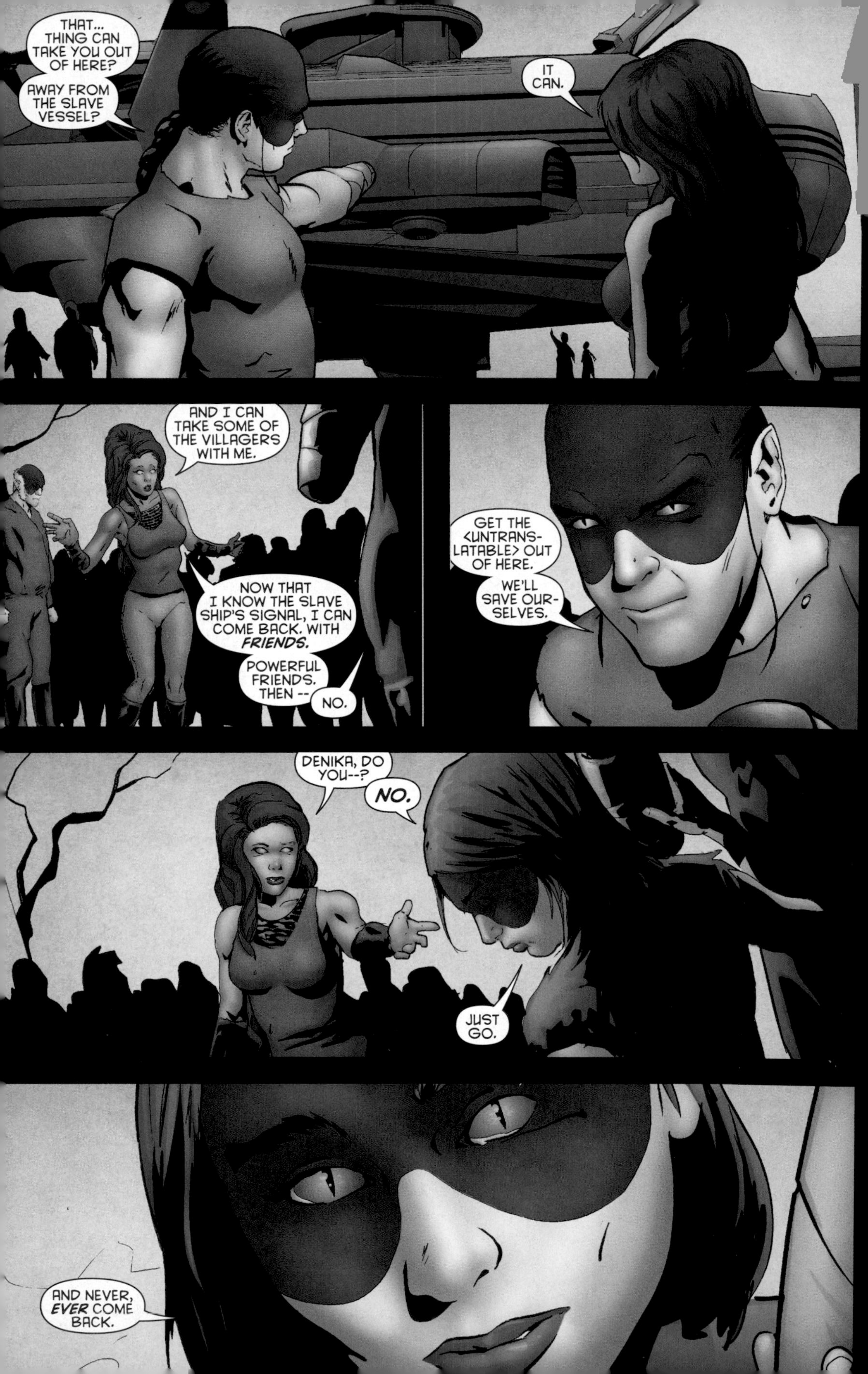
THAT... THING CAN TAKE YOU OUT OF HERE?
AWAY FROM THE SLAVE VESSEL?
IT CAN.
AND I CAN TAKE SOME OF THE VILLAGERS WITH ME.
NOW THAT I KNOW THE SLAVE SHIP'S SIGNAL, I CAN COME BACK. WITH *FRIENDS.*
POWERFUL FRIENDS. THEN --
NO.
GET THE <UNTRANSLATABLE> OUT OF HERE.
WE'LL SAVE OURSELVES.
DENIKA, DO YOU--?
NO.
JUST GO.
AND NEVER, ***EVER*** COME BACK.

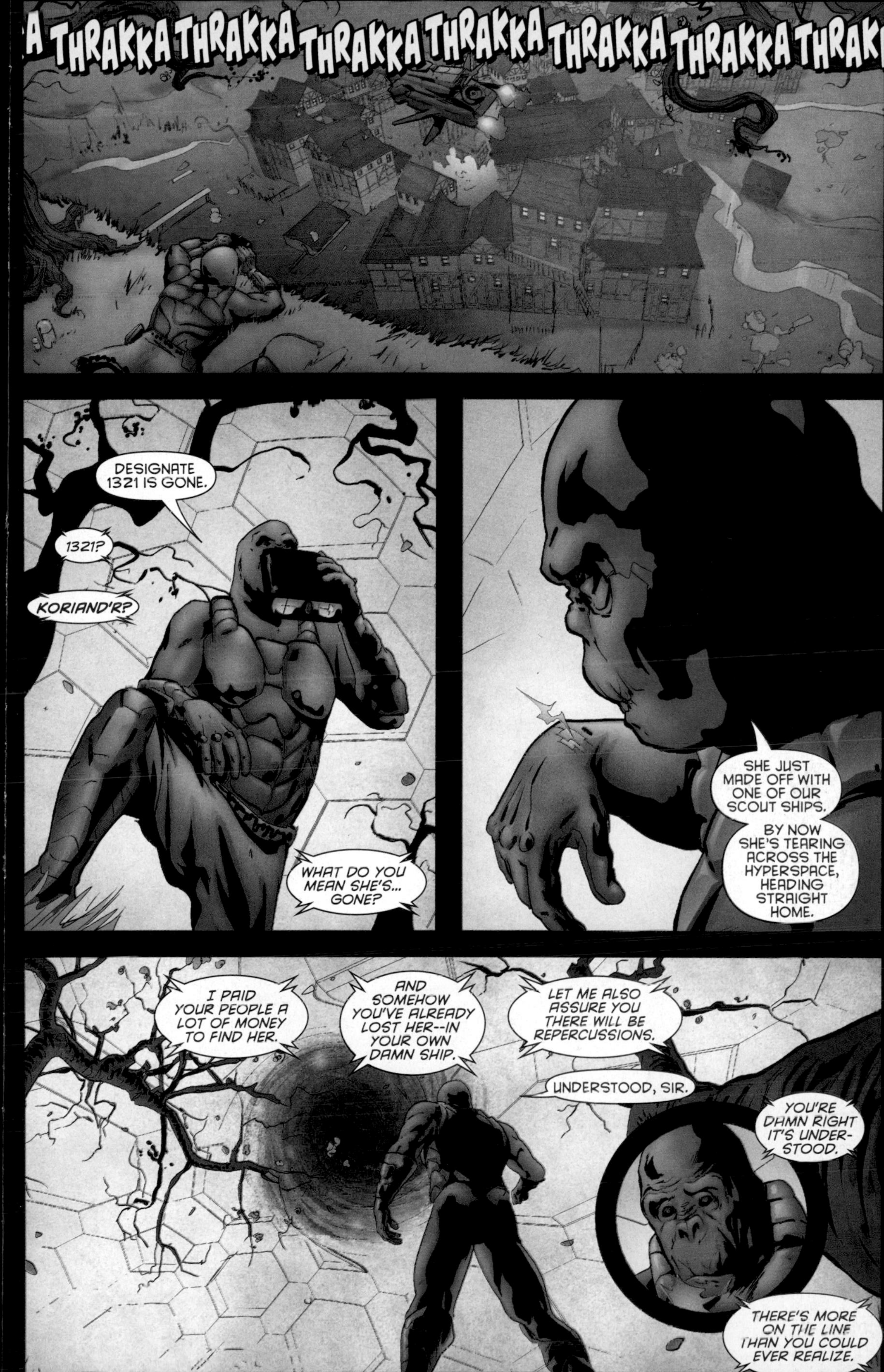
THRAKKA THRAKKA THRAKKA THRAKKA THRAKKA THRAKKA THRAKKA THRAKKA
DESIGNATE 1321 IS GONE.
1321?
KORIAND'R?
WHAT DO YOU MEAN SHE'S... GONE?
SHE JUST MADE OFF WITH ONE OF OUR SCOUT SHIPS.
BY NOW SHE'S TEARING ACROSS THE HYPERSPACE, HEADING STRAIGHT HOME.
I PAID YOUR PEOPLE A LOT OF MONEY TO FIND HER.
AND SOMEHOW YOU'VE ALREADY LOST HER--IN YOUR OWN DAMN SHIP.
LET ME ALSO ASSURE YOU THERE WILL BE REPERCUSSIONS.
UNDERSTOOD, SIR.
YOU'RE DAMN RIGHT IT'S UNDER-STOOD.
THERE'S MORE ON THE LINE THAN YOU COULD EVER REALIZE.

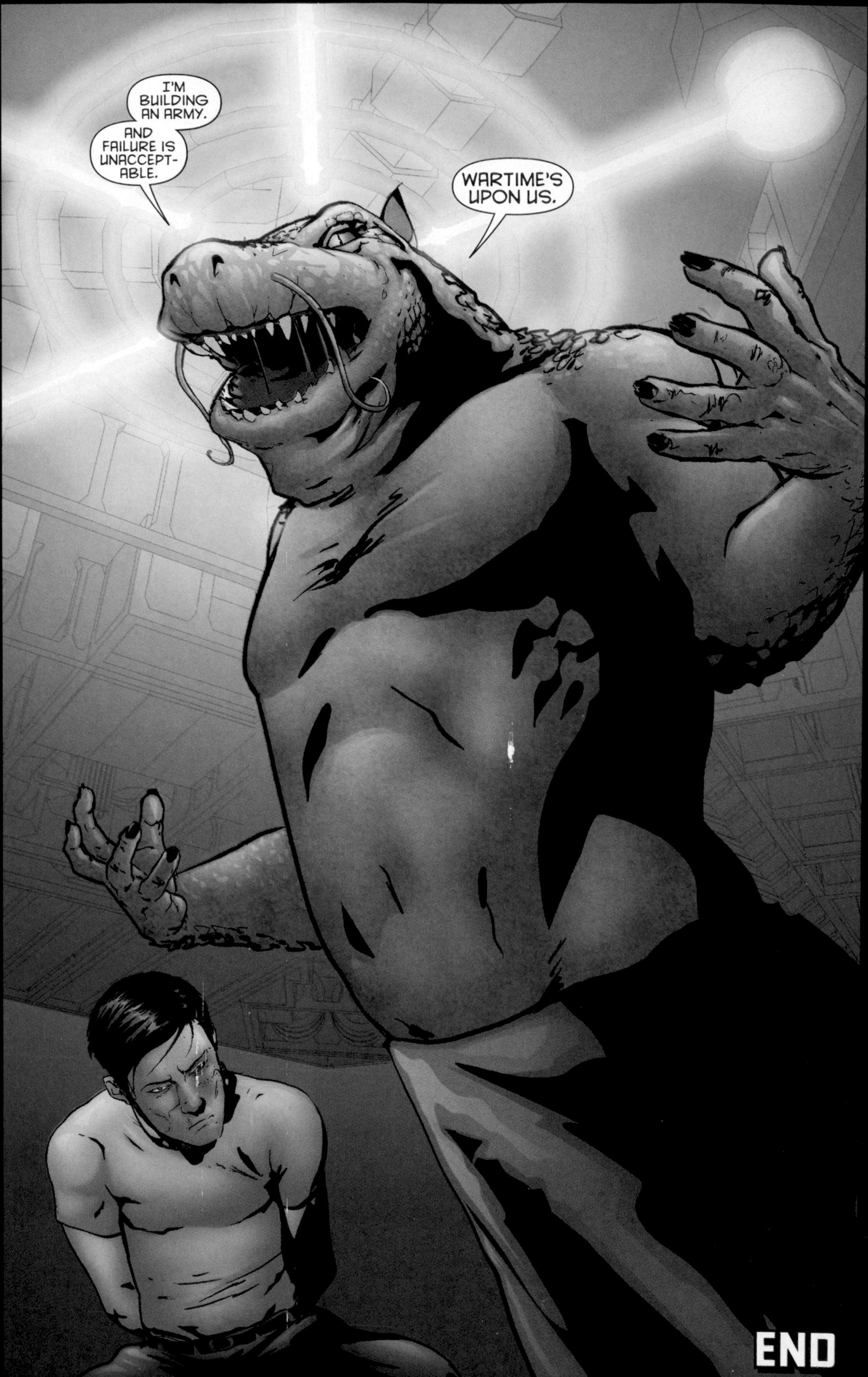
I'M BUILDING AN ARMY.
AND FAILURE IS UNACCEPT-ABLE.
WARTIME'S UPON US.
END

Unused cover by Philip Tan

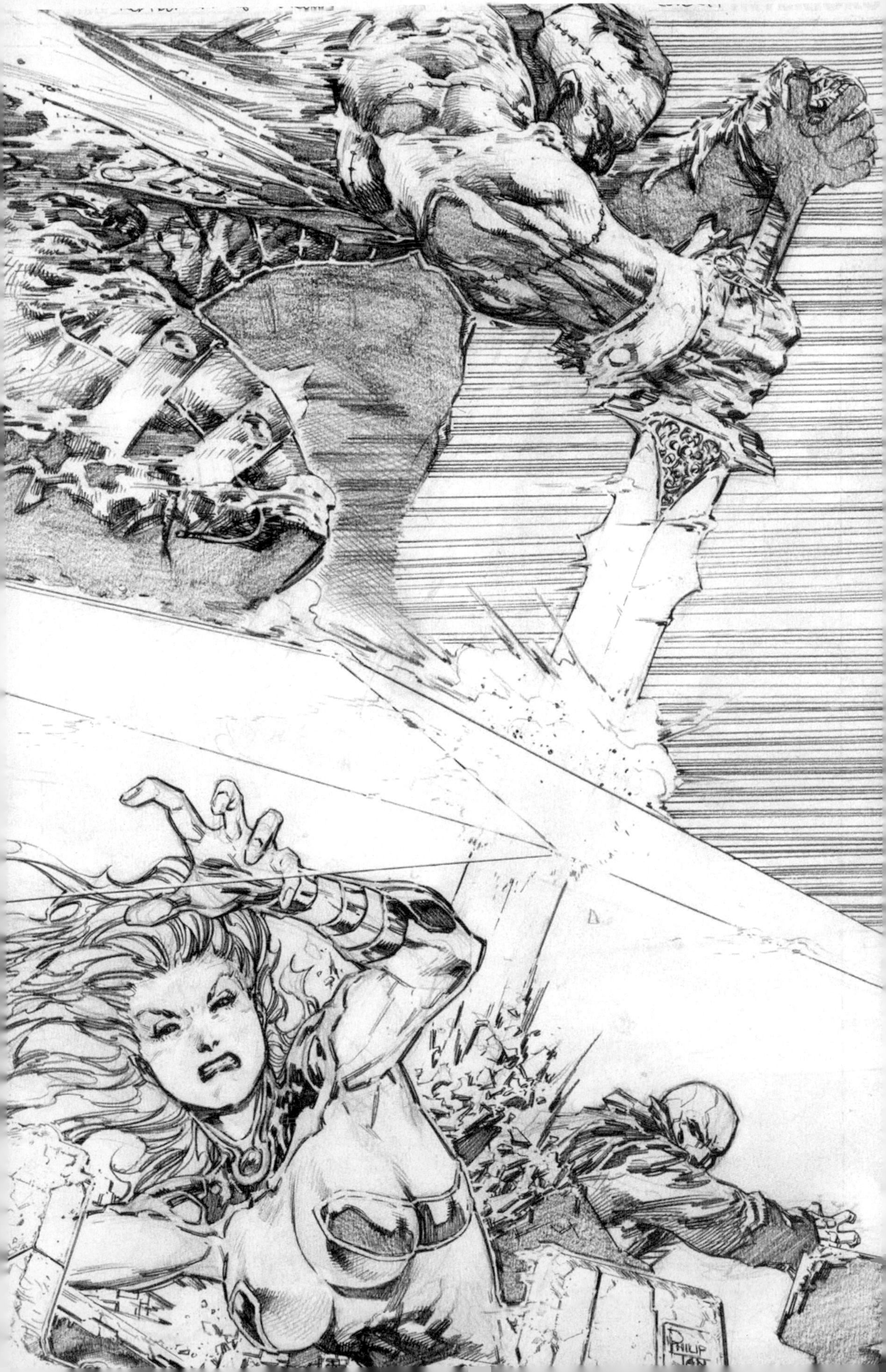
PHILIP TAN